SUPERVISION
First Line Management

SUPERVISION
First Line Management
Fifth Edition

LAWRENCE L. STEINMETZ
President
High Yield Management, Inc.

H. Ralph Todd, Jr.
American River College

Homewood, IL 60430
Boston, MA 02116

Sponsoring editor: Kurt L. Strand
Developmental editor: Joanne Dorff
Project editor: Rita McMullen
Production manager: Bette K. Ittersagen
Designer: Jeff Davidson

Compositor: Carlisle Communications, Ltd.
Typeface: 10.5/13 Palatino
Printer: R. R. Donnelley & Sons, Inc.

Library of Congress Cataloging-in-Publication Data

Steinmetz, Lawrence L.
    Supervision : first line management / Lawrence L. Steinmetz, H.
Ralph Todd, Jr. — 5th ed.
      p.   cm.
    Rev. ed. of: First-line management. 4th ed. Plano, Tex. : Business
Publications, 1986.
    ISBN 0-256-06669-8
    1. Supervision of employees.   2. Personnel management.   I. Todd,
H. Ralph.   II. Steinmetz, Lawrence L. First-line management.
III. title.
HF5549.S84286   1992
658.3'02 — dc20   91–20510

This edition is dedicated to four special women and two special young men whose support and encouragement kept this book in progress through some rough times for all of us. With grateful pride and thanks to: Zallia, Aleta, Deirdre, Marla, Jason, and Christen.

Preface

Changes in the underlying philosophy of management in the United States have influenced organizations more profoundly in recent history than in any previous period. Many managers have recognized that problems of competitiveness, balance of trade, and the world's image of the United States as a producer of largely second-rate goods and services rest with them and not their foreign counterparts. Supervision, the first line of management, is affected directly by these changes.

Our primary emphasis in this edition of *Supervision: First-Line Management* is on the changing nature of organizations and the way they are managed. As in the past, our primary focus is on supervisors and their unique role as the link between upper levels of management and the people who actually perform the services or make the products of an organization. Mid-level management perspectives have been expanded to provide a more complete understanding of management-management interactions as well as the interactions between management and nonmanagement employees. In addition to exploring the effects of organizational interaction with the social, political, economic, and technological environ-ments, we also include current trends in management action.

Briefly summarized, some of the major changes between this and earlier editions of *Supervision: First-Line Management* include:

1. An expanded history of management thought in the United States to help students understand the evolution of management practices and philosophy. We feel that knowing the foundations of present managerial thinking makes it easier to recognize what works and what doesn't.

2. Discussions on the impact of technology on organizational life and the vastly more complex job of managing in the information age than in any previous historical period.

3. Emphasis on the emerging importance of total quality management concepts as proposed by Jurand, Deming, Ishikawa, and Imani.

4. Applications of some of Tom Peters' *Thriving on Chaos* concepts for supervision.

5. Problems and promises of multicultural, multiethnic work forces and the

growing impact of internationalization on much of organizational life.

6. Sensitivity to the concepts of cooperation and partnership rather than competitiveness as paths to more successful organizational life.

7. Increased attention to dealing with lifestyle issues, such as AIDS, drug abuse, and alcoholism.

8. Current concerns with issues such as wrongful termination, compliance with civil rights law, and related workplace issues.

9. A return to the expanded "Things to Remember" section found in earlier editions of *Supervision: First-Line Management*.

10. A new instructor's manual with new chapter tests suitable for direct copy as well as computerized tests for both IBM and Apple computers.

11. *Endnotes* have been added to cite major sources and to suggest further reading.

12. Discussions of the self-assessment exercises are now in an appendix at the end of the text rather than in the instructor's manual.

In recognition of the continuing importance of ethical, legal, and social issues that affect organizations and frequently impact the job of supervisors, discussions of these issues have been strengthened.

Our text is directed toward practicing supervisors and mid-level managers, those preparing for promotion, and some who are interested in the world of work and management functions. We find that many disciplines other than supervision and management programs currently use the text and may well continue its use in the future. It is used in food service management, recreation supervision, a variety of vocational courses, criminal justice supervision, and as a supplement to engineering and industrial management programs.

In addition to emerging trends in the complex and difficult-to-comprehend environment of today, we have concentrated on emerging trends without neglecting the *how it is* frame of reference. A balance of both theory and application has always been a primary objective of our writing.

We would like to thank those instructors whose reviews provided many excellent ideas for this revision:

Catherine J. Gold
Mohawk Valley Community College

Carnella Hardin
Glendale Community College

Charles Yauger
Arkansas State University

Naz Chaudhry
University of Alaska

Edward R. Goettl
University of Minnesota

Donald Cappa
Chabot College

Rita Hall
Sullivan Junior College

Michael White
University of Northern Iowa

Wendell V. Fountain
Jacksonville University

Tonya Y. Hynds
Purdue University at Kokomo

Russ Holloman
Augusta College

Olene L. Fuller
San Jacinto College

James H. Boyle
Glendale Community College

We would also like to give special thanks to our colleagues at colleges and universities throughout the United States, Canada, Europe, Mexico, and South America who have used our text in all of its editions and to express our special appreciation to the splendid editorial staff at Richard D. Irwin for their intelligence, professionalism, good humor and, most importantly, patience.

Users of the text may call or write us directly if they have questions or comments, or if they would like to discuss specific issues. Ralph Todd may be reached at (916) 484-8613 or (916) 484-8361 (messages for return calls). Larry Steinmetz may be contacted at (303) 442-8115. We have attempted to retain the same level of writing and sense of real life examples as in the past. It is our belief that both instructors and students will find the fifth edition interesting, enjoyable, and most importantly, useful.

Ralph Todd
Larry Steinmetz

Contents

Part I

Linking Management and Employees

■ Sometime early in the history of humankind, leaders of people emerged. They planned and directed the activities of others. Although we don't know when management began, we realize that it was and still is necessary. People need guidance in accomplishing group goals. From these prehistoric beginnings modern management has evolved.

Chapters 1 and 2 introduce historical influences on today's management thought and practice and identify major trends in management thought. They also define basic management functions—responsibility, authority, and accountability—and the role of first-line and middle management in day-to-day activities.

Chapter 1

Supervision–Linking Management and Employees

Objectives

Chapter 1 introduces fundamental management processes and traces major historical developments that have led to current practices. Like all events that affect our lives, organizations have been required to adjust to social, political, economic, and technical change to meet increasingly complex demands. In no period of history has management found it necessary to know and to do so much. After completing the first chapter, readers will be able to

- Define responsibility, authority, and accountability.
- Use fundamental organization terms correctly.
- Recognize the effect of classical management concepts on current supervisory practice.
- Appreciate contributions of more recent management thinkers.
- Utilize three basic management questions correctly.

Thought Starter

Bradford Boyd, a management professor at Stanford University, points out that employees ultimately control how much work is accomplished, its quality, and whether or not it will be completed. Boyd then asks, "If employees control work, then what is the purpose of supervision and management?"[1]

In our first chapter we show why supervision is important and necessary. When work expands to the point that more than one person is needed to accomplish organizational goals, supervision is required. Work must be planned, organized, directed, and controlled. Every manager performs these basic functions. Supervisors, management's first line, also link employees with higher levels of management and other parts of their organization.

■ *Julie Thompson had been with U.S. Banking and Loan Services for almost two years before her promotion to department head of Loan Processing Services. Eight people, all of whom had previously worked with her and who reviewed loan applications, conducted appropriate research, and submitted recommendations for approval or disapproval, now reported directly to Julie. As the department's supervisor, she recognized that no one person could do all of the Loan Processing Services work. It required the entire team of eight people. Her job, she learned very quickly, involved many new activities. Some were concerned with determining priorities, making schedules and work assignments, being a source of information, analyzing problems and taking appropriate corrective action when needed, as well as being the primary link between higher levels of management and nonmanagement employees in her department. Her job was to get work accomplished through the efforts of others. In Julie's case, others were the people who reported to her.*

■ SUPERVISORS—MANAGEMENT'S FIRST-LINE

Supervisors are responsible for planning, organizing, directing, and controlling the work of employees.

Supervisors are the first line of management. They are responsible for planning, organizing, directing, and controlling the activities of employees who perform the necessary tasks and services of organizations. Depending on the type of organization for which they work, supervisors may have titles such as office manager, chief X-ray technician, police sergeant, section head, department manager, or any of a variety of others. Regardless of title, they are the essential links that implement action required to meet the objectives of an organization and of those who make policy. No other level of management is directly concerned with job performance, coordination of activities with other parts of an organization, and interpreting job objectives to employees.

■ MAJOR SUPERVISORY CONCERNS

Effectiveness means doing things completely and correctly.

Not only must supervisors be human relations specialists, coaches, technical advisors, disciplinarians, evaluators, motivational experts, team builders, record keepers, and cost specialists, but they must also constantly strive for effectiveness and efficiency in their organizational units. **Effectiveness** means doing things completely and correctly. An effective supervisor is concerned with doing the right things right.

Efficiency means performing work with minimum waste of time, effort, money, and other resources.

Efficiency is achieved by performing work with the minimum waste of time, effort, and resources, such as people, supplies, and materials. Painting a room, as an example, can be done effectively with a very small brush and carefully applied paint. Although it would be effective because the room would be very neatly painted, it would not be efficient. If a roller or airless paint sprayer were used, less time, energy, and paint would be required. Both effectiveness and efficiency would be achieved.

Successful supervisors must also be responsible. **Responsibility** is the obligation to perform necessary job requirements both effectively and efficiently. When an individual accepts an assignment, she or he has the responsibility for completing it to the best of her or his ability. To do otherwise would be irresponsible. In a less formal sense, responsibility also means doing what we know is right even though it may not be part of a regular job assignment. Assisting others, providing information, and reporting needed actions may all be part of informal responsibility.

Responsibility is the accepted obligation to perform necessary job requirements effectively and efficiently. Informal responsibility means doing what we know is right.

Managers are responsible for the actions of the employees in their work units. Supervisors are responsible for the actions of all of the nonmanagement employees in their sections or departments. Middle managers are usually responsible for the performance of a number of first-line managers and upper management is responsible for an entire organization. While responsibility is shared, it is never totally granted to another person lower in an organization. If an employee makes a significant error, upper levels of management see the supervisor as responsible, not the employee who made the mistake. Each higher level of management is also responsible for the employee's error. Without authority, however, responsible job performance may be impossible.

Authority is the right to act and implement necessary organizational activities including supervision of employees.

Authority is the right to act, assign, or use resources of an organization. Supervisors usually have the authority to assign jobs, evaluate and correct performance, organize work, and determine priorities, as well as implement a wide variety of other activities. It is granted by both their job description and higher levels of management. To some extent, authority is always limited. A supervisor may have the right to recommend termination of an employee but not to give final notice until specifically authorized. In most cases supervisors have budgets for their operations but must get higher-level approval for purchases in excess of a designated dollar value. In nearly everything they do on the job, supervisors have limited authority.

In addition to having both responsibility and authority, supervisors are accountable for their actions. **Accountability** involves reporting achievements and failures to higher levels of management. Like responsibility, it is the obligation to report personal or work-unit activities. Most organizations require supervisors to complete daily or weekly reports of the amount of work accomplished, schedules achieved, problems, and goals attained. A great deal of accountability reporting is accomplished through computer-generated reports, as well as through oral and written information. Without accountability there is no way for others in an organization to understand what is being accomplished, what problems exist, and how well supervisors are performing.

Accountability involves reporting achievements and failures to higher levels of management. It is a component of fully accepting responsibility.

Supervisors must also coordinate the activities of others. **Coordination** involves informing everyone directly concerned with performing a job or series of tasks what, who, when, where, how, and why the work must be accomplished. It ensures that the right actions are taken at the correct time. While coordination is primarily concerned with communicating what is necessary to others, it also helps ensure a smooth flow of work. Effective supervisors find coordination one of their most essential tasks.

Coordination means informing others what, when, where, how, and why work must be accomplished. It is getting things done in an organized sequence of activities.

▪ LEVELS OF MANAGEMENT

In all but the very smallest of organizations there may be several layers of responsibility and authority. At the highest or top level is executive management. Top managers often have titles such as chief executive officer (CEO), president, or general manager. In very large organizations, top management may include the board of directors, CEO, and executive committees. CEOs may have the title of chairperson, president, or a combination of the two. Top-level managers are responsible for defining the overall goals and making or approving decisions that affect their entire organization. While they may serve several roles, executive managers set the tone for the total organization.

Executive (top level) management includes chief executive officers, boards of directors, and executive committees that make key organizational decisions and formulate policies that affect the entire organization.

Mid-level or middle managers are responsible for interpreting the policies of top management in their own areas of specialization. Most mid-level managers have titles such as controller, chief purchasing agent, marketing director, operations manager, manager of administration, or similar titles depending on their organization and position. In very large organizations there may be

Middle management interprets top level policies in terms of its own areas of specialization.

several layers of mid-level managers. Managers of purchasing, human resource management, and financial operations often report to a manager of administration or some related title. To ensure a smooth flow of both communication and coordination of related activities, mid-level managers have the difficult task of linking first-line managers with higher levels of management.

Reporting to middle-managers are first-line managers, or supervisors. Supervisors, as the first line of management, are responsible for the work of individual employees who perform the vital tasks of an organization. They are the essential link between employees and higher levels of management, as well as other parts of their organizations.

First-line management consists of the supervisors responsible for the work of individual employees and groups in performing the vital tasks of an organization.

Individual nonmanagement employees are responsible for accomplishing their assigned jobs. As shown schematically in Figure 1.1, organizations can usually be viewed as triangles with very few managers at upper levels and many employees at lower levels. In small organizations, one person may serve all of the functions of top, middle, and first-line management.

■ FROM PAST TO PRESENT

No one knows exactly when management began. It is very likely that among the earliest prehistoric people there were leaders who decided on courses of action and planned what was necessary for survival. Some of the earliest writings found by archaeologists were made approximately 6,000 years ago by the people of Sumer. They recorded business transactions that involved directing activities of many people. Management, in a fairly sophisticated form, must have existed. Since a great deal of labor in early civilizations was accomplished by slaves, motivation was based on threats of punishment, whippings, and sometimes public beheadings.

Although employees are no longer whipped or beheaded, the whip-and-sword type of management is still in use. Many managers use threats, fear of job or pay loss, unfavorable assignments, and unfavorable performance evaluations as whips and swords to control employees. This "do it or else" management has persisted even though for nearly 100 years serious studies of management have demonstrated better approaches. As depicted in Figure 1.2, roles of supervisors in the 1990s have become both more complex and people oriented.

FIGURE 1.1 ■ Management Levels

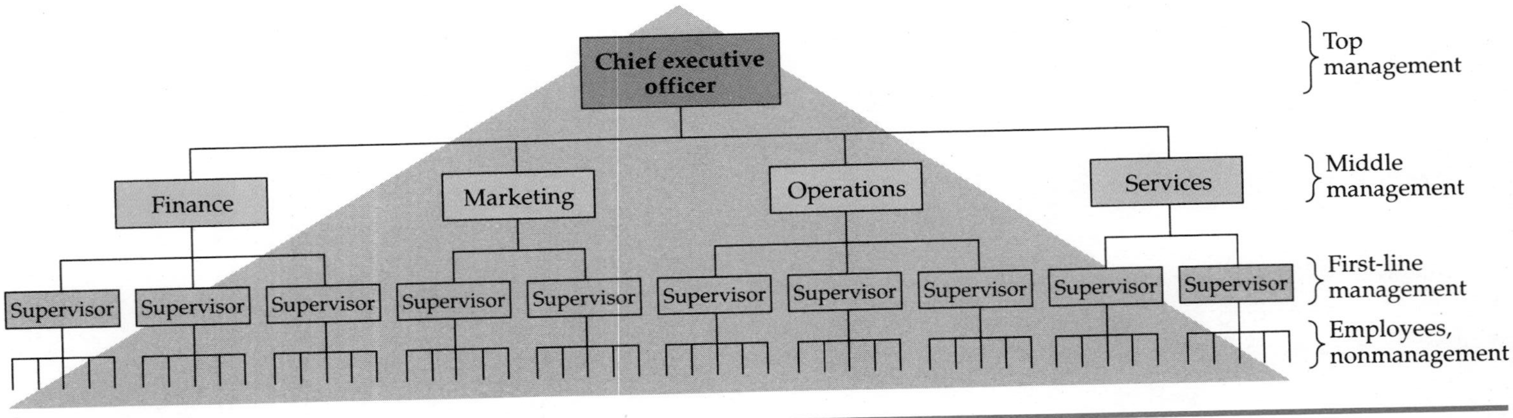

FIGURE 1.2 ■ Supervisory Roles for Effective Employee Relations

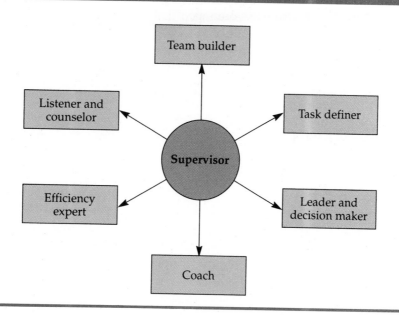

■ SCIENTIFIC MANAGEMENT

Scientific management was founded by Frederick Winslow Taylor and was dedicated to the use of scientific methods to find the one best way to perform every job.

At the beginning of this century **Frederick Winslow Taylor** was a young engineer at the Midvale Steel Company in Pittsburgh, Pennsylvania. Taylor had been successful as an inventor and spokesperson for improved work methods. He was convinced, based on his observations, that there was one best way to do every job. Scientific principles, Taylor believed, could be applied to work as they were to the laboratory. Although his methods antagonized his highly unionized employees, Taylor demonstrated that discarding nonessential components of a job and combining other parts in the correct sequence could greatly improve productivity. After leaving Midvale to become a consultant, Taylor conducted some of his most important experiments in job improvement at Bethlehem Steel.

In a famous experiment Taylor trained a common laborer, whom he called Schmidt, although his correct name was Knolle, to shovel pig iron (small blocks of iron that were converted into steel) at almost four times the normal standard. "Schmidt" increased his productivity from 12 ½ tons per day to 47 ½ tons per day. Taylor accomplished this seeming miracle by redesigning Schmidt's shovel, providing rest periods, and increasing pay from $1.15 to $1.85 per day when Schmidt attained the new standard of 47 ½ tons.[2]

Taylor was convinced that scientific principles applied to management could improve work and make employees more satisfied with the results of their efforts. He felt strongly that employees who exceed expected standards should be rewarded for their efforts and developed a **piece-rate system.** Employees were granted extra pay for each unit or piece produced in excess of a pre-established standard. Taylor's *Principles of Scientific Management*, published in 1911, established methods that still influence management thought, although some of his concepts do not apply in today's workplaces. Perhaps most significant were his concepts that:

1. **There is one best way to perform every task.** Management has the responsibility to define, through time and motion study, the most efficient method of performing every job. Most of Taylor's early experiments were designed to improve efficiency through the one best way for each job he studied. Time and motion studies measured precisely (Taylor used a stopwatch) the time each motion required and then reduced the number of motions for each job. He also developed techniques for location of equipment and tools that would make work easier and more efficient.

   Standards are the expected levels of performance for specific tasks. They may be measured by amount of productivity in a given period of time, quality, and schedule adherence.

2. **Standards should be established for each job.** A **standard** is the expected level of performance for completing a task. Taylor felt all jobs can be measured and standards developed for performing them by computing the average time for a number of "first-class" workers doing a given task. Over a period of time the average of these employees would be the expected performance of all employees. Those who met the standard would be meeting management expectations. Lower performance levels were considered less than adequate. A first-class worker, according to Taylor, was an employee who "could and would." A second-class worker "could but would not."

3. **For each task there were optimum efforts. Optimum effort** meant the amount of work that could be done without exhausting an employee. In his experiments with shovels, Taylor found that for different tasks, the optimum shovel size was different. Shoveling pig iron was different from shoveling ash from a furnace. In both cases, however, 21 ½ pounds was the optimum weight that the average employee could repeatedly

lift and sustain for a work day. For lighter materials a larger shovel could be used. More weight would tire most employees; less would not be efficient. Taylor established the concept that optimum effort is more productive over a long period of time than maximum effort for a shorter period.

In today's world we know that many new automobiles can be driven over 100 miles per hour. At that speed, however, their engines will last for a relatively short time. If speed is kept under 65 miles per hour, the automobile can usually perform for over 100,000 miles with recommended maintenance. The optimum speed is probably between 55 and 65 miles per hour for most automobiles.

4. **Taylor also pioneered work measurement.** Careful measurement of each job movement helped determine optimum standards, the one best way to perform tasks, and ways of improving efficiency. We measure the correct temperature of water when bathing by feeling the water. Taylor assumed that every job could be precisely measured. A thermometer in water is far more precise than one's hand in determining exact temperature. Countable measurements, such as distance, time, and amount, are far more accurate than the guesstimates of a hand in water or observations by a supervisor.

As one of the true classical thinkers in management, Taylor had a profound effect on work methods. Other researchers in efficiency improvement extended the application of scientific management techniques. Frank and Lillian Gilbreth, who were some of the true efficiency experts of their era, and Henry Gantt, developer of methods for tracking productivity through charting techniques, also helped establish scientific management as the model for industry during the first quarter of the century.

Henri Fayol formulated management principles that became the foundation for many modern management principles.

Another significant step in management thought was formulated by **Henri Fayol,** a French mining executive during the period scientific management was gaining recognition. He is often considered the founder of modern administrative principles. Fayol formulated 14 principles of management, many of which persist today. Although his 1917 text on general principles of industrial administration was not translated into English until 1930, his work became the foundation for much of the language of management. Concepts such as planning, organizing, and controlling were central to Fayol's thinking. Many other present-day organizational terms can be traced to Fayol. *Chain of command, unity of command,* and *span of management* are still active parts of management vocabulary. Chain of command, sometimes called **scalar chain,** is the reporting relationship from top to bottom in an organization. Unity of command states that an individual employee should not be required to report to more than one person, and span of management was concerned with the number of employees who report to a single manager. Fayol advised managers to beware of rigidity in their use of any set of guidelines. He used his principles as checkpoints to be applied if needed. Not every situation, he realized, required application of all fourteen.

Fayol's principles of management are listed in Table 1.1.

Although his ideas were generally considered academic during the early part of the century, **Max Weber,** a German sociologist who was also a contemporary of Taylor and Fayol, described the ideal organizational form as a bureaucracy. Although the word *bureaucracy* is usually associated with red tape, inefficiency, and

TABLE 1.1 ■ Fayol's Management Principles

1. Division of work: Specialization of labor both by employees and managers.
2. Authority: Right to give orders and extract obedience.
3. Discipline: Respect between employees and managers. Success is based not on fear but mutual respect.
4. Unity of command: Employees should receive orders from one manager only.
5. Unity of direction: One head and one plan for a group of activities having the same objective.
6. Subordination of individual interests to general interests: Objectives of the organization must prevail over individual interests.
7. Renumeration: Wages, bonuses, and profit sharing as incentives to make employees more valuable.
8. Centralization: Uses either centralization or decentralization to find the optimum use of facilities and personnel.
9. Scalar chain (line of authority): Chain of management from employees to supervisors to middle-managers to top management.
10. Order: A place for everything and everything in its place.
11. Equity: Kindliness and justice for all.
12. Stability of tenure of personnel: Orderly personnel planning. Promotion of a stable workforce.
13. Initiative: Zeal and energy in all efforts.
14. *Espirit de corps:* Use verbal contacts rather than formal written instructions when possible to promote a feeling of unity and to promote speed and clarity.

Bureaucracy, an organizational structure built on authority, control, reporting, limited responsibility, and impersonality in treatment of employees, was advocated by Max Weber.

inflexibility, Weber did not use it in that sense. A **bureaucracy** was, in Weber's framework, an organization that depended on formal rules and regulations, selection of personnel based on merit, and a well-defined chain of command. Bureaucracies also included, according to Weber, clearly defined responsibilities, systems of reports, and impersonal relations between management and employees. Many governmental organizations have adopted Weber's model and nearly all large organizations utilize at least some of his recommendations.

Neither Taylor, Fayol, nor Weber were seriously concerned with relations between managers and employees. Although Taylor often talked and wrote about employees, he, like Henry Ford, believed that people worked for "bread and bread alone." Taylor and his adherents failed to consider the workplace as a social environment where people talked, developed friendships, and were concerned about relations with their management. Fayol recognized the importance of effective on-the-job relations, but his concepts of respect rather than fear and reduction of formal communication had only minor impact on management at the time of his writings. Weber felt management-employee relations should be impersonal. Taylor, Fayol, and Weber are considered the founders of classical management. It wasn't until the mid-1920s, however, that the human element at work was seriously studied.

Many activities that are seen by supervisors as routine in today's organizational environment can be traced to the contributions of earlier management thinkers. Like most contributions that came later, their principles were either largely ignored or incorrectly applied in all too many organizations.

■ ELTON MAYO AND HUMAN RELATIONS

At the Hawthorne Works of the American Telephone and Telegraph Company near Chicago, a series of experiments were made between 1924 and 1930 to determine the effect of different conditions on work performance. In one series of experiments spanning the period from 1924 to 1927, the amount of light in various departments was systematically varied. It was believed that as light increased, productivity would also increase. Conversely, it was thought that when lights were dimmed production would decrease. Contrary to the experimenters' predictions, production increased whenever lighting was changed. When lights were dimmed, production tended to rise just as it did when they were brightened. In other experiments similar results were achieved. To help fully understand what was taking place, **Elton Mayo,** a professor at Harvard University, was asked to review the studies.

Mayo realized that a number of human factors affected work that were not directly related to factors such as lighting, ventilation, or other physical conditions of work. He found that when experimenters talked with and got to know individual employees personally, productivity improved. In short, any action that employees perceived as attention from management seemed to improve both morale and productivity. This improvement in performance because of management attention is known today as the **Hawthorne effect.**

Several other conclusions were reached by Mayo. Briefly stated he found that

1. Money was only one motivating factor for employees at work. Relations with other employees and supervisors also helped shape attitudes toward jobs.

2. Effective supervision went beyond control, discipline, and corrective action. It included establishing relationships of trust, confidence, and mutual respect. This finding was, unfortunately, interpreted as meaning supervisors should work to make people happy rather than productive.

3. Groups influenced the amount of work individual workers produced. Since standards were set for each type of work, groups tried to prevent highly effective employees from becoming "rate busters" by producing substantially more than the standard. Social pressure in the form of persuasion by other employees, threats, and isolation from informal group activity was used to bring rate busters into line with other employees. There was fear that standards would be increased.

4. Informal work groups also influenced both attitudes and productivity. People became part of informal groups through mutual interests, having similar likes and dislikes, need for security, membership in a group, or any of a number of other reasons. Members of informal groups did not necessarily work together in the same formal department or section. *Formal* in this case means an organizational unit with all employees reporting to the same supervisor.

Although the **human relations movement,** as it came to be known, was a direct outgrowth of the Hawthorne studies of Mayo and his associates, its recommendations were often poorly applied. Some managers felt that the only actions necessary were to make people happy. A happy worker is a good worker, it was thought. Some managers still adhere to this belief.

While still popular until the late 1950s, traditional human relations concepts began to gradually fade. Managers began to fully realize that being happy was not as important as being productive. If both could be achieved, then an ideal would have been reached. Employees who were well-trained, productive, and who felt their jobs were worthwhile also seemed to enjoy their work more than those with simple tasks and few responsibilities.

■ HUMAN RELATIONS REVISED

Like scientific management, human relations approaches set the stage for a great deal of current management thinking. Its findings were well-founded but, for a number of reasons, poorly applied. In the reality of work it is recognized that a number of conditions make "human relating" difficult at best. Some are

1. Supervisors are often chosen because of aggressive, achievement-oriented personalities rather than natural human relations skills. They are frequently impatient with those less knowledgeable and less skilled than the supervisor feels they should be. Human relations skills may be given lip service but in reality receive a relatively low priority by some first-line managers. When attempting to become better "human relaters," these managers often are seen by employees as insincere and manipulative.

2. Some employees do not like being too close to the boss either socially or in working relationships. They prefer to be told what needs to be accomplished and then left alone. Frequently a supervisor's attempts to establish better relations are viewed with suspicion and disbelief. They prefer not to be "human related with."

3. Human relations is often interpreted by higher levels of management as good pay, good working conditions, adequate supervision, and good benefits. As Daniel Bell noted, much human relations was "cow psychology."[3] Workers, he strongly stated, were not contented cows, nor should they be complacent and easily manipulated. Managers must go beyond making the workplace *nice*. They must also remember that productive and competent employees are usually the most satisfied with their work.

As originally conceived, the human relations concepts developed by Mayo and his experimenters were very important to the development of modern management practices. They failed largely because they were poorly implemented. Table 1.2 briefly summarizes some of the contributions of the early founders of management thought and practices in this century.

■ INTO THE PRESENT

In the face of increasing evidence that traditional human relations and efficiency-oriented approaches were not working adequately, a series of new researchers strongly influenced management from the late 1950s to the present. Although their work is very briefly summarized here, several are treated in greater detail in later chapters. These writers are often referred to as *revisionists* because they revised earlier concepts.

TABLE 1.2 ■ Founders of 20th Century Management Thought

Frederick Winslow Taylor	Originated and developed *Scientific Management.* Recognized the importance of standards, believed that there was "one best way to do every job," formulated piece work incentive systems. Considered to be first efficiency expert.
Frank and Lillian Gilbreth	Following Taylor's lead, developed highly precise methods of job analysis and ways of reducing both time and motion in assembly work. Refined efficiency concepts. Modern industrial engineering can be largely traced to their work.
Henry Gantt	A friend and admirer of Taylor, most remembered for developing graphic aids for management. "Gantt charts," bar graphs to chart whether standards are being met, are still used. Is considered to be the founder of modern scheduling techniques.
Henri Fayol	Is considered to be the founder of organizational theory. In his famous *Industrial and General Administration*, Fayol outlined 14 organizational principles, many of which are still used. Fayol was the first to recognize the importance of planning, organizing, controlling, and directing as primary management functions.
Max Weber	Believed strongly in the concept of centralized authority and bureaucracy as a model. Although much maligned in management texts, bureaucracy is still a reality of many, if not most, large organizations.
Elton Mayo	Realized that work organizations are social structures. Identified the reality of group norms, the influence of informal groups, and the necessity for management to recognize the importance of management-employee interaction at work. Is considered the founder of the *Human Relations School* of management thinking.

1. Peter Drucker has been a major force in management thinking for almost 50 years. In 1954 his *Practice of Management*, published by Harper & Row, set the stage for what later came to be known as *management by objectives*. Drucker is still a prolific writer and continues to be a powerful influence on management thinking.

2. Abraham H. Maslow pioneered applied motivational concepts in his famous *Motivation and Personality* (Harper & Row), also in 1954. Maslow is best known for stressing the importance and complexity of needs in motivation. His influence has extended long after his death in 1970 at age 62.

3. Douglas McGregor demonstrated that management style is determined to a large extent by assumptions managers make about employees. In his landmark text, *The Human Side of Enterprise* (McGraw-Hill, 1960), he set the tone for a great deal of today's management theory. McGregor, a social psychologist turned professor of management, died in 1964 at age 58. He is best remembered for his Theory-X and Theory-Y descriptions of management leadership. **Theory X** managers assume employees are naturally lazy, irresponsible, and work only for pay. They must be motivated by prodding, special rewards, and fear. **Theory Y** managers see work as a natural human activity and believe that properly trained and encouraged employees seek responsibility, want to contribute to their organization, prefer challenges to idleness, and control their own behavior.

4. Frederick Herzberg is still an active management thinker and writer. Some of his works have been republished several times. Famous for his "motivation-hygiene" two-factor theory of motivation, he is equally well known for his efforts in demonstrating that employees perform best when work is designed to allow them substantial control over their own performance. Herzberg's concepts have been applied to many of the best-operated organizations. People seem to favorably respond, as he predicted, to added responsibility, control over their own work, and participation in decisions that affect their jobs. This concept of increased employee responsibility and control over their own efforts is called **job enrichment.** Work, according to Herzberg, should be structured to encourage employee involvement. Scott Meyers, a former vice president of Texas Instruments Incorporated and a strong supporter of

Herzberg's concepts, stated that every employee should be trained to be a manager of their own work. His book *Every Employee a Manager* is one of the classics in management literature.

5. In the early 1960s Joan Woodward, an English industrial engineer, began an important series of studies of management styles in various types of business. Her findings indicated that each type of organization (mass production, craft, or automated) required different management styles. Out of her studies grew the realization that appropriate management style depended on the situation.

Contingency-based management recognizes that there is no one best way to manage. Forces in the manager, employees, and conditions of work determine appropriate management approaches.

6. From the late 1960s until the mid-1980s many very excellent management writers influenced management thinking and still continue to do so. Some who have received the greatest public exposure are Rensis Likert, Chris Argyris, Frederick Fiedler, Leonard Sayles, William Ouchi, Tom Peters, and Kenneth Blanchard. Many others equally knowledgeable, though less publicized, have had a profound effect on current management thought.

■ MANAGEMENT STYLE AND ORGANIZATION

Very early in management research it became apparent that *no one management style was best.* Three major factors seem to influence approaches that managers take.

1. **Type of work or situation.** In times of crisis or when an organization is failing to achieve major objectives and crisis is imminent, an authoritarian style may be more appropriate than a more participative one. **Authoritarian management styles** are characterized by decisions being made almost solely by management with little or no employee involvement. Authoritarian supervisors tend to dictate orders and assignments. **Participative management styles** solicit information and assistance from employees in decision making that affects the employees' work or work unit. Managers and employees view their relationship as partnership in making the work unit successful.

   Employees want someone who is decisive, makes accurate, rapid decisions, and is perceived to be in command as their leader in crisis conditions. As conditions improve, employees seem to respond best to a more participative style that allows added self-control. In addition to the quality of the organization's health, the type of work is also important in determining appropriate management style. On a construction site or in a factory, employees expect and usually respond to a directive type of management. Their specific assignments, schedules, and amount of work expected are clearly defined. In general office, sales, or administrative assignments, employees usually have greater control over their personal priorities in achieving work objectives. Professional employees, such as engineers, marketing experts, accountants, teachers, and purchasing agents, usually make their own decisions about what is needed and inform higher levels of management of potential problems, lengths of time required to complete a general assignment, and potential solutions for existing difficulties. Appropriate management style is contingent on (depends on) the situation.

2. **Employee expectations and level of employee skill and knowledge.** Employees with low levels of skill or knowledge often seek and require greater specific direction than those with higher levels of competence. Nurses, as an example, are expected to recognize problems and obtain appropriate assistance when needed and are essentially self-directed. Aides, who may assist nurses, are not expected to have the same level of skills and receive far more specific direction from their supervisors. Type of employees and level of knowledge and experience are major influences on appropriate management approaches.

3. **Management assumptions and perceptions** also influence workplace relations. Managers who assume people are capable of learning and accepting responsibility will take significantly different actions than those who assume employees are incapable without close supervision. They perceive employees as intelligent, capable human beings and often act as coaches, trainers, and sources of information and guidance. One of their major roles is being developers of people. Those who think employees are unable to make decisions and solve work problems view their roles as directors and implementers of corrective action.

Management perceptions, employee characteristics, and the situation or type of work all interact to determine the way organizations are managed. By *interaction*, we mean that each affects the other. Employees view their jobs, the conditions of work, and management from their personal frames of reference. Managers, with different perceptions than those of employees, act in accordance with their assumptions about employees and job requirements. Work conditions and type of activity also influence both management and employees.

■ SYSTEMS AND SUPERVISION

Organizational systems are designed to convert resources, called inputs, to products and services, known as outputs, by use of systematic steps, defined as processes.

First-line managers are directly involved in organizational systems. In workplaces, a **system** refers to converting resources into reality. Supervisors use ideas, policies, experience, knowledge, equipment, supplies, and people to accomplish organizational objectives. All of these resources are combined to produce the service or product of an organization. Each step in converting resources into desired outcomes is called a **process.** Organizations may be viewed as systems that use many types of resources as **inputs** that are processed into required **outputs.**

First-line managers have the primary responsibility for ensuring that processes work properly and that outputs meet organizational objectives. Activities such as selling, maintaining records, developing reports, advising clients or customers, or performing some type of repair or assembly are all processes. They all require the use of resources and all are used to help ensure customer satisfaction, profits, and organizational growth as outcomes.

■ CREATIVE DISCONTENT

Creative discontent is the concept that perfection is never reached in organizations. Good managers stress continuous improvement.

No manager should ever be content with the way things are, regardless of how good they may seem. In a world that is far more competitive than any before, it is essential that managers in the United States seek constant improvement. Masaaki Imai in his book *Kaizen* points out that Japanese competitive success is built on continual improvement.[4] There is little doubt that their management expertise has proven to be extraordinarily effective. To help focus on improvement, first-line managers, as well as others, must repeatedly ask themselves three essential questions:

1. Where are we now? Effective managers must constantly assess how well their organizational unit is performing, whether it is meeting its goals, and if employees are developing increased levels of competency. Areas of potential improvement must be continually identified.

2. Where do we want to be? Based on careful organizational analysis, new goals, targets, and levels of performance can be defined. Better ways of accomplishing tasks and improving quality are primary concerns in building realistic, achievable goals.

3. How do we get there? Having goals does not ensure success. Plans are required. For each part of a goal, specific ways of attaining it must be developed. Experienced supervisors directly involve employees who will be most affected in the planning process. Often people who actually do the work can best identify areas of potential improvement. Once the plans have been formulated, they must be implemented through schedules, assignments, and training, as well as systematic follow-up to determine if required actions are being accomplished according to the plan.

Figure 1.3 pictorially represents the impact of key management questions on creative discontent. These three steps (four, if implementation is counted separately) are a never-ending sequence. They involve defining what is needed, implementing action, and evaluating results in order to determine new possibilities for improvement. During the past few years many U.S. organizations have started to take more seriously the challenge of Japanese, other Asian, and European competition for world markets.

Sadly our improvements have lagged behind those of other developed or developing areas of the world. Emerging trends, however, offer promise of our regaining some of the management

FIGURE 1.3 ■ Creative Discontent

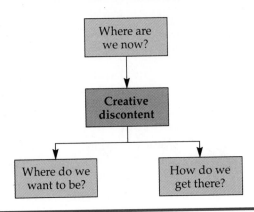

leadership that this country has been known for. In early 1990 many U.S. corporations saw improvements in quality of goods and services in this country as being significant. They predicted the trend will continue until equity with other developed countries is achieved or surpassed for most American-made products and services.[5]

■ TRENDS AND PROMISES

At one time the United States was the model for the world in productivity, innovation, and diversity of products and services. One by one other countries began to take over major markets. Among early casualties were the steel industry, photographic equipment, television and video equipment, automobiles, shoes and clothing, and many other consumer and industrial products. In the mid-1980s this country began to import more food than it exported for the first time. While many of these products are still manufactured here, they are not always viewed as the highest quality on world markets. Some managers are actively seeking ways of increasing competitiveness. Trends, some unfortunately weak, that will take management into the next century and that offer hope for survival of U.S. businesses have started to emerge.

1. **Recognition of change and change management.** Tom Peters has lead the way in voicing the necessity for recognizing and taking advantage of change.[6] While some view Peters's ideas as extreme, his insistence that organizational health and survival in

a complex world often means living with constant change is important. Managers content with doing things the same old way will fail personally, as will their organizations. Although change management has been a significant factor in organizations for many years, it is more important now than in any previous period.

2. Emergence of total quality management. W. Edwards Deming, J. M. Juran, and others have greatly influenced Japanese management thought for over 40 years. Their statistical process-control techniques for improving quality have been developed into a system of total quality management. During the past 10 years, total quality concepts, going well beyond the somewhat limited quality circle concept, have been accepted by some U.S. organizations. Contractors with the federal government must now show they have a total quality program. In many areas of the United States total quality management councils are training management in quality improvement concepts that apply to both service and product-oriented organizations. Some dramatic results have been attained by the United States Air Force in its logistics operations through the use of these concepts. Companies such as Intel, Hewlett-Packard, Procter & Gamble, Genesis Corporation, parts of Ford Motor Company, and many other organizations now view improving quality in every process as an absolutely necessary factor in their growth and survival.

3. Emphasis on continuous training. Marginal workers, those who lack experience and skills, are being viewed as a source of employees. Unusual training methods are often required to develop required skills and motivation. While it is difficult to instill a genuine work ethic in employees who have never been encouraged to develop productive habits, it is sometimes successful and worth the effort in both time and money.

With increasing changes in technology, demands of world competition, and complexity of organizations, training is the keystone to developing and maintaining an effective work force. Continuous upgrading of competencies in a constantly changing, technology-driven environment is necessary. It must apply not only to those who lack necessary skills and knowledge but to all segments of an organization as well.

4. Concern for customers, both internal and external. Management in some organizations is beginning to recognize nearly everyone they deal with is a customer in some sense. Employees who receive instructions, learn of organizational goals, and have schedules defined are internal customers. Other internal customers are first-line managers in other departments, technical specialists, and higher-level managers. External customers include vendors, clients, and many others, such as union leaders, government agents, insurance carriers, and representatives of local public agencies. Total quality management is based on concern for meeting or exceeding customer satisfaction, both external and internal. This may be one of the most significant trends in helping U.S. management successfully build a competitive, aggressive, and assured role in world markets.

5. Concern for organizational culture. During the late 1980s it became apparent that one of the factors that influenced how well organizations function was its attention to organizational culture. *Culture* refers to the primary values of most of the people who work in a company or governmental agency. Ideally organizational culture emphasizes excellence, service, competency, and dedication. It reflects the way people feel about their workplace. It is the willingness of employees to support the concept that personal well-being is directly tied to the well-being of the organizations for which they work. Many larger companies are beginning to attempt to create a work climate that encourages all employees, management and nonmanagement, to support the organization's goals and aspirations. Improved, positive culture can also mean improved positive workplaces.

■ REALITIES FOR SUPERVISORS

Although future trends hold many positive promises, other types of change are creating unusual realities for supervisors. Four of these are becoming increasingly evident. Increased dependence on technology-driven workplaces, changing demographics, multicultural work forces, and an increasing pool of marginally acceptable employees are among those most easily identified. In many offices, typewriters, a primary tool for the past 75 years, have disappeared. File cabinets have also been reduced to storage for only the most essential documents. Paper has been largely replaced for internal information by electronic systems. Regardless of type of organization, supervisors must rely on computer-based information systems to accomplish their work. A novelty in some organizations as recently as the early 1980s, computers, especially desktop varieties, are now necessities. Supervisors who do not understand or use computerized systems are often at a real disadvantage. Schedules, information sources, work monitoring, and data that allow analysis of group as well as individual performance is usually computer-based. Both the programs and hardware used to provide information and analysis is always becoming more sophisticated. Supervisors must be able to effectively utilize information systems as well as the efforts of their employees to achieve organizational goals.

Each year the total work force grows faster than the number of teenagers available to fill entry-level jobs. As a result, older people are now found in jobs that were once the almost exclusive domain of entry-level employees just out of high school. Many younger supervisors are finding that their employees are older and often more experienced in a variety of work than they are.

Managers at all levels also recognize that women are breaking barriers that formerly slowed their entrance into higher levels of management. Both female and male supervisors, with increasing frequency, find that their managers are women. There is evidence that much larger numbers of women and minorities than Caucasian males will enter the active work force of the United States during the foreseeable future. Changing demographics of the work force is a major factor with which management at all levels must be concerned. First-line managers are most directly affected.

Although it has always been a "melting pot of the world," the United States continues to become more varied than ever. In many large cities people of European descent are no longer the majority. Supervisors frequently find their employees have difficulty understanding both the language and customs of the United States. Some companies are attempting to bridge the cultural, linguistic, and employee expectations gap by providing special training in dealing with multicultural work forces, including language training. There is no evidence that the trend toward diversity will reverse during the remainder of this century.

A major difficulty is that there will continue to be a shortage of educated, trained employees available. It will be necessary for employers to increase training and motivational efforts to convert what were once considered marginal employees into useful members of the work force. A long-range benefit of these efforts may be a general upgrading of what was once considered a highly questionable segment of the labor pool.

Supervision, already a difficult and challenging job, will continue to grow in both complexity and skill requirements. With changes in the social, economic, and political climate of the world, top-level managers must constantly develop strategies to retain

TABLE 1.3 ■ Supervision—Present, Past, and Future

Here yesterday, here today, and here tomorrow.	Since earliest recorded history, supervisors have managed by use of fear, coercion, and manipulation. Many of today's supervisors and their immediate managers, unfortunately, still view their primary roles as rule enforcers, error correctors, and punishers of mistakes. They use fear as their primary motivational tool.
Efficiency experts and task masters.	After thousands of years of management by force, some managers in this century recognized that improved methods, well-developed standards, established procedures, and clear direction improved productivity. People, like machines, had to be programmed to perform. Job simplification, limited responsibility, and "no-brainer" work appeared to be the way to increased productivity. Some still believe employees do not want to work and, most of all, do not want to think.
Participation and common management-employee goals are the keys to organizational success.	Over a long period of time, primarily during the latter part of this century, managers began to realize that employees are individuals with different interests, different ways of viewing their organizations, and unique needs. By encouraging participation in job-related decisions, both morale and productivity can be improved. It is a concept preached loudly but only partially heard and rarely understood.
Elimination of fear, team development, and emphasis on constant improvement.	When it became blatantly clear that managers in other countries were frequently more successful in achieving goals than their United States counterparts, some organizations have recently encouraged their managers to try new tactics. Quality, freedom from fear, self-managed work teams, emphasis on achievement, and constant improvement are already making their mark in better-managed organizations.
Into the future.	Old concepts, some dating from antiquity, die hard. Progressive organizations realize that employees and managers both must contribute more than skills, knowledge, and energy for organizational survival. All members of organizations are partners who must react together in an era of rapid technological, economic, and social change. Flexibility, adaptability, openness, and voluntary cooperation are emerging norms in the best organizations.

their competive positions in world economies and world markets. Supervisors, as the final management step in making such goals realities, are under constant pressure to improve both quality and quantity. As the first line of management, supervisors will find themselves as developers of people through coaching, encouraging, training, and providing information. It can be a personally rewarding as well as highly demanding experience. A brief review of some of the past management thinking that is still present as well as trends toward the future are reviewed in Table 1.3.

■ THINGS TO REMEMBER

I. Supervisors are the first line of management.

    A. Supervisors accomplish organizational objectives through the efforts of their employees.

    B. No other level of management is as directly concerned with the actual performance of the services or products of an organization as are supervisors.

II. Major supervisory concerns include:

    A. Effectiveness.

    B. Efficiency.

    C. Responsibility.

    D. Authority.

    E. Accountability.

    F. Coordination.

III. Levels of management are:

    A. Top-level managers concerned with the overall goals of their organizations.

    B. Mid-level managers responsible for interpreting the policies of top management.

    C. Supervisors (first line of management) responsible for the work of individual employees who perform the vital tasks of an organization.

IV. Frederick Winslow Taylor is considered the founder of scientific management.

    A. Taylor advanced the concepts of work measurement, standards, piece rate incentive programs, and one best way to do every job.

    B. Taylor's work and that of his followers provided the basis for time and motion studies.

V. The importance of human relations at work was defined by Elton Mayo in studies made at the Western Electric Plant in Hawthorne, Illinois. His findings include:

    A. Both formal and informal groups influence productivity.

    B. Effective supervision requires establishing relationships of trust, confidence, and mutual respect with employees.

VI. Into the present.

    A. Major changes in management theory were developed in the period from the mid-1850s to the present.

B. Major concepts include management by objectives, contingency management, job design, management assumptions about people, and motivational theory.

VII. Management style and organization.

A. No one management style is best for all sets of conditions.

B. Management style is affected by the situation, employee expectations, and management perceptions.

VIII. Organizational systems.

A. First-line managers have primary responsibility for ensuring work processes result in the desired outputs of their organization.

B. Efficient and effective use of resources is a primary supervisory responsibility.

IX. Creative discontent—no manager should be content with the status quo.

X. Trends and promises:

A. Emergence of Total Quality Management.

B. Emphasis on training.

C. Concern for both internal and external customers.

D. Concern for organizational culture.

XI. Realities for supervisors.

A. Changing technology.

B. Changing demographics.

C. Multicultural, multilingual work forces.

D. Necessity to train and motivate what were once considered marginal employees.

■ KEY TERMS

supervisors	Frederick Winslow Taylor
effectiveness	scientific management
efficiency	standards
responsibility	piece-rate system
authority	optimum effort
accountability	Henri Fayol
coordination	scalar chain

Max Weber	**job enrichment**
bureaucracy	**authoritarian styles**
Elton Mayo	**participative styles**
Hawthorne effect	**system**
human relations movement	**process**
Theory X	**inputs**
Theory Y	**outputs**

■ DISCUSSION QUESTIONS

1. In what ways does the job of first-line managers differ from those of employees in organizations with which you are familiar?

2. What type of special challenges do organizations you are familiar with face during the next few years?

3. Based on articles in business magazines such as *Fortune, Forbes, Business Week, Harvard Business Review,* and others available in your library, what are some current problems faced by management at all levels?

4. What contributions of past management analysts and writers are evident in organizations with which you are familiar?

5. Which of the many emerging trends in management do you feel will be most significant in the future? Explain your selection.

■ SELF-ASSESSMENT

Listed below are 10 statements designed to help you evaluate your supervisory characteristics. Choose the response that best represents your feelings. An answer of 1 or 2 means that you strongly disagree or that the statement is not true. Answers of 5 and 6 mean you strongly agree or that the statement is totally true in your case. Answers less than 6 but more than 1 represent lower-strength responses.

1. I usually take full responsibility for my own actions and the performance of those who report to me.

    1   2   3   4   5   6

2. When faced with a potentially unpleasant decision or task, such as reprimanding an employee, I usually request the assistance of higher levels of management.

    1   2   3   4   5   6

3. Happy people are productive people. A supervisor's first responsibility is to make people happy.

1   2   3   4   5   6

4. It is best for supervisors to act like one of the employees rather than as a member of management in dealing with work problems. This will keep employees from resenting the supervisor for being a big shot.

1   2   3   4   5   6

5. In the real world of work, effective supervisors realize that they must learn to manipulate employees to ensure quality and productivity.

1   2   3   4   5   6

6. Scientific approaches to management have demonstrated that there is one best way to manage all types of work.

1   2   3   4   5   6

7. Technology has improved to the point that less knowledge is required by employees than in the past.

1   2   3   4   5   6

8. Managers should not change the way things are done once a procedure has been proven to work well.

1   2   3   4   5   6

9. At the present time the United States has the reputation for making the best-quality products in world markets.

1   2   3   4   5   6

10. Good supervisors concentrate on control, corrective action, and taking disciplinary action when employees make mistakes.

1   2   3   4   5   6

■ SHORT CASES

Connie's Concern

After just one and one-half years Connie Preaker was made supervisor of the small business liability claims-processing unit for Advanced Security Knowledge (ASK), a major small business insurer. All of the people who now reported to her were co-workers who started with ASK at approximately the same time as Connie.

Most of the 12 employees whom she now supervised either supported or were neutral toward her promotion. Four, however, were definitely antagonistic. They felt George Carney would have been a better selection since he was the first choice of Paul Rankin, Connie's former supervisor.

In order to establish herself, Connie called a meeting of her entire staff. "Here are some things I'd like to do," she began. "First, I'd like to appoint two group leaders—one to head accounts for retail organizations and the other for those that are wholesale distributors. They are the bulk of our business. I also feel that many of our procedures need revising. Your help is expected in upgrading the way we do most of our work. Another plan I have involves a job rotation system in order for everyone to learn all the jobs in our department. During the next two weeks we will have meetings to finalize the details of these suggestions. If you have any comments, please make them now."

To her surprise, Connie was greeted by total silence. As the meeting ended, Connie heard one of the employees remark, "Doesn't she think we work hard enough already?" "Paul sure wouldn't have done it that way," was the reply.

1. Even though she was sincere, what could Connie have done differently?
2. What are some special problems new supervisors have when their group is made up of people whom they once worked with?
3. New supervisors can usually expect some resentment when they are promoted over people who were their peers. Why does this often happen?

Ask Someone Else

Connie found herself with a number of problems as the new supervisor of ASK's small business claims-processing unit. From time to time she had to send audit teams of two or three people to various client locations to gather data for accident, health, and safety violation claims. Some of the trips required travel of one or two days in cities serviced by ASK.

Claims investigators were evenly balanced between men and women. They took their jobs seriously and had helped ASK build an enviable reputation in insurance research and assistance. When a need arose for a team to go to Lincoln, Bonnie selected Steve Salz and Sherill Raze as the audit team. Both were experienced and competent in their jobs.

On the day following their assignments, Al Raze, Sherill's husband, called Connie. "You know as well as I do," he began, "that Steve is the worst person to send on a trip with a married woman. He only has one thing on his mind. You know as well as I do that Steve is a single guy that plays around a lot and I don't want him playing with Sherill."

1. How should Connie respond to Sherill's husband?

2. If Connie assigns someone other than Sherill to the audit team, how will Sherill feel and how will other employees react?

3. Should Sherill say anything to Steve? Why?

■ ENDNOTES

1. Bradford Boyd has written extensively on supervision and management for many years. His most recent text, *Supervision* (McGraw-Hill, 1986), continues the tradition.

2. For an excellent discussion of Taylor's experiments, see Arthur Bedian, *Management* (Dryden Press, 1986).

3. Daniel Bell's *Work and Its Discontents* was published in 1956 by Beacon Press. His "cow psychology" description has been quoted in many texts.

4. Masaaki Imani, *Kaizen* (Random House Business Division, 1986) is highly recommended reading for serious management students. It describes the basis for Japan's success in modern work-improvement techniques.

5. Quality improvements in the United States have been reported in many sources, including *Forbes, Fortune, The Wall Street Journal, The Christian Science Monitor, Business Week,* and *Nation's Business.*

6. Tom Peters is author of several texts and a popular spokesperson for excellence in management. Some of his concepts are discussed more specifically in Chapter 7 of this text. His concern with excellence has made him one of the most popular management lecturers.

Chapter 2

Supervisors at Work: What They Do and How They Act

■ ▬▬▬▬▬▬▬▬▬▬▬ ■

Objectives

Chapter 2 focuses on primary areas of management knowledge and basic concepts that effective supervisors must learn. Its information will enable readers to

■ Identify major supervisory functions.

■ Recognize basic causes of supervisory failure.

■ Define the major categories of skill supervisors must have to be effective.

■ Understand the impact of organizational size on supervision.

Thought Starter

Just as all people are different, so are organizations and those who manage them. Supervisors in a bank act differently from those on a construction site or in a department store. Within organizations, supervisors differ in their roles and functions. Accounting department supervisors have different concerns from those in marketing or maintenance. Individual supervisors often have other methods for achieving desired results, even though they may work for the same organization.

Even in highly standardized places of work like McDonald's or the Gap clothing stores, supervisors find their roles somewhat different from their counterparts in other locations. Regardless of differences, however, all have many common concerns and must have similar skills and knowledge. All must deal with people, all are involved in planning and directing the activities of employees in their work unit, and all are responsible for the performance of those whom they supervise. In addition, they are accountable to higher levels of management for the performance of their group.

Like other levels of management, first-line supervisors often find their jobs constantly increasing in complexity and requiring skills and knowledge not needed by nonmanagement employees. Their jobs are often frustrating, nearly always demanding, and often highly rewarding.

■ *Paul Plesica was hired as training coordinator for James and Watters Scientific Company (JAWS) specifically to develop supervisory training programs. JAWS had received a significant NASA contract to design a variety of devices for applications in advanced space shuttle flights. JAWS had, for over 15 years, been in design, marketing, and sales of equipment used in chemical analysis. Their customers ranged from food processors and cosmetic companies to pharmaceutical and medical instrumentation organizations.*

One of Paul's major concerns was that many types of supervisors needed to be trained in the rapidly expanding company. Some were in administrative departments such as accounting and purchasing, others in manufacturing, and still others in sales, research, maintenance, quality control, and a variety of other activities. His primary task was to identify a common body of knowledge needed by all supervisors. He could then conduct classes for supervisors in a variety of organizational units.

■ SUPERVISORS AND ORGANIZATIONS

Nearly all organizations have a surprising variety of activities that must be accomplished. Employees in service organizations such as restaurants, hospitals, insurance companies, airlines, colleges, automobile repair services, and governmental agencies are usually in direct contact with clients or customers. Supervisors in service organizations must constantly be aware of the reaction of users of their services far more than those in manufacturing, research, or construction organizations. For the most part these supervisors have a wider variety of tasks to accomplish and different problems from those in production, research and development, or construction.

In organizations where little direct contact exists between employees and customers, work may have less variation and different areas of emphasis. Supervisors are usually concerned with motivational problems, maintaining high levels of quality and at the same time maintaining schedules. They also must plan the activities of others, organize work, delegate tasks to employees, and be the leaders of their work teams in accomplishing what are often repetitive tasks.

Regardless of whether they are working in an insurance claims department, medical supply company, personal computer assembly operations, or telephone installation services, supervisors share a common set of activities. All must deal with people, all are concerned with the way various tasks are accomplished, and all are involved in analyzing present conditions and planning new activities. They must also be decision makers, problem solvers and innovators.

In nearly every type of organization, there are constant challenges. Experienced supervisors know that the types of major activities for which they are responsible are also performed with different emphasis by higher levels of management.

■ MAJOR SUPERVISORY SKILLS AND FUNCTIONS

In order to be effective, managers must have many skills. Robert L. Katz, a highly regarded analyst of management action, observed most management skills were either technical, human, or conceptual.[1] Each is necessary and constantly used, but the proportion of time spent on each skill varies with the level of management, as shown in Figure 2.1.

Technical supervisory skills are those concerned with the knowledge and skills of performing a specific task.

Technical skills involve the "doing" part of a job. Salespeople must know how to approach, inform, and assist clients or customers. They must also assist in the selection of merchandise or service that is most suitable and must complete necessary sales documents. Accountants must know proper accounting procedures for cost analysis, completion of income statements, computation of net worth, and many other types of accounting activities. In manufacturing operations employees must be able to use equipment properly, complete assembly or machine operations, meet quality specifications, avoid waste, and meet schedules. Whether in sales, accounting, or manufacturing, supervisors are required to train, recognize when work is not being performed adequately, know procedures and equipment, and analyze methods for performance improvement. All of these require job knowledge. While

FIGURE 2.1 ■ Essential Management Skills

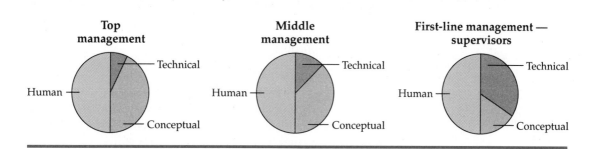

employees can perform specific jobs better than their supervisors in most instances, supervisors have the responsibility for being coaches, evaluators, and problem solvers. First-line managers, with the responsibility for supervising nonmanagement employees, are more directly involved with technical skills than any other level of management.

Human skills are necessary for all managers. They must relate effectively to employees, other managers, customers, union leadership, vendors, government agencies, and others.

Human skills are those that involve other people. Most supervisors know that learning the technical side of their work is not nearly as difficult as developing effective interpersonal skills. People problems are usually more difficult to diagnose and solve than those involving technical aspects of work.

Communication, conflict resolution, building confidence and trust, empathizing with the feelings of others, being willing to inform and assist, and behaving in ways that serve as a model for employees are all interpersonal human relations skills. Supervisors have the unique requirement of linking employees with other levels of management and other parts of the organization. Their human relations skill requirements are often difficult since they must be able to recognize employee viewpoints and also be managers. All levels of management from supervisors to the highest levels in an organization must have effective human relations skills for an organization to function adequately.

Conceptual skills are those that require analysis, concept formulation, and visualization of the way things must be accomplished.

Conceptual skills are those that require visualizing future events, speculating on the consequence of a decision, analyzing data and drawing logical conclusions, planning both long and short-range actions, organizing work and people, deciding on the direction of an organization, and formulating guiding policies. Any activity that does not directly involve the technical or human side of work is likely to be conceptual in nature. Conceptual skills are the "thinking" part of work. Just as technical skills more directly involve supervisors, conceptual skills are utilized to a greater degree by higher levels of management. Table 2.1 briefly summarizes the primary features of Katz's classification of essential management skills.

Major Supervisory Functions

Management functions are a group of related activities that managers must perform.

In addition to utilizing the major skills defined by Katz, managers also perform several essential functions. A **function** can best be understood as a group of related activities, some technical, others either human or conceptual. Henri Fayol was among the first writers, as stated in Chapter 1, to identify the importance of what he

TABLE 2.1 ■ Summary of Katz's Essential Management Skills

Technical skills	More important to supervisors than other levels of management. Involves ability to use and coach employees, use tools, techniques, procedures, on-the-job skills, and necessary job knowledge.
Human skills	Important to all levels of management. Includes communication, building effective interpersonal relations, demonstrating trust and confidence, resolving conflict, and behaving in ways others admire.
Conceptual skills	Utilized more at each higher level of management. A primary activity of top management and important to middle managers. Used to a degree by supervisors. Involves the "thinking into the future" part of managing. Long-range planning, analysis of business trends, determining marketing strategy, and developing more effective organizational formats are all conceptual in nature.

called the *elements of management.*[2] These are now recognized as primary management functions. Fayol's list included planning, organizing, commanding, coordinating, and controlling. In 1934 Luther Gulick coined the acronym *PODSCORB* to identify management processes.[3] Gulick based his famous acronym on Fayol's earlier writings. PODSCORB means planning, organizing, directing, staffing, coordination, reporting, and budgeting. Over many years, Fayol's and Gulick's list has been shortened. Today planning, organizing, controlling, and directing are generally accepted as the **primary management functions.**

These general management functions are accomplished in many ways. Communication, motivation, delegation, coordination, information, and organizational analysis are just a few of the methods managers use daily. Supervisors are responsible for being the initiators of the ultimate purposes of the organizations.

Typical Supervisory Activities

In every organization supervisors have different functions from those in other organizations. They also have unique expectations of their performance by both higher levels of management and by employees. It is impossible to catalog all of their individual roles. Some activities, however, are typical of most supervisory functions.

1. Through communication, coordinate the activities of employees to ensure that work is accomplished smoothly with a thorough understanding of individual responsibilities.

2. Act as leaders in motivating employees to meet both organizational expectations and to satisfy their needs for accomplishment. Involve employees in decisions affecting their work.

3. Plan, schedule, and delegate duties to ensure minimum duplication of effort as well as optimum efficiency in job performance. Identify potential problems and develop methods for minimizing their impact.

4. Provide information, assistance, and encouragement to employees. Help resolve on-the-job problems.

5. Keep higher levels of management informed of developments in the supervisor's area of responsibility and authority.

6. Evaluate both group and individual performance and take necessary corrective actions to ensure that work is accomplished as planned.

7. Coordinate activities with other sections or departments in the organization.

8. Help resolve conflicts between employees; maintain control and ensure that reasonable rules of behavior are being met.

9. Act as coaches, counselors, and trainers in assisting employees who have difficulties in performing their assigned tasks.

10. Constantly act as a developer of people, monitor of quality and productivity, and organizer of activities.

Most experienced, competent supervisors find it difficult to do all of the things they think are necessary. They are successful because they see their jobs as constant challenges and learning experiences. Less competent supervisors fail to realize that constant effort and dedication to excellence is always required.

Importance of Major Supervisory Activities

Although we know that supervisors are not limited to the basic functions of planning, organizing, controlling, and directing, the importance of these activities cannot be overlooked. Rarely do supervisors view these activities in any particular sequence. They plan when planning is required, reorganize both people and work to improve effectiveness and efficiency, control when corrective action is needed, and direct to ensure that people know what is needed and expected. Managers, including supervisors, all plan, organize, direct, and control. In order to carry out these basic functions they utilize a number of skills or tools. Figure 2.2 shows the relationship between managers, functions, and tools used to complete essential activities.

▪ PLANNING

Planning involves deciding on a course of action for the future. Although it is considered one of the key elements of effective

FIGURE 2.2 ▪ Supervisory Functions and Activities

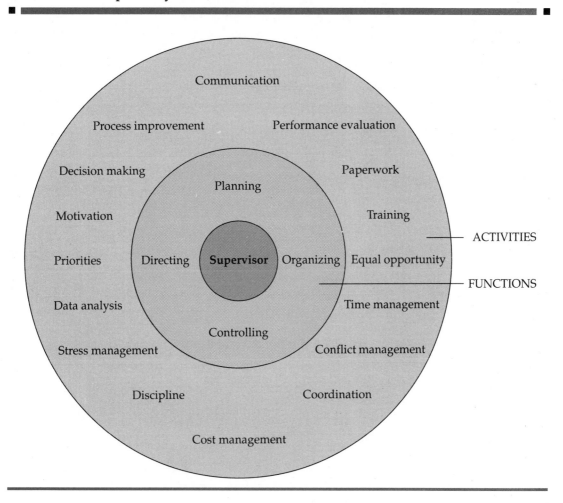

Operational planning is the day-to-day planning required to make work flow smoothly.

management, many supervisors fail to take either the time or make the effort to carefully plan their activities and those of their employees.

Most supervisors are concerned with day-to-day or **operational planning.** Typical operational plans include schedules, work assignments, equipment and materials usage, inventory procedures, and any other activities required on a regular basis. Operational plans convert the strategic and tactical planning of higher levels of management into reality.

Mid-level managers are concerned with interpreting policy within the framework of their departments and making plans to accomplish major projects. These functions are considered to be **tactical planning.** Top-level managers are often concerned with **strategic planning,** or long-range planning, designed to ensure the competitive position of an organization. Strategic plans usually become guidelines or policies that direct the organization over relatively long periods of time. They set the direction of the organization and help mid-level and first-line managers define ways of contributing to overall organizational objectives. Steps that lead to achieving management objectives are pictured in Figure 2.3.

Tactical plans are concerned with accomplishing major projects that support strategic plans.

Strategic plans are the long-range plans designed to ensure the competitive position of an organization.

When managers ask "Where do we want to be?" and then formulate a series of answers, they are setting objectives. This essential decision concerning what is needed to improve effectiveness and efficiency in meeting organizational goals is the first step in the planning process. Planning details stem from the question, "How do we get there?" Some plans may have a single use, others have multiple uses, and some are standing plans.

Single-use plans are composed of a series of steps necessary to accomplish a specific action.

Single-use plans are composed of a series of steps necessary to accomplish a specific action. If a supervisor knows that a vital report is due, a series of actions may be considered. A typical single-use, operational plan for completing a marketing report may include considerations such as these: Janet Mendez will do the statistical calculations, Bob Duran will compile the data, Paul Hanrahan will write the narrative explanation, and Susan Hodges will be responsible for the final editing. **Multiple-use plans** can be used in a variety of situations. Many multiple-use plans are in the form of **procedures.** They provide step-by-step instructions on ways to accomplish certain types of work. In a shipping department, as an example, regardless of where or by what means, the procedure is followed. **Standing plans** are usually those that apply to an entire organization and rarely change. An example is an emergency evacuation plan.

Multiple-use plans can apply to a variety of situations.

FIGURE 2.3 ■ Building a Yellow-Brick Road—Strategic, Tactical, and Operational Planning

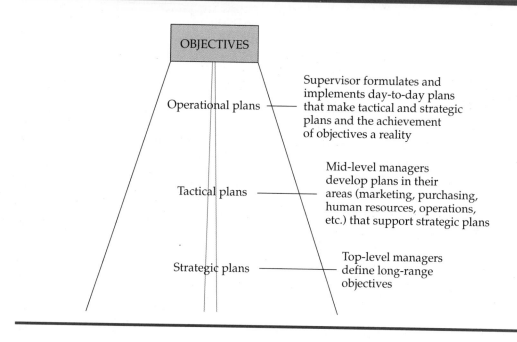

All of the employees involved in completing a report must complete their work within a limited amount of time. Effective supervisors know that formal plans are usually better than those that are informal. **Formal plans** are put into writing and can be used by both the planner and others whom the plans affect. **Informal plans** are often written on calendars or to-do lists and are not distributed to others. Informal plans may also be a sequence of ideas that are never put in writing. Effective supervisors quickly learn that formal plans are far more reliable and include many steps that informal plans may omit.

There are usually several layers of plans. A concept—or objective—is often the basis for what some managers designate as *preplans*. A **preplan** is usually a statement of what is needed and the overall steps for accomplishing it. If a person wants to build a doghouse, his or her preplan consists of knowing where it will be located, why it is needed, how it will be constructed, who will do the work, and when it will be completed. Each of these steps will have detailed subplans for their completion. How it will be built will include the type of flooring or foundation, materials, roofing,

Formal plans are in writing and are formatted so they can be used by all people affected by them.

Informal plans are usually for the sole benefit of the planner.

size, and may include descriptive drawings. Where it will be located may state the actual site and which direction the front will face. Both the preplan and the several subplans make up the total plan. Defining what, why, where, when, who, and how are important parts of most plans.

Planning Steps

Even though it is less formal at the operational level, planning has become increasingly important for supervisors. As the final step in the management chain, supervisors have direct responsibility for the services or products that customers use. Employees implement their plans to achieve the ultimate tasks of an organization.

In his popular text *Thriving on Chaos* Tom Peters points out that the length of a plan is not as important as the process of planning.[4] A good planning process involves everyone who is affected by the plan, can be easily changed as conditions change, and points the direction an organization or organizational unit needs to go.

In the *Wizard of Oz*, Dorothy must find the Emerald City in order to ask the Wizard how to return to Kansas. Formulating a plan is in a very real sense building a yellow brick road, as depicted in Figure 2.3. A supervisor's goal is the Emerald City and the plan tells how to get there, brick by brick. Unlike Dorothy, supervisors must recognize that even the best plans may not work well and that changes are often required. While change for change's sake is not recommended, neither is an inflexible or rigid adherence to outdated and often unworkable plans. Some of the basic steps in operational planning are briefly summarized in Table 2.2.

Supervisors and Planning

There is little doubt that planning will increase in importance for supervisors in the foreseeable future. In a world of almost constant change in technology, services, product demands, societal values, economic shifts, and organizational realignments, planning is an essential tool in helping ensure that work is accomplished with minimum difficulty. To fully appreciate the importance of good planning, it is helpful to understand the difference between reactive and proactive styles of management.

Reactive managers see their primary role as taking corrective action when necessary.

Reactive managers see their primary roles as waiting for problems to occur and then taking corrective action. This approach is

TABLE 2.2 ■ Fundamental Planning Processes

1. Organizational analysis	Organizational analysis is the systematic review of every aspect of a total organization or one of its parts. Supervisors must constantly review how well they are doing in terms of schedules, costs, labor utilization, quality, and related activities. It involves answering the question, "Where are we now?"
2. Setting goals or objectives	Answers to the question "Where do we want to be?" stem from organizational analysis. Once objectives are well understood, effective plans can be made to achieve them.
3. Planning to achieve objectives	Careful formulation of step-by-step actions, including what is being accomplished, why it is being done, who has major responsibility for individual tasks, when each step will start and be completed, where each step will be performed, and how it will be accomplished, including procedures, equipment, materials, and activities.
4. Plan implementation	Organizing activities, assigning specific areas of responsibility, obtaining necessary human resources, space, materials, and equipment. Initiating and coordinating each step of the plan.
5. Follow-up	Includes assessment of progress in implementing the plan as well as final determination of plan's effectiveness in meeting objectives. Can be used as a basis for necessary change.

sometimes known as *fire fighting* or *crisis management*. Reactive managers are constantly running from one problem to another trying to solve every problem that arises. They frequently complain that they do not have time to plan. Reactive managers exhibit little real confidence in their employees. Their insistence on checking every detail of work, even though employees actually performing a given task may be fully capable, communicates a lack of confidence. In a very real sense they are relieving employees of major responsibilities. Often reactive supervisors do work themselves rather than trust their employees. As a consequence, they increase their own inefficiency by not attending to other management responsibilities.

Proactive managers concentrate on problem prevention through planning. They want to minimize the necessity for corrective action.

Proactive managers know that problem prevention is far better than problem correction. Planning is the key ingredient in achieving success. Experienced supervisors realize that unless everyone in their work unit fully understands the steps necessary to complete

FIRST-LINERS

a given job, no plan will work. Two major factors, often neglected by reactive managers, serve as guides for proactive managers:

1. Plans must be flexible. It is better to use a poorly designed plan than none at all. While we recommend that supervisors try to utilize existing plans, they must also realize that as conditions change, plans must change also.

2. Employees should be involved in plans that directly affect their work. One of the most useful techniques of obtaining employee support is to involve them in all plans or decisions that directly affect their work.

Just as long-range strategic planning is a fundamental top management concern, proactive supervisors plan the operations of their work units. They know what must be accomplished, why it is required, when it will be done, who has responsibility for its completion, where work will take place, and how it will be performed.

Planning Realities

For a number of reasons, plans, even when carefully and skillfully formulated, fail. One of the most common reasons is simple failure to follow a plan carefully once it is made. Both supervisors and employees often think they know what needs to be done based on past experience. They fail to realize that good plans include changes, improved efficiency, and guidelines for action. A second major cause of planning failure results from unforeseen circumstances, such as equipment failure, power outages, poorly trained employees, and pressures that interrupt work already started. It is often said that management, especially first-line management, is a series of interruptions, interrupted by interruptions. Another major reason for planning failure is poor implementation. Having a plan isn't enough. Supervisors must assign specific tasks, communicate what needs to be accomplished, coordinate work effort, evaluate and analyze progress, and monitor progress to ensure planning steps are not overlooked.

Just as plans may not be completely successful in every situation, they have many very real benefits. Among the more obvious are

1. Work is accomplished on time.
2. Duplication of effort may be avoided.
3. Effort is utilized more efficiently and effectively.
4. Costs can be minimized.
5. Employees have a better understanding of organizational goals.
6. Quality as well as productivity can be improved.
7. Wasted effort, materials, equipment, and time is minimized.

When both supervisors and employees in their work group fully realize planning benefits, plans are more likely to succeed.

■ ORGANIZATION OF WORK BY FIRST-LINE MANAGERS

In an early "Sesame Street" program, a king called his subjects together to announce that the annual picnic would be held Friday in Central Park, beginning at 11:00 A.M. To let everyone contribute, he made a request of the crowd gathered in the plaza in front of his castle. "I would like some of you to bring sandwiches, some lemonade, and some watermelon. We will have a wonderful time." When Friday came, everyone brought lemonade to the park. A major error in organization had been made by the king. He forgot to let his people know who was to bring lemonade, who was to bring sandwiches, and who was responsible for supplying watermelon. Effective organization of work is designed to ensure that employees know not only what is needed,

Organizing means putting things in order.

but who is responsible for specific activities. *Organization* means to arrange elements of work in logical systematic ways that can be understood by all of its members. In very simple terms, it means *putting things in order.*

There are three major aspects of organization that supervisors must understand: structure, processes, and behavior.

Organizational Structure

Organizational structure defines who reports to whom and major areas of responsibility.

Organizational structure is primarily concerned with defining the way work is divided, who reports to whom, and major areas of responsibility. Like other aspects of management, there is no one best way to organize. A file cabinet may be organized in alphabetical order, by date, geographical area, subject, numerical code, or a combination of these. To be organized, it must be divided into logical segments that can be easily located and used when needed. Work is structured much the same way. It is divided into logical units, such as type of work, customer or client served, geographic area, or major project. All employees, including supervisors and mid-level managers as well as nonmanagement employees, know to whom they report and activities for which they are responsible.

Organizational charts delineate organizational structure, areas of responsibility, and lines of authority.

Most organizations define their overall structure with an organization chart. Organization charts graphically depict major functions, who reports to whom, major areas of responsibility, lines of authority, and how work flows. Unlike plans, organization structure may define what work unit will accomplish specific tasks but it does not show how, when, or why a specific task must be accomplished. Boxes on organization charts usually contain names and titles of key people in an organization. Each box depicts an **area of responsibility.** A department manager's area of responsibility includes all of the people and types of work reporting to her or his box. Lines on the chart that connect areas of responsibility to those above and below individual boxes represent **lines of authority.** Authority is granted by the function above an individual box and extends downward to other functions. Figure 2.4 is a schematic example of an organizational chart with both areas of responsibility and lines of authority.

When supervisors divide work, they usually think of who does what in their section, department, or other organizational unit. Their major task is to divide projects into logical units and assign parts of the overall job to individuals in their work group. Experienced supervisors recognize that for work to flow smoothly it must be assigned evenly. Every employee must exert approximately equal effort. Supervisors must also be able to determine if the way they have assigned jobs allows accurate determination of whether tasks are being accomplished within budget, on time, and with the required level of quality.

Depending on the type of organization, its size, and long-range goals, supervisors may divide work in several ways. No one

FIGURE 2.4 ■ Areas of Responsibility and Lines of Authority

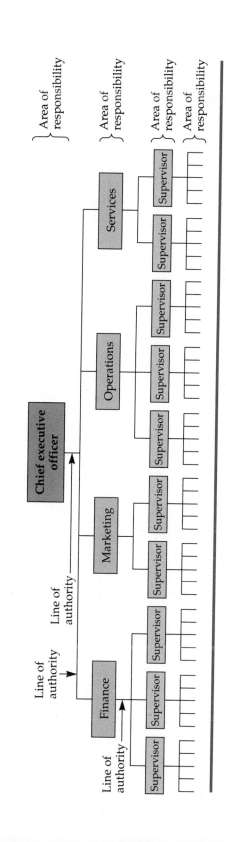

49

way is best for all organizational units within a given company or public agency.

Organizational Processes

Organizational processes consist of the step-by-step activities necessary to accomplish the work of an organization.

Every organization has its own ways of ensuring that work is accomplished in ways that meet objectives. These step-by-step procedures are called **processes**. A process is a series of actions necessary to accomplish a specific task. For most organizations to hire a new employee, they must perform several types of activities:

1. Identification of the type of job to be filled must be made. This usually requires a job description and a job specification. A description is essentially a list of all of the types of tasks an employee must perform to do the job. A clerk may be required to make data entries on a computer, maintain files, answer telephone requests for information, design and write reports, and put letters in proper format. These activities constitute a description of duties. A job specification is a list of training, education, experience, and physical requirements required to adequately perform the job description.

2. Recruitment involves attracting qualified applicants through announcements within an organization or advertising outside of the organization.

3. Selection is concerned with screening applicants, testing applicants, if necessary, interviewing, and making a final choice of a person to fill the job opening.

Each step is part of the process of employment. In every organization there are many—often hundreds—of processes. Each contributes to the overall goal of the organization. A current trend in organizations is to carefully analyze each process to ensure that every step is appropriate and correctly performed.

Organizational Behavior

Organizational culture consists of the primary values of an organization.

Every organization has its own personality. One part of its personality is the organization's **culture**. Culture refers to the primary values of the organization and the type of image it tries to portray, both internally and externally. As stated in Chapter 1, culture is an important and frequently overlooked component of organizational life. Many organizations, especially larger ones, are trying to create a culture of optimism, excellence, and customer service.[5]

Policy statements, internal communications, and image advertising in these organizations set the tone for their culture. Top management commitment is an essential ingredient of culture development. A significant part of culture involves the way organizations see their employees as well as their customers. Some treat employees as subordinates who obey the will of managers. Conformity to rules and limited employee involvement characterize this type of work environment. These organizations view customers as people who must be persuaded to buy their services or products.

Other organizations view employees as partners in the enterprise and not just hired hands. Employees participate in decisions affecting their jobs and are treated as key members of a team composed of managers, "doers," and specialist advisors. Customers are also treated as partners whose needs the organization must fulfill.

Supervisors and Organizational Processes

Supervisors are involved in organizational structure primarily through assigning specific tasks. A significant component of effective organizations is a thorough understanding of who is responsible for completing specific jobs. One of supervisors' most important tasks is refinement of existing processes to improve both their effectiveness and efficiency. In some instances they may create new processes, eliminate those no longer needed or that are inefficient, and work with employees to ensure that each step is performed correctly and will contribute to the overall purposes of the organization.

Organizational culture is, to a large extent, maintained and enhanced by supervisors. Effective first-line managers support the overall goals of their organization and work to promote its values in the work units they supervise. By developing their organizational skills, supervisors are also contributing to the total work environment.

■ SUPERVISORS AND CONTROL

There are many misconceptions concerning the definition of *control* in work environments. Some interpret control as manipulation. Others see it as rule enforcement. Neither usage is totally correct. **Control** is the corrective action—derived from

Control is corrective action, derived from measurements, necessary to ensure that desired standards are being met.

measurements—taken to meet expected standards of performance, costs, schedules, customer satisfaction, equipment utilization, vendor relationships, supply usage, and all other job factors.

When we drive an automobile, we control both speed and direction. We determine how fast we are going by observing the speedometer, and we visually check to determine if we are driving correctly. If we are taking a shower, we control the temperature and water flow by adjusting valves. In work organizations we take corrective action when our expectations are not being met.

Precontrol is planning that minimizes the necessity for corrective action.

Concurrent control is corrective action taken while a job is being accomplished.

Experienced managers know that **precontrol** is the starting point of effective control implementation. Precontrol consists of careful planning, identification of potential problems, and assigning work to competent employees. **Concurrent control** is accomplished by observing work while it is being accomplished and taking corrective action immediately, if possible. If a piece of equipment such as a computerized workstation is not operating properly, trained technicians can be called in to correct the problem. It is unfortunate that most control is not concurrent. **Postcontrol** is corrective action that occurs when reports and other sources of information indicate standards are not being met. It is usually based on measurements of what has occurred rather than what is occurring. Computerized reports make it possible in many organizations to obtain data very rapidly. In such cases corrective action can often be taken much sooner than it was before advanced technology was available.

Postcontrol is corrective action taken after a job or process has been completed.

Control utilizes three basic steps. First, expectations must be clearly defined. Expectations are what we want to occur. They are our standards. In some instances we can determine expectations with a degree of preciseness. Data-entry workers are usually expected to make 13,000 keystrokes per hour with 1/2 percent error rate or less. Failure to perform at this level means the employee failed to meet the standard. Most retail managers know the amount of sales an average salesperson should be able to generate in an average day. In restaurants, cooks know precisely how long steak must be broiled on each side in order to meet customer expectations. In well-managed organizations, expectations of supervisors are usually met. Good supervisors train employees to successfully achieve desired standards.

Establishing standards is not enough. There must also be a way of measuring performance to determine if standards are being met. Measurements may consist of actual observations, analysis of reports made while work is in process and, in many instances, after it has been completed. In each case the supervisor must determine if work is meeting quality, cost, schedule, and productivity requirements. Supervisors must often rely on feedback in the form of reports or computer-generated data to assess how well standards are being met. Accuracy of feedback is essential in determining the necessity for corrective action.

If expected performance is not being met, corrective action must be taken. Depending on analysis of feedback information, such action may include assigning additional people to a task, reducing advertising costs, obtaining improved equipment, or altering work processes. Corrective action is the essential control activity. Standards and measurements through feedback are of little use without needed corrective action being taken. It must be noted that corrective action may involve people, equipment, processes, or any of a combination of factors. Major control steps are summarized in Table 2.3.

Well-run organizations involve employees in developing standards, measuring their own work, and taking corrective action when possible. Managers in well-run organizations know that self-control is often more effective than control imposed by managers. Both individuals and work teams often set their own standards, measure their performance, and take appropriate corrective action. Management serves as coaches, advisors, information gatherers, and suppliers of assistance when assistance is needed.

■ SUPERVISORY INFLUENCE—DIRECTING

Directing includes all of the activities associated with influencing employees to perform at the level required to meet established standards.

Directing includes all of the activities associated with influencing employees to perform at the level of required standards. Leading, delegating, explaining, correcting, and praising are included in the directing function. While all of these are discussed in chapters that follow, it is necessary to recognize that directing is part of the essential communication activities that effective supervisors must learn. There is no supervision unless the supervisor communicates task requirements and expectations to employees. Most management communication is designed to influence others. Directing is an essential set of skills that effective supervisors must constantly practice.

Many supervisors are, unfortunately, poor communicators of what is needed and as a consequence are inadequate at directing the activities of others. In an orchestra each musician must understand the signals given by the conductor. If a single person fails to

TABLE 2.3 ■ Major Control Steps for Supervisors

1. Precontrol	Precontrol consists of carefully planning each activity and assigning trained, competent employees to accomplish each component. Planning includes alternatives, or backup plans, in the event conditions change.
2. Establishing standards	Standards are the expected level of performance for each job. They may be formal—based on a series of measurements and written in a manner that can be used by those involved in implementing the plan—or informal—based largely on judgment and experience. In either case standards are a necessary starting point for evaluating whether the work of individuals or a team of employees is being adequately achieved. Standards may include costs, schedules, quality, or quantity. They can also include factors related to customers, suppliers, equipment, and processes.
3. Measuring to determine if standards are being met	This activity includes both observation of work while it is in progress and analysis of feedback in the form of written and oral reports. It is essential that feedback data be accurate. Poor corrective action decisions are often made on the basis of information that is either incomplete or inaccurate. Good data are the basis of good decisions.
4. Taking corrective action	Corrective action is the essential step of the control process. If it is determined that expected performance is not being met, then corrective action must be taken. Ideally corrective action should be taken as soon as it is learned that standards are not being met. In some cases, however, it is necessary, after careful analysis of data, to develop corrective action plans. Ideally people performing work needing corrective action should also be involved in the corrective action planning process and its implementation.

either understand or follow the conductor's signals, the entire orchestra fails to achieve its goal. Football or basketball games can be lost when players do not understand the strategies and positions designated by the coach. In a work environment lack of understanding of a supervisor's directions by one or two employees can cause a needed task to either not be completed as desired or not be performed at all. In our next chapter the directing activity is treated more fully, with special attention given to delegation as a key to building employee involvement and responsibility.

■ ORGANIZATIONAL SIZE AND SUPERVISORY FUNCTIONS

Organizations with 100 or fewer employees are often quite different from larger ones. In very small organizations the only supervisor may also be the owner, chief executive officer, and department head all wrapped into a single person. Smaller organizations differ from larger ones in several ways.

1. Smaller organizations tend to be less formal. Procedures and written plans are relied on less and responsibility is limited.

2. In small organizations jobs are usually far less specialized. Employees do what is needed rather than what a job description designates as their area of responsibility.

3. Managers often perform many of the same functions as employees. They assist customers or clients, help with inventory, maintain records, and perform a variety of other tasks.

4. Because of the size and informality, employees in small organizations tend to know each other more intimately than those in large organizations. Quite often a family atmosphere exists.

5. Small organizations often have disadvantages for employees. Pay and benefits are generally less than those of their larger counterparts. Resources in the form of equipment, supplies, and training opportunities are nearly always better in larger organizations. There are usually fewer opportunities for promotion and personal growth in small organizations unless it is undergoing widespread expansion.

Supervisors in small organizations often have complex jobs. They must usually know how to do virtually everything required. In larger organizations with greater specialization, supervisors may be more restricted by limited areas of responsibility and far greater numbers of formal procedures.

Small organization supervisors are often the *total* boss. They hire, discipline, inform, counsel, get to know their employees very well, and on occasion may terminate nonperformers. Their level of influence is greater than many middle managers of large enterprises. Often their degree of satisfaction with their work is quite high. Lack of restrictions on their activities gives them very broad as well as significant responsibilities. Relations with other segments of their organization is usually less formal than in large organizations.

Frequently there is lack of visibility in large organizations. Employees view their total work organization based on their feelings about their immediate work group. It is difficult for them to understand organizational levels above their department or section and virtually impossible to grasp the functions of departments with whom they have little direct contact. Often there is frustration and a feeling of anonymity. Employees in very large organizations often view themselves as individually unimportant. In reality they have little real contact with the total organization other than other employees in their immediate work area.

Because of the diversity of tasks for which they and their employees are responsible, supervisors in small organizations often have more technically difficult tasks than their counterparts in large enterprises. In general, complexity is offset by informality, more personal contact with employees, and a clear view of total operations and organizational goals.

■ PUTTING IT TOGETHER—SUPERVISORY SUCCESS AND FAILURE

Planning, organizing, controlling, and directing are basic management activities that every supervisor must be skilled in performing. They do not include *all* supervisory activities, but they are recognized core requirements of work. Employees who demonstrate leadership characteristics, are willing to expand personal responsibility, and display ambition and dedication usually are the favored candidates for supervisory assignments. Many employees are promoted to supervisory positions with little preparation and training. They find themselves in a sink-or-swim environment. Until they learn essential supervisory skills, they often perform poorly and in some cases fail. Table 2.4 summarizes some of the reasons for supervisory failure.

■ A FINAL VIEW

While organizations may be the same size, serve similar purposes, and have nearly identical goals, no two are exactly alike. As a consequence supervisory duties vary greatly. Regardless of size, purpose, or location, all supervisors must be able to plan by conceptualizing the future, organize work into logical segments, control by taking corrective action when measurements indicate standards are not being met, and influence through directing the activities of those performing the essential duties that meet organizational goals.

TABLE 2.4 ■ Primary reasons for Supervisory Failure

Rigidity	Some supervisors resist ideas that they did not originate. Others try to succeed with unworkable procedures. In either case they refuse to recognize the reality that as conditions change so must plans and work. Flexibility and willingness to accept change is mandatory. We are not advocating change for change's sake. Plans that work should be followed. Flexibility, however, is a requirement of all successful managers.
Relationships	Lack of ability to effectively interact with others is the single most prevalent cause of supervisory failure. This includes employees, other supervisors, managers, and people who interface with the organization.
Organization	Supervisors who know that systematic arrangement of work elements, including assignment of employees to specific tasks, succeed in attaining goals when others fail. Those who do not know what is happening in their work units or how to find out are disorganized and will, doubtlessly, fail.
Attitude	Some supervisors, once promoted, take an "I don't care" attitude. Because of their fear of failure, they ignore problems, fail to make essential decisions, and refuse to listen to employee suggestions. Their primary motive is to survive. Other people's suggestions and information is ignored.
Commitment	Being a good supervisor is often difficult. While it can be very rewarding, it is often frustrating, demanding, and plagued with tiresome problems. Some supervisors give up and demonstrate little real commitment to their job.

No single factor determines organizational success or failure. Supervisors, employees, and job factors all interact to determine effectiveness and efficiency. Supervisors, depending on personal factors such as training and experience as well as their basic personalities, see employees and the work they perform through their own judgment of *what should* occur. Employees view their management at all levels and their jobs from different perspectives than do first-line managers. Their concern is primarily with the type of rewards the job and the organization offers. If the work is interesting, relations with their supervisor adequate, pay is equitable with normal expectations, and the job is one that encourages self-development beyond immediate tasks, then they tend to both perform well and like their work.

Organizational survival depends on upper management accurately assessing what society needs or wants, mid-level managers defining ways to support top management's policies and goals, and first-line supervisors interpreting and implementing actions necessary to make goals a reality.

■ THINGS TO REMEMBER

I. Supervisors and organizations.

    A. All organizations have a variety of activities that are unique.

    B. Service and manufacturing organizations differ in purpose but supervisors in each have a fundamental core of skills.

II. Major supervisory skills include:

    A. Technical skills

    B. Human skills

III. Importance of major supervisory activities.

    A. Supervisors rarely look at major functions in any particular order.

    B. Regardless of level, all managers perform certain common functions.

IV. Planning involves deciding on a course of action for the future.

    A. Executive management is concerned primarily with strategic planning, mid-level managers develop tactical plans for their departments or divisions, and supervisors translate these into operational plans.

    B. Informal plans are based on judgment, experience, and thinking ahead.

    C. Planning will increase in importance to supervisors in the foreseeable future.

    D. Reactive managers do little planning.

    E. Flexibility and employee involvement are keystones to effective operational planning.

V. Organization of work by first-line managers.

    A. Organizational structure is concerned with the division of work.

    B. An area of responsibility defines everything for which a single manager is responsible.

    C. Lines of authority show both reporting relationships and the way authority flows through an organization.

    D. Steps used to complete a specific task are called a *process*.

VI. Supervisors and control; control is the corrective action taken if measurements indicate that standards are not being met.

VII. Supervisory influence—directing.

    A. Directing includes all activities that influence employees to perform at the level of required standards.

    B. Leading, delegating, explaining, correcting, and praising are all included in the directing function.

VIII. Organizational size and supervisory functions.

    A. In small organizations an owner may also be executive, middle, and first-line management.

    B. Large organizations offer greater opportunities and usually have better pay, benefits, and available resources than most small organizations.

    C. Supervisory functions in small organizations may be less formal but more complex.

IX. Putting it together—supervisory success and failure.

    A. Planning, organizing, controlling, and directing are basic management activities.

    B. Supervisory failure may result from rigidity, relationships, organization, attitude, and commitment.

X. A final view.

    A. No single factor determines organizational success or failure.

    B. Organizational survival depends on upper management, middle management, first-line management, and employees working together to achieve organizational goals.

■ KEY TERMS

technical skills

human skills

conceptual skills

function

primary management functions

operational planning

tactical planning

strategic planning

single use plans

multiple use plans

procedures

standing plans

formal plans

informal plans

preplans

reactive managers

proactive managers

organizational structure

area of responsibility

lines of authority

processes

culture   concurrent control

control   postcontrol

precontrol   directing

■ DISCUSSION QUESTIONS

1. In an organization with which you are familiar, determine how employees view their immediate supervisor.

2. Why is planning often not done as carefully as it should be by first-line managers?

3. Employee job expectations often differ from those of management. Explain how this can occur.

4. Give examples of where coordination may be a problem in accomplishing a specific set of activities.

■ SELF ASSESSMENT

Evaluate your knowledge of first-line management skills by answering the following questions on a scale of 1 to 6. Answers 1, 2, or 3 mean you either totally disagree or somewhat disagree. Responses of 4, 5, or 6 indicate either agreement or very strong agreement.

1. Most supervisory jobs are alike regardless of the organization.

   1   2   3   4   5   6

2. Because organizations are different, there are no management functions that all effective supervisors must know.

   1   2   3   4   5   6

3. Since mid-level managers are held accountable for every activity in their division, first-line managers have little real responsibility.

   1   2   3   4   5   6

4. Most supervisors have training and experience when they are promoted to ensure effective human relations skills.

   1   2   3   4   5   6

5. Planning is essentially conceptual in nature and is not necessary in lower levels of management.

   1   2   3   4   5   6

6. Directing simply means making work assignments.

   1   2   3   4   5   6

7. At times, direct, forceful behavior is required in a supervisor.

   1   2   3   4   5   6

8. Good supervisors rarely act seriously. A sense of humor should prevail in all sets of conditions.

   1   2   3   4   5   6

9. Control is, in the final analysis, manipulation. In organizations of the 1990s, control will become an outdated function.

   1   2   3   4   5   6

10. More people are fired because of personality difficulties than because of performance ineffectiveness.

   1   2   3   4   5   6

■ SHORT CASES

Is Fairness Enough?

As crew chief for Columbia Area Telephone System, Rand Gurrero felt he knew his business. While enrolled in Columbia College, Randy had started as a system installation helper on a part-time basis. After completing two years of college, he was promoted to full-time installer and the company elected to pay for his remaining education if he wished to attend college at night. A year later he was made crew chief. Randy and his crew were responsible for installation and maintenance of business and commercial telephone systems.

Driven by a need to succeed, Randy became a demanding but generally fair first-line manager. His crew members admired his ambition and energy, but none felt close to him as a person. All crew members were cautious when they talked to him, and they tended to avoid making on-the-job decisions unless they checked with Randy first.

In day-to-day operations Randy would carefully review installation plans with sales engineers and analysts, make out a materials and equipment list, check equipment loading, and give his crew of eight installers and helpers a general outline of what needed to be done. On the job Randy would assign work to each person. If there was an especially difficult hookup, he would do the job himself rather than assign it to an installer. Eventually Randy felt he was working harder and harder, and his crew, although competent, seemed to take too long to complete required work.

In looking at his own performance, Randy felt he was supervising correctly. He was careful, worked hard, treated his employees fairly, and tried to make work go smoothly. Yet he knew he wasn't doing something right.

1. What can Randy do to improve?

2. How would you rate Randy as a first-line supervisor? Explain.

3. What will happen to Randy if he fails to change his current management style?

Growing Pains

Linda Tittle knew about the expansion of Minden Electronic Service Systems (MESS) almost a week before it was publicized. As supervisor of shipping and receiving, she attended weekly review meetings where preliminary discussions of the company's new undertaking took place. The company was enlarging its service area to include a number of nearby cities and communities. As a major service company, MESS provided repair, special assembly, and standard services for computers and computer equipment. Grace Gil, Linda's immediate manager, had asked each of the first-line managers to develop a plan for expanding their departments. "We're going to go from a single-shift operation to a double-shift operation as a first move. In addition most departments, especially the receiving area, will be expanded to include more room for the increased volume of material we'll be handling. I would like a preliminary plan of what you feel will be necessary to make the expansion successful. Try to have a rough draft ready today."

As Linda returned to her office, she thought about Grace's instructions: second shift, more space, and handling a greater volume of materials. "It may be a little tough," she mused, "but I have a few ideas."

1. In developing her preliminary plan, what major factors should Linda consider?

2. Why did Grace Gil want a preliminary plan rather than a final, detailed plan?

3. How would plans differ if MESS decided to decrease its operations rather than increase them?

▪ ENDNOTES

1. Robert L. Katz is a highly respected management writer. His classification of management skills first appeared in "Skills of Effective Administrators" in the *Harvard Business Review* (September–October 1974). Since then his model has been quoted many times in management texts and is still considered one of the best descriptions of necessary management expertise.

2. Fayol's contributions were first recognized in the United States in the 1930s when the original English translation of his work was made. His work gained its greatest popularity in the 1950s after the second English translation was published.

3. Luther Gulick wrote extensively with Lyndall Urwick. Both are considered pioneers in the development of management theory.

4. Tom Peters has written or co-written several popular management texts, including *In Search of Excellence* with Bob Waterman, *A Passion for Excellence* with Nancy Austin, and *Thriving on Chaos*.

5. Numerous articles on organizational culture can be found in current magazines, management texts, and academic journals. One of the discussions easiest to understand is in John Schermerhorn, Jr., *Management for Productivity*, 3rd edition (John Wiley & Sons, 1990).

Part II

Fundamental Supervisory Skills

Knowledge of what managers do is not enough. Supervisors must also be able to implement plans, make decisions, and motivate employees. These three chapters are concerned with how different levels of management implement plans at different levels in an organization. They also review the steps essential to the decision-making processes that are a major factor in every management function. What motivation means and different approaches to motivating employees in work environments are also examined. Although many texts treat motivation as a human resource management function, we see it as part of an organization's essential efforts to achieve its primary goals.

Making Policies and Plans a Reality: Initiating Work

Objectives

Chapter 3 is directed toward creating an understanding of how plans and policies are implemented at various levels in an organization. It traces work from the highest levels in an organization to actual performance of services or manufacturing. Readers will, after completing the chapter, be able to

- Identify major differences in the way work is assigned by top, mid-level, and first-line managers in organizations.

- Recognize the importance of the vital shift in the development of managerial expertise.

- Accurately evaluate factors in assigning work that lead to understanding or lack of understanding.

- Utilize techniques that help in effective work assignment.

- Identify supervisory skills necessary for implementing work and maintaining effort.

Thought Starter

At the beginning of this last decade of the current century, Donald Petersen was among the most admired chief executive officers in the United States.[1] As CEO for the Ford Motor Company he introduced new automobile models designed to rival those of foreign competition, was among the first U.S. executives to recognize the importance of quality in every aspect of operations, and attempted to develop innovative programs to increase employee involvement in their jobs. Although his work force was strongly unionized, both management and employee responses have been generally favorable. Ford improved both design and quality under Petersen's leadership during most of the 1980s.

Whether or not his efforts will continue to succeed into the next century depends on a number of factors. Among the most important is how well first-line managers implement top-level policy. Often the way required jobs are assigned is a key factor in shaping future success or failure. It involves more than just telling people *what* to do. Creation of understanding and enthusiasm are also essential components of assigning work. This chapter discusses the chain of work assignment in organizations, factors that lead to successful job assignment, and reasons supervisors often fail in assigning work. Many of its concepts are based on studies made by High Yield Management, an international management consulting firm, over a period of many years.[2]

■ *Denise Fajaro was faced with one of the most difficult tasks in her four years with Leland Insurance Programs Company (LIP). Top management at LIP had developed a plan for assisting small business owners in providing low-cost health care insurance. Based on a briefing by Susan Ross, manager of Client Services, the work load in Denise's area would increase dramatically if the plans were as successful as predicted. New procedures would be needed to process claims from literally hundreds of small concerns spread out over a wide geographic area. Work would be less routine than it is in dealing with larger employers, LIP's primary customers until now. It would require extensive training in new procedures, increased reliance on sophisticated computer programs, and close contact with a far greater number of clients than at any time in the past.*

Denise's section dealt directly with its clients in helping them manage health insurance claims. Her 12 employees received claims, contacted firms for additional data, audited claims forms for correctness, and authorized payment to hospitals, doctors, and other health care professionals. Denise recognized that as she reassigned people to new types of work there would be some resistance. Of all problems she faced, Denise knew that getting a commitment from her employees to making new systems successful was going to be the most difficult.

■ REALITIES OF EMPLOYEES AT WORK

Plans are converted into effort in a wide variety of ways. In some circumstances each day begins with specific assignments. These are usually brief and involve activities with which employees are familiar and competent to perform. Often employees get their assignments from work records left by a previous shift, memoranda, orders, requisitions, letters left in their in-basket, or telephone calls taken by an answering machine. Their supervisors are seen as sources of help and information and sometimes annoyance.

After learning their jobs, many employees develop a routine that takes them through a workday with little or no contact with their immediate supervisor other than casual discussions of job issues. They report for work, begin their daily tasks and work virtually without supervision most of the day. They feel, most of the time correctly, that they don't need to be told what to do. Often they resent changes in their regular assignments unless there are clear-cut benefits. If asked to do something different from their originally assigned tasks, they frequently reply, "It ain't my responsibility." Assigning work in ways that motivate rather than create resentment is a major supervisory skill.

Primary Factors Affecting Job Assignments

Joan Woodward, in a study of management styles in different types of industry, found that the type of work employees performed affected supervisory style.[3] Highly directive supervision with little participation is common for jobs where little training and experience is needed. Employees expect close supervision to help them meet minimum levels of performance. Levels of dissatisfaction and "don't care" attitudes tended to be higher in jobs requiring low-level skills and little knowledge beyond an immediate task.

In organizations where routine jobs with little variation are common, such as most assembly work or offices where data-entry clerks perform repetitive tasks, employees work within fairly rigid job descriptions. They have specific activities assigned by supervisors and expect explicit instructions on what needs to be accomplished. Jobs have often been simplified to the degree that only low-level skills are required. This type of work environment often fosters first-line managers who make nearly all significant decisions for their employees. Real responsibility lies with supervisors, not with employees.

In jobs that require significant training, experience, and knowledge, supervisors recognize and respect the expertise of their employees. They depend on employees to identify problems, develop solutions, and determine the most efficient and effective methods for performing a given task. Where "knowledge workers" are the primary employee group, supervisors tend to expect higher performance levels. In many knowledge-based occupations, such as nursing, law enforcement, fire protection, computer programming, laboratory work, graphic design, and similar occupations, employees are essentially self-directed. Keith Davis has pointed out that employees who utilize their training and experience fully tend to be more satisfied with their jobs.[4]

Bright people with dull jobs often feel that, "A job not worth doing is not worth doing well."

Often bright people are hired for dull jobs. Their resentment, boredom, and reluctance to perform better is, all too frequently, based on the perception that management doesn't care, their jobs are worthless, and they are payroll numbers, not people. Abraham Maslow, a noted psychologist whose work will be discussed later, stated that "a job not worth doing is not worth doing well."[5]

In dealing with such employees, supervisors are often frustrated and angered by what they perceive as laziness. Employees, on the other hand, see their jobs as inconsequential and not worth real effort. United States Bureau of Labor Statistics studies show that the highest rate of employee turnover is in jobs that require minimum skills.

An additional influence on initiation of work is the way managers see themselves and their roles in an organization. Some supervisors feel they must make all significant decisions in their work units. They firmly believe that employees are being paid to do what they are told, not to make decisions or suggest ways of doing things differently. Such supervisors are highly directive and often believe fear is a primary motivator.

Other supervisors believe employees have the responsibility for performing their jobs and managers are providers of information, guidance, and encouragement. Regardless of organization or type of work, every manager ultimately has a different style or method of managing. Their approach depends, to a large extent, on personality, training, and the way they perceive both employees and their primary goals. Managers, employees, and job conditions interact constantly. Each influences the other in determining how work is initiated.

General supervision is preferred by most employees. They do not mind being informed of priorities and what needs to be accomplished. "Over the shoulder" direction, however, is resented.

For many years it has been recognized that most employees prefer **general supervision** rather than **specific supervision.** They do not mind being informed of priorities, what needs to be accomplished, schedules, and potential problems. If, however, they know their jobs and are told *how* as well as *what*, resentment is almost inevitable. Effective first-line managers recognize the way employees view their work and avoid giving orders as much as possible. They use consultive, participative approaches unless conditions warrant otherwise. Most importantly they have a realistic view of themselves, the perceptions of their employees, as well as the nature of their organization. Figure 3.1 shows that bright people with dull jobs soon act like dull people.

Specific supervision involves close observation and direction by supervisors of employee efforts.

■ ORGANIZATION LEVEL AND DELEGATION OF WORK

Supervision, to a degree, occurs at every level in an organization.

Supervision, to a degree, occurs at every level in an organization. Supervisors assign, evaluate, coach, and correct the activities of employees who perform services or make products for an organization. Middle managers supervise first-line managers. Top managers supervise middle managers. In Figure 3.2 we point out that

FIGURE 3.1 ■ Bright People, Dull Jobs

supervisors are supervised and managers are managed. Each level in an organization, however, works differently from the level either below or above.

Organizational hierarchy refers to the ranking of managers from top to first-line.

At each higher step in the hierarchy of an organization, problems are different, responsibilities vary in breadth, and work shifts from technical matters to increased involvement in administrative and conceptual concerns. **Hierarchy** refers to the ranking of managers from top to middle to first-line. An organization chart is a primary map of the hierarchy of management. When employees are promoted to first-line supervisory management of the "doing" position they once held, they make a shift away from the doing of a job to its management. This movement away from the actual performance of specific productive tasks is called a *vital shift*. Figure 3.2 depicts the vital shift process as a series of steps in reaching areas of greater responsibility.

Vital Shifts

Vital shifts occur when people are promoted to higher levels of management.

If an employee moves from a nonmanagement position in an organization to a position that requires greater responsibility, not only for their own work but for that of others, they make a **vital shift.** Their responsibility shifts from "doing" types of work to management. In some organizations the first shift is into a role that is not management in the true sense but that entails some

FIGURE 3.2 ■ Vital Shifts

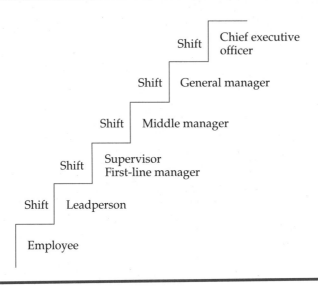

management duties. These employees usually have titles such as lead person, senior clerk, shift leader, or any of a number of similar titles. A **lead person** continues to do the same type of work as fellow employees and also assigns necessary tasks to others. He or she also acts as a source of information and help and is frequently a spokesperson for employees in the work team when dealing with managers in identifying employee problems. A general rule of thumb identifies lead positions: if an employee spends approximately 80 percent of her or his time performing primary work and about 20 percent in assigning work and assisting employees, he or she may be correctly identified as a lead person. With the exception of very small organizations or some retail establishments, true first-line managers spend all or most of their time in supervisory activities of nonmanagement employees and little or no time in performing nonmanagement job duties.

Supervisors plan the activities of both groups and individuals, define what needs to be accomplished in their work unit, and have a wide variety of evaluation and decision-making activities. Frequently they spend a significant part of their workday in meetings with their manager and other supervisors, special committee work, analyzing data, making reports, and dealing with people outside of their immediate work area, such as safety specialists, cost analysts, and others. For the most part they have made a true vital shift away from doing to managing. They are concerned with both assigning and delegating work to others.

Assigning Work

Directing the activities of employees is a key first-line management function. Directing includes a variety of activities, such as assigning tasks to both individuals and groups of employees, delegating authority, training, providing information, coaching, and correcting performance. Of all directing activities, assigning work seems the most simple. It is, in reality, an often confusing and difficult task.

When employees are interviewed for a job, they are usually told what the job will entail, basic requirements, and any special conditions of work, such as weekend assignments or travel. It is not until they report for work that actual day-to-day job duties become a reality. Often jobs are learned from a buddy system or observation, with little true assignment of specific tasks by the boss. They begin work by watching others, sharing tasks, and receiving assistance from other employees. Even in sophisticated organizations where orientation and training programs for new employees exist, difficulties in work assignment often occur. Supervisors, all too frequently, neglect making basic assignments that obtain desired results. Employees do what they think is needed rather than what they are told if instructions are not fully understood.

Communication specialists know that what may seem perfectly clear to one person is often either not clear or misinterpreted by another. A request by a supervisor of an employee to "please let me have a report on travel costs for last month as soon as possible" can be interpreted in several ways. Some employees may interpret "as soon as possible" to mean, "Drop all other work and get the report immediately." Others may think that the boss wants the report as soon as other work-in-progress is completed. Still others may not know exactly what is to be included in the report. Unless the supervisor defines what is needed more completely and checks for understanding, results may be unexpected.

While it is true that both experienced employees and supervisors generally understand each other, good work assignment requires not only full explanation but discussion of the job to be accomplished, identification of potential difficulties, and clear designation of employees responsible for its completion. Both supervisors and employees must fully agree on job requirements. All too frequently supervisors assume employees know what is expected and pay little attention to what is actually being accomplished. Effective work assignment means a clear understanding of what is specifically required by both employees and their managers. It is more than just telling people what to do.

Delegation

Delegation involves giving both authority and work to employees that was formerly done by their immediate manager. Granting authority is the heart of delegation.

When a supervisor assigns work, the responsibility of each level in the hierarchy changes very little. Supervisors tell, and employees do. Effective supervisors learn very quickly that a great deal of work that they do can be delegated to others. **Delegation** involves giving employees both authority and work formerly done by their immediate manager. Granting authority to others is the heart of delegation. Good supervisors know that checking reports for accuracy, analyzing cost data, developing schedules, writing routine reports, obtaining information, ordering standard supplies, and responding to client calls for information as well as many other types of work can be done as well or better by employees than themselves. Major components of the delegation process are summarized in Figure 3.3.

There are several advantages to delegation other than freeing the supervisor from routine activities that others can do. It sends a message to employees that the supervisor has confidence in their ability to perform successfully at a higher level of responsibility. It is also a powerful motivational tool. Employees (and managers as well) who have had additional responsibilities delegated to them tend to live up to the added obligations. Most importantly, employee loyalty to both the objectives of the organization and to an immediate supervisor is usually enhanced. Rather than resent additional responsibility, employees tend to perceive their supervisor's confidence in their ability as a valuable personal asset. Delegation is also one of the most effective training tools for those who have leadership potential. Rather than being a threatening challenge, delegation is more often an uplifting experience for both employees and supervisors.

For the most part top-level managers delegate activities to upper level middle managers. Important parts of these activities are delegated to lower-level middle managers, who in turn delegate to first-line managers. Delegation at upper levels of management

FIGURE 3.3 ■ Basic Delegation Processes

usually occurs through staff meetings and discussions of general plans and policies. Managers of different areas of specialization, such as finance, human resources, purchasing, marketing, and other areas of an organization, identify components they can complete. Delegation occurs by mutual agreement as much as by directives from higher levels.

Most middle managers are concerned with broad areas of responsibility, with first-line managers handling specialized areas. In marketing, as an example, a mid-level manager is usually designated as manager of marketing. Her or his major concern is usually with market research, advertising, sales, and distribution. First-line managers reporting to the marketing manager are responsible for specific areas of specialization. Sales managers, usually first-line supervisors, have major responsibility for a segment of a sales force; advertising managers for type and placement of advertising; and other managers for remaining areas of specialization. These areas, usually a department or section, depend on first-line managers to assign specific activities and delegate various functions to their employees. Delegation, giving authority and obtaining commitment, is one of the most powerful tools available in the development of responsible, full-functioning employees.

■ TO DELEGATE OR NOT TO DELEGATE

Experienced supervisors know that delegation frees them from many routine duties that can be performed by nonmanagement employees. Through delegation they are able to spend more time in planning, analysis of work problems, evaluation of group and individual performance, providing assistance to employees, and coordination of their group's activities with other sections or departments. They also understand that when work is assigned, it must be carefully discussed to ensure full understanding of what is expected. Even though the benefits of delegation and systematic methods of assigning work are easily understood, they are all too often neglected.

Supervisors often fail to effectively delegate or assign work for a number of reasons. Many of these are related to lack of confidence in employee competence, belief that sharing power with employees weakens management influence, and conviction that if they want it done correctly, they must do it themselves. Table 3.1 lists a few of the many types of activities that can and should be delegated to nonmanagement employees.

One of the earliest recorded examples of the necessity for delegation may be found in the Judeo-Christian account of Moses leading his people out of Egypt. It elegantly explains reasons for delegation.

In the book of Exodus, Moses leads his people out of Egypt into the desert to escape persecution by the pharaoh. One of his

TABLE 3.1 ▪ Activities That Can Be Delegated

1. Response to letters of inquiry and review of routine information and procedures for summary reports.
2. Maintenance of records, such as budget expenditures, purchase orders, and overtime records.
3. Most scheduling activities that do not involve personnel.
4. Job-related technical problems.
5. Analysis of data related to costs, labor utilization, and job-related information.
6. New projects that are within an employee's scope of training and experience or ability to learn.
7. Control of expendable materials, equipment utilization, and meeting schedules.

first stops is at the home of his friend and father-in-law, Jethro. Jethro observes that Moses is trying to make decisions for everything that must be done as well as solve every problem encountered. He tells Moses to designate leaders of tens, leaders of fifties, leaders of hundreds, and leaders of thousands. These leaders will make decisions for their groups, and Moses will only be required to make decisions that affect everyone. "It is too much of burden," Jethro counsels Moses, "to make all judgments."[6]

Chief executive officers of modern organizations, like Moses, cannot make all decisions and must delegate some of their functions. Lower levels of management must, in turn, delegate portions of their work to others. Jethro's advice is as valid today as it was over 4,000 years ago. *Delegate as much as you can downward.*

What Not to Delegate

Some supervisory activities, like those of all managers, should not be delegated. In general, problems involving people that report directly to first-line managers cannot be delegated. Additionally some specific responsibilities may be delegated only to a limited degree. Typical limited delegation activities are briefly described in Table 3.2.

Common Causes of Failure in Delegation and Assigning Work

Often a supervisor's desire for success prevents effectiveness in the key tasks of delegating and assigning work. Their personal

TABLE 3.2 ■ Limitations of Delegation

1. **Planning.** Planning a specific job or completing details of a general plan may be delegated. Planning that affects a group, organization of work, or individual assignments is an exclusive supervisory responsibility.

2. **Morale problems.** First-line managers may be faced with a group of employees who are discouraged, burned out, or not working as a team. Rebuilding and maintaining a cooperative, productive work force is a supervisory responsibility.

3. **Conflict resolution.** While some conflicts between employees may be resolved by those directly involved, supervisors have the responsibility for preventing destructive or demoralizing behavior. Conflict resolution cannot be delegated.

4. **Performance evaluation.** Determination of the adequacy of group performance, as well as that of individuals, is a primary supervisory responsibility. Even in self-governing groups that have developed in some organizations, determination of overall level of performance remains a primary supervisory task.

5. **Coaching.** Often buddy systems are used in on-the-job-training. While they often work well, supervisors have primary responsibility for evaluating performance. Determination of whether or not a task is being performed correctly and coaching employees in ways of improving performance is a first-line management responsibility.

6. **Personal assignments.** Upper-level management may give supervisors specific tasks to perform. Usually these involve determination of feasibility of schedules, projected costs, or development of operational plans. None of these can be fully delegated, although the supervisor may enlist employee assistance in data gathering, suggestions for improvement, and estimations of time required to complete specific jobs.

7. **Disciplinary action.** Correcting inadequate or inappropriate behavior on the job is exclusively a supervisory task. This is especially true when counseling or reprimands for rule violations are necessary.

8. **Exclusive qualifications.** At times a supervisor may be the only person in a work group qualified to do some types of work. Others may lack necessary knowledge, resources, information, interpersonal skills, or authority. Supervisors, in these circumstances, cannot delegate required actions.

values, beliefs about employees, and attitudes toward their jobs are barricades to truly effective management. In general terms two fears concern some first-line managers.

1. Many supervisors fear their immediate managers will see them as failures if they do not succeed in every endeavor. Rather than delegate difficult jobs, they perform many easily delegable tasks themselves. As a consequence they have little time for other supervisory duties and often try to complete tasks that may be done better by employees in their work group.

2. Some first-line managers do not want to offend or disturb employees with whom they've worked for long periods of time. They frequently fear that delegation of difficult tasks

may alienate members of their work group. Doing tasks that can be assigned to others is seen as a way of maintaining good relationships with employees.

Supervisors often fail to recognize that they are managers. While effective interpersonal relationships are mandatory, supervisors are not in a popularity contest. At times they must make decisions that others may see as unfair or harsh, assign work that challenges employee knowledge and ingenuity, and correct inadequate or incorrect employee efforts. They must never forget the old adage that "when you are up to your rear in alligators, never forget you're there to drain the swamp." In simple terms supervisors must never forget that completing work effectively and efficiently is their primary task.

■ INTRAPERSONAL REASONS FOR SUPERVISORS FAILING TO ASSIGN WORK

Interpersonal relations involve the way individuals deal with others.

Intrapersonal factors are those within individuals that may prevent them from being effective.

Interpersonal relations involve the way individuals act in dealing with others. **Intrapersonal factors** are those within an individual that may prevent her or him from being totally effective. Although fear of failure is the most prevalent intrapersonal reason for not assigning some types of work, there are a number of other reasons. Some of the major beliefs that prevent supervisors from being totally effective include

1. "I can do it better myself." Some supervisors feel that they can do every job better than their employees. A case in point will illustrate this fallacy.

In a large northern California aerospace company, Sue Samuelson was promoted to head of Design Engineering. When she moved into her new office, she brought both her drafting table and her personal computer that was networked to all of the computer-aided design software of her organization. When complex designs were required by the engineering staff, she would make rough layouts on her drafting table and then enter them into the computer for final design. Rather than assign such jobs to others, she did them herself. Sue felt that she was the top designer and did not trust others to complete difficult tasks. As a consequence she had little time for supervisory responsibilities, such as coaching other designers, operational planning, developing improved methods, or evaluating overall group effectiveness. Her obsession with "if you want it done right, do it yourself" prevented her from being an effective first-line manager.

Ultimately, the manager of Engineering, Sue's immediate manager, told her that her job was to direct the efforts of others, not to do their work. He knew she was a competent designer. Her job as a supervisor was not that of designing but managing the activities of her section. He had her drafting table removed and told her that the computer was there to assist her in evaluating the work of others but not doing it for them.

It has been estimated that employees who work at a given task every day can perform individual tasks better than their supervisors 80 percent of the time. Regardless of the previous skill level of the first-line manager, those who perform a given task on a regular basis usually have the greatest skill in doing it correctly.

2. Recognizing what needs to be accomplished. Effective supervisors constantly appraise current conditions, develop new objectives, and plan how they are to be accomplished. They know which direction their work unit is going and how it is going to get there.

It is unfortunate that many supervisors lack the competence to recognize what needs to be done to improve conditions. They feel that their primary task is to relay directions from higher levels of managers. If something goes wrong, they see it as the fault of their employees, their immediate manager, or others in their organization with whom they have contact on a daily basis. They typically do not attempt to understand the long-range objectives of their organizations or how they contribute to its success or failure. In ancient Greece, sailors on the Mediterranean had a saying: "If you don't know where you're going, any wind will get you there." Some supervisors do not recognize what is needed and respond only to crises or problems in their work unit.

3. Lack of confidence in employees. Often supervisors feel that their employees are not competent to handle anything other than routine tasks that require little imagination and have limited responsibility. They are concerned that any employee failure will reflect on their ability as first-line managers. In an era of multicultural, ethnically diverse work forces, prejudice often feeds the conviction that employees have neither the skills nor the knowledge to adequately complete complex tasks. Simple behaviors, such as an unfamiliar accent or inability to understand common slang, may be interpreted as lack of intelligence. Beliefs by some male supervisors that women cannot perform physically demanding tasks also contribute to lack of confidence.

Lack of confidence also arises because of the so-called generation gap. Older first-line managers, with values formed 20 years earlier than those of the majority of their employees, may think that younger workers lack commitment and are not interested in the success of the organization. Younger first-line managers of older employees may feel intimidated and frustrated by workers with far more experience and confidence than themselves.

Objective studies indicate that job performance is not dictated by age, sex, or ethnicity. Good employees may be any age, gender, or from any cultural group. Poor performers may also come from these same identifiable groups. Effective supervisors recognize that individual performance counts more than preconceptions about race, religion, color, national origin, sex, age, or physical ability.

4. Need for control. In addition to lack of confidence in employees, some supervisors have a strong need to manipulate others. They see control not as corrective action to ensure that standards are being met but as exertion of personal power. Typically they adopt a highly authoritarian style of management and do not allow significant decisions to be made by anyone other than themselves. They constantly look for mistakes made by their employees and are critical rather than analytical. Punitive corrective action is far more significant to them than gathering data to determine causes of problems. Sharing authority and power with employees is seen as a sign of weakness. Like ancient slave drivers, fear and punishment are seen as the most powerful motivators.

5. Fear of risk. Frequently supervisors perceive delegation as an unacceptable risk. They feel that the safest path to follow is one where they do all of the administrative work, including much that is routine, rather than delegate it to others. If there is even the slightest doubt about an employee's competence, no additional responsibilities will be assigned. While this type of caution may seem prudent, it results in supervisors being burdened with work that others can do as easily. This type of thinking prevents employees from developing the additional skills and knowledge to perform complex tasks.

6. Martyr complexes. Often deliberately and sometimes without awareness of their actions, some supervisors seek the sympathy and admiration of employees, peers, and higher-level managers by seeming to be constantly busy. If asked to go to lunch with friends, they respond with a sorrowful, "I'd like to, but I'm loaded with work." Rather than delegate, they deliberately burden themselves with routine work and often invent reasons to stay busy. Their desire for others to see them as overwhelmingly burdened with work dominates their lives. On a regular basis they take extra work home, work late, and appear to be burdened with work. They are not workaholics in the sense of seeing work as a primary reason for their existence, but want to be seen by others as sacrificing their personal lives for the good of their organizations.

Supervisors with martyr complexes have a built-in justification for inefficiency, poor performance of their work group, and lack of necessary interpersonal contacts with employees. Work becomes a socially acceptable method of avoiding contact with others and an excuse for poor performance. It provides the false security of "I was too busy to do all of the things that needed to be done."

7. Guilt drives. While similar to martyr complexes, guilt drives in supervisors stem from feelings that it is necessary to be busy all of the time. Any lull in work is seen as inexcusable in themselves and others. Unless they are extremely busy and know that additional work needs to be accomplished, they have gnawing feelings of guilt. Unlike supervisors with a martyr complex, being seen as busy is not as important as constant, unrelenting work.

Supervisors are frequently faced with what seems to be overwhelming work requirements. Even in such cases, most will take occasional breaks, talk with other supervisors and employees, and try to prioritize work in ways that allow them to combine tasks, eliminate unnecessary effort, and delegate most routine activities. They are not driven by guilt. Guilt-driven supervisors often do not delegate in order that they will always have work that must be completed.

There are a number of additional factors that prevent supervisors from delegating tasks or simply assigning work to employees. Nearly all originate in lack of confidence in employees or beliefs that only supervisors understand what really needs to be accomplished. Some of the common reasons given by supervisors for not delegating work are listed below. Most have little real legitimacy.

1. Feelings that employees are too inexperienced.

2. It takes longer to explain than to do it myself.

3. A mistake may be too costly.

4. I can get quicker action than any of my employees.

5. It's something I like to do and can do well.

6. Some things can't be assigned to employees.

7. Employees don't understand the big picture.

8. My employees aren't ready for complex assignments.

9. Employees in my group are too busy for additional assignments.

Only reasons 6 and 9 have any validity. It is true that some things cannot be delegated and that excessive work loads require the supervisor to pitch in and help. These instances are usually rare and last for brief periods.

■ EMPLOYEES AND RESPONSIBILITY

Employees learn to either accept or not accept responsibility. In organizations that encourage employee participation, self-control, and job-level decision making, employees accept and respond to added responsibility. It is an important indication that management trusts and has confidence in their ability. Those organizations that stress top-down decision making, minimal participation, and conformity to standard ways of performing work build resistance to responsibility beyond an employee's immediate task. Effective first-line supervisors understand employee expectations.

Supervisors should not attempt to solve all employee job problems.

Supervisors, in an effort to increase employee commitment, will often attempt to encourage employees to accept greater responsibility. Management training programs in which they have participated have emphasized that responsibility is a powerful motivator of performance. Unfortunately some employees see added responsibility as both unfair and unwanted. They feel the supervisor is trying to get them to do the "dirty work" of the organization. Unless there has been a systematic, step-by-step set of actions to increase employee participation, employees may feel that their jobs are exclusively limited to their job descriptions. This is especially true when the work force is unionized. Labor contracts often specify that work assignments are limited to precise job descriptions. Under such conditions supervisors are faced with almost insurmountable difficulties in increasing employee responsibility and commitment. In addition to expectations based on previous work experience and attitudes toward management, a number of other factors affect employees' willingness to accept full responsibility for their efforts.

Reasons Employees Resist Delegated Responsibility

Some of the reasons employees resist accepting full responsibility for work assigned by their supervisors include

1. Employees quickly learn that some supervisors will solve problems that the employees do not want to handle themselves. Ineffective supervisors, in an attempt to favorably impress employees, will try to solve *all* employee problems. They fail to recognize that effective managers help develop employee competence and confidence by *not solving* most employee difficulties. When employees learn that they must make decisions and take responsibility for their own efforts, they grow in job effectiveness and commitment to their work.

2. Fear of unjust or unreasonable criticism is another reason that employees avoid additional responsibility, reject delegated authority, and develop less dependency on specific management instructions. Some employees, because of very negative experiences with supervisors, feel that the best way to stay out of trouble is to do only what they are told. Supervisors who use threats, punishment, and a constant search for mistakes as their primary tools in accomplishing work breed dependency and inefficiency in their employees.

3. Employees are reluctant to attempt work that they do not understand. Effective first-line managers are also good communicators. They define what is expected, check with employees

to ensure understanding, and do not make assignments that set an employee up for failure. Good supervisors know that they must establish a relationship of trust and confidence with their employees. If an employee needs additional information or explanation of what is required, they can ask their supervisor without fear of criticism or being made to feel incompetent.

4. Sometimes employees are overloaded with work and new assignments are either put on the bottom of the pile or simply remain incomplete. Experienced first-line managers prioritize work in ways that make sense to their employees. They explain what needs to be done first and what is less urgent. Work is distributed as evenly as possible in order to avoid overloading individual employees. Most employees will make an extra effort to complete added work if they feel their managers are being fair and support their efforts.

5. In large organizations, employees often feel anonymous. They see themselves as a payroll number and little more. Unless their first-line manager recognizes their efforts and lets them know their importance to the organization, they will consistently work at a level that will keep them out of trouble, but little more. In essence, they work to meet minimum requirements.

6. Employees often are reluctant to accept work they see as boring, too simple, or unnecessary. Effective supervisors recognize this reluctance to do low-level work and try to distribute it evenly, make it enjoyable, and explain its necessity. Tom Peters and other management writers have pointed out that routine, dull work can be an opportunity for everyone to work together to complete a task.[7] Rather than a dull, boring experience, it becomes a social event in which everyone participates and celebrates its completion.

7. Lack of confidence in their supervisor's judgment, expertise, and ability can inhibit effort. When employees think their first-line manager is incompetent, they often doubt the necessity for accomplishing assigned tasks. Effective supervisors establish their roles as managers strongly and purposefully. They do not make the mistake of trying to be one of the crew. While they prefer to be liked and have good relations with their employees, they never forget that their primary task is to build conditions where employees will work to accomplish organizational objectives.

■ MANAGEMENT, LEADERSHIP, AND INFLUENCE

Many management writers have noted that most employees in the United States are overmanaged and underled. Supervisory influence is based, to a large extent, on position power. A person's title is their chief source of getting employees to complete day-to-day assignments. Experienced first-line managers know that real influence comes from mutual respect between employees and supervisors, being seen as experts in their roles as team leaders, and influencing efforts of others through encouragement and enthusiasm.

Making Work Assignments the Right Way

Effective assignment of work requires practice, a good understanding of people, patience, and communication skills. Here are some of the techniques that are often helpful.

1. **Clearly explain what is expected and check to ensure that the employees fully understand their assignment.**

2. **Give trained employees the opportunity to decide the best way of accomplishing an assignment.** Discuss potential problems if there are any and offer assistance if it is needed.

3. **Set reasonable goals.** Encourage employees to participate in establishing standards, such as length of time to perform a task, and ways of improving work effectiveness.

4. **Be accessible.** Don't be impatient if employees ask for instructions to be repeated.

5. **Make in-process checks.** Helping employees to develop confidence and responsibility requires allowing them to solve difficult and challenging problems. Be sure the employee can't handle a troublesome assignment before "jumping in." Make the follow-up positive and nonthreatening.

6. **Demonstrate trust and confidence in employee ability.** Have high expectations. Winning coaches expect their players to be the best.

7. **Praise correct work.** Employees interpret approval of work as belief in their competence. Help employees correct poor efforts. Analyze rather than criticize in helping solve problems.

8. **Don't accept excuses.** If valid reasons for poor performance exist, such as incorrect information or faulty equipment, help solve the problem. If the employee is making excuses for poor work, discuss the work and the effects of poor performance.

9. **Don't assign work that is not fully understood.** Employees may be able to do some types of work in which their supervisors lack expertise. If, however, they fail in a task that neither they nor their supervisor fully understands, the supervisor has major responsibility for the error.

10. **Avoid overloading highly competent and effective employees and underloading those who do not perform as well.** Sometimes poor performers respond to added responsibility.

Step by Step—Getting Work Started

Initiation of work requires a number of steps.

Initiation of work includes a number of steps. Briefly summarized, the process includes

1. Identification of actions that need to be accomplished. Without clear objectives, work is often confused and meaningless. Not only must objectives be identified, but they must be communicated to others in clear, unambiguous terms.

2. Planning the most efficient and effective ways to achieve objectives is necessary. As previously stated, planning identifies what, why, who, where, when, and how objectives are to be accomplished.

3. Delegating and assigning specific segments of a plan to others is an important supervisory activity. Unless employees clearly understand what their task is, how it contributes to major objectives of the organization, and supervisory expectations, goals may be only partially attained.

4. In-process follow-up is vital in helping to ensure that plans are adequately completed. Corrective action must be taken as soon as it is determined that standards are not being met. All too frequently supervisors wait until a job or series of tasks is behind schedule, over budget, and incorrectly done before taking action.

5. Final assessment of results assists in planning future activities, improving processes, and defining training needs for employees. Supervisors who are not content to do things the same old way but make continuous improvements are most likely to be seen as true first-line managers both by employees and higher levels of management.

Assignment of work and delegation of authority are often difficult skills for inexperienced supervisors to learn. In many ways they are some of the most critical for first-line managers to master. As leaders and communicators, supervisors' effectiveness often depends on the understanding employees have of required performance standards. Commitment to meeting or exceeding assigned tasks by supervisors depends on the level of trust and confidence employees have in their organization, management, and assigned tasks.

■ THINGS TO REMEMBER

I. Realities of employees at work.
   A. Some employees do not get assignments directly from their supervisor.
   B. Routine, repetitive tasks usually are supervised differently from those requiring extensive training and experience.
   C. Bright people are sometimes assigned dull jobs.

II. Organizational level and delegation of work.
   A. Supervision, to a degree, occurs at every level of work.
   B. When a person, regardless of level, is promoted in an organization, they make a vital shift.
   C. Delegation involves giving employees both authority and work formerly accomplished by their manager.

III. Delegation of work.
   A. Delegation frees supervisors from routine duties.
   B. Activities that involve evaluation, discipline, morale, and conflict resolution cannot be delegated.
   C. Fear of failure and reluctance to offend employees are major reasons supervisors fail to delegate.

IV. Intrapersonal reasons for failure to delegate.
   A. "I can do it better myself".
   B. Supervisors' failure to realize what needs to be done.
   C. Lack of confidence in employees.
   D. Need for control, fear of risk, martyr complexes, and guilt drives.

V. Employees and responsibility.
   A. Employees learn to either accept or not accept responsibility.
   B. Some employees reject added responsibility.

      C. Systematic, step-by-step approaches are necessary in obtaining employment commitment.

VI. Management, leadership, and influence.

      A. Many employees are overmanaged and underled.

      B. Supervisor power is most frequently based on position power.

      C. Getting work started includes a number of systematic steps.

■ KEY TERMS

general supervision	lead person
specific supervision	delegation
hierarchy	interpersonal relations
vital shift	intrapersonal relations

■ DISCUSSION QUESTIONS

1. From your own experiences, identify examples of poor assignment of work or failure to delegate. What could have been done to make them more effective?

2. Many managers are reluctant to delegate work, even though they like their employees and work is being accomplished as it should be. Why does this occur?

3. Why do some supervisors develop martyr complexes or guilt drives?

4. Explain why some employees may fail to successfully make the vital shift to higher levels of management.

5. Why are higher-level managers often not directly concerned with the technical aspects of doing a particular task?

■ SELF-ASSESSMENT

Here is another opportunity to evaluate additional supervisory skills. As in other self-assessment exercises, low numbers (1, 2, 3) indicate disagreement or a negative response. High numbers (4, 5, 6) mean you agree or respond positively. If you are not a supervisor or mid-level manager, answer as if you were.

1. Do you feel comfortable telling people who report to you what needs to be accomplished?

   1   2   3   4   5   6

2. When you are not truly busy on your job, do you feel uncomfortable or guilty?

   1   2   3   4   5   6

3. Do you sometimes feel that you have to do all of the real work and can't really rely on others?

   1   2   3   4   5   6

4. Do you frequently have difficulty in organizing work so it will flow smoothly?

   1   2   3   4   5   6

5. For middle managers who supervise first-line managers, administrative matters are more important than technical aspects of accomplishing work.

   1   2   3   4   5   6

6. It is better for a supervisor to do a job rather than try to explain it to an employee who is not familiar with its requirements.

   1   2   3   4   5   6

7. It is not always necessary to assign specific jobs to the person who can best perform them.

   1   2   3   4   5   6

8. People understand what you want. You only have to give directions once. If employees listen, they will understand.

   1   2   3   4   5   6

9. Fear of criticism can be a major reason employees avoid responsibility.

   1   2   3   4   5   6

10. How much do you trust the judgment of employees who report to you?

   1   2   3   4   5   6

CASES

Poor Richard

As manager of the Metropolitan Utility District (MUD) Customer Relations Section, Richard Beymer was responsible for handling customer complaints, routing repair and emergency requests to proper departments, recommending solutions to customer problems, and keeping upper-level management informed of probable trouble spots as well as occasional positive feedback from customers. It was a difficult job and it had to be done with 12 employees who spent most of their time either on the telephone responding to customer inquiries or entering data on their computer terminals regarding customer requests.

To help his employees, Richard instructed them to "transfer all problem calls to me. I'll handle them for you. I also want to review all letters to customers and sign them myself. That way you'll be protected. Any other reports or documents that leave the office will also be approved by me before they are released. If you have questions or need information, ask me directly and I'll get it for you. When contacts are needed with other departments, I'll make the contact for you."

Employees quickly learned to overload Richard with work. Everything had to be checked by him. They asked him to handle many routine matters. Richard wondered, "Why do I seem to be working harder than any of the other supervisors? I'm the only supervisor who takes paperwork home. Their jobs can't be that much harder."

1. What is Richard's most obvious problem. Why?
2. Why does he want to check all of the details in his department?
3. What activities can he delegate to reduce his load?
4. Rate Richard as a supervisor. Explain.

Lisa Wong is not Wrong

After three years as supervisor of statistical analysis for MUD, Lisa Wong was promoted to department manager for Engineering Services. As department manager she found herself responsible for technical report writing, graphics for statistical analysis, and research information used by MUD's engineering department. Since she was a supervisor of supervisors, many of Lisa's functions changed. She spent most of her time in consultation with other department managers, in meetings with the four supervisors who reported to her, and in meetings involving long-range planning, status reports, and problem solving. It was a vital shift from her previous assignment.

Lisa was an experienced and well-respected department manager. In an effort to help her supervisors develop their management skills, she refused when asked to solve problems that she felt the supervisor could handle. Lisa also suggested sources of help and information but did not require that they be used. In her weekly meetings with the supervisory staff, she asked supervisors to review their major accomplishments for the week and tell how they helped other departments or what types of problems they had handled. She stressed that they should train their people to be on-the-job problem solvers and to "own" their jobs.

When higher-level management reviewed Lisa's performance, they placed a star by Lisa's name in their highly confidential file of people who had strong management potential. Lisa Wong was not wrong. She was on the way to even greater responsibility.

1. Why do you think Lisa was well-liked by her employees as a supervisor?

2. In what ways was Lisa coaching her employees rather than directing them?

3. Is there a danger in letting people solve their own problems? Why?

■ ENDNOTES

1. Don Petersen has been written about in *Fortune, Forbes, The Wall Street Journal, Nation's Business, Business Week,* and many other periodicals. He has been consistently considered one of the most effective chief executive officers in the United States.

2. High Yield Management, located in Boulder, Colorado, is owned and operated by Larry Steinmetz. His consulting activities with many national corporations has provided invaluable information on organizations and management activities.

3. Joan Woodward, mentioned in Chapter 1, found that the type of industry influences management style and the way work is initiated. Her primary studies were made in England during the 1960s. In 1965 the Oxford University Press published her *Industrial Organization: Theory and Practice.*

4. Keith Davis has written some of the landmark texts in human relations during the past 20 years. He has been an editorial staff advisor for McGraw-Hill Publishing Company for a number of years. Since his retirement from

the School of Business at Arizona State University, Davis has continued to be active in consulting and writing in organizational behavior. His original human relations series is considered a pacesetter in the fields of human relations in organizations and organizational behavior.

5. Exodus, chapter 18, verses 16–20. Moses leads Jewish slaves out of Egypt into the Promised Land beyond the Red Sea.

6. In his PBS series on excellence, Peters cites the case of a bank at which the president as well as all other managers and staff pitch in at the end of the month to mail bank statements. It becomes a social event looked forward to rather than drudgery.

Chapter 4

Decision Making— Management's Real Test

Objectives

After completing Chapter 4, readers will be able to identify

- Internal forces that keep managers from making decisions.
- Major "sins" of decision making.
- Ways of identifying objectives.
- Methods for developing and implementing alternatives.
- When group decisions may be better than individual decisions.
- Easy-to-remember rules for making good decisions.

Thought Starter

Decision making is a thread that runs through every aspect of our lives. In work organizations employees decide whether to work or to stay home, and managers decide what will make their organizations function more efficiently. It is impossible to be a fully functioning person without making numerous decisions throughout any given day.

Many forces make people hesitant in decision making. In some instances first-line managers do not want to offend employees. In others they are concerned with the way higher levels of management will view their actions.

Effective managers know that their skill in making decisions is the basis for success or failure. Faced with problems on a daily basis, managers make many routine decisions based on experience and judgment. At times, however, they are required to make decisions that affect their entire organization. In many instances critical decisions are concerned with people, money, equipment, facilities, and other essential resources.

First-line managers must constantly choose courses of actions from many possibilities. They recognize that their performance is often judged by their effectiveness in making decisions. Delaying or ignoring critical decisions often results in disaster. Incorrect decisions may have the same consequences. Chapter 4 discusses ways managers, especially those in the first line, can improve decision-making skills.

■ *In March of 1991 Stan Salzman was faced with a major problem. As supervisor of the state real estate licensing board's examination unit, he was recognized as the authority on requirements for qualification as broker. He was respected by employees, admired by higher levels of management, and often cited in the real estate sections of newspapers as a vigilant protector of consumers who dealt with the real estate industry. His problem? Two large companies offered him executive positions that would more than double his present salary.*

His wife and children were excited about the possibilities of his moving up in his profession. Stan was concerned, however, with who would take his place. He asked himself, Would being an executive be as worthwhile as influencing the quality of people who deal with home buyers in a complex world that is especially difficult for first-time buyers? On the other hand, increased income and the prestige of being a top executive in a major firm was also attractive. It was a tough decision. After a week of thinking it over, he made his decision. What was it? Why did he make it?

■ DECISION MAKING—CHOOSING A COURSE OF ACTION

Decision making entails choosing a course of action from several possibilities or alternatives.

There is little doubt that decision making is a critical management skill. It involves every management function. **Decision making** entails choosing a course of action from several possibilities or alternatives. While most decisions are concerned with routine, day-to-day selections of courses of action, some are critical to the success or failure of organizations. Management effectiveness is strongly influenced by decision-making skills. Good managers are willing to make decisions, even those that are difficult, and use methods that help ensure their correctness.

It is important for supervisors to understand decision levels, types of decisions, and forces that prevent good decision making. Decisions made by top-level managers are different from those made by middle and first-line managers. Equally important is the recognition that forces within individual managers often delay and sometimes stop necessary decision-making processes.

Increasing reliance on computer-based information has made an additional impact on managerial actions. While a number of computer programs can integrate data and draw logical conclusions, none have the experience and judgment of qualified managers. In spite of their impressive speed in calculations and ability to organize and store vast amounts of data, computers cannot predict the future or deal with human problems. Although

FIRST-LINERS

computers are, in today's environment, essential tools, they are not yet replacements for the training, experience, and intelligence of experienced managers.

■ DECISION LEVELS AND TYPES OF DECISIONS

Strategic decisions are long-range decisions that affect the operation of the total organization.

Top-level managers are often concerned with long-range decisions that affect their entire organization. Most of these strategic decisions are made in consultation with experts on their staff. Usually they are expressed in the form of policy statements, objectives, or general guidelines for plans. **Strategic decisions** are fundamental purposes of an organization; they change as the organization's environment changes. Poor strategic decisions can mean success or failure of organizations.

When Richard Clark, chief executive officer of Pacific Gas and Electric Company, the nation's largest utility company, announced his company's intention to support major environmental concerns, it was a strategic decision that had very long range implications. Rather than fight environmentalists, as they had often been accused of doing, PG&E would join in their efforts to ensure minimum damage to the ecosystems in which PG&E power plants and transmission systems were located. Not only was the strategy designed to improve the corporation's public image, but it also had the potential of improving long-range profits by more closely examining new alternatives for producing and delivering energy to homes and industry.[1]

Strategic decisions set the course for all other decisions made in organizations. In the case of Pacific Gas and Electric many other lower levels of decisions must be made in the future to support those of Richard Clark and his top staff. Middle managers in purchasing, marketing, human resource management, facilities planning, production, engineering, finance, and all other major segments of the organization must make tactical decisions that support the strategic decisions and make them a reality.

Tactical decisions are decisions that support and make strategic decisions a reality.

Tactical decisions are the step-by-step actions that make strategic decisions possible. Tactical decisions involve planning and organizing to meet long-range corporate goals. As stated earlier, decision making is a part of every management action. Whether the function being carried out by managers is planning, organizing, directing, or controlling, decision making is involved. Each action is designed to make the strategic decisions of upper-level management successful and to integrate them into the operations of the organization.

Operational decisions are the day-to-day decisions made by supervisors.

First-line managers convert tactical decisions into reality. For the most part their decisions are operational. **Operational decisions** are the day-to-day decisions that all managers must make. Managers decide which tasks must be completed first, who will be responsible for various activities, and what needs to be done to make their units function more effectively. Most operational decisions are directly related to employee assignments, equipment utilization, supplies, schedules, priorities, and methods of improving work. Although first-line managers may be involved to a degree in tactical decisions, most of their work, whether planning, organizing, directing, or controlling, is making operational decisions that keep their organizational unit functioning. Results of indecision from procrastination and vacillation are shown in Figure 4.1.

■ FORCES THAT PREVENT DECISION MAKING

In the early part of this century William James stated that unmade decisions were a fundamental cause of many human problems.[2] His insights into decision-making difficulties are still valid. People are reluctant to make decisions, James believed, because of conflicts within themselves. At best, decision making always carries a degree of uncertainty.

Both **procrastination** and **vacillation** occur as a result of the lack of certainty. Procrastination is doubtlessly one of the most

FIGURE 4.1 ▪ Indecision and Results from Procrastination and Vacillation

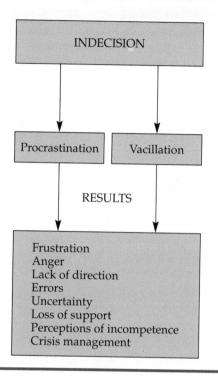

Procrastination means to delay or postpone. It is a chief reason for lack of decisions.

Vacillation is the inability to decide between alternative courses of action. It means being "wishy-washy."

Approach-approach conflicts delay decisions because choices are similar and any choice will likely be satisfactory.

common problems. If the results of a decision, such as reprimanding an employee who is consistently disruptive, can be unpleasant, some managers will delay action. Delays can also occur when the result of a decision is not clear. Fear of failure is a strong reason for procrastination.

In some cases a choice between two or more possible decisions, each with equally uncertain results, can cause delays. First one course of action is chosen, but before it is implemented, another is selected and the first may be reevaluated. Decisions go unmade because the decision maker is unwilling to make a clear, definite choice. Like procrastination, vacillation can also be a major reason for unmade decisions.

Three other types of internal conflicts often impede decision making. **Approach-approach conflicts** occur when any choice is likely to be satisfactory. In a restaurant the menu may list a number of choices that are well liked by the customer. Any choice will be satisfactory, although the person may spend some time deciding. In such cases the customer may follow the lead of others at the table rather than lengthen the decision process.

At work people are often faced with a number of different tasks that need attention. If all have equal priority, any choice is likely to be satisfactory, although making the choice may take longer than necessary. Approach-approach conflicts are usually resolved satisfactorily but are an identifiable cause of delay.

Approach-avoidance conflicts occur when the results of decisions are either uncertain or potentially harmful.

Most internal conflicts involve **approach-avoidance conflicts**. A decision is needed but the outcome is uncertain or potentially unsatisfactory. Some approach-avoidance conflicts are relatively simple. A decision to assign an employee to a job she or he has not done before carries the potential for delays and even failure, but it may also be necessary if the employee is to learn new skills. She or he may also be the only person available. Most decisions carry a degree of approach-avoidance conflict. Effective managers recognize that part of their job is to take some risks and that there will be occasional failure. Major decisions, usually made by upper levels of management, can literally save an organization or ruin it.

Supervisors are often faced with approach-avoidance conflicts. When faced with the necessity for meeting an important schedule, overtime work by most of the employees may seem to be a possible solution. Costs of the overtime work, however, would also impact budgets and could, in the long run, be a self-defeating decision. In such cases supervisors must weigh the importance of both schedules and budgets to arrive at well-reasoned priorities.

Avoidance-avoidance conflicts are the result of the inability to perceive alternatives that are not painful, harmful, or have a negative outcome.

In work organizations **avoidance-avoidance conflicts** are, fortunately, relatively rare. Faced with the necessity of laying off employees due to a loss of business, a supervisor may find that the reduction in number of employees will severely impact both schedules and customer services. If the layoff does not take place, the organization will suffer financially. Any choice appears to be a bad one. Avoidance-avoidance conflicts are the most difficult for most people to resolve. There often seems to be no way to make a decision that will solve a current problem without creating others. Three are described in Table 4.1.

External Decision Blockers

At times, forces that a manager cannot control impede decision making. First-line managers are often faced with limitations of authority, policy restrictions, schedule demands, lack of personnel, financial constraints, and restrictive union contracts, all of

TABLE 4.1 ■ Types of Internal Conflict That Block Decision Making

Approach-approach	When decisions have highly predictable outcomes and any choice is satisfactory, indecision may occur over which is "best." Like a donkey trying to decide which of two bales of hay to eat first, people often have difficulty making decisions when the choices have equal or near-equal value.
Approach-avoidance	Most decisions have an element of uncertainty. Outcomes can be potentially incorrect or even harmful. This uncertainty over decisions that need to be made (approach) and the possibility of error (avoidance) may result in delay. Most decisions involve a degree of approach-avoidance conflict.
Avoidance-avoidance	When any choice appears to be unsatisfactory, avoidance-avoidance conflicts result. Decisions are not made because negative outcomes are the only ones apparent. It is the "out of the frying pan, into the fire" situation. Fortunately avoidance-avoidance decisions are relatively rare in most people's lives.

which may delay or prevent needed decisions and subsequent initiation of action from taking place. Decisions must be limited to the realities of the workplace and its built-in limitations.

Regardless of the cause, delaying a decision can be devastating. Employees who need decisions in their jobs become frustrated. Higher levels of management see such delays as a weakness, and the longer a decision is delayed, the weaker the responsible manager's position becomes. During the time of the delay, the problem remains unsolved and becomes even more pronounced. Managers, including supervisors, are judged both for the quality of their decisions and the time required to make a decision.

It is true that in rare instances delaying decision making to obtain additional information or to let events develop further is justified. In such cases, the reason for the delay must be communicated in detail to all that will be affected.

■ STEPS IN DECISION MAKING

Most decisions are relatively routine and are made on the basis of experience, well-known procedures, or directives from higher-level management. Ideally most routine decisions are largely **programmed decisions.** They have been anticipated, are usually recurring, and procedures and practices that direct managerial

Programmed decisions are those dictated by policies, procedures, or established practices.

action have either been deliberately developed or have evolved over time. Proactive managers, as described in Chapter 2, try to look ahead and develop procedures for handling as many problems as can be anticipated. Unlike reactive managers, they work to reduce potential crisis and fire fighting that occurs when managers are forced to run from one problem to another. Part of effective decision making requires envisioning future possibilities. Experienced hikers and campers will often bring anti–snake venom kits with them on long summer treks. While snake bites are rare, it pays to be prepared. Managers who are able to foresee potential problems are also prepared. As an example, if an employee is absent, proactive supervisors know how to rearrange work sequences and still accomplish most or all of what was expected for a given day's effort.

■ SYSTEMATIC DECISION MAKING

Systematic decision making involves a set of step-by-step actions that lead to carefully considered decisions.

Good managers are decisive. In addition to willingness to make decisions, they also accept responsibility for results. They know that effective decisions require a systematic approach. By **systematic decision making** we mean a well-thought-out sequence of steps that are more likely to achieve desired results than a random, top-of-the-head solution. Successful, experienced managers engage in organizational analysis on a continuing basis. They know that assessment of their organizational unit's needs is an ongoing process. If they recognize a problem or need for action, the decision-making process is initiated. In cases where procedures, policies, or established practices act as guides, the decision process is relatively simple. When, as is often the case, there are no guidelines, seven systematic decision-making steps are followed: recognize need for decision, problem definition and objective determination, alternative development, alternative selection, action implementation, follow-up, and development of policies and procedures for future similar decisions. Table 4.2 summarizes these major steps.

Organizational analysis is not, in itself, a step in the decision-making process. It is, rather, an ongoing assessment of the general health of the manager's major organizational unit. Supervisors are concerned with the flow of work in their area of responsibility, the degree to which quality, productivity, cost, schedules, and other standards are being met, and whether specific areas need attention. To an extent all managers use what is often called the

TABLE 4.2 ■ Systematic Decision Making

1. Recognize need for a decision.
2. Define problem; state in terms of goals or intent.
3. List alternatives; do not evaluate feasibility, costs, or side effects.
4. Develop evaluation criteria, i.e., feasibility, costs, schedules, side effects.
5. Implement decision; prepare and utilize implementation plan.
6. Follow up, both in-process and results. Make in-process corrections if necessary or advantageous.
7. Develop policies or procedures for future similar decisions.

Management by exception means to put more energy and time into those aspects of the organization that have problems than those that are meeting expected levels of performance.

Objectives are the aims and goals of individuals, groups, and total organizations. They embody the intent of those who develop the objectives.

exception principle or *management by exception.* Those activities or areas of concern that are not meeting expectations receive the greatest amount of attention. If the number of hours required to complete a specific task or group of related tasks has increased, experienced supervisors immediately gather enough data to analyze the difficulty and take corrective action. If changes are needed or a problem is recognized, the first step in the decision-making process takes place: objectives are defined.

An **objective** is the desired result of a decision and the actions that follow. A common error is the incorrect definition of a problem. If, as an example, on the day of an advertised sale 3 of a small department store's 15 salespeople are ill and unable to report for work, the manager is faced with a difficult problem. Inexperienced supervisors will often define the difficulty as not enough people. Experienced first-line managers recognize that providing high-quality service to an increased number of customers is the true problem and objective. Like planning, good decision making is dependent on having well-defined objectives that will meet the organization's needs or improve its operations and processes. First-line managers with poorly defined objectives are likely to make equally faulty decisions.

Decision making starts with the recognition that decisions are needed and ends with a follow-up while the decision is being implemented and after it is completed. Briefly summarized, decision making includes:

1. **Recognize the need for a decision.** Effective managers are able to identify problems and recognize that decisions are required for their solutions. Managers who fail to recognize problems or potential problems are certain to fail.

2. **Accurate definition of the problem.** One of the most important steps in good decision making is accurate definition of the problem. Many problems are inaccurately defined. If, as an example, a month-end report is due and the best word processor operator is ill, the problem is not necessarily a lack of competent assistance but finding the best way to complete the report in time. Problems are best defined in terms of goals or intent. In the case of the missing word processor operator, the goal is to complete the report in time.

3. **Alternatives.** After the problem has been defined, alternatives need to be considered. What are possible ways of accomplishing the goal and solving the problem. Call in another word processor operator, borrow one from another department, assign an operator not familiar with the report, work overtime with a less competent person, or, as supervisor, do it yourself?

4. **Develop evaluation criteria.** Before selecting an alternative, factors such as schedules, costs, feasibility, and side-effects must be considered. Which is more important? Test alternatives against criteria and decide which ones to implement and which to reject.

5. **Implement the decision.** Prepare and utilize an implementation plan for turning the selected alternative into a reality.

6. **Follow-up.** Once a decision has been implemented, follow it up both while the implementation is under way and after it is completed.

7. **Develop policies and procedures for future similar situations.** Many decisions can be programmed or preselected by sound policies and procedures that delineate what should be done in specific circumstances.

One of the more common definitions of decision making is *making a choice from a number of alternatives.* In rare instances the number of available alternatives may be very small. For most decisions a number of alternatives are usually available, with more than one that will help solve the problem. Faced with the need to provide adequate services to customers, our manager of the small department store can quickly draw up a list of possible alternatives:

1. Call in temporary help.

2. Have all salespeople on the floor; work overtime to restock shelves and straighten storeroom.

3. Have manager work as salesperson.

4. Rearrange assignments so existing people can do tasks absent employees normally perform.

5. Ask employees to take short breaks rather than the standard 15 minutes.

6. Pay overtime for shortened lunch periods.

There are probably several other alternatives an experienced retail sales manager can formulate. Once alternatives have been listed, those most likely to help meet the objective will be selected for implementation. While a single alternative may solve some types of problems, in most cases two or more are selected for implementation.

In **alternative selection** a number of factors must be considered. Most important is the question of whether or not, if selected, the alternative will accomplish the objective. Bringing in temporary employees, alternative number one, may not be a good choice. Untrained employees, even those experienced in retail sales, may be more of a burden than any real assistance. Our manager will reject this alternative. Working overtime is a possibility but it will increase costs and may also have the undesirable side effect of tired, irritable employees and increased absenteeism on following days. Although many routine office duties will be delayed, the manager can work as a member of the salesforce. A side effect will be extra hours of catch-up work. Reassigning duties is also a good selection. There is no additional cost, but some employees may resent the extra load. If it is for a short time, most will realize the necessity for everyone sharing the additional work. Altering breaks is possible but may cause some discontent. Paying overtime for shorter lunch periods is also possible but will be an additional cost.

Our manager will, after evaluation, reassign duties and work on the floor as a salesperson. If implementation of these two alternatives does not seem adequate, shorter breaks and lunch periods will be considered. General overtime will be a last resort. Some planning will be required in work reassignment but experience and judgment will help in making equitable rearrangement.

It is likely, if our example was a real-life situation, that the manager has experienced absenteeism before this incident. Practices or even written procedures have probably been established to serve as decision guidelines. If not, a systematic approach will allow a choice of workable alternatives. Many grid formats are

TABLE 4.3 ■ Decision Grid

ALTERNATIVE EVALUATION—PROVIDING SERVICE TO CUSTOMERS

Alternative	Meet Objective?	Add Costs?	Feasible?	Side Effects
Temporary help	Do not know	Probably	Doubtful	Slow others
Manager work in sales	Yes	No	Yes	Some work delayed
Reallocate assignments	Probably	No	Yes	Some resentment over extra load
Work overtime on storeroom and stocking	Probably	Yes	Yes	Fatigue, potential for increased absenteeism
Reschedule breaks and lunch times	Will help	If overtime is necessary for short lunch	Yes	May cause resentment if prolonged

possible. Table 4.3 depicts a grid approach to decision making that helps ensure a systematic evaluation of alternatives. It considers costs, feasibility, and side-effects. In reviewing the grid, it should be noted that many possible variations can be used. Managers can identify factors that are most important and evaluate alternatives using their own criteria. Success of **decision grid** techniques depends on accurate problem definition and objective selection of alternatives.

Supervisors can use many other systematic decision-making methods. In those involving significant amounts of money, careful cost analysis is necessary. In some instances schedules may be an overriding concern. Quality considerations, equipment and materials utilization, delivery times, and many other variables may affect the way alternatives are evaluated and chosen. In most instances decisions first-line managers make are relatively routine and are based largely on experience and judgment. When important problems are recognized and defined as objectives, good decision making often depends on analysis of many possibilities.

■ GROUP DECISIONS

Compared to individual decisions, group decisions have advantages and disadvantages. Japanese managers have long had a tradition of not implementing any decisions until other managers

Group decisions have the advantage of greater acceptance and accuracy if group members have expertise in the problems being addressed.

agree that they are in the best interests of the organization. In many instances significant decisions are also reviewed with members of employee groups before any changes are made. Although the process of gaining approval and acceptance from everyone in an organization can be slow, there is usually broad-based support. Although many managers are tired of reading and hearing about Japanese techniques, there is little doubt about their success.

Involving employees as well as managers in decision making is relatively rare in the United States, although it is gaining support in some areas. We have developed some relatively simple guidelines that have proven helpful to supervisors who recognize the need for both group and individual involvement in decisions.

1. Involve employees, when feasible, in decisions that directly affect their work, assignments, or work methods, such as more sophisticated technology.

2. When broad-based acceptance is needed, group decisions are usually accepted more readily than individual or top-down decisions.

3. Group decisions made by well-informed people will usually be as good or better than those of equally knowledgeable individuals.

4. Group decisions made by poorly trained or inadequately informed people are likely to be worse than those of knowledgeable and well-informed individuals.

5. Group decisions are much slower than individual decisions and are often less precise.

6. In a crisis environment well-informed decisions by acknowledged leaders are both desired and expected.

Table 4.4 depicts some advantages and disadvantages of both group and individual decisions.

Decision-making groups can be committees, portions of an organization, a small group of employees with similar jobs and concerns, or in some cases an entire work force. Regardless of group composition, employee involvement in organizational decisions has positive benefits. At the New United Motors International (NUMI) plant in Fremont, California, union employee grievances against management have dropped from approximately 200 per month to less than 2 per month.[3] It is significant that management techniques emphasizing high degrees of employee involvement result in increased commitment to the objectives of their organization.

TABLE 4.4 ■ Group versus Individual Decisions

Type	Accuracy	Speed	Acceptance	Communication
Group	Depends on group members; often more creative than individual	Slower than individual decisions in most instances	Usually higher than individual	Faster than individual
Individual	More accurate if individual has greater expertise and knowledge than group	Usually much faster than groups if individual has expertise	Usually much less; resistance is predictable and expected	Usually slower except in crisis conditions

■ GAINING ACCEPTANCE OF DECISIONS

Several factors are important in gaining general acceptance of a decision. Supervisors who make decisions and implement them without providing discussion, information, or any degree of employee involvement are likely to find resistance and resentment. Two simple guidelines have been developed to help management in gaining support as well as acceptance of decisions:

1. Employees tend to reject decisions that they were not involved in or that have uncertain and possibly negative impacts on their jobs.

2. Most people accept decisions to which they have contributed or that have clearly positive benefits.

Managers who involve employees in decision-making processes are most likely to get a high degree of acceptance and support, especially if the decisions directly affect the employee's work. If involving employees is not feasible, discussing the necessity and potential benefits of the decision will help alleviate fear and uncertainty.

Not all decisions have positive outcomes. In some instances lack of work may require a reduction in the number of employees in a given work area. In such cases open, candid discussions of the reasons for the reduction is far better than trying to hide conditions until lay-off notices are given to affected employees. Bad news, carefully and honestly presented, is better than rumors, suspicion, and fear. Decision-acceptance conflict resolution actions are shown in Figure 4.2.

FIGURE 4.2   Resolving Decision-Acceptance Conflicts

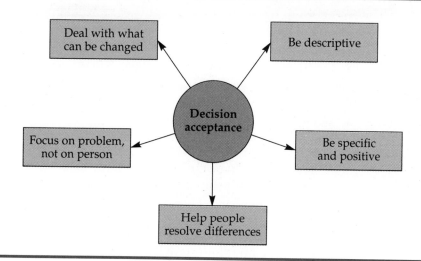

Resolving Decision-Acceptance Conflicts

At times conflict may arise between employees, employees and supervisors, and supervisors and other supervisors over the correctness of a decision or its implementation. It is important to recognize that a degree of **decision acceptance conflict** in any organizational setting is inevitable, normal, and beneficial as well as potentially destructive. New ideas, new ways of accomplishing tasks, and innovative uses of resources can be developed from disagreement.

When conflict escalates to a point that strong emotions are involved, anger and frustration are often dominant feelings and differences go unresolved. It is necessary for the supervisor to intervene. Simply telling people involved to "knock it off" rarely resolves anything. It may temporarily get people back to work, but the issues remain undecided. Conflict resolution requires that the supervisor avoid emotional involvement, be analytical rather than critical, approach the difficulty as an information gatherer, and avoid embarrassing or making the participants feel like losers. Effective managers attempt to provide solutions that both sides in a conflict situation will find acceptable.

While not all conflict can be easily resolved, a number of guidelines are helpful in reducing tension, anger, and frustration:

1. Be descriptive, not judgmental. Approach the conflict with a willingness to listen to all points of view. Often there is no clear right or wrong, just different points of view. Experienced first-line managers will describe rather than evaluate. If, as an example, a conflict arises over work schedules, the supervisor should restate facts rather than emotions. "Mary has worked on the second shift for the past four months while John has been assigned to the first shift during the same period of time. Mary would like to be changed to the day shift and John would like to stay on his present schedule." Rather than point out that it is unfair for an employee to "get his or her own way all of the time," the descriptive statement is not likely to be challenged. In this instance the supervisor is in a much better position to explain scheduling procedures and rationale and have a degree of acceptance.

2. Be specific and positive. It is much better to state that "Bill has been on time all but four days in the past three months" than "Bill is late a few days every month." While the second statement is general and essentially negative in tone, the first is specific and is likely to be received more positively. It also lets the employee know that the supervisor is informed and concerned about employees reporting to work late. Being specific provides a focus for eventual conflict resolution.

3. Deal with what can be changed. Often conflicts arise over issues that cannot be changed by a supervisor. Union contract rules, personnel policies, or schedule procedures may dictate shift assignment in the case of Mary and John. It is time-consuming and futile to enter into extended discussions of issues beyond the control of both managers and employees.

Work environments always have some limitations. Equipment, supplies, time, policies, costs, schedules, and lack of trained employees are just a few of the more common types of restraints faced by first-line managers. In such cases a simple, straightforward explanation is all that can be done. Most people will accept logically presented, sincere explanations of why some things cannot be changed.

4. Focus on the problem, not on the person. When John objects to working on a weekend, it is better to state, "We have to determine how to accomplish all of our work and still be fair to all employees," than, out of exasperation, "John, you always have an excuse for not working when you're needed." Experienced supervisors will also listen carefully to John's explanation. He may have worked weekends for an extended period of time and feels other employees should also have similar assignments. A realistic view of the problem is how to get needed work completed, not John's objections. Perhaps other alternatives are available. It would be ideal to make John part of the problem-solving process. If he recognizes that there are no other viable alternatives, his objections may be less emotional.

5. Help people resolve their own differences. Supervisors can often minimize conflicts by facilitating employee decision groups. In work schedule conflicts, a group of employees may be able to develop rules that they feel are fair and will meet work requirements. While there may be some objections, all participants will understand the group decision. Although they may not be in total agreement, they are provided an opportunity to state their position to peers as well as managers.

Experienced first-line managers recognize that many decisions cannot be made by employees. Specialized knowledge and expertise, familiarity with established policies and procedures, level of responsibility and authority, and effects of decisions on other aspects of work mandate decisions by the supervisor. Many aspects of work do not directly affect employees. Reports to higher levels of management, development of budget information, labor projections, and analysis of performance by both individuals and their work unit are just a few of the types of problems that necessitate supervisory rather than group decisions.

■ TAKING THE HEADACHES OUT OF DECISION MAKING

While many decisions made by first-line managers are routine, some require careful analysis before implementation. Objectives must be clearly defined, possible alternatives developed, courses of action selected based on careful evaluation, and implementation originated from well-formulated plans. Both in-process and completion follow-up are necessary. Effective supervisors recognize that many problems can be solved by employees who understand and are skilled in performing their jobs. Other decisions are made on the basis of established practices, procedures, and policies. A few simple guidelines may help in taking some of the stress out of decision making resulting from *exceptions*.

1. Recognize the difference between little problems and big ones. Effective supervisors recognize that most problems they are faced with on a daily basis can be easily resolved. In many instances these small problems, if left alone, will settle themselves. Others may take some degree of analysis and research as well as concentrated attention. Most demanding, however, are those rare problems that are very difficult and require a clearly defined, systematic approach.

Inexperienced and, often, ineffective supervisors fail to recognize that not all problems warrant time-consuming effort or emotional reaction. During any given period some things will not meet standards, plans, or expectations. These are usually easily resolved. Major problems that may potentially delay schedules, increase costs, lower efficiency, or affect employee morale require careful attention and analysis. They are, fortunately, usually rare and with systematic analysis can usually be either fully or partially resolved. First-line managers who see every problem as a crisis not only make their own existence difficult but that of others as well.

2. Rely on established procedures when possible. Over a period of time procedures are developed in most organizations that define courses of action. In some instances general practices that may not be explicitly defined in writing are also valuable in assisting decision making. General policies often provide direction for especially difficult problems. Regardless of the source these established guides should be utilized. There are many instances, however, when no procedures, past practices, or policies exist that will adequately assist the first-line manager. In such cases they must use their skills in problem definition, alternative development and analysis as well as solution implementation efforts to resolve on-the-job difficulties.

3. Seek help from others. No one knows everything. In an organization there are usually many people who have experience and expertise that others lack. When faced with unfamiliar problems it is often better to seek information from others than make decisions based on lack of both experience and knowledge. Many organizations have a variety of specialists who can be helpful in the resolution of many different problems. Seeking assistance is not an indication of weakness, but an intelligent approach to problem solution.

4. Avoid crisis decisions. Over 20 years ago a crisis occurred during the third Apollo moon mission. Onboard computers shut down and astronauts had to fly their space capsule back into the earth's atmosphere. Their angle of entry had to be correct within one half of a degree. It was one of the most perfectly timed and accurate entries of the six major Apollo missions. When asked later by reporters if they felt lucky at being able to get back, the commander replied, "Luck had little to do with our success. We were well-trained and knew exactly what to do."

Like the astronauts, effective first-line managers know how to act when faced with a crisis. Their *proactive* planning and self-development tends to minimize the stress others less prepared may face. Like Boy Scouts with their motto, "Be prepared," knowledgeable supervisors develop the skills and attitudes that enable them to diminish the effects of most crisis conditions. Rather than "freeze" and fail to take action when needed, they are able to quickly review possibilities, select appropriate solutions, and take action quickly.

All too often, postponed decisions, failure to utilize systematic steps in reaching conclusions, and inadequate preparation for possible crises can lead to disaster. Although their actions may seem instantaneous, people in critical occupations in medical care, protective services, such as police work and fire protection, and public transportation are constantly trained in keeping cool, evaluating, and acting rapidly as well as correctly.

Supervisors can develop their own crisis skills by recognizing possibilities, learning from their own experience and the experience of others, and taking advantage of training programs that help them minimize panic decisions. Rather than delay crisis decisions, they are able to rationally evaluate possibilities and choose correct courses of action without unnecessary delay. In many instances what seemed to be a crisis can be changed to less critical conditions by calm, deliberate, carefully timed, and well-thought-out management action.

5. Don't anticipate calamity. Some people feel their lives are built on crisis. In most organizations true crisis situations are rare. Less-effective supervisors may act like children being taken to a doctor's office for a booster shot. They start crying long before the needle touches their arm, only to find out that it did not really hurt. Supervisors who perceive every situation as one that can lead to disaster make life difficult not only for themselves but for their employees and immediate manager as well.

6. Not all decisions are correct ones. Most problems supervisors encounter in organizations have many possible solutions that can potentially result in satisfactory outcomes. One of the real strengths of systematic decision making is the examination of many possibilities or alternatives. Regardless of how thorough an analysis is made and how well specific decisions are implemented, some won't work as well as planned. No decision maker is likely to have a perfect record. In-process follow-up during implementation can often detect if outcomes are likely to not meet objectives. When a difficulty is detected, the decision may be corrected before too much damage has occurred. Even when errors are not evident until an action is completed, corrective actions may still be made. Effective supervisors know that some decisions will be better than others. They also recognize that by adhering to sound principles, errors can be minimized.

7. Develop decisiveness. Indecisive managers are in reality nonmanagers. Supervisors who fail to make decisions and take responsibility for their actions are seen as message carriers and little more. Both employees and higher levels of management have little professional respect for the way indecisive supervisors fulfill their roles. Deciding and doing are both necessary keys to leadership at any level and especially for first-line managers.

8. Implement decisions. Once a decision has been made, implement it. Successful people know that once a set of objectives has been designed and the implementation steps defined, the next step is to *do it!* Without action the very best decisions are worthless.

Cognitive dissonance refers to holding two or more conflicting ideas at the same time.

Plan actions, assign responsibilities, and begin work. While some managers want perfection, it is often more of a goal than a reality. While implementation is in-process, check for problems and make appropriate corrections. Psychologists sometimes use the term **cognitive dissonance** to describe holding two opposing ideas at the same time. In decision making it occurs when a decision is made and doubts occur about its accuracy before implementation. As discussed earlier, vacillation and procrastination are the cardinal sins of decision making. Delays caused by anxiety over the correctness of a decision can be as harmful as no decision when decisions are critical. It is true that there are circumstances where no decision is the correct decision. These, however, are rare and usually entail situations that are, by nature, self-corrective. First-line managers who are smart, work hard, are ambitious, and are nice (SWANs) need to recognize that their performance is often judged by willingness to make decisions and implement action to make their choices a reality.

9. Follow up, follow up, follow up. Once a decision is made, it is necessary to do both in-process and results follow-up. Even those decisions that have doubtful outcomes can often be corrected while action is taking place. Careful monitoring of each step, evaluation of potential impact, and in-process corrections can have positive results. In some instances follow-up is difficult or impossible during implementation. Evaluation can be based only on results. Final follow-up to determine if additional decisions are necessary and if the original action can serve as a basis for standard procedures is also beneficial. Proactive managers view decision follow-up as an opportunity to make future implementation easier, more effective, and more efficient.

■ DECISIONS, DECISIONS, DECISIONS

Like communication, decision making is one of several first-line management activities that involve every function supervisors perform. It is part of planning, organizing, directing, controlling, and support activities. Decision-making skills are involved in coordination, time management, cost control, scheduling, performance evaluation, and the many other types of work first-line managers do. Decision making is always coupled with other activities. Effective managers develop expertise in many activities.

In a world of increasingly sophisticated technology it is necessary for managers to understand the advantages and limitations of computer-based decisions. Mathematical models that are extremely valuable in dealing with complex decisions have been formulated over many years of experience. Many of these have been incorporated in computer software that can draw information from large databases (information stored in computer files). Because of their speed, computers can sort out relevant data, apply correct mathematical tools, and develop recommended decisions much quicker than people can. While their conclusions are often very useful, computers do not have the experience, judgment, and sense of what works and what doesn't that competent managers possess. Computer-based decisions are best viewed as helpful and perhaps necessary analytical tools rather than completely flawless responses to problems or needs.

Effective first-line managers constantly try to improve skills in every aspect of work for which they are responsible. Coordination, communication, analysis, evaluation of performance, reporting, budgeting, staffing, and training activities all require sound decision making. Good decision makers are also good thinkers.

■ THINGS TO REMEMBER

I. Decision making.

   A. Decision making entails choosing a course of action from several possible alternatives.

   B. Types of decisions differ at each level of management.

   C. Computers cannot replace training, experience, and intelligence in decision making.

II. Decision levels and types of decisions.

   A. Top-level managers make strategic decisions.

   B. Middle managers are concerned primarily with tactical decisions.

   C. Supervisors make operational decisions that keep work units functioning on a day-to-day basis.

III. Forces that prevent decision making.

   A. Decision making always carries a degree of uncertainty.

   B. Procrastination and vacillation are common barriers to decision making.

   C. Approach-approach, approach-avoidance, and avoidance-avoidance conflicts also impede decision making.

   D. External factors that prevent or delay decision are often uncontrollable by managers.

IV. Steps in decision making.

   A. Some decisions are programmed and are automatically made.

   B. Programmed decisions work on the principle of being prepared.

V. Systematic decision making.

   A. A systematic decision is a well-thought-out sequence of steps, usually involving a seven-step process.

   B. Decision-making grids are useful for some types of decisions.

VI. Group decisions.

   A. Group decisions may gain approval and acceptance but take longer than individual decisions.

   B. Group decisions are best when members of the group have expertise in the area of concern.

VII. Gaining acceptance of decisions.

   A. Employees tend to reject decisions that they were not involved in or that have uncertain impact on their jobs.

   B. Most people accept decisions to which they have contributed and view them as having potentially positive benefits.

VIII. Resolving decision acceptance conflicts.

   A. Effective managers provide solutions that both sides of a conflict situation will find acceptable.

   B. Conflict resolution involves a number of steps including being specific, focusing on the problem rather than the person, being descriptive rather than judgmental, and helping people to resolve their differences.

IX. Taking the headaches out of decision making.

   A. Objectives must be clearly defined before good decisions can be made.

   B. Good managers recognize the difference between little problems and big ones, rely on established procedures when possible, seek help from others, avoid crisis decisions, don't anticipate calamity, know that not all decisions are the best ones, develop decisiveness, and implement and follow up decisions.

X. Decisions, decisions, decisions.

   A. Decision making involves every activity performed by first-line supervisors.

   B. Good decision making requires good thinking.

■ KEY TERMS

decision making	**procrastination**
strategic decisions	**vacillation**
tactical decisions	**approach-approach conflicts**
operational decisions	**approach-avoidance conflicts**

avoidance-avoidance conflicts   alternative selection

programmed decisions   decision grid

systematic decision making   decision acceptance conflict

organizational analysis   cognitive dissonance

objective

■ DISCUSSION QUESTIONS

1. What are some fundamental steps that a supervisor can take to develop proactive management practices that assist in decision making?

2. Organizational analysis is used to identify both strengths and potential problem areas in an organization. How would the supervisor of a shoe department in a large department store make an organizational analysis?

3. List three difficult decisions (job-related, educational, personal) that you have had to deal with in the past year. How were they resolved?

4. In what ways does prioritizing what needs to be done relate to effective decision making?

5. In decisions you have faced, what have been some of the major difficulties? Describe significant factors that influenced your choices.

■ SELF-ASSESSMENT

To evaluate some of the knowledge you have developed about decision-making processes, respond to the following questions or statements with a 1, 2, or 3 if you totally or somewhat disagree. Positive responses should be answered with a 4, 5, or 6.

1. I rarely have difficulty making either personal or work decisions.

    1   2   3   4   5   6

2. The first step in good decision making is to develop alternatives.

    1   2   3   4   5   6

3. Good decision makers rarely change their minds once a decision has been made.

    1   2   3   4   5   6

4. Side effects of selecting a particular alternative can be either positive or negative.

   1   2   3   4   5   6

5. Follow-up is necessary only when decision outcomes are uncertain.

   1   2   3   4   5   6

6. In some cases the acceptance of a decision by employees and other managers is almost as important as the decision itself.

   1   2   3   4   5   6

7. Some decisions are best made by groups, others are best made by individuals.

   1   2   3   4   5   6

8. General descriptions of a problem or conditions requiring a decision tend to reduce arguments more than specific descriptions do.

   1   2   3   4   5   6

9. I tend to procrastinate when making important but potentially unpleasant decisions.

   1   2   3   4   5   6

10. Most problems have clearly right or wrong answers.

   1   2   3   4   5   6

■ SHORT CASES

Sophie's Choice

In just four hours Sophie Lomax, supervisor of New Products Research for American International Marketing, is scheduled to give a presentation on sales figures for new high-density computer laser disks. Sophie had the data but the report was not typed, reproduced, stapled, or ready for distribution at the meeting. It would be embarrassing to her and her immediate boss if she attempted to give the presentation unprepared to distribute the report to the top-level managers attending the conference.

Sue Hoover, who normally did the word processing and related work, was late and had not called in. When Sophie called Sue's home, no one answered. All of the other employees were working on other important projects and none knew the report format or could access data as effectively as Sue. As the minutes kept ticking away, Sophie noted that if the report was going to be finished in time, it would have to be started in the next hour.

1. Define the problem in terms of objectives.

2. List alternatives that Sophie may realistically consider.

3. Choose from your list the alternatives you think will help Sophie most.

4. How can Sophie avoid a crisis atmosphere?

Norval's Nightmare

As terminal supervisor for Baker-Air Regional Flight, Inc.'s (BARF) central terminal, Norval Wellsfry was faced with a tough decision. BARF specialized in short-range, critical freight shipments to cities with major air-transportation facilities. Because of demand, BARF's management decided to expand into other cities and to use a hub system. Flights from smaller cities would all bring their shipments to the central terminal where they would be redistributed for shipment to their designated areas. It would be a system very similar to that used by major airfreight handlers, such as Federal Express, Emery Air Freight, and others.

Frank Litz asked Norval to assess the impact the hub system would have on the central terminal. It would require careful planning and decision making. More space, more personnel, and perhaps more shifts would be needed. Should the company rent extra space or build a larger terminal? Package handling equipment would also have to be increased. Phasing the new business in to meet demands without overexpanding appeared to be a critical decision area. Norval knew that his opportunity for future promotion was tied directly to how well he completed this assignment.

1. What are some of Norval's key objectives in deciding what to do about the expansion plans? How should he prioritize them?

2. What are some potential side effects of the alternatives he may select?

3. Both costs and schedules are important to BARF. How should Norval approach ensuring prompt schedules without undue costs?

▪ ENDNOTES

1. David Kirkpatrick, "Environmentalism: The New Crusade," *Fortune*, February 12, 1990, pp. 48–49.

2. William James, *Psychology,* Henry Holt & Company, 1910.

3. NUMI's management achievements have been published many times. This report is especially unusual because it came from a publication of the American Federation of Government Employees, *Government Employees*, in October of 1989.

Chapter 5

Motivation and Demotivation at Work

Objectives

In 1910 William James, the father of American psychology, studied a number of questions concerning the reasons people do the things they do.[1] Although James knew a great deal about human behavior, he was, like us more than 80 years later, uncertain about motivation. There are *no* easy answers. In Chapter 5 you will learn some major motivational theories and their applications to everyday life.

Readers of Chapter 5 will be able to

- Define the uses of money as a motivator.
- Recognize job assignments that are demotivators.
- Apply several motivational principles.
- Utilize techniques that tend to improve employee performance.
- Define principal demotivators for most employers.

Thought Starter

Frequently the difference between a winner and a loser is determined by who most wants to win. In his lecture tours Ken Blanchard, author of the *One Minute Manager,* urges managers to develop winners. A few people seem to be high achievers while many others seem content to just get by. Why do some people want to be the best and others feel it isn't worth the effort? We know that activities that arouse enthusiasm and energy in some people lead to apathy and boredom in others. Managers find themselves with the difficult task of developing conditions that allow most people to be winners at work.

Motivation is one of the most studied areas of human psychology. After many years of speculation and experimentation numerous questions concerning why people do what they do remain unanswered. For very practical reasons supervisors are usually not interested in motivational theory. Their primary concern is *how to get people interested in doing their jobs.* It's not an easy task.

In Chapter 5 we explore both theory and applications of motivation. Every approach we discuss has practical applications in a typical supervisor's place of work. We feel that no matter how sophisticated or how recent, no one theory answers all questions relevant to the behavior of people.

■ *Darleen Bissel's complaint about her job was straightforward. "My company is a good one and the pay for what I do is better than most places. It's hard to be motivated, under any circumstances, in an electronic sweatshop. As a telemarketing specialist, everything I do is monitored by computers. When I report to work, turn on my workstation, hook up my headset, start answering calls from customers or telephoning them with additional information, it's all monitored by computers. I haven't read George Orwell's books, but Big Brother is the computer. It even records how long it takes me to go to the restroom. At this point my strongest motivation is to find another job."*

Motivation is a primary management problem, especially in the highly competitive customer-driven environment of today's organizations. Yet management, the most concerned party, designs jobs that are demotivators rather than motivators. It is one of the many extremely difficult problems managers face for the rest of this and on into the next century. How can an organization take advantage of technological tools and still maintain a motivated work force?

■ MOTIVATION

One experiment developed by psychologists that anyone can do is to have two people pretend to throw a ball back and forth to each other as if the ball really existed. At first it is an interesting game. After a few short minutes interest begins to fade, and the game becomes a boring set of motions. If the experimenter insists that it continue, the subjects in the experiment start complaining of being tired and will ultimately quit.

If the same two people were using an actual ball and playing catch, the game would go on much longer and there would be far fewer complaints. People who realize that they have "nothing" jobs are like the players without a ball. They are also bored, tire easily, and complain about their jobs. One of the real challenges of first-line management is to keep people motivated and help make their jobs more meaningful than a "pretend" game.

Motivation is concerned with the forces within individuals that cause them to act to satisfy needs.

Like many other terms, *motivation* has no single definition. From a practical point of view, **motivation** is concerned with the *forces within individuals that cause them to act to satisfy felt needs.* These forces are triggered by factors or stimuli within themselves or their environment. Motivation always results in some type of activity. Many theories attempt to explain motivation. Some deal with identification and strength of needs. Others focus on expectations that goals will be achieved, the importance of learning, choices people make, and genetic characteristics. Managers are usually not as concerned with theories as they are with practical methods of getting people to display interest in their work and to improve their performance. Supervisors are often the most frustrated in this effort since they deal directly with employees on a daily basis.

On-the-Job Motivation

All too often managers see their primary role as taking corrective action when something goes wrong. Employees are left alone until some error is discovered, then they are "zapped." These managers are driven by the need for personal power and control of others. One stated, "I want my employees to dance when I wiggle my fingers, just like puppets." Fear is viewed as the great motivator.

Fear teaches employees to avoid certain actions or behaviors but has little long-range motivational value.

It is true that people react to fear. Often they do what they are told in order to avoid unpleasant consequences. For the most part, fear teaches employees to avoid specific types of behavior rather than to do things correctly. Over time their fear is frequently converted to resentment, apathy, lack of respect, and finding ways of getting even with the offensive boss.

Some managers firmly believe that a happy employee is a good employee. While it is true that unhappy employees may be less productive and cause more problems than happy employees, happiness does not guarantee adequate performance. Employees can be perfectly happy working ineffectively, inefficiently, or simply incorrectly. It is better to have employees who are pleased with their accomplishments and have confidence in their ability to learn and achieve. Good managers try to build the type of self-discipline and enthusiasm that drives employees to continually try to improve.

Another common management technique is the **carrot-and-stick approach** that combines the fear and happiness methods. People, some managers believe, will work for rewards if they are highly visible. Employee of the month, no errors for a month, and special awards for individual achievement are all tangible rewards for effort beyond what is normally expected. Often those who fail to achieve the same level of performance as those who do are punished with unfavorable assignments, ridicule, and even threats. Managers who use the carrot-and-stick approach to motivation fail to realize that in every work group a few employees are capable of performing at higher levels than others. In sports,

not everyone can run a mile in four minutes regardless of how much they try or are trained. Work situations are similar. A few high-performing employees may consistently demonstrate outstanding performance while others try but can never produce quite as much or as well. Outstanding employees consistently earn rewards. Performance of those with average ability often declines rather than improves in the face of what seems to be a no-win set of conditions. Figure 5.1 summarizes the carrot and stick approach to management in terms of potential punishment and rewards.

Reward and punishment management is known as jackass management.

Reward-and-punish management is often known as the jackass style because employees are treated like animals—rewarded for performing better than others and punished for not being as good as the best, even though they worked at the top of their ability.

FIGURE 5.1 ■ Carrot and Stick Motivation

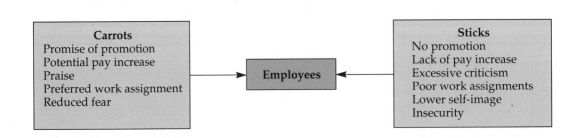

In a few of the better-operated organizations managers have learned that people are often motivated by a sense of responsibility, involvement in decisions affecting their jobs, and trust in their manager's sense of fairness, support, and competence. Corrective action takes the form of analysis, mutual problem solving, and a sense of helpfulness rather than punishment. Rewards are based on group rather than individual achievement.

■ MONEY PROBLEMS AND PROMISES

Early in the 20th century Frederick Taylor wrote that people worked for bread and bread alone.[2] Later Henry Ford, a friend and admirer of Taylor credited with development of the modern assembly line, echoed Taylor's beliefs. Money was the *only* reason people worked. A closer examination by either Taylor or Ford may have yielded different results. People use money to help them obtain those things they identify as needs. Figure 5.2 asks if money is the ultimate motivator. We don't think it is. People accept a particular job for many reasons in addition to money. If the salary or hourly wage is too low, people will not accept certain jobs for any reason. Money is important but not the sole determiner of why people select specific occupations or career paths. A college student may accept a low-paying job to be able to continue his or her education. While, in this case, money pays for necessities, it is

FIGURE 5.2 ■ The Ultimate Motivator?

used to help achieve longer-range goals. Money is used to make other goals possible. Self-esteem and promises of a career in a chosen field may be the real motivators.

Some people accept work because it is available, they can learn the necessary tasks, and it is in a convenient geographic area. Others have friends who have recommended them, the work is the type they have been trained to do, and the organization has a good reputation in their community.

Money as an Incentive

For many years Frederick Herzberg has pointed out that people tend to be more dissatisfied with inadequate pay than they are satisfied with adequate pay.[3] If, as an example, everyone receives a cost-of-living increase in pay every year, they like the pay increase but do not increase their level of effort on the job or improve work habits. In this case money is not a motivator. On the other hand, if an anticipated cost-of-living increase does not materialize, employees become dissatisfied even though their average level of income has not been reduced.

Money will trigger increased effort in many people if it is used as an incentive. **Incentives** are goals that are designed to increase motivation. Money becomes an incentive when it is associated with productivity, quality, or opportunity for promotion. Possibilities of a higher standard of living and greater responsibility are the motivators rather than the money itself. Money is a means to achieve other goals. Not all people, however, take full advantage of monetary incentives even when they exist.

One of the more common types of incentive systems is **piece-rate work.** Employees are paid a minimum hourly wage for achieving a predetermined standard. Piece-rate standards are usually set slightly below what an average employee can achieve with an easily attainable effort. Most employees will earn an amount slightly above standard. A few will earn substantially more than standard and still fewer may double or in some instances triple average wages. These high achievers are frequently seen as rate busters whose productivity pushes the standards higher so everyone has to work harder to meet minimum requirements. Studies in the garment industry, where piece rates are common, have shown that most employees will perform at a level that earns more than minimum but does not seriously threaten easily achievable standards. High-productivity employees are scorned, disliked, and excluded from association with average performers.

Commission sales is another form of incentive that is somewhat like piece rates. A percentage of the profits of each item or service sold is given to the salesperson. Some commission salespeople will work hard to make sales, but when a certain level of income is reached, other priorities such as time with their families, sports events, or other interests become more important than the potential income of an additional sale.

One of the most successful and publicized individual incentive plans is that of Lincoln Electric Company in Cleveland, Ohio. Lincoln relies on "intelligent selfishness." Lincoln rewards people for their contributions to the company. Contributions may be productivity, quality, new ideas, improved methods, or any activity that improved the profitability of the organization. Individual productivity at Lincoln has, historically, been higher than that of comparable employees anywhere else in the world.

Group Incentives

Profit sharing, by granting employees a percentage of organization profits, is the oldest and best known form of group incentives.

Organizations that use group incentives seem to have substantially greater success than those that rely solely on individual performance. Profit sharing, stock ownership, and gainsharing are the primary types of group monetary incentive programs. **Profit sharing** is the simplest and perhaps best known of group incentives. A percentage of an organization's profits are distributed to all employees. When a company makes money, everyone gets a share of the profits. One of the most successful types of profit sharing was established by Joseph N. Scanlon in 1958. Scanlon believed in a group reward for suggestions, joint labor-management committees for discussing and proposing labor-saving techniques, and employees sharing in reduced costs rather than net profits. Although Scanlon's plan is more than simple profit sharing, it has proven, in medium-size organizations, to be a powerful method of involving employees.[4]

ESOP plans use stock ownership by employees as an incentive to increase productivity and quality.

Employee stock option plans (ESOPs) allow employees to purchase company stock at reduced prices and usually without the usual brokerage fees. In some instances all stock is sold to employees and ultimately the organization is owned solely by employees. Stock ownership, like Scanlon plans, have proven to be effective incentives.

In ways similar to the Scanlon plan, **gainsharing** offers rewards for suggestions, improvements in quality or quantity methods, process improvement, schedule maintenance, or any other activity that may either improve methods, attract customers, ensure quality, enhance productivity, or reduce waste. Any action that reduces costs or otherwise improves profits results in rewards for everyone. People are rewarded for their efforts as well as the end results.

■ IT'S NOT ALL MONEY

Although money is an important consideration, other factors are important in motivational studies. During the early 1980s the United States Department of Human Services began a continuing series of studies entitled *Work in America.*[5] Managers who have looked at the publications have found the results disturbing.

What supervisors thought was important in the work environment was far different from ratings by employees. Other researchers have learned virtually the same thing. Employee's views are often different from those of the first-line managers who supervise their on-the-job activities. Kenneth A. Kovach verified these findings and reported them in *Business Horizons* magazine.[6]

In order to understand his research, it is important to remember that all employees who participated were fully employed and reasonably secure in their jobs. Table 5.1 summarizes the results of Kovach's studies. They are very similar to those found by the Department of Human Services.

TABLE 5.1 ■ What Employees Want, What Supervisors Think They Want

Employee Ranking	What People Want from Their Jobs and Their Organizations	Supervisor Ranking
1	Interesting work	5
2	Appreciation for work accomplished	8
3	Feelings of being in on things	10
4	Job security	2
5	Good wages	1
6	Opportunity for advancement and development	3
7	Good working conditions	4
8	Personal loyalty to employees	6
9	Tactful discipline	9
10	Sympathetic help with personal problems	7

DEMOTIVATION

Demotivation is any action or set of actions that negatively impacts employee performance.

It is evident from studies that what supervisors think employees want and what workers feel is most important are, in most instances, different. Most managers think they understand what motivates their employees. All too frequently their perceptions are incorrect. Rather than motivate employees, managerial actions often demotivate them. A **demotivator** is any set of conditions or actions that negatively impacts employee performance. Since individuals perceive their jobs and the actions of their managers differently, it is impossible to list all of the potential demotivators, but some are easily understood. Some common demotivators that can be controlled by management are shown in figure 5.3.

Equitable pay means being paid essentially the same rates as those with similar training, experience, and job classification.

While important, money, most managers' first choice as a motivator, is not as significant as interesting work, provided employees view their pay as equitable. **Equitable pay** means that employees believe they are being paid what other people in similar jobs with similar levels of skill and training are being paid. Money becomes a demotivator when employees, because of low pay, feel their personal worth to the organization is very little. An often heard expression, "They only pay me to do this job, and that's all I'm going to do," indicates that pay can be a demotivator if it is perceived as inequitable. Inadequate pay is, in many instances, less of a demotivator than other job factors.

FIGURE 5.3 ■ Typical Management Demotivators

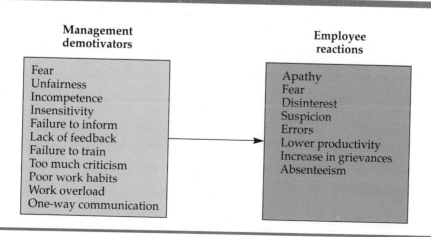

Management demotivators

Fear
Unfairness
Incompetence
Insensitivity
Failure to inform
Lack of feedback
Failure to train
Too much criticism
Poor work habits
Work overload
One-way communication

Employee reactions

Apathy
Fear
Disinterest
Suspicion
Errors
Lower productivity
Increase in grievances
Absenteeism

On-the-Job Demotivators

Management incompetence is a primary demotivator.

Although many factors can contribute to lower productivity, increased errors, excessive absenteeism, poor quality, carelessness, and wasted time, management incompetence and insensitivity are primary contributors. Poor decisions and indecisiveness, failure to thoroughly explain and discuss job requirements and objectives, failure to provide help and information when needed, underutilization of employee capabilities, lack of empathy with employee difficulties in performing new tasks, unreasonable performance expectations, preferential treatment for some employees and exclusion of others, and unfair criticism rather than analysis and provision of assistance are just a few of the more common demotivators.

Managers at all levels, including supervisors who use fear, threats, and manipulation as attempts to increase productivity or quality, are certain to be frustrated by lowered rather than improved performance. They assume employees are incapable and treat them as incapable. Employees respond by fulfilling the managers' assumptions. When employees feel they are treated as hired hands who park their brains at the door when they report for work, contribute only their labor, and have little involvement in the organization other than being a payroll number, they become apathetic, resentful, resigned, and sometimes destructive. Achievement of minimum standards or less becomes the norm.

Poor physical working conditions, lack of materials and supplies, inadequate facilities, and the perception that the organization does not care about its employees can also be strong demotivators. Frederick Herzberg, whose work is discussed later in this chapter, found that employees become dissatisfied with money, policies, facilities, benefits, relations with supervision and other employees, and their work assignments if any of these seem either inadequate or threatened. To better understand employee demotivation, it is necessary to have a good grasp of some of the factors that act as motivators. Maslow recognized that people have needs of different strengths. While other explanations of motivational factors have become popular, Maslow's point of view remains a useful starting point in understanding human needs.

■ MASLOW'S HIERARCHY OF NEEDS

Few theories of human behavior have been quoted more than those of Abraham H. Maslow.[7] Maslow believed that people had

Lower-level needs are those required for physical survival and maintenance.

Higher-level needs are those needs for social contact, self-esteem, and self-fulfillment.

five major types of needs. Two of these he considered to be basic or lower level needs. **Lower level needs** are those associated with physical survival. Three other types of needs are viewed as higher level needs. **Higher level needs,** such as social needs, psychological needs, and self-actualization could not occur until lower-level physiological and safety needs were at least partially satisfied. Figure 5.4 depicts the relationship between needs identified by Maslow.

Maslow felt that only two needs could be satisfied by money: the need for physiological survival and the need for safety. **Physiological needs** are the most basic of all. Water, air, food, warmth, and sleep are typical of those needed for survival. No other needs are important unless these are at least partially satisfied. **Safety needs** are also survival oriented. These include personal security, such as a safe place to sleep, freedom from fear of physical attack, and knowledge that physiological needs will be met. Both physiological needs and safety needs can be satisfied to a large degree by money.

FIGURE 5.4 ■ Maslow's Hierarchy of Needs at Work

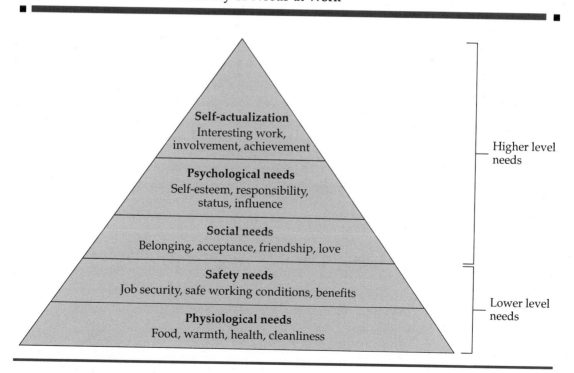

Higher-level needs cannot be entirely satisfied with money. They include social, psychological, and self-actualization needs. **Social needs** include belonging, being accepted by others, having friends, and loving and being loved by others. In work organizations supervisors can help employees feel accepted by letting them know they were hired because they were needed, introducing them to other employees, showing support, offering assistance, and being willing to listen. Social needs, Maslow pointed out, are extremely strong in our culture. We try to make ourselves more attractive and appealing to others in many ways. For proof we only need to look at advertisements on television, in newspapers, and especially in magazines.

Psychological needs are those that make us feel better about ourselves. They include self-esteem, status, both self-respect and respect of others, and influence. Like social needs, supervisors can, by simple approval of work well done, help satisfy psychological needs. Other techniques include willingness to solicit employee ideas, assigning meaningful jobs, and letting employees know the importance of their work.

Maslow identified **self-actualization** as the highest need. It is the knowledge that we are able to define and accomplish those things that are both personally important and satisfying. Self-actualized people are able to have a sense of fulfillment for their accomplishments. They are not as concerned with praise, recognition, and status as much as they are with doing what they feel is meaningful in their lives. In work situations employees who are doing what they like and can do well usually have a feeling of self-actualization. Their job is important to them as well as to others.

Several needs may operate at any given time. A person can have some concern for being accepted, feeling worthwhile, and doing interesting work at the same time. Although higher-level needs are rarely satisfied, they can be satisfied to a large extent by having the right type of assignment, management, and working environment. Maslow pointed out that a *satisfied need is not a motivator.* As our need for status and self-esteem becomes better satisfied, the need for self-actualization becomes more important. People who feel they are accepted by others often seek status. In general as lower-level needs in Maslow's five steps, often called a **hierarchy of needs,** become at least partially satisfied, then the next higher level of need becomes increasingly important.

Although Maslow's hierarchy-of-needs theory is useful, it is also somewhat limited. Human behavior is very complex and behavior doesn't always follow predicted patterns. It is helpful for managers to understand other types of motivational theory in developing on-the-job actions.

■ HERZBERG'S MOTIVATION-MAINTENANCE THEORY

Motivation-maintenance theory is based on the concept that some needs are necessary for personal maintenance and others for motivation to produce more and better.

Frederick Herzberg has received both wide approval and criticism for his work in motivational theory. There is little doubt that in many circumstances many of his concepts work very well. Herzberg recognized during some of his very early studies that some needs are not necessarily motivators.[8] Increases in job security, improved company policies, good relations with other employees as well as adequate pay are all liked and needed by employees. They do not, however, improve performance. Additional vacation time, as an example, will be something most employees see as valuable. But it is doubtful that performance will change if management institutes policies that provide additional vacation time. He also recognized that it is possible to be both efficient and human.[9] Herzberg's conclusions were that job environment factors such as responsibility, recognition, interesting work, opportunity for advancement, and recognition motivated employees.

Two types of needs were evident. **Motivational factors,** which were directly related to improved performance and job satisfaction, and **maintenance factors,** which employees saw as necessary for personal security and comfort. Herzberg found that absence of motivators, strangely, did not necessarily create discontent. Employees became excessively concerned with maintenance needs when motivational factors were absent. He also learned that maintenance factors could be dissatisfiers far more often that satisfiers. People who believed their pay was not equitable for the jobs they performed became very dissatisfied. When given a pay increase to align their wages with those of other in similar classifications, the satisfaction experienced was far less intense than the dissatisfaction they had known when their pay was too low. Dissatisfaction with inadequate maintenance factors such as benefits, company policies, and physical work environment is usually much more intense than satisfaction experienced when inadequacies are corrected. Table 5.2 summarizes some of Herzberg's primary maintenance and motivational factors.

As can be readily seen, Herzberg's maintenance factors are similar to what Maslow identified as lower-level needs, while motivational factors are those Maslow classified as higher-level needs.

TABLE 5.2 ■ Herzberg's Two-Factor Theory of Motivation

Motivational Factors	Maintenance Factors
Achievement	Job security
Recognition	Interpersonal relations with peers and management
Interesting work	Organizational policies and administration
Responsibility	Salary
Opportunity for advancement	Working conditions
Self-esteem	Supervision, skills, and competence

Job Design

Herzberg's most lasting observation has been his belief that improvements in **job design** could build in both job depth and job scope. **Job depth** refers to the degree that employees are responsible for and control their own work. Clerks who produce reports or letters on a word processor or spreadsheet and then give them to their supervisor for review, editing, and signature have very little depth to their jobs. If, on the other hand, they schedule their own work, determine priorities, check their output, and sign their own documents, their job have considerable depth.

Job depth is measured by the amount of control and responsibility employees have for their own jobs.

Herzberg was convinced that one of the best ways to increase motivation was to design tasks in ways that gave greater control and responsibility to employees. Supervisors in organizations that give employees optimum depth of work find their roles change to advisors, developers of people, information providers, and evaluators. They are no longer "traffic cops" obsessed with rule enforcement.

Job scope refers to the number of different tasks in a job.

Job scope refers to the number of activities in a task. Some jobs are highly repetitive with little or no scope. Angela Ditmar checks employment notification cards for the Employment Development Department of her state. She reviews Social Security number placement, name sequence (last name first), address, and last job held. She can check approximately 4,000 cards per day with little overt effort. A good scanning machine could do the job even faster and perhaps better. There is very little depth or scope in her job. If she is promoted to management analyst, as she hopes, she will have a wide variety of tasks ranging from policy review, to auditing, interviewing, providing information, and acting virtually as her own supervisor. Her new assignment will have both *depth* and *scope*. Of the two concepts, job depth is far more important. A. H. Maslow is credited with stating that "a nothing job plus a nothing job is still a nothing job." Job scope, unless coupled with job depth, can be virtually meaningless.

It is unfortunate that not all tasks can be easily redesigned to meet Herzberg's criteria for effective job redesign. When possible, it can be an effective technique for adding motivators to otherwise mundane, boring, and repetitive tasks.

■ EXPECTANCY THEORY

Expectancy theory states that behavior is a function of the value of a reward and the expectancy of achieving the reward.

Approximately 30 years ago a series of studies by an outstanding staff of psychologists at Ohio State University provided a different type of insight into certain types of motivation. First postulated by Julian Rotter and then amplified by a number of others, **expectancy theory** was seen as having particular value to managers. Many writers today feel that it is a plausible and useful approach to building motivational programs in the workplace. In simple terms expectancy theory states that *behavior is a function of the value of a reward and the expectancy of achieving the reward*.

If, as an example, people feel a promotion is something that they would like and that increased effort will help them achieve it, they will work harder to achieve their goal. In this case the promotion represents the reward, their belief in achieving it is their expectancy, and their behavior is represented by increased effort. According to expectancy theory two conditions must be present for any increase in effort. How much effort will be expended depends on both of these factors.

1. A goal or potential reward, which is anything that is perceived as being desirable or needed. Goal attractiveness is often referred to as **valence.**

Valence refers to the value or attractiveness of a reward.

2. An expectancy of achieving the goal or reward.

Managers who help employees define goals or who provide rewards, some as simple as showing approval for good work, and demonstrate that their efforts will achieve those rewards are demonstrating the basic expectancy theory concepts. Increasing reward value and providing expectancy of achievement can be powerful motivational tools.

Expectancy alone can have some motivational value. Managers who expect their work teams to be successful often achieve their goals. When employees know they are expected to perform

Self-fulfilling prophesies and the Pygmalion effect are both forms of expectancy. In each case the individuals involved attempt to make their expectations or wishes come true.

well, they tend to achieve more. One of the real compliments that managers can pay to employees is to have high expectations of both individuals and work groups. It conveys belief in the employees' ability to achieve and perform well. This type of motivation is sometimes called the **Pygmalion effect** or the *self-fulfilling prophesy*. It is based on the observable fact that most people try to perform as expected. Managers who have low expectations will get poor results. Those with high expectations are far more likely to achieve good results. In George Bernard Shaw's famous play, *Pygmalion,* later to become the movie "My Fair Lady," Eliza Doolittle, a flower girl who meets Professor Higgins's expectations of learning to act like a lady, states, "You see, really and truly, apart from the things anyone can pick up, the difference between a flower girl and a lady is not how she behaves but how she is treated. I shall always be a flower girl to Professor Higgins because he treats me as a flower girl, but I know I can be a lady to you because you treat me as a lady and always will."

Some time ago Jay Sterling Livingston wrote this paragraph that still applies to today's managers:

> Some managers always treat their employees in a way that leads to superior performance. But most managers, like Professor Higgins, may intentionally treat their subordinates in a way that leads to lower performance than they are capable of achieving. The way managers treat their subordinates is subtly influenced by what they expect of them. If a manager's expectations are high, productivity is likely to be excellent. If expectations are low, productivity is likely to be poor. It is as though there were a law that caused a subordinate's performance to rise or fall to meet the manager's expectations.[10]

Coaches who expect their teams to win are more likely to have winning teams. Managers who expect their employees to be the best are likely to have the best employees.

■ A PRACTICAL POINT OF VIEW

While theory is an attempt to explain why things occur, most managers are interested in practical actions they can take to develop effective work forces. Robert Presthus has found basically three types of people in most places of work:[11]

1. Ascendants. Ascendants are sometimes confused with workaholics. They are typified by high achievement drives, desire to please higher levels of management, high energy levels, and consistently high performance. Ascendants are typically strong

Ascendants are people driven to do their best at all times. They work hard and usually achieve their goals.

supporters of their organizations and higher levels of management. Because they place personal success above relationships with fellow employees, they are often impatient with those who lack their intensity and willingness to work. Once ascendants have been given assignments, they are very reluctant to share them with others, even when they are clearly overloaded with work.

Managers tend to develop a dependency on ascendants to handle assignments that need to be completed well without delay. Approval of higher levels of management, recognition for their work, and increased influence are their primary goals and rewards. Typically ascendants rarely question organizational policy or decisions of their immediate supervisors. They require almost no supervision other than knowledge of what is needed. Supervisors recognize that ascendants are self-motivated and that they are always attempting to improve their own performance.

Indifferents work for money and little else. They perform to minimum standards to keep from being fired.

2. Indifferents. Unlike ascendants, indifferents work to minimums. Their jobs are not the primary motivators of their lives. While supervisory praise may be liked, it is neither sought nor expected. Indifferents know just how much work is required to keep from getting reprimanded or terminated. They will do their assignment and then wait for further instruction before starting anything else. Motivational efforts have little long-range effect. Work is merely a means for earning money to satisfy basic needs and to be able to associate with friends away from the workplace. Typically indifferents do not seek promotion or added responsibility. They have little or no desire to know more about the organization other than their own immediate assignment.

If an ascendant is asked about their job, they will answer in great detail with descriptions of the organization, their assignments, and their position. If asked, "Where do you work?", the indifferent will reply, "Downtown." "Where downtown?" "In one of those big buildings." "What do you do?" "Whatever they tell me."

Interestingly, indifferents, like ascendants, pose no real motivational problems. They have a pace at which they will work, and managers soon recognize that indifferent employees will always do the "grunt" work of an organization and little more.

3. Ambivalents. Organizational work units, such as departments and sections, usually have very few ascendants and, fortunately, few true indifferents. Ambivalents form the bulk of most work forces. If challenged by interesting work, ambivalents will act very much the same as ascendants. When work is seen as dull or

Ambivalents are people who act like ascendants if they are doing work they enjoy but take on indifferent characteristics if they are bored or faced with work they do not like.

repetitive, they will seem to be indifferent. Ambivalents are often creative and intelligent. They enjoy displaying their knowledge and analytical skills. Of all employees ambivalents are most likely to challenge management policies and directions from their supervisor. They will procrastinate in completing work that they see as routine or in which they have little interest.

Ambivalents pose a constant motivational problem for first-line managers. Their performance can be superior if their assignments are interesting, challenging, and have a degree of depth. Often, in nearly all organizations, many assignments are relatively routine and once mastered become uninteresting to ambivalents. Experienced supervisors attempt to challenge ambivalents with responsibility, new types of assignments, and recognition for good work. Like ascendants, ambivalents respond to approval, recognition, and opportunity for personal development or promotion. They often distrust management and can be a source of problems.

Although Presthus's model is somewhat simplistic in that it categorizes employees into three rather stereotyped groups, it seems to fit what managers frequently find in their own work units. In the early part of this century Frederick W. Taylor testified at a congressional hearing that there were first-class workers, second-class workers, and third-class workers. First-class workers were those who know how to work and do work. Second-class workers were those who know how to work but don't, and third-class workers were those who don't know how to work and don't. Taylor's observations were quite similar to those of Presthus.

A weakness in Presthus's model is that people are very complex and do not always fit into classifications. Some employees who seem to be indifferent may, under the right conditions, change and become better performers. Both ascendants and ambivalents can burn out if they are overworked and under constant stress. Regardless of its appeal, effective managers should recognize the limitations of the Presthus model. It must be tempered with the realization that as conditions change, so do the needs, aspirations, and dedication of employees. Experienced managers try to understand people as individuals rather than as members of a predetermined category.

■ INTERNAL AND EXTERNAL ORIENTATION

Numerous studies have been made at universities as well as places of work to determine if people respond more to external circumstances or to their own sense of responsibility. Their findings

External orientation is defined by dependency on luck, coincidence, being liked, and higher authority for quality of life.

indicate that some people feel their lives are controlled by luck, coincidence, higher authority, people with power, social tradition, and forces over which they have little or no influence. These people are considered to be **externally oriented.** If they are successful in some endeavor, they feel it was because of luck or that someone in power likes them. Failures or unfortunate events in their lives are always blamed on others, including parents, supervisors, the society in which they live or have lived, or bad luck. Their **locus of control** (i.e., what controls their lives) is outside of themselves. They tend to be dependent on others and often see life as a gamble. Externally oriented workers are most strongly motivated by praise, approval of those in power, and the values of those that they see as higher authorities.

Internally oriented people depend on their own resources, are motivated most by personal achievements, and tend to be existential in their approach to life.

Internally oriented people tend to believe that their success or failures are due to their own choices and actions. They tend to be existential. All of their activities, especially their work, are seen as enriching experiences. Internally oriented people derive pleasure from their own accomplishments and do not rely on the approval of others. Their sense of personal responsibility often gives them an objectivity lacking in others. Internally oriented employees are often difficult for supervisors to understand. In work activities internally oriented people are often seen as effective but independent. Most set high standards of performance for themselves and tend to achieve most of their goals. Work is usually a self-actualizing experience.

Studies by Robert B. Morton, president of The Organizational Laboratory, an organizational development group, indicate that many higher-level and top managers are internally oriented.[12] They are self-reliant, unafraid to make difficult decisions, and tend to be analytical rather than critical. While they may seem ideal employees, they are often more loyal and dedicated to their profession than to their organization. Although they will work diligently to succeed, they will not hesitate to change jobs if opportunities for challenge and personal development seem greater.

No person is entirely internally or externally oriented. Those who gain in competence and belief in their own ability tend to move toward greater degrees of internal orientation. Morton and others have found that conditions may affect an individual's locus of control or orientation and, in some situations, move them toward greater dependency and less internal orientation. Managers who see themselves as developers of people—by providing constant training and challenging but attainable goals for continuous improvement—tend to move their employees toward less dependency on external factors and toward greater internal orientation. As knowledge, skill, and total competency increases, so do self-confidence and the realization that work itself can be a rewarding experience.

■ SOME ON-THE-JOB REMINDERS

Motivational programs work best when the entire organization is involved. Although first-line managers can do a great deal to increase performance levels in their work teams, top management commitment to creating conditions that make work interesting and worthwhile in addition to economically rewarding is necessary. Supervisors, as management's first line, can take a number of actions that will help their own as well as their work unit's level of interest and achievement.

1. **Learn to listen.** Employees respect managers who are willing to actively listen to their ideas, concerns, and suggestions. Good managers do not stop at listening. They act on employees' suggestions and give credit to those who originated the idea.

2. **See yourself as a developer of people.** Managers are judged by the competency of their employees. Good managers encourage employees to take additional responsibility, attempt challenging assignments, and continuously learn to build competency and confidence. They also gain the respect of employees who recognize management's interest in building employee competence.

3. **Avoid being a manipulator.** One of the worst slogans that has persisted over the years is "let them think it was their idea." People recognize insincerity and attempts to manipulate. "Let them know it was their idea" may be a far better approach.

4. **Recognize effort as well as results.** Don't wait until a job is completed to tell people that it is being done correctly. Equally important is to correct mistakes as soon as they occur. Be analytical rather than critical. Correct causes rather than symptoms. This requires gathering data, listening, and constant learning.

5. **Have high expectations of the performance of your team.** Let them know you think they are capable of developing methods for doing jobs smarter and better. Often hard work alone is not enough. There is a great deal of truth in the old adage that "it's

better to work smarter, not harder." Motivation to be innovative and creative can be great performance improvers.

6. **Don't be afraid of your own employees.** Some managers fear that they will be displaced by more competent, better-trained and educated employees. They fail to realize that competent, effective employees are far more likely to push them up rather than out.

7. **Never forget that all of your actions send messages to your employees.** Enthusiasm is catching. Managers who show a sense of excitement about new ideas, ways of continuously improving, and belief in the competence of their employees have high-achievement work teams. Learn to keep your cool even in the tensest situations. Always show up, show up on time, and show up prepared to do your best. Like it or not, supervisors are models for their employees. Those who have poor work habits will have employees with the same habits. Be the type of manager you admire most.

Good managers are also good leaders. Their enthusiasm, fairness, and concern for excellence in both work and individuals is always apparent. Others recognize they want their employees as well as themselves to succeed.

■ THINGS TO REMEMBER

I. Motivation.

   A. There is no single definition of motivation.

   B. Motivation is concerned with the forces within individuals that cause them to act.

   C. Motivation results in some type of activity.

II. On-the-job motivation.

   A. Fear teaches employees to avoid specific behavior rather than to do things correctly.

   B. Carrot-and-stick approaches to motivation use both punishment and rewards.

III. Money problems and promises.

   A. Ford and Taylor failed to realize there are many motives which influence choice of jobs.

   B. Money will trigger increased effort only if it is directly related to other rewards.

IV. Money as an incentive.

    A. Herzberg recognized that people are more dissatisfied with low pay than they are satisfied with high pay.

    B. Studies of piece-rate systems indicate that people tend to work at a given pace regardless of rewards for extract effort.

V. Group incentives.

    A. Profit sharing, ESOP programs, and gainsharing are all excellent group incentives.

    B. A work force reacts more favorably to group incentives than to individual incentives.

VI. It's not all money.

    A. Supervisors' perceptions of employee needs are often different from those of employees.

    B. Most employees rank interesting work as the most important job consideration.

VII. Maslow's hierarchy of needs.

    A. Maslow's basic categories of needs are: physical, safety, social, psychological, and self-actualization.

    B. Lower-level needs (i.e., physical and safety) are most directly related to money.

VIII. Herzberg's motivation-maintenance theory.

    A. Herzberg identified two classes of needs: motivational and maintenance factors.

    B. Herzberg believed that job design could build in motivational factors.

IX. Expectancy theory.

    A. Unless there is an expectancy of achievement, there will be little increased effort.

    B. Managerial expectations directly impact employee performance.

X. A practical point-of-view.

    A. Robert Presthus proposed that employees fall into three categories: ascendants, indifferents, and ambivalents.

    B. Ambivalents are the most difficult to supervise. Ascendants are the easiest, and indifferents expend minimum effort to avoid getting fired.

IX. Internal and external orientation.

A. Internally oriented people rely on luck, coincidence, and higher authority.

B. Externally oriented people rely on their own resources.

XII. On-the-job reminders.

A. Motivational programs work best when the entire organization is involved.

B. Good managers are also good leaders.

■ KEY TERMS

motivation

carrot-and-stick approach

incentives

piece-rate work

profit sharing

Employee Stock Option Plan (ESOP)

gainsharing

demotivator

equitable pay

hierarchy of needs

lower-level needs

higher-level needs

physiological needs

safety needs

social needs

psychological needs

self-actualization

motivational factors

maintenance factors

job design

job depth

job scope

expectancy theory

valence

Pygmalion effect

ascendants

indifferents

ambivalents

externally oriented

locus of control

internally oriented

■ DISCUSSION QUESTIONS

1. Describe the level of motivation where you work or have worked. What are some motivators and demotivators that you have observed?

2. If you are or had the opportunity to be a manager at your place of work, what would you change to improve motivational practices? Explain your actions.

3. What types of actions or treatment do you find particularly demotivating? How have these affected you personally?

4. In what ways can managers make work more exciting and interesting?

5. List and explain some of the most important characteristics of managers for whom you like or would like to work.

■ SELF-ASSESSMENT

As in other self-assessment exercises, respond to the questions or statements below with the number that indicates your degree of agreement or disagreement. Remember that a 1, 2, or 3 indicates disagreement while 4, 5, and 6 show agreement.

1. In dealing with new employees, it is a good practice to emphasize penalties that will result from rule violation or poor performance.

   1   2   3   4   5   6

2. Money and security are more important as motivators for most people than interesting and challenging work assignments.

   1   2   3   4   5   6

3. Managers can do very little to help people satisfy their needs for belonging and self-esteem in a work organization.

   1   2   3   4   5   6

4. Do you believe that you can only get promoted if you are in the right place at the right time?

   1   2   3   4   5   6

5. To what extent do you agree with the statement, "In the final analysis, all management involves manipulation of people"?

   1   2   3   4   5   6

6. It is easy to classify people into those who will be good employees, those who may or may not be satisfactory, and those who will not be satisfactory.

   1   2   3   4   5   6

7. Managers who have high expectations of their employees are likely to create dissatisfaction and disrespect for their leadership.

   1   2   3   4   5   6

8. Good managers reward good performance and punish poor performance.

   1   2   3   4   5   6

9. Managers should treat all employees exactly alike in order to be fair.

1   2   3   4   5   6

10. One way to build motivation is to make decisions and then make employees think it is their idea.

1   2   3   4   5   6

■ SHORT CASES

Sony in San Diego

Many if not most Sony television sets sold in the United States are not made in Japan but in San Diego, California. "Mike" Morimoto, general manager of Sony—San Diego, has achieved what seems to be an American worker revolution. There is no union, quality and productivity matches or exceeds Sony plants in Japan, and absenteeism is almost nonexistent. Employees are intensely loyal, and almost none leave for other employment.

Before major decisions are made at the plant, Mike meets with all employees in groups of 100 each. It requires 18 meetings to talk with everyone. He listens carefully to objections to proposed changes and often changes plans in ways employees have suggested.

An excellent company-subsidized cafeteria exists at the plant, and there is no executive dining room. Managers are told to eat at a different table each day with employees, not managers. Nearly all 1,800 employees are personally acquainted with Mike and each of the other managers in the plant. The only reserved parking place is for the company nurse to ensure care in case of an emergency. There have been no layoffs at the plant, even when sales of television sets have slumped.

Employees receive pay comparable to other industrial workers in the area but consistently report that money is not as important as the "great work attitude" at Sony.

1. What makes Sony management's approach different from a typical U.S. organization?

2. Why do Sony employees in San Diego outperform workers in similar facilities in the United States?

3. Will Mike Morimoto's methods work for managers who have not had his type of Japanese training? Explain your response.

Power Down at Pacific

Customer service representatives at Pacific Area Telephone (PAT) sit at computer terminals and provide both information and complaint correction services for customers. A part of their job assignment is to suggest different types of equipment or services that will improve their business customers' communication capabilities. In some cases they also suggest similar types of services for individuals who have large numbers of telephone calls.

In an effort to improve productivity, PAT instituted an electronic monitoring system that automatically checks on the length of time employees spend on a single call, the number of calls returned to customers, sales of new services or equipment, and the length of time the employee actually spends in customer contacts. If an employee goes to the restroom, the monitoring system measures exactly how long the employee was away from the workstation. Employees have frequent reviews of their productivity with their supervisors.

Although the new system has been strongly endorsed by management, including supervisors, it has not had the desired effect. Sales of new services and equipment have actually declined and numbers of calls to customers has either dropped or remained the same. In an effort to put pressure on employees to produce more, daily reports are now generated and distributed to employees showing their productivity compared to company goals.

1. Why haven't the new practices had the desired effect?

2. How will employees react to the new daily report?

3. What measures can be taken to improve both morale and productivity?

■ ENDNOTES

1. William James, *Psychology,* vol. 2 (New York: Henry Holt & Co., 1902).

2. Frederick Taylor, *Principles of Scientific Management* (New York: Harper & Row, 1911).

3. Frederick Herzberg has written many texts and articles dealing with work improvement. His most famous article is probably "KITA, One More Time How Do You Motivate Employees," *Harvard Business Review,* January–February 1968. In 1987 the *Harvard Business Review* republished the article with commentary from Herzberg. He reaffirmed that money tends to dissatisfy more than satisfy.

4. Dale Wren, *The Evolution of Management Thought,* 3rd edition (New York: John Wiley & Sons, 1987), pp. 282–83.

5. Work in America studies have been in progress for several years. Many have been conducted by the Survey Research Institute at the University of Michigan.

6. Kenneth A. Kovach, "What Motivates Managers? Workers and Supervisors Give Different Answers," *Business Horizons,* October–November 1987, pp. 58–65.

7. A. H. Maslow first came to the attention of management with the 1943 publication of *Theory of Human Motivation.* Maslow died an untimely death in 1970.

8. Frederick Herzberg, Bernard Mauser, and Barbara Snyderman, The Motivation to Work (New York: John Wiley & Sons, 1959).

9. Frederick Herzberg, The Managerial Choice: To Be Efficient and to Be Human (Dow Jones-Irwin, 1976).

10. Jay Sterling Livingston, "Pygmalion in Management," *Harvard Business Review,* July–August 1969, pp. 81–82.

11. Robert Presthus, *The Organizational Society* (New York: Alfred A. Knopf, 1962).

12. Based on "The Grass Valley Studies," currently being prepared for publication by Robert B. Morton, Ph.D., Fellow in the American Psychological Association.

Part III

Tools of Influence — Communication, Leadership, and Politics

■ Peter Drucker is fond of saying that employees in the United States are overmanaged and underled.[1] Managers learn to plan, organize, analyze, and prioritize much of their work. Many fail, however, in building positive work climates with employee teams that are achievement oriented and strongly supportive of their organizations's goals, Other management analysts have noted that a primary problem is not only lack of inspirational leadership but communication of goals. People often do not understand what is expected.

In Chapters 6, 7, and 8, major sources of influence that have the potential for improving understanding and developing effective individual and team effort are examined. Communication skills and willingness to communicate are essential. Supervisors must also build their own leadership skills and learn to use power to build and achieve rather than solely correct and control.

Our concern is with practical methods that first-line managers can use to build credibility and influence in their organizations. Effective supervisors exert influence not only on their employees but on higher-level managers as well. To do so they must be skilled communicators, effective leaders, and know how to use and acquire power.

Communication and Supervisory Influence

Objectives

Communication in organizations is a relatively new field of study. During the eras of scientific management and the human relations movement the value of good communication was recognized but not given the attention it receives today. During the past 20 years it has evolved into a major area of organizational study. Readers of Chapter 6 will be able to

- Identify basic communication processes.
- Define the differences between messages and meanings.
- Recognize common communication barriers.
- Analyze four basic communication patterns.
- Delineate types of communication codes.
- Identify common organizational communication difficulties.

Thought Starter

John Wilson is a management consultant and analyst who has spent many years identifying the characteristics of people who get promoted in organizations and of those who do not. "One of the most significant skills that help people move upward in organizations," Wilson states, "is the ability to communicate effectively. Those who are able to express their thoughts and feelings in ways that are interesting and easily understood by others have a definite advantage. They are often promoted over equally knowledgeable people who lack oral and written communication skills."[2]

Managers frequently complain that people they recruit from college campuses usually have adequate knowledge of technology but are often poor communicators. In the world of change that organizations exist in today, effective communication is more essential than ever. It is ironic that while advances in electronic technology allow instantaneous worldwide communication with automatic language translation, communication is still a major problem both on and off the job.

Chapter 6 examines factors that affect communication. Both barriers and methods of overcoming them are identified.

■ *Ace Plumbing and Pipefitting is a large contractor specializing in installing plumbing in large commercial buildings. Their expertise has been recognized in major projects in many countries. During the late 1980s and early 1990s their profits began to fall. "Our major problem," reported Marilyn Morales, Ace's manager of accounting, "was cost overruns for almost everything. Our overtime budgets, materials costs, and special tooling were major problems. Employees seem to like the company and we did not feel they were the major problem. When our supervisors told everyone to do their best because of our cost problems, they tried but without results."*

"Susan then had an idea that really made a difference," added Ken Miller, general superintendent. "She suggested we show our actual cost figures to our employees and ask for their ideas. We made copies of reports that highlighted major problems to everyone in a general meeting. Individual crews then met and, after going over problems, submitted many workable suggestions for shortening processes, making our special tooling less costly, and improving efficiency. Six months later we were not only out of trouble but able to give everyone a bonus for their efforts. We communicated with our employees in a different way. There were no secrets." Open communication pays off for everyone, often in unexpected ways.

■ COMMUNICATION—UNDERSTANDING AND BEING UNDERSTOOD

A working definition of **communication** *is understanding and being understood. It involves sharing thoughts, information, and feelings.*

There are many definitions of **communication.** It is, according to some experts, the process of sharing ideas, information, and feelings. Others define it as an exchange of messages to which meanings are added. While both statements are correct, a definition easier to remember for practical application is *understanding and being understood.* There is no communication unless both conditions are met. People must not only understand messages sent by others but be able to make themselves understood.

Most people rarely stop to evaluate their success or failures at understanding and being understood. Table 6.1 is a simple test that helps define this concept. In the left-hand column of the table, names of people that most of us work with are listed. On the top line are the numbers 1 through 6. If you feel you are better at understanding and being understood by the person or people listed in the first row, check 4 (slightly better), 5 (somewhat better), or 6 (much better), depending on how much better you are than the person or people with whom you compare yourself.

TABLE 6.1 ■ Understanding and Being Understood

Compare yourself to:	1	2	3	4	5	6
Your immediate supervisor						
People at your level						
People at lower levels						
All people in the organization						

Should you feel your ability to understand and be understood is less than the person or people listed, check 1 (much less), 2 (somewhat less), or 3 (slightly less). Remember, you are comparing yourself to people with whom you currently work or have worked in the past. To fully understand the purpose of the comparisons, *do not read further until all items have been completed.*

How well do you understand and are you understood compared to others? We have given this simple rating test to hundreds of people in all types of organizations and occupations. Most rate themselves in the 4, 5, or 6 categories for all of the comparisons. Only a few rate themselves in the 1, 2, or 3 blocks. Our evidence indicates that people tend to think they are usually better than others in understanding and being understood. A major communication difficulty is that many people think not understanding and not being understood is the other person's problem. They fail to acknowledge their own communication errors and omissions. Most assume that, "If it's perfectly clear to me, it should also be perfectly clear to you."

In addition to the complacency of feeling that communication problems are caused by others, people generally fail to recognize the difference between messages and meanings. When a person converts an idea, feeling, or information into some form of communication, he sends a **message** to others. Those who receive the message interpret the message and give it **meaning.** Senders often make the mistake of thinking that receivers interpret their messages as intended. Many factors other than the sender's intent, however, act as *filters.* A **filter** is any set of conditions, either within the person or the situation, that influences the way a message is interpreted. One of the most important is an individual's frame of reference.

*People send **messages** to which **meanings** are added by receivers of the messages.*

*A communication **filter** is any set of conditions, either within a person or the situation, that influences the way a message is interpreted.*

Frames of Reference

Frames of reference are all of the internal and external factors that affect interpretation of events, situations, and messages.

When a person receives a message, it is interpreted in terms of their personal frame of reference. A **frame of reference** consists of all of the internal and external factors that may affect interpretation of events, situations, and messages. If, as an example, Robyn tells Dick, "I'm sorry, I can't go out tonight. There's just too much work to finish," he may interpret it as meaning, "Robyn is overworked, I'll try again tomorrow," or, "I guess it's all over between us. She doesn't want to go out with me," or, "Robyn probably has something else planned. I'll call someone else." Dick can interpret Robyn's message in many ways, depending on his own knowledge, feelings, and past experiences. He receives the message and gives it the meaning that fits his frame of reference.

Effective supervisors recognize that employees frequently have a different perspective or frame of reference from theirs. Employee frames of reference depend on their relationship with the supervisor, their interpretation of job requirements, their feelings toward the organization, and countless other factors. As a manager, the supervisor's frame of reference when dealing with employees is often work centered. What is very personal to an employee may be only one part of many concerns the supervisor has with the overall functioning of the work unit. Effective communicators recognize that each individual has a unique way of interpreting the content and intent of messages. They attempt to communicate as much as possible from the other person's frame of reference. Frames of reference are, as shown in Figure 6.1, similar to looking through a window with many panes that represent different aspects of our lives and experiences.

Feedback

Feedback is information gathered in response to a communication.

In a work environment supervisors often fail to realize that each individual in their organizational unit has a unique frame of reference. As a consequence, message interpretation is often different from the supervisor's intention. To minimize misinterpretation, first-line managers must learn the effective use of feedback.

Feedback is information gathered in response to a communication. It can be based on observation or statements from people receiving the original message. Competent supervisors encourage employees to ask questions, restate their understanding of an assignment, or to demonstrate what they are going to do. It is far

FIGURE 6.1 ■ Factors Influencing Frame of Reference

Personal needs	Psychological maturity	Knowledge
Physical well-being	Life experiences	Job conditions
Self-esteem	Perception of situation	Relations with others

better to grasp the meaning attached to a message and clarify understanding before errors are made. Learning to obtain accurate feedback is a necessary but often neglected skill. Busy supervisors often do not take the time required to obtain feedback. They assume employees fully understand everything that they have been told. Some may ask an employee, "Do you understand?", and receive a nod of agreement, only to find later that what the employee *thought* and what was *needed* were not the same. Communication skills involve far more than words. Everything a person does communicates something to others. It is helpful to recognize some of the variety of ways we transmit information to others.

Communication Skills and Channels

Top managers often complain that many employees may have good technical knowledge but lack effective communication skills. Those who rise in management ranks must be able to speak, write, make presentations, or express concepts in other ways, such as graphs, tables, lists, and pictures. Each of these types of communication is called a **channel**. Information is transmitted. It can be spoken, sent by voice, body language, telephone, television,

Channels *are the ways*
information is
transmitted. It may be
by language, pictures,
nonverbal symbols,
electronic, or any other
means that senses can
detect.

computer, in writing, by pictures, gestures, or face-to-face communication. Channels are the ways information is conveyed from one person or group to others.

A major advantage of face-to-face communication is its simultaneous use of multiple channels. Nonverbal as well as verbal channels are used. A person's expressions, voice characteristics, movements, distance maintained from others, posture, and all other observable characteristics convey messages, often more significant than the words being used. In this context *verbal* means the use of spoken or written words to send messages. *Nonverbal* refers to all of the other factors heard and observed that influence the way messages are interpreted. It is estimated that approximately 35 percent of meanings given to messages are verbal and the remaining 65 percent are nonverbal.

■ COMMUNICATION CODES—VERBAL AND NONVERBAL

Communication codes
may use language or
some type of nonverbal
communication.

Communication professionals recognize that the use of words is only one of the many ways we communicate. Each method that is used is considered a **communication code.** Codes include a variety of communication methods. It is generally agreed that there are two major classifications of communication codes, each with many subparts. Figure 6.2 portrays the relationship between communication codes and the total process of communication. Some of the major types of communication that comprise total communication are summarized in Figure 6.3.

FIGURE 6.2 ■ Communication Codes

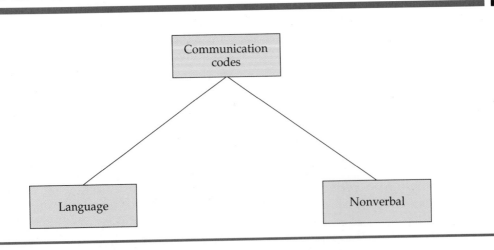

FIGURE 6.3 ■ Factors Influencing Face-to-Face Communication

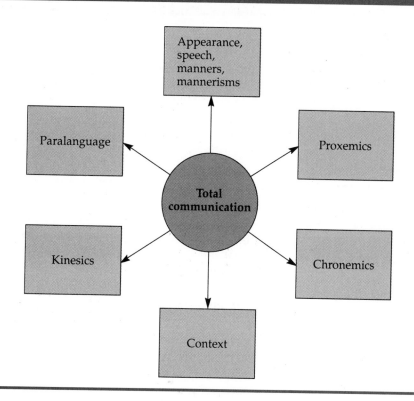

1. **Language.** We use words in combinations with each other, either orally or in writing, to express our ideas, feelings, information, and questions to others. Verbal expressions, both oral and written, are used by every society. Regardless of the wide diversity of sound patterns used by the earth's many national and cultural groups, all share information, concepts, questions, and feelings with others through the use of language. Language codes are very complex. In some societies the method of pronunciation determines the message as much as the actual word. In most languages individual words may have many meanings depending on pronunciation as well as when and how they are used.

2. **Nonverbal codes.** In addition to language a great deal—perhaps most—of our communication is nonverbal. Sounds that may not be words in themselves are one of the many types of nonverbal signals. Cries of pain, laughter, or disgust may be unspellable, but we recognize their intent. Facial expressions,

gestures, posture, speed of speech or movement, pictures, lights (such as those that tell us to stop or go, get our attention, or are used in searches), and display of shapes all communicate meaning. Music, sculpture, drawings, and paintings also send messages. An almost endless variety of symbols that communicate nonverbally are used all over the world. They range from those as simple as trail markers in the form of cuts on trees to show direction, to styles of architecture designed to communicate both beauty of form as well as function. We can usually recognize a house of worship, an office building, a bridge, or a dam by its shape, location, and apparent use.

In a work environment, nonverbal signals are very important. Managers are often unaware of the importance of the nonverbal messages that they send to their employees, clients, and other managers.

■ NONVERBAL COMMUNICATION

Although language is an important code, **nonverbal communication** is often more significant. An understanding of some of the more important nonverbal methods of communication in the workplace is essential. Nonverbal communication is considered to be "communication rich." It carries messages that language alone cannot express. Feelings, intensity, mood, urgency, and response clues are all transmitted primarily through nonverbal codes. Every move we make, or sometimes fail to make, communicates to others.

Appearance, Speech, Manners, and Mannerisms

Appearance, speech, manners, and mannerisms are the first nonverbal communication that is transmitted by people in face-to-face contact.

When people contact each other, even casually, inferences about the other person are made based on their appearance, speech characteristics, social skills, and special mannerisms as well as a variety of other factors. Judgments based on these characteristics strongly influence the way a person treats others and, in turn, is treated by others.

1. Appearance. Correctly or incorrectly, we interpret the appearance of others within the first few seconds of seeing them. Their dress, age, sex, height, weight, posture, grooming, and facial expression all carry messages. We make inferences about their type of work, health, socioeconomic status, mood, and life-style. Depending on our sensitivity to the way others appear and our preconceptions of how they compare to ourselves, we try to determine if they are our type of people.

Appearance is a powerful and persuasive communicator. Lawyers coach criminals to dress and act like model citizens at trials. People who are preparing for job interviews dress and groom themselves to make favorable impressions. We learn, from a very early age, that appearance often makes the difference between acceptance and rejection, especially by our peers.

Supervisors often neglect the importance of their appearance and its effects on both employees and higher levels of management. Good grooming conveys a sense of confidence, pride, and self-respect. Sloppy appearance often sends the message that the person probably thinks and behaves the way he or she looks.

Career advisors often tell those who are ambitious to dress one level above their current position if they want to rise in an organization. There is little doubt that appearance is a major communication factor.

2. Speech. After appearance, speech is usually the next type of communication on which judgments are made. Grammar, slang, jargon, tone of voice, voice quality—such as pitch, timbre, accents—pronunciation, and use of idioms communicate much more about a person than the words being used. Vocal characteristics, such as a high-pitched, squeaky voice, harsh or abrupt tones, mumbles, and nasal twangs may cause immediate unfavorable reactions. Some voices are almost musical in quality or acceptably cultured. These make more favorable impressions.

Studies have shown that both oral and written communication skills are very important when people are being considered for promotion. Personal credibility is often directly related to good communication skills, especially in face-to-face situations.[3]

3. Manners. People who treat others with respect, maintain an even temperament, and are generally friendly and pleasant make a much better impression than those who seem arrogant, rude, ill-at-ease, or aloof. Good manners, an important set of social skills, are a significant asset. They profoundly influence reactions of others, although they are only one part of the total communication mix. Supervisors who are well mannered are usually held in high esteem by employees, peers, and higher levels of management.

Social skills are best defined as the way we treat others. Those with poor social skills are often seen as people to avoid. A characteristic of top managers is referent power, the influence that a person gains from having a great deal of personal credibility and being respected by others. (This concept will be discussed in greater detail in later chapters.) An important part of gaining referent power involves social skills. Along with appearance and speech characteristics our manners help create those important first impressions as well as having longer-range effects on the way individuals are perceived by others.

4. Mannerisms. Many of us are unaware of the way some of our unconscious habits affect others. Some people will sit with their "motor running." One of their legs will be rapidly moving up and down, from ankle to knee. Such movements convey impatience, tenseness, and eagerness to leave. Others refuse to look at the person to whom they are talking. Some will bend a paperclip or roll a piece of paper when listening or talking with others. Excessive hand movements, common in many people, are often distracting and make conversation, at best, difficult. Habits like pulling on an ear, head scratching, finger popping, and other body movements are all too common.

Effective communicators know that distractions created by habitual mannerisms often communicate uncertainty, fear, impatience, and stress. Effective communicators train themselves to avoid mannerisms that may transmit unwanted messages about themselves.

Paralanguage

Paralanguage conveys meaning by the way things are spoken rather than by what is said.

Mirrors are often seen on the desks of people who answer telephones and take orders for classified advertising in large newspapers. These people want to be sure that they are smiling when they answer the phone. Our voices carry messages other than our words. **Paralanguage** refers to a *parallel language.* Our voice characteristics, such as emphasis on specific words, emotional state, sincerity, and degree of interest, are interpreted by others before our words are given meaning. Telephone salespeople who read scripts are heard by potential customers as readers rather than salespeople who believe in their products. Insincerity is often easily diagnosed. Paralanguage transmits many messages that are not in words.

Others can tell our probable mood, degree of interest, and our true meaning by the way we say things as well as what we say. If a supervisor tells an employee, "That was a good job," it may be interpreted several ways. In a sarcastic tone, "*That* was a good job?" usually indicates a poor job. A neutral tone may be interpreted as satisfactory but no better, while an enthusiastic "that was a *good job!*" indicates strong approval. Although the words are the same, the way they are presented determines their meaning.

Our paralanguage is very important. First-line managers who give directions or relate problems in a joking, nonserious manner, even though the problems are important, may be incorrectly interpreted by employees. Paralanguage often carries the real intent of a message more than words. It is important that supervisors recognize that the way things are said is often more important than what is said.

Touch and Response

Touch and response are powerful forms of communication that are, with the exception of the handshake, usually socially unacceptable in our society.

It is unfortunate that our society has become essentially nontouching. Due to highly publicized descriptions of sexual touching involving children, accusations of sexual harassment, and fear of identification of sexual preference, touching has been greatly limited in our society. A pat on the shoulder to show approval, a hug of affection or support, a warm squeeze on a hand, and a light touch to the face can often convey messages that words cannot. Touching has been proven to be essential to the normal development of infants. Some people, however, feel so uncomfortable with displays of nonsexual touching that communication by touch in a work environment has been reduced to the handshake.

Supervisors should not underestimate the importance of the socially acceptable handshake as an important form of communication. A warm, firm handshake transmits a message of friendliness, confidence, and acceptance. Limp, unresponsive handshakes convey disinterest, lack of self-direction, and a generally flat personality. Supervisors and employees interested in developing their social skills need to pay attention to accepted good manners and the importance of offering a hand. They should avoid bone-crushing contests to prove dominance and "wet-fish"— damp, cold, and lifeless—contact. Cultivating a confident, firm, warm greeting through a handshake often conveys more than words. One of the best ways of making a good impression on others is a handshake that conveys both warmth and interest. Some advisors to management suggest a mild antiperspirant if a tendency to perspire in the palms exists. A wet handshake often conveys stress, fear, and lack of confidence, regardless of other nonverbal clues.

Proxemics

Proxemics involves all of the forms of communication through the use of space. It ranges from personal and social space to seating arrangements, office layout and size, to office location.

Proxemics, or use of space, is also an important form of communication. If a large corporation is located in a tall building, its top management staff will usually be located on the top floors. *Top* on the corporation's organization chart also means top in location in a building. By the same token, the senior manager in a meeting will also be seated at the head of a conference table during a regular meeting. Position, size, and quality of space provides information regarding status to others.

People in power are given more space by others. They also have better office furniture, greater privacy, and location. Office arrangements also communicate personal characteristics. Managers who center their desks in an office convey a sense of power and dominance. Those who arrange office furniture to accommodate visitors send a message of warmth, consideration, and less social distance. Providing an employee with added space conveys approval and is often interpreted as a type of promotion.

Most people have a **personal space.** Invading personal space, except in very intimate communication, can cause discomfort and aversion. People who stand too close to others, especially face-to-face, are often guilty of not considering the importance of the personal space of others. **Social space,** the distance we usually feel comfortable with when talking with others, is approximately 20 to 30 inches, or about the length of a casual handshake. **Public space,** the distance used to talk with groups, is usually 4 to 10 feet or even farther, depending on the situation. Our use of space and consideration of the space of others is an important nonverbal source of information.

Those who understand proxemics are aware of the "magic 90°." Many studies indicate that people who discuss issues with each other do so best when a table corner or 90°-angle arrangement of chairs exists. Supervisors who talk with employees on a one-to-one basis can use the magic 90° to great advantage.

Kinesics

Kinesics is the use of body positions and movement to communicate. It is commonly known as body language.

Kinesics is often known as *body language*. Posture, facial expressions, gestures, body movement, and eye movement are typical examples of kinesics. Books have been written on body language.

Some body language is deceptive. People learn to control their facial muscles, posture, and general appearance to mask true feelings. Most adults can consciously control much of their body language. They can look interested when bored, smile when angry, and be apparently sincere when lying. A great deal of body language, on the other hand, is involuntary. People react to events in their lives with facial expressions, posture, hand movements, degree of relaxation or tenseness, as well as speed of movement and general grooming. All of these transmit messages.

Although books have been written on uses of body language, care must be taken in interpreting its meanings. Some people stand with arms folded over their chests as a matter of habit rather than defensiveness. Whole chapters have been written on the significance of the way legs are crossed. Serious study indicates that habit and comfort are factors as well as other interpretations.

Some body language is deliberate. We frown, smile, or nod our heads to signal our feelings to others. Hands are used to express size, height, and shape. Movements are also used to urge people to stop, slow, move faster, or proceed in an indicated direction. Supervisors must learn to use their own body language appropriately, control it when necessary, and avoid prejudging employee reactions solely on kinesics. Combined with other nonverbal clues, however, it often provides insight into the feelings and reactions of other people.

Chronemics

Chronemics is the use of time to communicate—being late or early to meetings, failing to meet schedules, or being exceptionally punctual.

Chronemics is the study of the way individuals use time to communicate. People are frequently unaware of the way their use of time affects others. Those who are constantly late, demand the time of others, provide information too late, or relate events in embarrassing moments communicate something about themselves by their use of time. Supervisors who report to work late, fail to attend scheduled meetings, and act too busy to talk to employees communicate ineffectiveness to employees.

As stated earlier those who show up, show up on time, and show up dressed to play are far more likely to be successful than those who do not show up, are late when they do, and are not prepared.

■ WORDS AND MISSED MEANINGS

One of the difficulties with most languages, and especially with English, is the many usages possible for a single word. It is estimated that the 500 most commonly used words have approximately 15,000 possible usages. A simple word like *fly* can often be interpreted only by the context in which it is used. **Context** refers to the situation in which a word or term is used or to the words that precede and follow the word.

Context refers to the situation in which a word or words are used or the definition of a term by the words that follow or precede it.

1. At a baseball game an outfielder may catch a *fly* ball.
2. A patient frog may also catch a *fly*.
3. The *fly* on his pants may be open.
4. We can *fly* from Miami to Boston in a few hours.
5. I ate on the *fly* from my office to the meeting.

Soda may be something to drink or a white powder used in cooking. *Cream* can be a color, a component of milk, a type of cheese, a cold confection, or the very best of any group of things. *Fast* can be speedy, going without food, a person with few morals, a true friend, or something that is strongly attached. Almost any descriptive term we use has many possible usages. It is important in communication to be sure that the receiver understands the term in the sense that it was intended to be understood. Good communicators know that meanings are not in words. *Meanings are in people.* Interpretation of words is a primary communication problem. Effective communicators are always aware that what is clear to them may be also clear to someone else and the two meanings can be entirely different.

Listening, the Missing Skill

We usually listen to ourselves and occasionally listen to others. One of the most effective communication tools is listening. Managers who are willing to listen to employees openly and without criticism build respect, confidence, and personal credibility. Listening can be one of the most effective motivational tools available. Supervisors who are willing to listen to their employees often are able to make better decisions, avoid problems, and plan more effectively.

Effective listening requires effort. It involves far more than being a human tape recorder. Good listeners are active. They signal understanding nonverbally with head movements and facial expressions, they paraphrase their understanding of important points, and they request clarification of points they don't understand. Most of all they do not interrupt with arguments against what a person is saying or give advice until the issue has been fully related, and only then when they have relevant information or data. Good listeners recognize that each person they deal with has had unique experiences, developed individual values, and has highly individualized attitudes. In listening they try to accept a person as they are rather that what they would like them to be or how they may have been in the past. Good listeners listen *totally.* Not only do they hear words but they are sensitive to paralanguage, body language, and other nonverbal as well as verbal messages.

Total listening involves both hearing, interpretation of paralanguage, and observing body language as well as use of space.

Most managers, including first-line supervisors, are often busy and preoccupied with many problems. Telling rather than listening becomes an unfortunate pattern of behavior. Those who fail to use their listening skills will, eventually, have employees who will not give them anything to listen to.

In his best-selling *Thriving on Chaos,* Tom Peters repeatedly recommends visible management.[4] It is a similar concept to his **management by walking around (MBWA).**[5] Peters states that managers who make themselves known to employees and carefully listen build trust, confidence, and make change much easier than those who institute policy from the ivory tower of a remote and somewhat mysterious office.

■ COMMUNICATION STYLES

Motivation and communication styles are directly related. Managers who are concerned with dominance and power often ignore the suggestions of others and insist that their own ideas, decisions, and concepts are the only ones that are workable. Those who are insecure become noncommunicators. The less a person says, these managers feel, the less blame they will receive for mistakes. Some people, including managers, hide their true feelings by seeming to be agreeable, pleasant, and wanting to please. Careful listeners will realize that they rarely express their true feelings about anything. Others try to be open, honest, assertive without being offensive, and willing to evaluate positions with which they may have originally disagreed.

Cheryl Hamilton and Cordell Parker have classified these styles of **communication** as **blind, closed, hidden,** and **open.**[6] They are careful to point out that no one style is best for all situations. A key to understanding these styles is the willingness to disclose. Disclosure involves sharing information, opinions, and feelings with others. It need not be all personal. Both individuals and organizations can have open communication that involves future plans, information from other sources, or descriptions. Table 6.2 summarizes some of the characteristics of the four styles.

Hamilton and Parker are careful to note that while the open style of management is far more human-oriented than others, there are times when other styles have advantages. In a crisis, decisive, hard-nosed, blind communicators may do best. If conflicts with no apparent resolution exist, closed styles are often the only realistic solution. Initial contacts are often made best by using a hidden style where too much disclosure may lead to discomfort or alienation. An open style is usually more appropriate after a person becomes known. Open managers are usually trusted, respected by employees, and are good team builders. When their openness is misunderstood, however, it may be perceived as a weakness.

■ BEYOND STYLES AND THEORY

People tend to adopt the type of behavior and communication patterns that work best to meet their perceived needs. Those who learn (very often early in life) that aggressively assertive communication

TABLE 6.2 ■ Management Communication Styles

Style	Characteristics	Comments
Blind	Egotistical; unwilling to listen to others; believe their way is the only way; usually poor listeners; critical; high control	Aware of what they want; leave little doubt about where others stand with them; not afraid to exercise authority
Closed	Are essentially noncommunicators; concerned primarily with survival rather than effectiveness; suspicious and fearful; seen as manipulative	Will do what is required; go by the book; are conformist rather than innovative; do not relate well to most others but may have a few true friends
Hidden	Tend to be well liked; agreeable; conflict reducers; socially oriented; want to be accepted and liked by others	Do not disclose their opinions; often seen as manipulative; typical "yes" people; flatter boss and others with power
Open	Good listeners; trusted by others; friendly; share feelings and knowledge; usually productive and flexible	May make others uncomfortable with their openness; often frustrated when changes they want are not made; accept personal responsibility for their actions

Tough battlers, give-up communicators, friendly helpers, and problem solvers are similar styles to those of blind, closed, hidden, and open communicators.

with little regard for the feelings of others gets them what they want may use that style. These **tough battlers** will often either achieve what they want or at least end in a stalemate. Tough battlers may force others into a **give-up pattern** that is consistently used by those with closed styles. They often reach impasses with **problem solvers,** typically open communicators. Tough battlers nearly always win in discussions with hidden communicators, who are usually **compromisers.**

Employees seeking promotion will often adopt the type of behavior that they observe works with their immediate manager. If the manager is successful using a blind, tough-battler communication style, some employees will feel that it is the key to success. Others may learn that open styles are achievement oriented and lead to problem solution rather than criticism and punitive action. Managers must constantly be aware of the effect their behavior has on others. Even the most apparently successful can set undesirable patterns for members of their work groups. Perhaps most importantly they must never forget that their personal success is tied directly to the success of their employees. Effective managers communicate in ways that build trust and confidence rather than fear or suspicion.

■ COMMON COMMUNICATION BARRIERS

There is no way that human beings can relate to each other except through some form of communication. It is unfortunate that forces in people and situations often make communication a difficult process. Three common types of barriers often occur. In work environments good supervisors can recognize such barriers and overcome them, to a large extent. Supervisors, as presented in Figure 6.4, may be, in reality, the head of bottlenecks to effective communication. Too many messages from many sources must feed into a single receiver. Only a limited number may be responded to at any given period of time, and many go unheeded.

Psychological Barriers

Fear, lack of confidence, traumatic events, preoccupation with other events in their lives both good and bad, and concern for the way they relate to others all can alter communication. Interpretation of messages is often distorted by psychological barriers. Employees who feel under pressure to achieve often distort, either

FIGURE 6.4 ■ Communication Bottlenecks—Too Many Messages through the Same Space

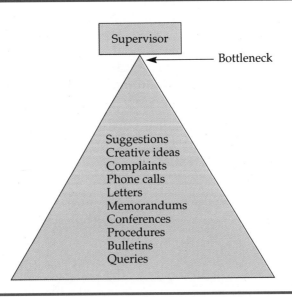

unintentionally or intentionally, what is being communicated. Supervisors, often faced with tight schedules, demands from higher-level managers, and their own desires to succeed, fail to listen.

Psychological barriers to communication include fear, lack of confidence, traumatic events, preoccupation with other events good and bad, and concern for the way others perceive an individual.

Psychological barriers can be overcome by development of a sense of *psychological maturity*. **Psychological maturity** means that an individual has learned to overcome internal barriers and can recognize and empathize with barriers in others. She or he recognizes difficulties that others may be experiencing and tries to understand from the other person's point of view. Keys to overcoming barriers, in addition to empathy, include

1. Concern for the problems and difficulties faced by others. This includes remembering that when good employees make errors, they feel worse than their supervisor does. Additional punishment in the form of lectures or threats is not needed nor appropriate.

2. Avoidance of defensiveness. If attacked, psychologically mature managers discuss perceived problems rather than defending past actions. They are analytical rather than critical, minimizing defensiveness in others. Problems rather than personal actions are the focus of their discussions.

3. Knowledge. Psychologically mature managers are knowledgeable. They know that without adequate information, opinions and decisions are meaningless.

Social Barriers

According to legend, when messengers brought news of a lost battle to the Roman emperor, they were often slain on the spot. This kill-the-messenger belief still exists in a modified form. Employees are reluctant to bring bad news to their supervisors. They do not want to be associated with potential disaster. Most people treat those with greater power or status differently from the way they relate to peers or lower-status individuals. Social barriers are based on perceived differences in power and status.

Social barriers are based on perceptions of differences in rank. Those perceived as having higher rank are often treated with deference. Communication upward is frequently intentionally limited.

One of the difficulties that supervisors may have in communicating with employees is the **social distance** that employees feel exists between themselves and management. Managers, many employees believe, often correctly, associate primarily with other managers and belong to a different social circle. Communication with higher-status people is often guarded, limited, and to a large extent hidden. Employees are often reluctant to reveal their true feelings for fear of offending or disagreeing with their managers.

A characteristic of better-run organizations is the effort of managers to reduce social distance. Total listening, including not only language but all of the nonverbal signals, is a powerful tool in reducing social distance. Limiting status symbols is another effective antidote to the social distance barrier. Managers who talk with employees at workstations rather than in the manager's office help reduce social distance. Social distance is reduced most effectively by managers who talk *with* rather than *down to* employees. *Talking with* means accepting employees as equal partners in the success of an organization rather than projecting an image of managerial superiority.

Sensory Barriers

Sensory barriers include any physical or physiological factors that interfere with understanding and being understood.

Sensory barriers are those caused by noise, distance, physical barriers such as walls, poor hearing, poor vision, or other physiological problems. In general they are the least difficult to overcome. In face-to-face communication it is important to select locations where people can adequately hear, see, and understand each other. If an employee has a visual acuity or hearing problem, it is necessary to create conditions where these barriers are minimized. In most cases managers have little difficulty with people who have sensory disabilities. Empathy, sensitivity, and willingness to recognize disabilities always makes communication less difficult.[7]

Information Overload

Information overload means giving more information to a person or group than can be fully absorbed and comprehended.

One of the most common management communication errors related to sensory barriers is that individuals cannot remember everything. Managers often make the mistake of giving both oral and written instructions that are lengthy, complex, and impossible for most employees to fully grasp. There is more information in the message than can be fully assimilated. Employees may remember part of what they have been told but not everything.

Simple activities, such as introducing a new employee to the other people in the group they are joining, can be, at first, a confusing experience. After the third introduction the name of the first person introduced has been lost. In any situation that involves too much information, much of it will be lost.

Organizational Barriers

With the exception of small organizations where communication is usually informal and two-way, management communication is often one-way. This is true even at the first level, where busy supervisors give instructions and rarely seek responses. Directives, policy statements, priorities, long-range plans, and other information regarding the organization most frequently originates at higher levels of management and eventually makes its way downward through each organizational level. In large organizations the originator of a message is often someone employees know only by name. Downward communication is relatively easy to send through regular organizational channels. Responses upward are often difficult or virtually nonexistent. Organization structure often makes upward communication difficult or virtually impossible.

Organizational barriers are bottlenecks that prevent upward communication created by both the structure and the size of organizations.

Upward communication requires that messages go through several bottlenecks. A supervisor with 12 employees can only spend a brief amount of time with each employee. Problems, suggestions, creative ideas, and complaints that are intended to go upward are often stopped, diluted, or reinterpreted by the supervisor. If a message is sent upward to the next level, the same type of bottleneck exists. Some organizations have attempted to improve upward communication through the use of open-door policies that encourage employees to feel free to discuss problems or suggestions with managers at any level. While these are good in concept, they rarely work as well as planned. Managers, especially those at upper levels of large organizations, do not have adequate time to spend with employees who directly provide services or products.

First-line managers can do a great deal to enhance communication with employees by being willing to listen, discuss job problems, and explore feasibility of suggestions. They can see their roles as trainers, information providers, facilitators, and team builders rather than rule enforcers or order givers. Higher-level managers who meet with employees on both a one-to-one basis as well as in groups, even if such meetings are infrequent, enhance employees' sense of being in on things. There is little doubt that visible management promotes feelings of confidence and loyalty far more than does management known by name only.

■ COMMUNICATION IN PRACTICE

Managers who communicate well are, unfortunately, the exception rather than the rule. Clarity, conciseness, and completeness, the traditional hallmarks of good communicators, are not enough. Whether conversing with employees or other managers, here are a few suggestions that may help improve communication effectiveness.

1. **If possible, be existential.** Do not blame others for having points of view different from yours. Recognize that not one second in a person's past can be changed. There is also no way of accurately predicting an individual's future. We must learn to accept people as they are *now* rather than as we think they were or how they will be in the future. *Acceptance,* in this example, means recognizing that every individual has a unique view of their personal universe. It may be radically different from ours or most others. It does not imply either agreement or disagreement. Acceptance is the recognition that every individual has their own frame of reference. First-line managers who recognize the importance of understanding from the employee's point of view are able to open avenues of communication that are both positive and productive.

2. **Keep your cool.** Good communicators control their emotions. If they disagree or are disagreed with, they do not get angry. A good practice is to be analytical rather than critical. Being analytical means looking at information and actual events rather than reacting emotionally to points on which there is disagreement. It also means being able to look at problems rather than personalities.

3. **Always listen totally.** *Total listening* means listening not only to words but also to paralanguage, body movement, facial expressions, and developing a sensitivity to the real mood and emotional status of message senders. It also involves encouraging, without directing, the message sender to fully state her or his feelings, ideas, information, or problems.

4. **Avoid defensiveness.** Good communicators try to understand another person's perspective, even when they are being criticized. Rather than defending their position, they try to learn why others disagree.

Halos are judgments based on superficial characteristics, such as appearance or speech characteristics.

5. **Avoid halos, stereotypes, and other biases.** A **halo** is a judgment of others based on one or a limited number of personal characteristics. People who look and speak intelligently, as an example, are often judged to be more competent than those who lack some of the same personal characteristics. Halos can also be negative. A person who has poor communication skills

Stereotypes are generalized biases derived from beliefs about behavior of those of certain ethnic backgrounds, national origins, religion, sex, type of work, education, geographical area, or other characteristics.

may be viewed as dumb even though their work is exemplary. **Stereotypes** are based on judgments about the group a person is identified with. Ethnicity, religion, previous employment, place of birth, type of education, neighborhood in which a person lives, and almost any other basis for generalization can create stereotypes. Biases, regardless of their cause or origin, often do a disservice to both parties in any face-to-face communication.

Communication is one of the most significant of all human activities. No relationship, formal or informal, can exist without some type of communication. Every type of behavior or lack of behavior communicates. We live in an environment filled with communication. It is essential that managers continually attempt to improve their communication skills. It will help both their work and their personal lives.

■ THINGS TO REMEMBER

    I. Communication—understanding and being understood.
   - A. Meanings are in people, not in words.
   - B. A frame of reference is composed of all internal and external forces that affect the way a person perceives the world in which he or she lives.
   - C. Feedback is the information gathered in response to a communication.
   - D. A communication channel is composed of the media that transmits a message.
   - E. Face-to-face communication uses many channels.

   II. Elements of nonverbal communication.
   - A. Appearance, speech, manners, and mannerisms.
   - B. Paralanguage.
   - C. Touching.
   - D. Proxemics.
   - E. Body language, or kinesics.
   - F. Chronemics.

 III. Words and missed meanings. Good listening requires effort.

 IV. Communication styles.
   - A. Blind communicators.

B. Closed communicators.

C. Hidden communicators.

D. Open communicators.

V. Beyond styles and theory.

A. People tend to adopt the type of communication patterns that satisfy their perceived needs.

B. Tough battlers, give-up patterns, problem solvers, and compromisers are similar to blind, closed, hidden, and open communicators.

C. Effective managers use communication to build trust and confidence.

VI. Communication barriers.

A. Psychological barriers include fear, lack of confidence, and preoccupation with other events.

B. Social barriers are related to differences in status or perceived power.

C. Sensor barriers involve physical barriers that affect the senses.

D. Information overload occurs when people are given more information than they can absorb at one time.

E. Barriers caused by organizational structure are often due to built-in bottlenecks.

VII. Communication in practice.

A. Good supervisors are existential in their beliefs and behavior.

B. Effective communicators keep their cool, avoid defensiveness, and are good listeners.

C. Stereotypes and halos are potential problems in all communication.

■ KEY TERMS

communication

messages

meanings

filter

frame of reference

feedback

channel

communication codes

nonverbal communication

paralanguage

proxemics

personal space

social space

public space

kinesics

chronemics

context

management by walking
around (MBWA)

blind communication

closed communication

hidden communication

open communication

tough battlers

give-up pattern

problem solvers

compromisers

psychological maturity

social distance

halo

stereotypes

■ DISCUSSION QUESTIONS

1. List three communication problems that you have encountered in work organizations. How could they have been prevented?

2. What are two realistic approaches that can reduce problems in upward communication in organizations? Explain your suggestions.

3. Most people born in this country of parents who were also born here share the same values and frames of reference. Explain your agreement or disagreement with this statement.

4. Which style of communication do you feel works best in most types of organizations? Defend your response.

5. Why should disclosure of personal feelings and information be somewhat limited when a person is not fully acquainted with those with whom they are communicating?

■ SELF-ASSESSMENT

Remember that in responding to these questions or items, a 1, 2, or 3 indicates disagreement while 4, 5, and 6 represent agreement, with 6 being the highest degree of agreement.

1. When communicating with a manager who is dominant, egotistical, and generally negative, it is best to seek compromises and show a willingness to cooperate.

   1   2   3   4   5   6

2. The best way to influence those who disagree with you is to show them examples and data that prove they are wrong.

   1   2   3   4   5   6

3. Clarity, conciseness, and correctness ensure that messages will be understood.

   1   2   3   4   5   6

4. In the final analysis managers are paid to make decisions. Employees are paid to carry out those decisions. Good managers spare their employees the responsibility of being involved.

5. A person's eyes will express their true feelings if a person looks closely enough.

   1   2   3   4   5   6

6. Modern organizations, especially large ones, are structured to make upward communication both easy and helpful.

   1   2   3   4   5   6

7. Information overload is not a reality but a smokescreen used by union leaders to overcome employee errors.

   1   2   3   4   5   6

8. A strength of the English language is that words have precise meanings and are not dependent on context or the way they are used.

   1   2   3   4   5   6

9. Good managers recognize social distance and work to minimize it by being highly visible and listening carefully to employees.

   1   2   3   4   5   6

10. People who seek compromises usually win more arguments than tough battlers or problem solvers.

   1   2   3   4   5   6

■ SHORT CASES

People Don't Listen

Most people have had amusing experiences with misinterpreted messages. Jack Maloney called a local weekly advertising bulletin and told the classified advertising clerk, "I'd like to list my radial arm saw for sale. It's in good condition and includes instructions." He was surprised four days later to see his ad: "Radio alarm spa for sale, fully instructed." Apparently Jack and the clerk did not fully understand each other.

Paul and Mae Plescia were visiting Gettysburg National Park. Just after they entered the park, they noticed that the excursion train had just left so there would be a short wait for the next one. A park guide approached them as they looked at the schedule and politely asked, "Missed your train?" "Glad to meet you M. Train," answered Paul, whose hearing is not the best. "My name is Paul Plescia and this is my wife, Mae. I guess we have to wait 20 minutes."

Near the end of World War II, General MacArthur issued a formal request to the Japanese to surrender. The reply contained the word *mokusatsu*. *Mokusatsu* has two possible meanings in Japanese. One is "no comment," the other is "we ignore." Unfortunately, the "we ignore" interpretation was given to MacArthur. The Japanese Diet (congress) wanted time to discuss possible surrender. MacArthur thought the offer was rejected. Shortly after the interpretation the first atomic bomb used in war was dropped. It would have never been used if the word had been interpreted the way it was intended.

1. Give examples of communication misunderstandings you have experienced.

2. What types of barriers caused the mistakes described in the examples listed in the case?

3. Can messages be deliberately misinterpreted? How and why?

Listen Closely

When Sheila Mendez was selected as chief of police by the Columbia City Council, Bill Tunstall, a high-seniority captain who was also a contender for the assignment, was bitter. "She got it because she is a woman and an alleged minority. She doesn't qualify."

In a meeting with her top staff, including Bill Tunstall, Sheila announced, "We are going to reorganize the way beats are assigned. Each area of town will have its own team and team leader. Our underlying strategy is to have police officers work in the same area and become fully acquainted with the people and problems on their beat. They can identify outsiders and develop credibility with local citizens. Each team will be autonomous but can request assistance from other teams when needed."

Later that day Bill met with his staff. "Here we go again," he started with a knowing smile. "Another reorganization by the downtown experts who know what's right for everybody. 'Each area of town,'"Bill drew a small square on the chalkboard of the meeting room, "'will have its own team.'" His stress on the words drew a flurry of laughter, "The underlying strategy. . . " At this point Bill repeated Sheila's announcement word-for-word.

On the morning after the announced change, the *Columbia Courier* carried the banner headline, "CITY COUNCIL AND NEW CHIEF OF POLICE ENDORSE REORGANIZATION—COPS HATE IT."

1. How did Bill change Sheila's message?

2. In what ways do paralanguage and body language modify message interpretation?

3. If asked what he told them, how would Bill's officers reply?

■ ENDNOTES

1. Peter Drucker has been a major influence on management for nearly forty years. Many of his articles have appeared in *The Wall Street Journal* and other popular business publications. His latest book, *New Realities*, is published by Harper & Row (1989).

2. Based on a personal interview with Dr. Wilson, "Advanced Management Skills" seminar, February 20, 1991, University of California-Davis.

3. Based on studies by John Wilson, management consultant. Most of Wilson's studies of promotions and communication skills were made in consulting with the Kaiser Corporation, Oakland, California.

4. Tom Peters, *Thriving on Chaos* (New York: Alfred A. Knopf, 1987).

5. Thomas J. Peters and Robert Waterman, *In Search of Excellence* (New York: Harper & Row, 1982).

6. Cheryl Hamilton and Cordell Parker, *Communicating for Results*, 3rd edition (Belmont, Calif.: Wadsworth Publishing Company, 1990).

7. In 1990 the Congress of the United States enacted the Americans with Disabilities Act. Discrimination against people with disabilities is prohibited. Employers may not set unreasonable physical standards. If a bona fide occupational qualification exists that would make it impossible for certain people with disabilities to qualify for the assignment, then reasonable accommodation must be made. *Reasonable accommodation* means searching for an assignment that the potential disabled employee may successfully fill.

Chapter 7

Leadership and Supervision

Objectives

Chapter 7 deals with one of management's most essential functions: being a leader. Several objectives are important:

- To define leadership.
- To be able to list the most common leadership explanations.
- To utilize Fiedler's leadership approach.
- To define contingency leadership, grid, and path-goal leadership theories.
- To recognize factors that contribute to leadership and those that do not.

Thought Starter

M. June Smith is a prototype of leaders for the next century. As brand director for Coors Beer she was instrumental in moving it from a limited, western United States market to become the third largest seller nationwide, just behind Miller and Budweiser. In 1990 the 40-year-old self-starter became general manager for Ceramicon Designs, a Coors subsidiary. She states that her job is not unique. "We manage by agreement and by collaborating. It's sort of like a think tank." June Smith is a manager and a leader, the best combination that can be found in any organization.[1]

■ *During the height of the Northern Ireland conflict with the Irish Republican Army, two young women, one Catholic and one Protestant, in Belfast, Northern Ireland, no longer wanted to see their Catholic neighbors and children uselessly slaughtered in an unending religious and national conflict. They went door-to-door throughout their neighborhood asking people to join in a protest against indiscriminate murder. On an appointed day over 10,000 Catholic and Protestant women and their children marched through the city. It was one of the most effective demonstrations in history as well as being an example of what real leadership can accomplish. Leadership involves recognizing that something needs doing and then getting it done.*

■ LEADING AND MANAGING

In 1990 Donald Petersen retired as chief executive officer of the Ford Motor Company. During seven of the nine years he headed Ford, its net profits exceeded those of General Motors Corporation, which is three times as large as Ford. Petersen attributes his success largely to three principles:

1. **Concentrate on products and services.** Profits will follow. Unless consumers are satisfied with what an organization has to offer, its efforts are meaningless. Never stop trying to improve.

2. **Turn your people loose.** Petersen is convinced that good managers are developers of people who can accept responsibility and interact with others to achieve results. Consultations between engineers and assembly workers at Ford is routine.

3. **Be consistent.** A hallmark of good management is knowing what is needed and never giving up good goals. This does not mean being inflexible, but it does imply that when excellence is set as a major organizational target, never do anything that will dilute or impede achieving it.

Good leaders are often heroes and role models. In national and international affairs they are highly visible, both supported and disliked but, most of all, recognized as people willing to get things accomplished. All leaders know what they want and strive to get it completed.

Like many other terms, **leadership** has no precise definition. Most of us recognize leaders when we encounter them. Defining precisely what they do that is different from what followers do is difficult. One common characteristic of leaders is their ability to

Leaders have the common characteristic of being able to influence others.

influence others. Leaders are people who get other people to do not only what the leader thinks is important but what followers also think is significant. They are able to define goals that others will accept and work to achieve. No single model of leadership describes the broad range of types of leader influence.

Mother Theresa labored for many years to help the poorest people of India. She was awarded the Nobel Peace Prize for her efforts. Many people in India as well as other countries volunteered, without pay, to support her efforts. Her influence in obtaining help for those unable to help themselves is undeniable. Saddam Hussein in Iraq was revered by many people of his country and other Arab states for his willingness to defy the greatest powers of the world, including the United Nations. Leaders have many motivations but the actions they take to separate themselves from others is difficult to define.

Leaders are able to get people to act to achieve goals.

Leaders are able to get people to act to achieve goals. In many cases this means that leaders must define for others what is needed and what is right. Historically there have been several types of leaders.

Charismatic leaders are characterized by their force of personality, determination, and willingness to take extraordinary risks.

1. **Charismatic leaders.** In the 1930s Mahatma Gandhi was able to influence most of his fellow Indians to resist British rule. Although Gandhi never used force or violence of any type, Great Britain gave rule to the Indians shortly after the end of World War II. Gandhi was able to define what the people of his country wanted and to exert the type of pressure needed to get it accomplished. When he was assassinated by one of his former followers, much of the world mourned.

   Martin Luther King, Jr. inspired many people to help free black people from segregation and discrimination in the United States. He was able to define what both many white and black people felt was right and then showed them ways of accomplishing their goals. Although he was ultimately assassinated, there is little doubt of his charisma and his leadership. In all societies there have been charismatic leaders. Their force of personality, determination, and willingness to take extraordinary risks are difficult to challenge.

Traditional leaders inherit their roles by birth or kinship.

2. **Traditional leaders.** Throughout history many people have been thrust into leadership roles by birth or kinship. Throughout most of the history of humankind, leadership has been inherited. Emperors, czars, kings, queens, and potentates of all kinds have inherited their leadership. In industry some

leaders have achieved their status by kinship. While many traditional leaders have been mediocre or worse, some have had remarkable success. IBM can trace its entrance into the electronic computer age to the insistence of Thomas Watson, Jr., son of the company's founder. Since its beginnings Ford Motor Company has had a succession of Fords become chief executive officers. Except for a few notable exceptions traditional, inherited leadership rarely exists in developed societies.

Emergent leaders achieve their status through personality, credibility, or willingness to speak for their group.

3. **Emergent leaders.** In every group some individuals, because of their personality, credibility, or willingness to speak for the group, become informal leaders. They are expected by other members to represent the work unit to which they belong. In some situations more than one informal leader may emerge. Frequently these informal leaders are promoted to formal leadership positions because of their dedication, willingness to represent others, and sense of what is needed. Although not all informal, emergent group leaders become formal managers, many succeed in entering management ranks. Their willingness to represent the views of others as well as a strong sense of purpose serve them well.

Appointed leaders are common in work organizations. Their leadership is based on recognized expertise, efficiency, effectiveness, and potential for learning management skills.

4. **Appointed leaders.** All managers are not leaders, even though they tend to think they are. Managership and leadership are not the same. In work organizations people are sometimes promoted because they are efficient and effective employees. They may have good organizational, planning, and analytical skills but do not do well in building enthusiasm and dedication in employees. Although their management skills are recognized, they lack the ability to inspire others to excel. Those managers who have both management skills and leadership ability are usually more successful in working with others to accomplish organizational goals. It is unfortunate that promotions, especially to first-line positions, do not always require leadership potential. First-line supervisors must learn to be leaders as well as managers or slip into mediocrity.

Authority, an integral part of all management activity, makes it possible to get work accomplished. But it is not an adequate substitute for leadership skills not granted by the organization.[2] Respect of others earned by actions, expertise in identifying problems as well as potential solutions, willingness to take risks to accomplish goals, and personal integrity are all important components of managerial leadership. One of the real difficulties in learning leadership skills is that no magical formula is successful in every situation.

In some instances individual employee knowledge, experience, and ability act as substitutes for leadership.[3] Highly cohesive groups can often work effectively without formal leaders. Some companies, such as General Mills, Procter & Gamble, Digital Equipment, Federal Express, 3M, and Johnsonville Foods, have been experimenting with self-managed work teams. Supervisors are either nonexistent or act as facilitators for the groups. Leadership is provided by top management and informal group leaders. Hiring, firing, scheduling, quality control, and other traditional management activities are accomplished by the group.[4] While the concept of self-managed work groups has a great deal of appeal, it works best in organizations that have strongly interdependent employee teams. Most of the experimentation has been in food processing and some types of manufacturing where teams may be easily identified. For organizations that have employees who are relatively independent, such as sales, advertising, and most clerical operations, the self-managed team concept would be difficult to successfully organize.

■ UNDERSTANDING LEADERSHIP IN ORGANIZATIONS

In work organizations people learn from others. What seems to be a successful pattern for one person is adopted by others. If a person works in an organization where all decisions are made by managers, supervisors see themselves primarily as rule enforcers and disciplinarians. Where punishment is swift but rewards few, then they will likely adopt the same type of behavior if promoted. They assume it is what the organization expects and it seems to work. In other organizations supervisors may see themselves primarily as message carriers, and employees are essentially self-managed. In such cases the supervisors take a hands-off approach. People learn by modeling their behavior after those in positions of power. Managers who set good examples train potential supervisors to take positive leadership roles. Those who work for nonleaders, who rely on granted authority for their supervisory actions, send a different message. It is important for workplace leaders to be **referents.**

A referent is someone who has the respect and confidence of others.

A referent is someone who has the respect and confidence of others. Their actions communicate competence. They are the type of person who others would like to be. Managers with leadership

skills are pacesetters for the organization. In nearly all instances they believe strongly in their own ability and those of their work team. Enthusiasm for achievement and concern for success of individuals and the group as a whole characterize their efforts.

"American workers are overmanaged and underled" is a much quoted saying that contains a great deal of truth. It implies that our managers have learned to plan, organize, and control both activities and people, but they have not been as successful in their efforts to build excitement and strong goal support in their organizations. A key to improving the current stance of U.S. organizations compared to those of Japan and other Asian nations as well as those of the "new Europe" may well lie in the ability to train managers to be effective leaders. Leaders are always needed. In this and the next decade, competent leadership will continue to be a much sought after set of management skills.

▪ LEADERSHIP THEORIES—TRADITIONAL AND ALPHABET-SOUP

Leadership is difficult to define and equally difficult to study. Ralph Stodgill and Bernard Bass have studied leaders and their actions for over 40 years. They point out that a person may be a leader in one set of conditions but not in others.[5] A still not fully answered question is, Why do some people become leaders and others do not?

Older Leadership Theories

One of the oldest leadership theories was based on the concept of biological superiority. People were *born* leaders. Originally called

Great person leadership theories state that leaders are born, not made.

the **great man theory** it is now sometimes referred to as the *great person theory*. Very early in life some children are able to strongly influence the actions of other children. This ability, in some instances, persists into adulthood. It is difficult, however, to prove that being able to influence others is inborn. Children learn many things and some have learned that if a person tells others what to do, some will comply. Most social scientists reject the notion that there is a leadership gene. Most seem to feel that leadership is a set of learned actions that come into play under certain conditions.

Traits common to all leaders have not been satisfactorily identified.

For a number of years, some management writers proposed a **trait theory** of leadership. Leaders were alleged to be intelligent, energetic, analytical, politically sensitive, attractive to their followers, and dependable. Interestingly many nonleaders could be identified with these or similar characteristics. Traits common to all leaders are difficult to identify and virtually impossible to assign. Most organizational analysts have looked for variables other than traits to identify leadership behavior. These more recent approaches to the study of leadership tend to support each other to a significant extent.

Alphabet-Soup Theories

Few texts have had the lasting impact of Douglas McGregor's *The Human Side of Enterprise*, originally published in 1960 and reprinted many times since.[6] In it McGregor identifies his famous **Theory-X** and **Theory-Y** styles of management. Table 7.1 identifies traditional, Theory-X beliefs contrasted to those of Theory Y, a more human-oriented approach.

Theory X, Douglas McGregor's designation for traditional management, assumes that people must be tightly controlled, that they dislike work, and are basically lazy and irresponsible.

Theory Y is based on the managerial assumption that, given the encouragement and opportunity, people will control themselves, prefer to do a good job, and will seek added responsibilities.

McGregor's most lasting contribution may not be either Theory X or Theory Y. McGregor was one of the first to recognize the importance of managerial assumptions. Managers who believe they have worthless, nonachieving employees get exactly what they expect. Those that feel that work is an important segment of every person's life and that it should be no less natural than play, hobbies, or other expenditures of energy represent the new view of management. Theory-Y managers are people-oriented leaders. Theory-X managers feel that fear, money, and getting the most for the least effort is what people really desire. Over 30 years later we are still concerned with control, rule enforcement, and reward and punishment. It is ironic that management consultants have for all of those years taught that McGregor was correct: *The assumptions that managers make about their employees determine how employees will*

TABLE 7.1 ■ McGregor's Theory X and Theory Y

Theory X Assumptions	Theory Y Assumptions
People do not like responsibility	Most people seek responsibility
People need to be prodded to work	People will work if encouraged
Fear is the best motivator	Fear is the worst motivator
Employees are not interested in their organization	Most employees want to work for a successful organization
People work for money and money alone	People work for money and many other reasons
At best, people are naturally lazy	Most people prefer to work than remain idle

behave. Managers who believe their people are winners have winning groups. Those who believe employees are losers have losers.

Theory Z

Theory Z is William Ouchi's extension of Theory Y. It states that people can be essentially self-directed, deeply involved in day-to-day job decisions, and can see themselves as partners with management in building the success of their organization.

William Ouchi has been a writer and consultant for many years. His clients have included some of the most management advanced companies in the United States. Ouchi believes that managers should go beyond Theory Y and adopt **Theory Z.** In his best-selling *Theory Z: How American Business Can Meet the Japanese Challenge*[7] Ouchi added another letter to McGregor's theories. Managers must provide a climate where employees are more self-directive, involved in on-the-job decisions, and see themselves as partners with management in building the success of their organizations.

While Ouchi's concepts are often advocated in the 1990s, they are, in reality, adopted by very few organizations. Ouchi agrees with other significant writers, such as William Edwards Deming, Ishikawa, and Imani, that organizations that are people-driven rather than management-controlled are the ones that eventually succeed. Managers at outstanding corporations such as Sony and Toyota are taught that success depends on good design, good materials, and good people. Of these three, good people are the most significant.

Neither McGregor nor Ouchi's messages are unique. Many other observers of organizational life have observed that managers who value employees and see them as the major component of any organization are most likely to be successful.

PEOPLE AND TASKS

One of the more popular approaches to managerial style and leadership was developed by Robert Blake and Jane Mouton.[8] In studies similar to those made at both Ohio State University and the University of Michigan, Blake and Mouton narrowed management's primary concerns to people and tasks. Their studies indicated that leadership style depended on the degree of emphasis managers placed on accomplishing work and on building relationships with people. Some managers, they found, concentrated primarily on getting work accomplished, while others felt relationships with employees were most important. Some managers did not seem to be strongly interested in either employees or the tasks they were assigned.

Blake and Mouton's conclusions were based largely on questionnaires that measured factors such as feelings about decisions, strength of convictions, approaches to conflict, control of emotions, amount of humor, and degree of effort. Based on the results of the questionnaires, they were able to graphically plot a manager's most probable leadership style. Their graphing technique, called the **Managerial Grid,** became a favorite tool for conducting leadership studies and improving management leadership effectiveness. Figure 7.1 shows the managerial grid as well as the style of leadership a person is likely to use. Grid scores are based on a scale of 0 to 9 for both people and tasks. Scores for concern for people are registered vertically in columns and dedication to task attainment is indicated by scores in rows. An individual can have a high task score and a low people score, a high people score and a low task score, or any combination from very low to very high on both scales. A person who, as an example, scores a 0 on the people scale and a 9 on the task scale has a very strong need to get the job accomplished but no concern for relationships with people.

Blake and Mouton identified five primary management styles. They are careful to point out that there can also be variations within a given style. It is possible to have a moderate concern for people and a high concern for work or little interest in people and a moderate task involvement.

Five basic leadership styles identified by Blake and Mouton were called impoverished management, country club management, middle-of-the-road management, task management, and team management.

Impoverished management is the result of a low involvement with both people and tasks. Although relatively rare, impoverished

Managerial Grids graphically plot a manager's most probable leadership style.

FIGURE 7.1 ■ The Managerial Grid and Management Styles

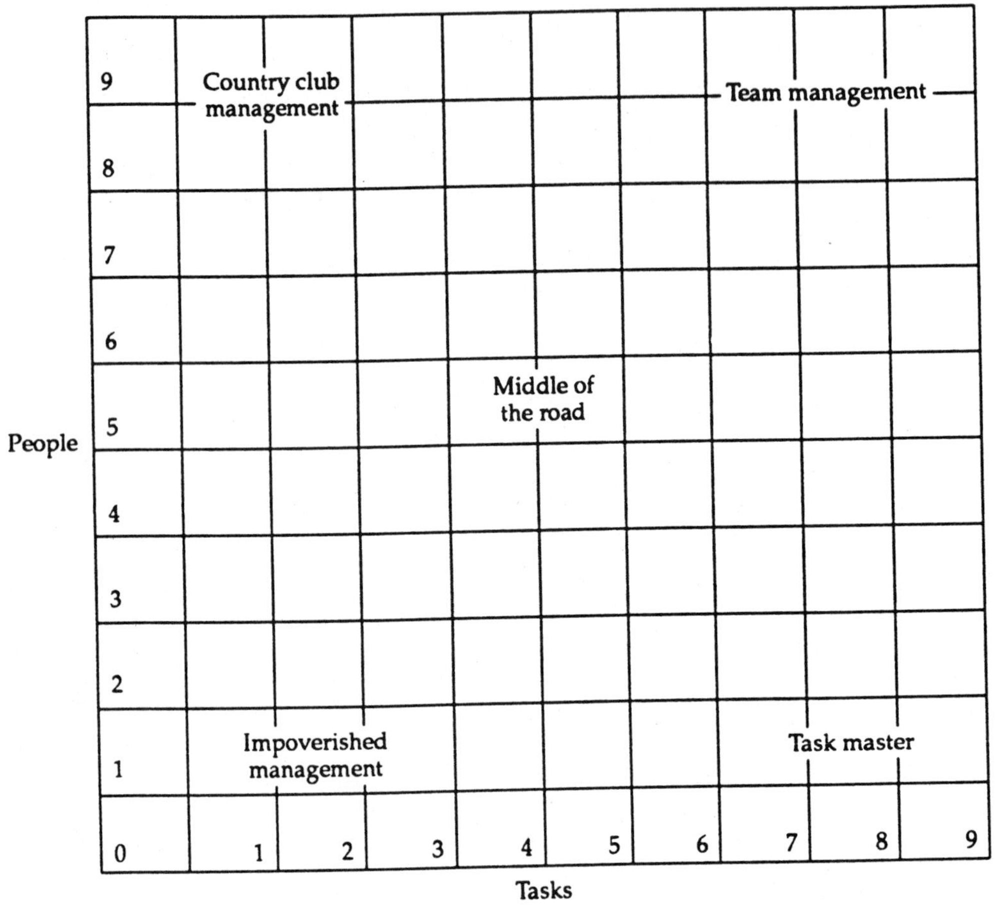

Impoverished managers see their role as message carriers.

leaders see their role primarily as message carriers. They leave most decision making, determination of priorities, and evaluation of work quality to employees. They have little direct involvement with employees or the tasks that need to be accomplished. Impoverished leadership styles can be acceptable for some types of groups, such as independent research and development efforts, but in most instances their lack of involvement creates a poor work climate. Impoverished managers rarely make decisions; they go by the book and do only what is required to keep from being fired. Their belief is that if a person doesn't make a decision, he or she will never make a bad one. Survival is the primary motivation of an impoverished leader. Their score on the Managerial Grid will be low on both task and people items.

Conntry club managers make their employees comfortable and content on the job.

Country club managers are committed to making their employees comfortable and content on the job, building strong relationships, and assuring that their employees take advantage of all of the benefits that the organization offers. They have a strong need to be liked—a need for friendship—and see their primary task as reducing conflict and complaints. Country club managers strongly believe that happy workers are good workers and, as a consequence, pay little attention to required tasks. On the Managerial Grid they score high on people and low on tasks.

Middle-of-the-road managers seek reasonable compromises, conforming to accepted norms for work and on-the-job behavior.

Middle-of-the-road managers are the most common leaders in most organizations. They have a moderately high interest in people and a moderately high interest in getting work accomplished. Their leadership style is based on seeking reasonable compromise, conforming to accepted norms for work and on-the-job behavior, adherence to policies, and building a stable work group. Their commitment to the organization, its employees, and its work is moderate. On the Managerial Grid their scores are usually in the middle, or 5, 5.

Task masters are strongly production and quality oriented.

Task masters do not care about people other than the need for their energy, skills, and effort in accomplishing work. They know what needs to be done, are strongly production and quality oriented, and impersonal in their relationships with employees. People are there, like machines, to complete jobs. Task masters will do whatever is required to complete assigned task on or before time. They make decisions for their group and see themselves as enforcers of rules, organizers, and controllers. Although they usually have good productivity, they also create tension and hostility because of their failure to treat their employees as individuals with unique individual needs. They score low on people and high on tasks. They are motivated by a desire to please higher level management and personal power.

Team management is characterized by a leadership style that has a high degree of interest in both people and the tasks that must be accomplished. Managers with team orientation are interested in their own success as managers in order to achieve goals, the development of employees in their work teams, and the success of their work unit as a whole. They want their people to be the best. In many work organizations, promotions often come from groups led by team managers. Their motivation is achievement, excellence, and continual improvement. On the Managerial Grid, team managers score high on both people and tasks.

Although Blake and Mouton's work is now somewhat dated, it views job leadership in an easy-to-remember-and-understand framework. It also offers the opportunity for individuals to examine their own methods of leadership and determine where they fit on the Managerial Grid.

■ WHERE ARE WE NOW?

Three other approaches to leadership in organizations have provided additional insights in organizational life. **Interactive theories** recognize that leadership depends on the interaction of managers, people, and conditions. Recognition that no one type of management style is best for all conditions forms the foundation for **contingency-**based management theory. **Path-goal theory** has concentrated on the complex relationships between leaders and followers. None of these is mutually exclusive of the others. All of them contribute to our understanding of leadership but do not contradict the others.

Path-goal theory concentrates on the relationships between leaders and followers.

Interactive Leadership Theories

Interactive theories of leadership state that forces within the manager, situation, and employees determine appropriate leadership style.

In what is considered to be a *Harvard Business Review* classic, Robert Tannenbaum and Warren H. Schmidt pointed out the importance of interaction between managers, employees, and the situation in determining leadership factors.[9] Forces within managers, forces within employees, and the situation interact to determine leadership behavior. The behavior of managers is influenced by their personalities, what they have learned, expectations of both employees and higher levels of management, and their assessment of the situation. They are also influenced by their evaluation of the skill of employees and both the difficulty and urgency of the task. Employees, like managers, are influenced by expectations of peers, their perceptions of the job, and their relationships with managers. Job factors include level of difficulty, urgency for completion, and availability of resources to adequately perform needed activities. Figure 7.2 depicts this relationship graphically.

As Figure 7.2 indicates, managers, employees, and situational factors are always interacting to shape courses of actions. Leadership style is strongly influenced by this interaction.

Contingency—It Depends on . . .

During the 1960s Joan Woodward studied many organizations in Great Britain. Her findings led her to the inescapable conclusion

FIGURE 7.2 ▪ Factors Influencing Leadership Style

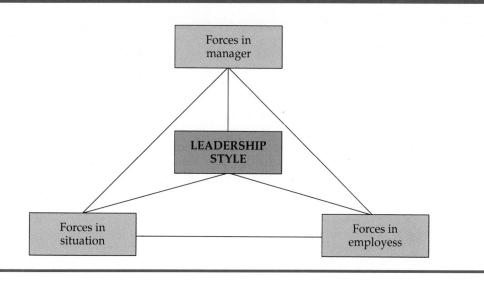

Contingency theory states that the appropriate leadership style depends largely on the situation. Leadership style should change as the situation changes.

that different organizations require different types of leadership styles and that the best type of management depends on the situation. In some instances highly directive, authoritarian leadership seemed to work well. She also found the permissive and participative styles also worked well if conditions dictated that they were correct. Her conclusion was that "no one type of leadership is best for all sets of condition."[10]

Woodward's studies were some of the first to recognize that the situation is an important consideration in determining leadership style. She was not the first to recognize style differences in managers, but she was one of the first to seriously study style applications in various work environments. Manufacturing industries tended to have greater numbers of directive leaders who were decisive, high-control people who took major responsibility for their decisions and expected employees to follow directions explicitly. Jobs that involved teamwork and relatively complex skills responded best to managers who consulted with employees before making a decision and relied on employees to identify and be involved in problem solving. When people had jobs that were relatively independent of each other and involved complex skills and knowledge, leadership was not sought or needed. A closer look at the styles Woodward studied may be helpful.

■ MAJOR LEADERSHIP STYLES

Authoritarian leaders see themselves as the ultimate decision makers. They take a parental role, either benevolent or judgmental, in dealing with employees.

Some leaders are authoritarian (sometimes called *autocratic*). **Authoritarian** leaders see themselves as ultimate decision makers. They take a parental role in dealing with employees. Some are benevolent parents who instruct their employees on what is right and wrong; others are judgmental parents who see correction as their major function. Neither the benevolent nor the judgmental authoritarian leader allows freedom or encourages increased responsibility, innovation, or creativity. Employees are paid to do a job and their function is to see that it is accomplished. If decisions are to be made, the leaders will make them. In jobs involving routine, repetitive work where minimal skills are needed or in crisis situations, authoritative management seems to work very well.

Participative leaders view employees as partners in decision-making processes. They encourage employee ideas, suggestions, and job involvement.

Participative leaders encourage employees in their work units to make decisions related to their jobs, to be a part of planning activities, and to consult with the manager on work problems and possible solutions. Participative supervisors see themselves and their employees as parts of a unit, not as we versus they. Everyone must contribute. Managers, they feel, are just another job classification requiring a different set of skills from those of nonmanagers. Participative leaders concentrate on team building. Work environments that involve diversity of job assignments, complexity of tasks, and close interaction with others respond well to participative leadership styles.

Permissive leaders are essentially nonleaders. They view their role as message carriers while employees decide what needs to be done and what decisions are needed.

In some sets of conditions **permissive** leadership seems to work well. Permissive leaders see their role as essentially nonleaders. They inform employees of what higher levels of management have directed but little else. Employees in their work teams are essentially self-directed and self-controlled. If employees are fully trained, competent, and rely on their own knowledge and skills to perform work, permissive leadership may be appropriate. Research and development operations where both individuals and teams act autonomously may respond well to permissive leaders.

Most contemporary theorists agree with Woodward's findings. Leadership style depends on the situation. It is important, in reviewing behavioral classifications such as leadership styles, to recognize that there is rarely a "pure" management style. In their roles as leaders, managers may vary their style to match conditions. A highly participative manager, as an example, may be authoritarian in crisis situations or in dealing with new, untrained employees. Authoritarian managers may reduce their degree of dominance in order to build effective work relationships.

A summary of primary leadership styles Woodward studied are depicted in Table 7.2. During the last few years management writers have developed other ways of classifying leadership actions. Some of these will be discussed later. Most organizational and leadership analysts use the basic styles shown in the table.

Fiedler and LPC

Fred Fiedler, like Woodward, is convinced that appropriate leadership style is dictated by the situation in an organization at a given time. When conditions change, so should management style. Like many other observers of management effectiveness, Fiedler recognizes that both people and the tasks they perform are the primary components of every work environment. Leaders must be concerned with both relationships and defining tasks.

Some leaders, Fiedler found, tended to be task-oriented while others were relationship-oriented. In an effort to identify leader orientation, he devised a preference test called the **least preferred co-worker (LPC) scale.**[11] People are asked to identify characteristics (pleasant or unpleasant; tense or relaxed; open or guarded; etc.) of people they least prefer as co-workers. **Task-oriented**

TABLE 7.2 ■ Summary of Leadership Styles

Authoritarian (autocratic)	Makes all significant decisions. Controls all actions. Often critical and demanding. Does not trust judgment and competence of others as much as their own. Sees their job as directing and that of others as doing.
Participative	Wants employees to be involved in decisions that affect their job. Often consults with employees on work problems. Views role as a facilitator, advisor, trainer, and motivator. Wants employees to succeed. Ties personal success to effectiveness of employees.
Permissive (laissez faire)	Sees role primarily as message carrier. Is essentially a nonleader. Wants employees to do what they think is correct. Tries not to be involved in employee problems at work. Exerts very little control and gives few directions. Believes employees should do what they think is correct.

people tend to see least preferred co-workers in a very negative perspective. Those who are **people-oriented** tend to recognize that even those who are not necessarily their favorite co-workers may have some positive behavioral and personality characteristics.

Those rating people positively are called high LPC leaders and those who rate people negatively are identified as low LPC leaders. Fiedler believes that in some situations, high LPC managers perform better and in others, low LPC leaders are more effective.

If a situation is moderately good, with few major problems but some degree of difficulty, people-oriented managers are usually more successful. When conditions are poor with many problems and frequent crises, an authoritarian, task-oriented leadership style is more effective. Fiedler states that as conditions become very calm and things are functioning without visible problems, an authoritarian, task-oriented style may also be appropriate to keep employees from becoming complacent with success.

Fiedler's most lasting contribution may be his identification of essential leadership characteristics. These are not personal traits, but are what Fiedler believes are the essential components of leading.

Leader-member relations are the most important leadership factor identified by Fred Fiedler.

1. **Leader-member relations.** Leader-member relations refer to the amount of loyalty, dependability, and support a leader receives from her or his group. Leaders who have strong group support as well as the support of higher-level managers do not have to rely on other sources of influence to be successful. This is the most important single element of what Fiedler terms *situational control*.

Task structure refers to the ability of leaders to define what needs to be done to achieve work objectives.

2. **Task structure.** In addition to relationships it is important for people to know what needs to be done. There should be a clear understanding of tasks involved in a job, goals to be accomplished, procedures, and organization. Good leaders are able to define task structure in terms understandable and acceptable to members of their team.

Position power is the amount of power a leader possesses as perceived by employees.

3. **Position power.** It is important that the leader be able to legitimately influence not only employees but other managers, both at the same and higher levels. Employees must recognize that the leader has the authority and degree of influence to make significant decisions, to evaluate performance, and to determine when change is necessary. Position power is the perception of power in the leader by members of the work team and is based to an extent on the support the leader receives from higher-level management.

Situational control is based on a combination of leader-member relations, position power, and task structure. Good leaders are perceived to have all three.

Situational control refers to the degree that a manager in her or his role as a leader is able to use leader-member relations, task structure, and position power to direct work activities toward achieving organizational goals. Supervisors who recognize the importance of leadership components as well as the importance of controlling conditions in their work unit are far more likely to succeed in their efforts than those who manage but do not lead. Factors influencing situational control are shown in Figure 7.3.

Fiedler and other contingency theorists have shown that *no one style of leadership is best for all situations*. They also point out that supervisors and other managers who can exert control over their work environment are far more successful in accomplishing organizational goals.

Path-Goal Theory

Path-goal theory defines the leader as a person who can define goals that lead to satisfaction for those that achieve the goals. It is based on expectancy principles.

Based largely on the work of Martin Evans and Robert House,[12] path-goal theory focuses more on the needs of group members than do other approaches to understanding leadership. In its simplest form it defines the leader as a person who can define goals that lead to satisfaction for those that achieve the goals. In such cases the leader defines the path or way that the goals can be achieved. In many ways it is similar to expectancy theory. Leaders show that effort to achieve can result in the satisfaction expected.

FIGURE 7.3 ■ Fiedler's Situational Control Factors for Contingency-Based Leadership

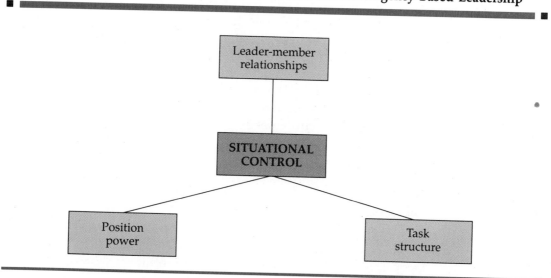

A major role of leaders is to define goals that are attractive to followers and then strengthen the expectation that the rewards of goal achievement can be attained. Leadership style in path-goal theory is defined somewhat more specifically than in other explanations of how leaders function.[13]

Directive leadership defines goals and tasks, set standards and priorities, and enforces rules, policies, and procedures.

1. **Directive leadership** defines goals and tasks; sets standards, schedules, and priorities; enforces rules, policies, and procedures; and exercises control over work activities.

Supportive leadership builds close working relationships, demonstrates concern for employee welfare and job satisfaction, and stresses cooperative work relationships.

2. **Supportive leadership** builds close working relationships, demonstrates concern for employee welfare and job satisfaction, and stresses cooperative work climates and good interpersonal relations.

3. **Participative leadership** encourages employees to be part of the decision-making process, consults with employees on work problems, uses employee ideas and gives credit to originator, and believes in empowering employees to make decisions affecting their jobs.

Achievement-oriented leadership sets challenging but achievable goals, has high expectations of self and others, and emphasizes competence and personal responsibility.

4. **Achievement-oriented leadership** has high expectations of self and employees, sets challenging but achievable goals, emphasizes excellence in all aspects of work, and works to increase employee competence, confidence, and feelings of personal responsibility.

As in contingency approaches, path-goal theory recognizes that situational factors influence the leadership style that is most effective. No single style is best for all conditions. Characteristics of employees, the job, and the manager's personality, as in interactive theory, determine the most effective approach. Complex tasks performed by well-trained, competent employees respond to both participative and achievement-oriented leaders. Employees faced with boring, repetitive, or stressful tasks often respond to supportive leadership, especially if they show strong affiliation needs. Directive leaders are more effective with employees who have strong security needs or who perceive management's role as task definers and rule enforcers. Figure 7.4 summarizes path-goal leadership styles.

■ FIRST-LINE MANAGERS AS LEADERS

A common complaint of many supervisors is their lack of power to make employees do what is needed. Rather than develop leadership skills, they rely on the legitimate authority that is part of their

FIGURE 7.4 ■ **Path-Goal Leadership Styles**

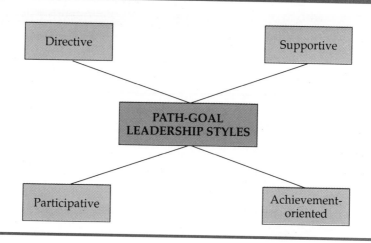

jobs. Pushing and threatening is not leading. Supervisors who recognize that they can be role models, pacesetters, people others can depend on for assistance when needed, and who recognize and support the efforts of employees will achieve many of their goals. Good managers recognize the need for continuous improvements. Small improvements in work activities every day can mean large improvements over time.

In work organizations those who directly supervise employees must show leadership skills in every activity that relates to their employees. Regardless of skills in planning, organizing work, analyzing and controlling activities, and defining tasks, being able to inspire enthusiasm, confidence, and competence as well as support for the goals of the organization requires leadership.

■ A LOOK BACKWARD AND FORWARD

Leadership theory is interesting but not useful unless it has applications in the workplace. Although there is a great diversity of theories, many of which are not covered here, they are similar enough that supervisors can utilize many of the approaches each suggests. Leadership skills can be learned, practiced, and perfected by people who are willing to accept responsibility for the actions of others, have strong beliefs in their abilities to get things accomplished, and who see developing as well as directing people as part of being complete managers. Their people skills and ability to define goals and control their work environment add leadership to the traditional role of managing. Some of the lessons from those who make the study of leadership their major work can be helpful.

1. **Managers with high expectations of themselves and others are more likely to achieve more than those who believe employees are basically lazy and work only for money.** As McGregor stated, the assumptions managers make about people are a key to job effectiveness. McGregor recognized that work is as natural as play in people's lives. Rather than "working for Friday," employees should see their jobs as an enriching experience.

   William Ouchi recognized that employees are not just hired hands. They are as essential to organizations as management is to leadership success, if not more so.

2. **Management style depends on conditions.** Managers who have the confidence and respect of employees are able to define goals and tasks, and who let people know what is expected build strongly supportive work climates. They are able to exert influence not only over their employees but over those to whom they report. Most importantly they are able to assess conditions and act to control them in ways to accomplish organizational goals. Effective supervisors can learn to behave in ways that are appropriate for the situation at any given time.

3. **Good leaders show others how to get things done.** In his short text based on personal notes, Maslow pointed out in his classic, *Eupsychian Management,* that baboons kept others in line by threatening, snarling, and punishing.[14] Chimpanzees led by teaching, showing adolescents how to best survive, and acting as protectors. Maslow stated that both styles work, but given a choice he would rather have a chimpanzee as boss rather than a baboon.

■ KEYS TO LEADERSHIP

In 1988 Kenneth Labich published the results of an extensive study of what successful executives felt contributed to high-commitment organizations. He quotes Harry Truman's famous statement, "Leadership is the ability to get other people to do what they don't want to do and like it." Not all definitions of leadership agree with Truman's. Labich focused on seven major keys to business leadership:[15]

1. **Trust your subordinates.** Mutual trust between employees and high-level executives is essential. Giving employees a voice in decision making is a fundamental part of building trust. James Burke of Johnson & Johnson, one of the most respected chief executive officers in the United States, is quoted as saying, "Leaders are developed by challenges." One of the most important challenges is obtaining the confidence and trust of employees.

2. **Develop a vision.** Employees like to know where the organization is going and why. Good leaders have a clear vision of where they are going, how they will get there, and what the role of their people will be. They also have the skills to communicate the vision to others and show them how it benefits everyone in the organization.

3. **Keep your cool.** In a crisis effective leaders don't let pressures make them ineffective. They continue to listen, analyze, decide, and act. An effective leadership skill is the ability to build a consensus on the correct courses of action.

4. **Encourage risks.** Effective leaders encourage employees to take risks and learn to accept errors. Good leaders set an example by taking chances and encourage lower-level managers and employees to do the same. Risk-taking requires that employees learn to take on responsibility and authority often reserved for higher-level managers.

5. **Be an expert.** Good managers, as Tom Peters is fond of saying, come dressed to play. They do their homework, know their products or services, and understand the characteristics of their business. First-line supervisors in their leadership roles must be able to identify problems, recognize needed actions, and be seen by employees as knowing what they are doing.

6. **Invite dissent.** One way of testing an idea is to invite others to critically evaluate its soundness. Effective leaders are not afraid of disagreement with their ideas. They are able to take their own ideas and combine them with those of members of their work team to build a consensus for action. Good decisions are often forged from input from many sources. A willingness to listen and use the ideas of others builds success. "Yes" people are not needed or wanted by effective leaders.

7. **Simplify.** Reports, recommendations, and data are often complex and difficult to explain. Good leaders are able to focus on

FIGURE 7.5 ■ Leadership at Work

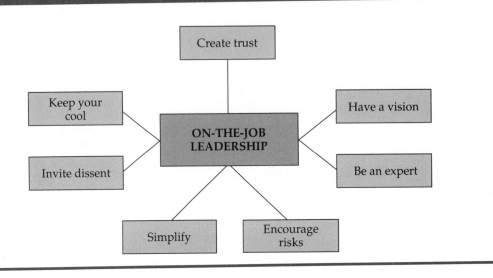

essentials and communicate needed actions in clear, understandable terms. They have the ability to lock in on the essential elements of information and data and recognize detail that can easily be left out of statements of action or change.

Figure 7.5 summarizes Labich's advice to managers.

Another characteristic of good leaders is their willingness to shake things up by instituting change if it is needed. They also prize personal integrity and their own sense of ethical worth. Leadership is difficult to teach, but a great deal can be learned by experience, judgment, and willingness to retain objectivity about one's personal strengths and potential limitations.

■ THINGS TO REMEMBER

   I. Leading and managing.

      A. Like many other terms, *leadership* has no universally accepted definition.

      B. Leaders are able to influence others.

      C. Leaders are able to define goals that others will support and work to achieve.

      D. There are several types of leaders including charismatic leaders, traditional leaders, emergent leaders, and appointed leaders.

E. Leaders may be either formal or informal.

II. Understanding leadership in organizations.

A. Those whose behavior serves as a model for others are known as *referents*.

B. Effective leaders are vital for the future of U.S. organizations.

III. Leadership theories.

A. McGregor stated that the assumptions managers make about people determine their management style.

B. Theory X describes traditional, strong-control, authoritarian management styles.

C. Theory Y describes managers who assume that employees want to work, like responsibility, and want to succeed.

D. William Ouchi extended Theory Y and named it *Theory Z*.

E. Interactive theories recognize that leadership depends on forces within managers, employees, and situations.

F. Contingency theory recognizes that as conditions change, management style should change.

G. Path-goal theory states that leaders define goals and show followers how to achieve those goals.

IV. Major leadership styles.

A. Authoritarian (autocratic) leaders believe in strong control.

B. Participative leaders work to involve employees in decisions.

C. Permissive (laissez faire) leaders abdicate decision making to followers.

V. Fiedler and LPC.

A. Fiedler believed that appropriate leadership style is determined by situational factors.

B. Leaders must have position power, good relations with followers, and an ability to define needed tasks.

VI. Path-goal theory.

A. Path-goal theory is closely tied to expectancy theories of motivation.

B. In path-goal theory leaders may be directive, participative, supportive, or permissive.

C. As in contingency theory, the most effective leadership style depends on the job, the employees, and the manager.

VII. First-line supervisors as leaders.

    A. Often first-line supervisors feel they lack the power to make necessary changes or to enforce rules.

    B. Pushing and threatening is not leading.

■ KEY TERMS

leadership

charismatic leaders

traditional leaders

emergent leaders

appointed leaders

referent

great man theory

trait theory

Theory X

Theory Y

Theory Z

Managerial Grid

impoverished management

country club managers

middle-of-the-road managers

task masters

team management

interactive theory

contingency theory

path-goal theory

authoritarian style

participative style

permissive style

least preferred co-worker (LPC) scale

task oriented leaders

people oriented leaders

leader-member relations

task structure

position power

situational control

directive leadership

supportive leadership

participative leadership

achievement-oriented leadership

■ DISCUSSION QUESTIONS

1. What type of leadership do you feel is most effective when dealing with untrained people just starting a new type of work? Explain your answer.

2. What is a potential weakness of charismatic leaders?

3. Why do most successful leaders stress the importance of being an expert as well as being a model for other members of their organizations?

4. Based on your own experience, give an example of an effective leader and describe what she or he did to become successful.

5. What styles of leadership do you think would be most effective for a group of technicians in a medical laboratory; a committee charged with improving communication within an organization; a group of manufacturer's representatives selling computer-based workstations to large corporations; a team of forest fire fighters?

▪ SELF-ASSESSMENT

Do you have what it takes to be a leader? If you have not had leadership experience, imagine you are in a work environment where you are being considered for promotion. Remember that a low number, 1, 2, or 3, indicates disagreement or a small amount. Numbers 4, 5, and 6 indicate agreement or a large amount. There may be more than one appropriate response for some items or questions.

1. Are you willing to take responsibility for being the spokesperson for a group when others are reluctant to do so?

   1   2   3   4   5   6

2. Studies show that participative leadership styles are the best.

   1   2   3   4   5   6

3. Controlling the actions of others is, in the long run, more important than spending time building confidence and trust.

   1   2   3   4   5   6

4. Effective leaders know that over a period of time, fear is a primary motivator in improving productivity and quality.

   1   2   3   4   5   6

5. Every manager should learn the leadership formula.

   1   2   3   4   5   6

6. In a crisis most employees want the manager to be decisive and to clearly communicate what is needed.

   1   2   3   4   5   6

7. Leaders who share power with their group or team members weaken their personal influence and lose the respect of their employees.

   1   2   3   4   5   6

8. Managers with high expectations of performance from their employees are less likely to be disappointed than those who have no expectations either positive or negative.

   1   2   3   4   5   6

9. Good leaders are more interested in achieving goals than how members of their group feel about them personally.

   1   2   3   4   5   6

10. It is important for leaders to recognize that there is one best style of leading in the same sense as there is one best way to do any particular job.

    1   2   3   4   5   6

■ SHORT CASES

It Always Hurts

Nadine Nystrom was a professional nurse for Health Underwriters Research Teams (HURT). HURT was a health service group sponsored by a number of related medical insurance companies that had pooled their resources to develop a facility for treatment and research on rare medical problems. They felt it was an effective effort to reduce constantly rising medical costs. Although she had been offered promotions, Nadine, who had a master's degree from a well-known medical college, saw her role as a member of a treatment/research team rather than as a leader.

Early in her employment with HURT Nadine received a set of X-ray photographs of a patient with a rare type of spinal tumor. She recognized immediately that the side-view pictures were missing and that the attending physician would need them. Rather than wait for the physician's review, Nadine rushed the patient back to the laboratory and supervised a new round of exposures.

During a conference the next day Nadine insistently voiced her opinion that a procedure needed to be established that would prevent omissions of needed laboratory information. Over the head of the chief of the X-ray laboratory, the procedure was adopted.

After the incident nurses who had problems involving patient care and information procedures would approach Nadine with their complaints. Nadine would investigate the problems and bring them to the attention of management during weekly conferences. Although some supervisors grew irritated with Nadine's knowledge of problems that they had failed to consider seriously, few denied she was wrong. Among nurses and technicians she became an unofficial spokesperson and was highly respected as a person willing to take personal risks of management disapproval in her pursuit of better-quality procedures and problem solutions.

1. What type of leader was Nadine? Describe her style according to theories presented in the text.

2. Is it possible to be an effective leader without formal authority? Give a real or imaginary example of how this can occur.

3. Do leaders seek followers or followers seek leaders? Explain your response.

Good Old Carl

Carl Washington was well liked, an effective and efficient employee, and was loyal to upper-level as well as his immediate management. When a vacancy occurred for a new executive housekeeper at HURT, Carl was a natural choice. He was well trained, certified by the National Administrative Housekeepers Association, and had received advanced training in cleaning and maintaining health care facilities. In a health care facility housekeeping is a vital function. Housekeeping departments are responsible for cleanliness, disposal of contaminated materials, and provision of needed housekeeping items throughout the facility. Technically Carl was both experienced and qualified.

His weekly reports on budget planning, inventory maintenance, equipment readiness, and emergency preparation showed that Carl was excellent as the new executive housekeeper. His employees liked him and many thought he was a perfect boss. If an employee needed time off from work, Carl would grant it. When employees made mistakes, they were excused. If someone was late for work, Carl would understand. Absences were rarely questioned. When employees fell behind in their work, Carl would pitch in and help get it completed. Everyone liked Carl.

When he was moved out of his position as executive housekeeper to that of administrative assistant to the chief of Plant Services, many of his employees were puzzled and felt he was being treated unfairly. Higher levels of management knew from complaints made by the medical staff, however, that too many housekeeping mistakes were being made, too many housekeeping employees were goofing off, and too many absences were being recorded. Even though Carl had been asked to run a tighter ship, he did not like correcting employees or telling them what to do. He felt they were experienced, trained people and should be left alone to do their jobs.

1. Was Carl a leader? Explain.

2. What did management fail to consider when selecting Carl for the job of executive housekeeper?

3. When is it necessary for leaders to be hard-nosed and authoritarian?

4. Who is respected more by employees? An achievement-oriented manager who sets challenging but achievable goals or one who concentrates on building a friendly work climate where the manager firmly believes that a happy worker is a good worker? Explain.

■ ENDNOTES

1. Adapted from Mark M. Colodny "Fortune People," December 3, 1990, p. 178.

2. Chad T. Lewis, Joseph Garcia, and Sarah M. Jobs, Managerial Skills in Organizations (Boston: Allyn & Bacon, 1990), p. 239.

3. Dan Costley and Ralph Todd, Human Relations in Organizations, 4th edition (St. Paul, Minn.: West Publishing Company, 1991), pp. 248–49.

4. Brian Dumaine, "Who Needs a Boss?" Fortune, May 7, 1990, pp. 52–60.

5. Ralph Stodgill and Bernard M. Bass, Bass and Stodgill's Handbook for Leadership, 3rd edition (New York: The Free Press, 1990).

6. Douglas McGregor, The Human Side of Enterprise (New York: McGraw-Hill, 1960).

7. William Ouchi, Theory Z: How American Business Can Meet the Japanese Challenge (Reading, Mass.: Addison-Wesley, 1981).

8. Robert R. Blake and Jane S. Mouton, The Managerial Grid (Houston: Gulf Publishing, 1964).

9. Robert Tannenbaum and Warren H. Schmidt, "How to Choose a Leadership Pattern," Harvard Business Review, May–June 1973, pp. 162–75.

10. Joan Woodward, Industrial Organization: Theory and Practice (London: Oxford University Press, 1965).

11. Fred E. Fiedler, Martin M. Chemers, and Linda Mahar, Improving Leadership Effectiveness (New York: John Wiley & Sons, 1976).

12. Martin Evans and Robert J. House, "Retrospective Comment," in The Great Writings in Management and Organizational Behavior, 2nd edition,

eds. L. E. Boone and D. D. Bowen (New York: Random House, 1987), pp. 354–64.

13. Adapted from Costley and Todd, *Human Relations*, p. 246.

14. A. H. Maslow, *Eupsychian Management* (Homewood: Richard D. Irwin, 1964).

15. Based on Kenneth Labich, "The Seven Keys to Business Leadership," *Fortune*, October 24, 1988, p. 58.

Chapter 8

Power, Status, and Politics

Objectives

Chapter 8 focuses on power, politics, and status in organizations, which are topics related to leadership discussed in Chapter 7. After studying the chapter, students will be able to

- Define and identify sources of power.
- Recognize and identify five major types of power.
- Distinguish between positive and negative politics.
- Characterize types of status and their role in organizations.
- Identify shared power and techniques for power enhancement.

Thought Starter

In a study of mid-sized city governments it was found that secretaries and administrative assistants of city managers and other officials often accumulate a significant amount of power. Since they handle most of the incoming telephone calls and answer routine questions, many callers relied on their information and advice rather than "bother the boss."[1] Lower-level managers would often attempt to cultivate the friendship of the secretaries and assistants in order to obtain inside information. Being in on things is important for ambitious people who work in the political climate of not only government but many other organizations.

Association with power leads to power. People who know or who are close to the boss are often perceived as having power. Their influence does not stem from either formal authority or responsibility but from being viewed by others as an extension of the power of people with whom they associate.

■ *"No single person,"* Matt Angus pointed out to Cheryl Sutton, *"can do everything by himself. The only reason we have managers is to plan, organize, direct, and control the efforts of others to accomplish predetermined goals. In a shoe store the goal is to sell shoes; in a computer assembly plant the goal is to make computers to meet customer needs."*

As a new supervisor, Cheryl listened carefully. "Just how do managers get others to do what needs to be done?" Her question caused Matt to hesitate but a brief second.

"Managers have power. They have the highest legitimate authority and greatest responsibility in their work unit. Employees recognize managers as being able to influence their job assignments, rate of pay, opportunity to learn and advance, and their feelings of self-worth. Managers also have influence because of their knowledge and expertise in analysis and decision making. In addition they are examples for others. Their attitudes and values are usually reflected in the attitudes and values of their employees. Power is the ability to influence others. Being able to influence others to achieve is one of the fundamental management skills and is frequently the most difficult to learn to use effectively." Matt smiled at Cheryl, "You'll do it, but it won't be easy."

■ POWER—INFLUENCING AND BEING INFLUENCED

Power is the ability to influence others.

Power is the ability to influence others. It is measured by the degree of influence. Historically power has been thought of largely in negative terms. Lord Acton's famous statement, in a letter to Bishop Creighton of England, that "power corrupts and absolute power corrupts absolutely" expresses the feelings of many people about power. While Acton's statement has a degree of appeal, it fails to recognize that power is necessary in nearly all aspects of life and especially in work organizations. Supervisors often complain that they do not have enough power. They are bound by personnel policies, union contracts, higher-level management edicts, and both federal and state law in performing their work. Some feel that there is little real corrective action that they can take when dealing with employee problems. They feel powerless or unable to adequately influence the actions of others. Part of their difficulty may be in understanding the way power is acquired and used.

Power—Where Does It Come from?

Power originates from many sources. Some power is formal, or granted. Other types of power are earned or are the result of a person's personality. Power is not always in people. It can be in a law, policy, contract, memorandum, or book. There is virtually no way that all of the sources of influence can be listed. Supervisors, however, are primarily concerned with influencing their employees and the managers to whom they report. To do this they use both formal and informal power sources.

Formal power is granted.

Formal power is an integral part of a position or assignment. It is based on the authority inherent in the job. Supervisors usually have the formal power to assign work, evaluate performance, schedule work, recommend hiring or firing, make decisions concerning work, and implement needed change. As they shift to higher levels of management, greater formal power is allocated to the position. Power is granted by higher-level management and is inherent in a position.

Informal power is earned.

Informal power stems from several sources. Assertive, ambitious people often are able to influence others simply by making and verbalizing decisions faster than others. Some people would rather let others decide. Others influence through their personal credibility and expertise. Charismatic personalities influence others because they are persuasive or have personal characteristics attractive to others. Simple physical attractiveness has been shown to be a source of influence. People often allow themselves to be influenced by those whom they find attractive. One way of influencing others, most of us recognize, is to allow them to influence us. Charismatic leaders are often dynamic, highly persuasive, and dedicated to ideals that appeal to their followers. Their power is highly personal and informal. It is not granted but developed by individuals who use such influence.

▪ OTHER TYPES OF POWER

Although it is difficult to classify all types of power in an organization, French and Raven identified five types often used by managers.[2] They were not meant to include every possible source of influence but to highlight major types of power used by managers.

Coercive power depends on the ability to threaten, punish, or affect an individual's self-esteem.

Coercive power. Like it or not, coercive power is inherent in every manager's job. If a manager can influence a person's performance appraisal, potential increase in pay, promotion, transfer, opportunity for training, and can legitimately reprimand for inadequate performance or rule violation, she or he is in a position to use fear as a form of influence. Coercive power is dependent on threats, punishment, withholding rewards, and even affecting a person's feelings of self-worth. Most managers use coercive power as little as they can. They recognize that it creates resentment, feelings of unfairness, and teaches people what not to do rather than motivate them to learn more and perform better. Coercive power is granted by the position. First-line managers who are dependent on coercion as a primary means of control will ultimately be seen as failures. They destroy employee confidence, trust, and willingness to do more than the minimum required by job descriptions or known standards. Employees of coercive managers may become concerned with getting even and engage in work-delaying activities or other types of minor sabotage. In the past the bull-of-the-woods approach to supervision was typical of many organizations. It still exists, to an extent. Most managers, fortunately, recognize that rule by threat points to their own inadequacies as leaders.

Reward power stems from the ability to praise, provide pay increases, grant special favors, and provide other rewards.

Reward power. Like coercive power, reward power is granted by the position. It is the power to approve, recognize good work, give preferred assignments, grant special requests, and recommend pay increases, promotions, or special training. In many ways reward and coercive power are similar. Both are inherent in a supervisor's job and withholding of rewards may seem to be coercive. Both coercive and reward power are limited. A supervisor may not, in many cases, be able to do more than recommend. Definitive action may require higher-level management approval.

Personnel policies and, in some cases, union contracts restrict much of what a supervisor can do. In many instances an employee may be paid at the top of their rate range and, other than cost-of-living increases, no additional money can be given to them. If promotional and training opportunities are also limited, there is little that a supervisor can do except provide recognition and approval for performance that exceeds normally expected standards. Although it has strong advantages when compared to coercive power, reward power is always limited.

Expert power is dependent on the perceived degree of expertise an individual possesses. Expert power is not exclusively vested in leaders or managers.

Expert power. Good managers know that expertise is one of the strongest sources of influence. Supervisors who constantly learn not only the technical aspects of their field but are aware of organizational changes, policy applications, and ways of solving complex problems are often considered to be experts. Employees who perceive their managers as having knowledge and the ability to use it to improve work develop both confidence in their managers and respect for their leadership.

Unlike coercive and reward power, expert power is earned. Over time employees who increase their own knowledge and skills also gain expertise and may be seen as experts in a particular area. Managers often rely on the expertise of employees in decision making, problem solving, and planning. Effective supervisors try to use the expertise of their employees as much as is practical. This does not diminish their perceptions of the manager as being an expert in managing and a reliable source of information and assistance. If, however, a supervisor is viewed as lacking management or technical expertise, employees will respond only to the supervisor's coercive or reward power. Managers who are not seen as fully competent receive little respect or loyalty from their employees.

Supervisors have greater sources of information than employees, deal with more conceptual problems, and consult with higher levels of management on a daily basis. If they prepare themselves well, keep their knowledge current, and make careful, systematic decisions, they will be perceived as experts by employees.

Referent power originates out of respect, admiration, perceived credibility, and behavior that others admire.

Referent power. Like expertise, referent power is also earned rather than granted. It is difficult to define and more difficult to describe. Referent power is the influence based on trustworthiness, credibility, belief in an individual's integrity, and their treatment of others. Good referents serve as models for others. They are viewed as having characteristics that others admire. Many chief executive officers are good referents for their employees. They are perceived as believing in themselves and their organization. Referents stress the importance of team approaches and recognize that no one person can do everything. They see their roles as facilitating, encouraging, and at times insisting on actions that help both the organization and its employees.

Supervisors can also become referents by the way they treat others, their willingness to defend their work group, and their honesty and candor when dealing with difficult problems. Good referents have a strong sense of what is ethically correct as well as right for their organization. They give and receive trust, loyalty, and confidence.

Advertising agencies often use well-known actors who have had roles in television or movie productions that portrayed honesty, competence, credibility, and willingness to stand by principles in the face of strong opposition. Since their roles build a highly positive image, the actors are used as referents in advertising.

In work organizations referents cannot pretend. They must be what others want and expect in their managers.

Legitimate power is the power of the position. It comes with the job.

Legitimate power. In military organizations it is said that "When you salute, you are not saluting the person. You are saluting the rank." Supervisors are part of management by virtue of their job title. They are no longer one of the girls or one of the boys. Their responsibilities, duties, and frame of reference at work is different from those of employees. This does not mean that they no longer can be friends with others or are entirely separate. It does imply, however, that a psychological distance separates them from their employees. Both employees and supervisors recognize that different job requirements require different types of skills and knowledge. Employees tend to be concerned with their immediate task and the benefits of work in terms of social interaction, pay, and benefits. They also know that recognition, approval, and their own future are dependent to an extent on their supervisor. Psychological distance is a reality. Legitimate power is granted and includes both reward and coercive powers. It also includes rights and responsibilities of management.

Figure 8.1 shows that managers use all types of power. Expert and referent power are the most important over a long period of time.

FIGURE 8.1 ■ French and Raven's Types of Management Power

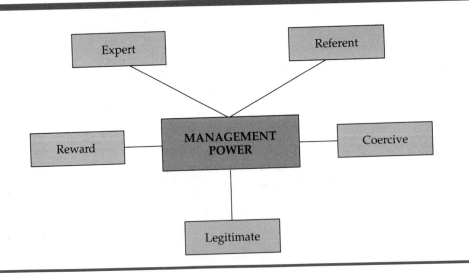

■ POWER AND ACHIEVEMENT

Research indicates that most top managers believe that over time referent and expert power are the only two types of power that have any real meaning.[3] First-line managers in their roles as supervisors also use legitimate power as a source of influence, especially during their initial months of management experience.

Personal power is used to enhance feelings of control, manipulate others, and position a person for further personal gain.

David McClelland points out that there are two categories of power that managers may adopt.[4] **Personal power** is used to enhance feelings of control, manipulate others, and position a person for further personal gain. It is essentially self-serving and contributes little to organizational achievement. **Institutional power** focuses on achievement. Managers who use institutional power believe firmly that power must be shared. Achievement-oriented managers recognize that empowering others also increases their own ability to influence others to succeed. Managers who utilize personal power are concerned with themselves first and others next. Achievement-oriented managers know that their own success is dependent on the success of those who report to them. Managers are judged by the effectiveness and efficiency of their employees. A manager who builds a sense of responsibility and independence in employees is making the most effective use of power.

Institutional power focuses on achievement, shared power, and is used to further the welfare of the organization and its employees and the leader's ability to use influence positively.

Keys to Positive Power

Robert Lefton is president of Psychological Associates, a St. Louis consulting firm. In a syndicated article Lefton points out that a person's speech, political skills, and recognition of the shifting needs in organizations all contribute to establishing and maintaining influence.[5] Table 8.1 summarizes some of Lefton's major points.

■ POLITICS IN ORGANIZATIONS

When people are chosen for promotion, past performance is often given first priority. The best employees, it is assumed, will make the best first-line managers. While some excellent employees are successful as managers, others are not. In an office, as an example, the most proficient clerical employee, who is excellent in computer in-put, who understands paperwork systems, and who excels in report writing, may not be the best candidate for promotion to office manager. In addition to technical skills those who make the

TABLE 8.1 ■ Lefton's Keys to Positive Power

Credibility	Expertise, trustworthiness, being well liked, and being seen as dependable all contribute to perceptions of credibility by others. A technique for gaining credibility is the willingness to argue against yourself.
Candor	Sincerity, honesty, being analytical rather than critical, avoiding criticism of others in the organization, and building a reputation for confidentiality in personal discussions all contribute to a sense of candor.
Political smartness	Empowering those of lower rank, encouraging others to build organizational skills, becoming part of networks made up of influential members of the organization, and building association with others perceived as having power are politically smart actions.

Politics is the acquisition, maintenance, and use of power.

vital shift from employee to manager must also have management and leadership skills and understand how organizations function. A knowledge of organizational politics is not only useful, but necessary.

Politics can be defined as the acquisition, maintenance, and use of power. Many supervisors and some employees attempt to use flattery, compliments, and providing favors to gain favor with those who they feel can affect their future. This obsequious behavior is most often rejected and seen as unwanted, but on occasion works. It is self-serving and often hides the true feelings of those who use it as a ploy to gain influence.

Nearly 40 years ago William Whyte recognized that every organization has a number of people who virtually dedicate their lives to its success.[6] Their place of work becomes the most important element of their existence. These **company people** are viewed as loyal, dedicated, and highly responsive to management. While they often rise to upper middle-management and higher-level administrative positions, they rarely become top managers. Rather than originate new ideas, company people are willing to follow, without challenge, the dictates of those above them. They are essentially "yes" people. Disagreement with upper levels of management, they feel, is almost sinful. Company people know the organization, where real power lies, and understand the nuances of change. They are valuable employees but are sometimes mistrusted because of their highly political orientation. When volunteers for committee assignments are needed, company people will usually be the first to offer service. Approval of higher levels of management is their strongest motivator.

Company people are loyal, dedicated to the organization, and responsive to higher levels of management.

Positive politics, as Lefton suggested, can stem from several sources. Strong support of employees increases perceptions of power by upper levels of management. Although a supervisor may not be a company person in the classical sense, building associations with higher levels of management is one of the most effective ways of gaining power. In large organizations people are often viewed as being on a track. Some tracks are fast, others are slow, and a number of people are no-track.

Fast-track employees work for recognition and promotion. Their political smartness and ability usually identifies them as promotable.

Fast-track employees. Well before they are selected for advancement or, in some instances, to join an organization, bright, ambitious people plan their future. They know that excellence in their performance and political smartness are vital ingredients to future advancement. Not only do they work effectively at their immediate assignments, but they deliberately seek out others who, like themselves, are knowledgeable and advancing in the organization. By volunteering for committees, special assignments, and willingness to make presentations, they are viewed by upper levels of management as those who will advance rapidly through the organization.

Fast-track employees work for recognition and promotion. A characteristic of fast-track employees is their belief in their own ability to perform at high levels. This self-confidence is apparent to others. Usually they deliver what they promise.

Fast-trackers are sensitive to where power lies and are willing to accept risks of failure to rise in an organization. Their political awareness gives them an advantage over others. From a pragmatic perspective fast-track people are usually more dedicated to their profession than to an organization. They want to excel in their chosen field. If opportunities seem limited they will move to other organizations, frequently with promotion or higher levels of compensation.

Slow-track employees are often competent and hardworking but advance slowly because of lack of involvement in organizational politics.

Slow-track employees. In some ways the backbone or real support of organizations is in those people who perform their work competently, do not cause trouble, and are supportive of the organization. They are not necessarily politically active, although they may be interested in their organization's changes, successes, and failures. They usually have a working knowledge of how the organization functions and are able to effectively use that knowledge to make their jobs more effective.

Unlike their fast-track counterparts, slow-track people are often viewed as competent and supportive in their existing jobs.

Promotions to management positions may come slowly because they are seen as needed in their present assignments. Their predictable, competent behavior is appreciated but their lack of practical politics tends to lock them into their existing positions.

No-track employees are satisfied without additional responsibility. They have few ambitions beyond their immediate assignments.

No-track employees. Most employees rise only in their existing job classification or general class of work. Although they may be competent workers, the organization is important only for its economic benefits and security. It provides money, security, and enjoyment of leisure. Management responsibility and power are neither attractive nor desirable. This does not mean they do not like their jobs or their organization. No-track employees may be dependable and reasonably satisfied with their jobs but have little desire to contribute more than their technical skills and required effort.

Occasionally no-track employees are promoted to supervisory positions. When this occurs, they are frequently ill-at-ease in their new assignment, identify their roles as closer to that of employees rather than managers, and often voluntarily return to employee status. While some no-trackers may learn to enjoy their supervisory role, few rise to higher levels. Added responsibility, ambition to gain greater influence, and taking greater personal risks have little appeal.

Negative and Positive Politics

Negative politics involve games playing, manipulation, and deception.

In an effort to gain influence, some people resort to games playing or **negative politics**. Common games include exaggerating small errors or personal traits of anyone seen as a competitor, spreading negative rumors about others, deliberately failing to provide needed information, conveniently forgetting to tell someone about an important meeting, or distorting a statement or report made by another person. Negative politics include any action that is self-serving and is at the expense of others.

If both Susan and Joe are competing for the same promotion, Joe may report to the manager's administrative assistant or directly to the boss that "I think Sue should be given full consideration for the job. It is my understanding that she no longer drinks before reporting for work every morning." Planting the seeds of doubt about a person's character or performance is one of the most destructive types of negative politics.

Some people, unfortunately, seem to make negative politics work. In many instances they discredit themselves rather than their opponents. Rumor spreaders, people who belittle or demean others or betray confidence, often alienate themselves. Experienced managers learn to identify games players and will stop their actions by challenging the validity of innuendos and half-truths.

Positive politics are based on common sense. Show up, show up on time, and show up dressed to play is a hallmark of positive politics. It means attracting the attention of higher levels of management without game playing.

Positive politics consist of actions that increase personal credibility without attacks on others or the organization. Supervisors who are interested in increasing their influence to be able to perform more effectively use positive politics. Power that they gain is used to help not only themselves but their employees and the organization. Some types of positive politics are inherent in good work habits. A few types of positive politics are briefly summarized below.

1. **Show up. Show up on time. Show up dressed to play.** Tom Peters is credited with giving the advice that one of the best ways to gain recognition and a reputation for responsibility is to always show up for meetings, appointments, and discussions. Showing up on time is equally important. Don't keep others waiting, especially those in positions of influence. Showing up dressed to play means being prepared and ready to participate, act, and implement. These same rules apply to work. Finish it, finish it on time, and finish it correctly.

2. **Look and act the part.** Image consultants often tell their clients to dress one level above their current position. People who exhibit concern for their appearance, speech, and manners send a positive image to others. Studies have shown that people who look and act successful are more likely to be successful. While dress and communication skills alone will not guarantee greater influence, they provide an advantage that may be lacking in others.

3. **Seek information and advice from the right people.** Learn who the real experts are in an organization. Be willing to discuss specific issues with them while not bypassing your present manager. Most people like to talk. Learn to listen and don't be reluctant to ask questions. It's a good way of making yourself known.

4. **Volunteer carefully.** Organizations are like mazes. It is difficult to work through all of their turns that lead in wrong directions. There is a saying that being maze-smart is more than the road to survival; it is the road to success. Maze-smartness means understanding how the organization works and who controls each of its components.

5. **Don't bite the hand that feeds you. It may bite back.** Disgruntled employees and supervisors who are openly critical of their management often find themselves in an unwanted situation. They lose the trust of both their employees and their managers. When this occurs they find that their career halts. Criticism is acceptable if it is open, warranted, and under the right conditions. If it is misplaced or unfounded, it can result in personal disaster. It is dumb to bite the hand that feeds you. It not only can but will bite back.

6. **Be an expert—avoid "it ain't my responsibility."** Politically insensitive and organizationally inept employees and supervisors are unwilling to learn how organizations really work. Rather than support the organization, they concentrate solely on their immediate jobs. If asked for information regarding another function, they will reply, "It's not my responsibility." Rather than learn, they lend truth to the saying, "Given a choice between ignorance and knowledge and between helpfulness and lack of concern, most people will choose ignorance and lack of concern."

7. **Support your people and your organization.** A primary indicator of good managers is their willingness to defend the actions of their employees and their organization. If attacked or criticized by outsiders, they listen, gather data, and are willing to correct mistakes. They also will not tolerate unfounded and unjust attacks on their employees. Political bright managers defend their employees but may take strong corrective action if there is evidence that performance has been inadequate.

8. **Stick to your personal values and ethics.** Korn-Ferry is one of the largest and most respected management search firms in the United States. Their research indicates that the most valuable tool of good managers who realize the political sensitivity of their actions is to always preserve their personal integrity. They adhere to their personal values of right and wrong and have a strong sense of what is ethical and what is not. It is important to be seen as a straight arrow who does not deviate from principles of fairness, honesty, and commitment to customers, employees, the organization, and those whom the organization may affect.

9. **Sycophants are often losers.** English writers at the beginning of the 20th century often wrote about people who tried to achieve power through excessive flattery, compliments, and

willingness to do anything that those in power asked. These **sycophants,** as they were called, were universally disliked and held in suspicion by others. Weak leaders often tolerated them as ego bolsterers and supporters. They were, in fact, self-serving seekers of power through association with power.

It is fortunate that most managers in the 1990s realize that flattery is often the worst comment on ability. Those who use excessive compliments and flattery are often losers in their attempts to gain influence and association with power.

10. **Keep your cool.** The inability to evaluate and logically counter criticism, even when unjust, blame for actions over which there was no control, and attacks by uninformed managers and others who deal with the organization is politically devastating. Rather than react emotionally, politically smart managers evaluate, gather and present facts, correct errors if they occur, and analyze rather than criticize.

Other practical politics include getting to know influential people outside the organization as well as those within. Joining professional associations, participating in client meetings, and attending special management seminars are all possible ways of meeting others. Although many are reluctant to do so, volunteering for participation in community service projects supported by a supervisor's organization builds positive images both inside and outside of their organizations.

Hard work, dedication, and loyalty are essential characteristics of those who rise in organizations. These characteristics alone, however, are not adequate. Knowledge of the organization, its power sources, people who make decisions, and expertise, not only in a single function but in the total system, are parts of both pragmatic and positive politics.

■ STATUS

Status is the rank given to others because of their perceived worth to a group, degree of influence, or position.

In every group some people are held in greater esteem than others. Although several managers may have the same apparent rank on an organization chart, one or two will be considered more influential than others. Their formal authority and power is equal to that of other managers but their status is greater. **Status** is defined as the rank given to others because of their perceived worth to a group, degree of influence, or position. **Formal status** is position-related. Those who have titles such as chief, president,

Formal status is granted by a job title or position.

vice president, director, or manager are perceived as having greater status than others in an organization. **Informal status** is based on the esteem people have for those who, while of equal rank to others, seem to have greater influence and be able to accomplish more for the benefit of the group or organization. Supervisors who are perceived as being able to effectively represent their work units, perceive problems and define solutions, implement corrective actions, and show a willingness to take personal risks are often ranked higher than others who are less assertive and more narrow in their perspective of their responsibilities.

Informal status is granted for the ability to accomplish more for the benefit of the group.

In addition to formal and informal status there is both general and specific status. **General status** is the rank given to people because of their occupations, perceived degree of influence, or social worth. In his classic text, *Humankind*, Peter Farb points out that "in all societies, people rate highest the occupations that involve power, material rewards, the authority to deal with crises, and service to the social group."[7] Nearly all societies stratify themselves in some ways. This is also true in work organizations. Skilled occupations are ranked higher than semiskilled ones. Management and professional jobs are ranked higher than nonmanagement, and top management is ranked highest.

General status is granted to people because of their perceived social worth or their job title.

Specific status is given to people for their skill or knowledge in a specific activity. In restaurants, as an example, senior waiters or waitresses are usually given higher rank because of their knowledge and skills. Rather than seek advice or information from supervisors, less experienced employees view these senior people as their primary sources for guidance and problem solving. This occurs even though their pay may be identical. Clerical workers faced with a statistical or analytical problem will contact those who have the knowledge and skills needed to help solve the problem before asking their immediate managers. Specific status is usually based on skills and knowledge in a type of work. Since they are perceived as being the best at what they do, they are ranked higher than others.

Specific status is based on an individual's skill or knowledge in a particular area of work.

Supervisors with special skills and knowledge are often contacted by other supervisors and higher levels of management for information and advice. Their status is based on expertise that gives them both greater influence and a higher ranking than their peers.

Status Symbols, Distributive Justice, and Status Congruence

During the 1920s and 1930s when the factories of the United States employed large numbers of people for manual assembly (most of which is now automated), it became important to identify a person's rank in an organization. In an era that saw few women in management assignments, a person promoted to a first-line management job changed clothes. Instead of the typical blue, open-necked shirt, the new supervisor would wear a white shirt and tie, much the same as those employees in administrative and higher-level management positions. Out of this practice the terms *blue-collar* and *white-collar workers* were born. White shirts and dress blouses became symbols of management and office employees. Blue shirts and work clothes were symbols of factory and maintenance employees. These became important status symbols.

A status symbol may be defined as any object, sign, adornment, or amount of space that identifies a person's rank or position.

A **status symbol** may be defined as any object, sign, adornment, or amount of allocated space that identifies a person's rank or position. There are literally thousands of status symbols. Type of dress, manner of speech, location and size of office, type of equipment, special privileges, and amount of education are all recognizable status symbols. People perceive status by symbols attached to a person as exemplified in Figure 8.2.

In many organizations there have been attempts to reduce these symbols in order to minimize social distance. Symbols, however, still persist. In our society distributive justice is still important. **Distributive justice** means that those who have greater responsibility, take greater risks, and exert more influence should

FIGURE 8.2 ■ Management Status Symbols

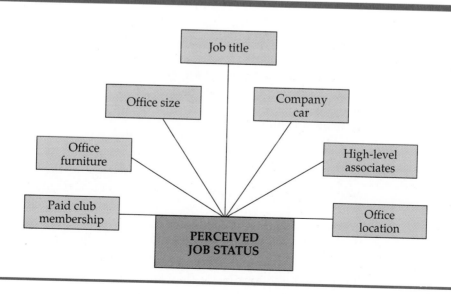

Distributive justice
means that people expect
those who contribute
more and take greater
risks to have more.

also have greater rewards. We normally expect the president of an organization to have a larger office, better location, and nicer furniture than those of lesser rank. Lack of these symbols may, in some instances, diminish perceptions of status and power. We want those we view as powerful to act the part and have the symbols to go with their rank. This matching of symbols and rank is called **status congruence.** Supervisors usually have few symbols that distinguish them from other employees. In some instances, an identification badge, a private telephone, or a new location are provided. Such symbols should not be rejected.

Status congruence refers
to the degree that status
symbols are appropriate
for a person's rank.

In 1988 the Chinese military restored symbols that distinguished officers from noncommissioned officers and noncommissioned from enlisted personnel. They found that without the symbols, which had been removed during the infamous Cultural Revolution, perceived authority was often absent. People needed to know who had legitimate power and who did not. Although some people feel that symbols of power are both unnecessary and unwanted, they are an ingrained part of our culture and should be carefully used as indicators of earned rank.

Supervisors, the first line of management, must also realize that their employees do not want them to be "one of the girls" or "one of the boys." They want them to be leaders and managers.

■ REALITIES OF WORK LIFE

Success is the ability to
define and achieve goals.

Many people define success in terms of money and the things that money can acquire. Our definition is in some ways similar. **Success** is the ability to define and achieve goals. It means knowing what you want and then being able to get it. In work organizations ability and hard work go a long way toward achieving the personal ambitions of many people. We know, however, that hard work is not enough. It is important that those involved project an image of competence, ability, and being in on the organization's network of information systems.

Experienced supervisors realize that hard work and competence are necessary components for advancement. They should also understand that hard work, knowledge of the organization, and the ability to use its channels are not enough to develop their full potential. Credibility, effective use of positive politics, learning to share power, and countering negative politics are all important. In today's environment success in organizations requires increasing knowledge, sensitivity to change, and the use of positive power and politics.

■ SHARING POWER, REDUCING STATUS, APPLYING POSITIVE POLITICS

Industry Magazine, in its October 15, 1990 issue, listed the Hewlett-Packard plant in Roseville, California, as having one of the best quality records in the computer industry. Failure rates of its series 3000 computers have decreased eightfold. Much of the plant's success can be attributed to Larry Mitchell, general manager.

Mitchell's management style reflects current trends in the use of power, reduction of status, and application of positive politics. "I rarely wear a tie at work," he states, "and like to think of myself as a coach—a person who teaches, inspires, and provides the tools necessary for employees to do their jobs." In northern California, Hewlett-Packard has a reputation for being one of the best places to work, not necessarily for its pay, but for its attitude toward employees. "We work for the best company and it makes us feel like the best in the business," one employee stated. Her feelings are reflected in statements by many others. Mitchell's approach to management is reflected in the actions of other managers at lower levels. Hewlett-Packard supervisors stress teamwork, encouragement, and personal responsibility. Employees make most job decisions and use their supervisor as a resource for information and assistance rather than as a disciplinarian and order giver. Consultive styles of management minimize the necessity for actions that employees may view as negative.[8]

Empowering others often means teaching and encouraging them to become members of an organization rather than be hired hands. In the best organizations employees don't park their brains at the door and pick them up on the way out, as those in less effectively managed organizations do. Supervisors may find that some employees, trained in more traditionally managed environments, initially resent the idea of sharing in decision making. They do not want to be responsible for most of the aspects of work that they are accustomed to their supervisor performing. In dealing with reluctant employees, supervisors must be patient and keep in mind the lessons of **kaizen:** *improve a little in every aspect of work each day.* Continuous improvement is easily assimilated by organizations. It is important to realize that many little changes over a long period of time are usually more effective than occasional major changes that require difficult periods of adaptation, frustration, and resentment. Once the benefits of having real job power are accepted, few employees ever want to return to older, high-control systems.

Kaizen means continuous improvement.

Managers like Larry Mitchell of Hewlett-Packard realize that the more power one has, the less one should use. Reducing status barriers by being highly visible, listening carefully, and developing an open communication style pays off in trust, confidence, and support of organizational goals.

■ THINGS TO REMEMBER

I. Power—Influencing and being influenced.

    A. Power is the ability to influence others.

    B. Formal power is granted; informal power stems from perceptions of others.

II. Types of power.

    A. French and Raven classified power into five types: coercive, reward, expert, referent, and legitimate.

    B. Current authorities believe that expert and referent power are the most long-lasting and effective.

    C. Personal power is essentially self-serving.

    D. Institutional power is used for achievement of both personal and organizational goals.

III. Keys to positive power—Credibility, candor, political smartness.

IV. Politics in organizations.

    A. Politics involves the acquisition, maintenance and use of power.

    B. Company people are viewed as loyal, dedicated, and responsive to management.

    C. Fast-track people are slated for rapid advancement; slow-track people advance to lower-level mid-management assignments; no-track employees typically remain in their original job assignment.

    D. Negative politics involve playing games; positive politics involve commonsense behavior that meets standards of excellence.

V. Status.

    A. Status is defined as the rank people assign to others.

    B. Formal status is granted by position; informal status is earned by actions on behalf of others.

    C. General status is associated with occupation or perceived degree of social worth.

    D. Specific status is granted to people because of their perceived expertise.

    E. Status symbols are adornments that reflect position.

    F. Distributive justice is the belief that those who have greater responsibility should have greater rewards.

    G. Status congruence means that symbols should fit the position.

VI. Realities of work life.

    A. Success depends on the ability to define and achieve goals.

    B. Politics are a reality of organizational life.

VII. Sharing power, reducing status, and positive politics.

    A. Managers in the best-run organizations view themselves as coaches, teachers, and providers of tools that enable employees to do their jobs.

    B. Empowering employees accustomed to managers making all decisions requires patience and consideration by supervisors.

    C. *Kaizen* means continuous improvement over a long period of time.

■ KEY TERMS

power	**informal power**
formal power	**coercive power**

reward power	**negative politics**
expert power	**positive politics**
referent power	**sycophants**
legitimate power	**status**
personal power	**formal status**
institutional power	**informal status**
credibility	**general status**
candor	**specific status**
political smartness	**status symbols**
politics	**distributive justice**
company people	**status congruence**
fast-track employees	**success**
slow-track employees	***kaizen***
no-track employees	

■ DISCUSSION QUESTIONS

1. Where does most first-line management power originate in large organizations?
2. How do you feel about the statement, "If in doubt, use flattery"?
3. Give an example of organizational politics, positive or negative, that you have encountered.
4. In what ways are status, politics, and power related?
5. To what extent are money and success related?

■ SELF-ASSESSMENT

If you disagree with or have a negative response to the questions and statements listed below concerning power and politics, answer with a 1, 2, or 3. A response of 4, 5, or 6 indicates agreement. Remember, some items may have more than one appropriate response.

1. Reward power and coercive power are closely related.

    1   2   3   4   5   6

2. Legitimate power is the power of the office or position rather than the power of the person.

    1   2   3   4   5   6

3. Legitimate power is probably more useful at lower levels than higher levels of management.

   1   2   3   4   5   6

4. Expert power is more useful to nonmanagers than it is to managers.

   1   2   3   4   5   6

5. Referent power is more tangible and easily identified than other forms of power.

   1   2   3   4   5   6

6. Nonmanagement employees with special expertise may exert power over their supervisors under specific conditions.

   1   2   3   4   5   6

7. Politics in large organizations always harm some while benefiting others.

   1   2   3   4   5   6

8. Flattery, compliments, and agreement are the foundation of effective political action in organizations.

   1   2   3   4   5   6

9. One way of increasing power is to empower others to make decisions related to their jobs.

   1   2   3   4   5   6

10. Supervisors need not be concerned with status symbols if, on an organization chart, they have equal power and authority with other supervisors.

   1   2   3   4   5   6

■ SHORT CASES

The Size of Things

When Nancy Rybody was promoted to supervisor of Employee Welfare, she found herself managing people with whom she had been a co-worker for the past three years. They were her friends, sources of information, and often sources of support. She was now faced with directing their activities. She knew that most of the 14 people in her group were pleased with her promotion. Approximately four senior employees, who had been with the organization an average of 10 years, acted as if she was the new kid on the block and did not deserve being promoted.

One of the more outspoken of the four seniors, Hank Samuelson, openly remarked, "Nancy is a nice girl, but she won't make it as a manager. She just doesn't have the experience or know-how." Nancy's first reaction to Hank's statement, when she was told of it, was anger. She wanted to go to her immediate manager and obtain permission to get Hank transferred. Her manager was a senior employee, however, who had hired Hank as well as the other three senior employees during the initial start-up of the company 12 years ago. "It would be politically stupid," Nancy thought, "to get Hank transferred just because he thinks he knows more than I do." She was now faced with the problem of preventing Hank from becoming an informal leader whose political connections could harm her status and degree of influence in her new position.

1. What actions can Nancy take to reduce Hank's influence on others in the work unit?

2. Explain the political ramifications of Nancy's relationships with the four dissenters.

3. How can Nancy best establish her status as leader of her work unit?

The Old Shell Game

Grant Rice was an expert at organizational games that enhanced his position as supervisor of Commercial Purchasing for Southern Utilities' Department of Environment (SUDE). His work team was responsible for the review and revision of procedures for handling hazardous materials used in electrical transformers, power converters, and related environmentally sensitive practices. To get his job done and impress others who felt his function was not only nonessential, but entirely useless, Grant issued memoranda relating to environmental concerns, made presentations at many meetings regarding SUDE's functions, and became a member and officer of several local environmental groups in the community. He had testified before the state legislature's Committee for Industrial Environmental Protection, during which he strongly supported the efforts of SUDE to make Southern Utilities a model for industrial environmental protection both within the state and perhaps nationally.

Many of Grant's critics saw him as a politically motivated but ineffective supervisor. They were shocked, however, when he was promoted over the head of his immediate manager, Lila Atkinson, to become corporate director of Environmental Actions and Development.

1. Why was Grant seen as political in his job as leader of environmental concerns for Southern Utilities?

2. What political tactics did Hank use to obtain the degree of influence that he apparently commanded?

3. Explain Grant's use of politics as well as expertise in obtaining his advancement from supervisor to director of Environmental Actions and Development.

■ ENDNOTES

1. Adapted from an unpublished study by Gordon McPherson, "Politics at City Hall," California State Department of Transportation, November 1990.

2. John R. French, Jr., and Bertram Raven, *The Bases of Social Power in Group Dynamics*, (New York: Harper & Row, 1969), pp. 259–60.

3. Thomas Steward, "New Ways to Exercise Power," *Fortune*, November 6, 1989, p. 54.

4. David McClelland and D. H. Burnham, "Power Is the Great Motivator," *Harvard Business Review*, March–April 1976.

5. Robert Lefton, "Rank Doesn't Always Determine Power," *Los Angeles Times*, March 25, 1989, sec. G.

6. W. H. Whyte, Jr., *The Organization Man* (New York: Simon & Schuster, 1956).

7. Peter Farb, *Humankind* (Boston: Houghton Mifflin, 1978), p. 373.

8. Adapted from an article by Larry Hicks, "Carrying the Load," *Sacramento Bee*, November 27, 1990, sec. C.

Part IV

Tools of Supervision—Enhancing First-Line Management

■ First-line supervisors, and all other levels of management as well, must have many types of specialized skills. Some of these involve human resource management, the personnel side of management. Other skills are concerned with utilizing time effectively and efficiently, being cost-effective, and training. These affect a host of skills and knowledge associated with areas of specialization. Purchasing directors must know both procedures and ways of handling customers and vendors. Financial managers find that budgeting, financial planning, and many other accounting functions stretch their expertise. Other managers in sales, manufacturing, marketing, distribution, plant services, and so on must all have a wide variety of specialized skills and knowledge.

In these next three chapters we look at three essential functions common to most supervisors. They must know how to utilize their time wisely, control costs in their sections or departments, and recognize the importance of constant training in a world of continuous change. Although there are many other management skills that supervisors must have, these three are of particular interest.

9

Taking Charge of Time and Change

Objectives

In a constantly changing work environment, management of time is an essential supervisory skill. There is usually more work to be accomplished than time available to complete it. In this chapter readers will learn to

- Develop awareness of how time is spent.
- Develop priority lists to assist in managing available time.
- Recognize common time wasters.
- Avoid principal time traps.
- Identify types of change and their impact on organizations.
- Link change management and time management for improvement of both effectiveness and efficiency.

Thought Starter

One of the most remarkable changes brought about by a combination of technology with new approaches to management has been dramatically shortened response times to customer requirements. Processes that once took months can now often be done in a few days. General Electric, Xerox, Brunswick, Ford Motor Company, Procter & Gamble, Hewlett-Packard, and many other companies have benefited from development of better time management techniques and improved quality.[1]

In a rapidly changing and complex environment, both time and change management are vital management skills. This chapter explores ways organizations and individuals can recognize change, use time effectively, and manage time to meet the demands of work life in a new era.

■ *Although she tried to with every bit of her energy, Shawn Eagleton felt she could never accomplish all of the work necessary to make her section the best for Altamont Production Enterprises. In many ways Shawn was considered by her 12 employees as the most eligible person for promotion to chief of Information Services. Shawn's feelings were different. "How can a person like me even be considered?" she thought. "I've never played the political game, never commented on my own work, and, most of all, never had time to do many of the things that need accomplishing." Like many dedicated supervisors, Shawn was faced with constant pressures of time. In an environment where conditions, organizational demands, customer requirements, and technology were constantly changing, her skills in managing time became more critical. She wondered what could be done to utilize her time more effectively.*

■ THE TIME CRUNCH

There are only 24 hours in each day, 60 minutes in each hour, and 60 seconds in each minute. Not one bit can be packaged, bottled, or preserved. Regardless of what efforts are made, time relentlessly speeds along. Many people are painfully aware of a **time crunch**. There never seems to be enough time to accomplish everything that needs to be done.

Although we all know that it is a limited resource, everyone wastes time. Some of us waste time due to our own inefficiency or reluctance to do what we know needs doing. We also waste time because conditions force us into useless activities. Waiting for availability of a copy machine, attending a meeting that has little real value, listening to unwanted visitors, dealing with computer and other equipment breakdowns, and being put on hold on a telephone are just a few of the countless, irritating time wasters.

Supervisors may not always realize the impact of improved time management for themselves and their employees. If one person reduces the time required to perform job duties by six minutes per hour, the results will be an improved efficiency of 208 hours per year—five full weeks plus one day of work time! Ten employees averaging the same six-minute-per-hour time improvement in performing their jobs would achieve a full work year in improved time utilization. If these same 10 employees earned an average of 12 dollars each for every hour worked, the total cost benefits would be almost $25,000 in the first year. Even a modest two- or three-minute improvement can have significant results.

Time and Money

In 1938 the **Fair Labor Standards Act** was enacted by the Congress of the United States. It included provisions known as the *Wage and Hour Law*. Several important definitions were established that profoundly influenced the way time is considered in a work environment. Although supervisors need not be accountants or payroll experts, it is helpful if they have a basic understanding of the way the law affects their daily activities as well as the policies of their organization. Four provisions of the act are of special importance.

*Standard work times are defined by the **Fair Labor Standards Act** of 1938.*

1. Any time worked in excess of 40 hours in a week must be paid at a rate not less than one and one half times the base hourly rate. If hourly paid employees work more than 40 hours per week, they must, under the law, receive overtime pay. A **standard workweek** is defined as a 168-hour period beginning at some time decided by organizational policy. Usually the period begins at midnight Sunday (in some organizations Saturday) and ends at midnight the following Sunday (or Saturday). Any time worked in excess of 40 hours in a standard workweek must be paid at a minimum of one and one half times the base hourly rate. Some state laws and federal contracts with private employers require that overtime be paid for work in excess of eight hours in a day. A **standard workday**, as defined by the law, is a 24-hour period beginning with the employee's regular starting time.

*A **standard workweek** consists of 168 hours beginning at a time defined by organizational policy, usually midnight Saturday or Sunday and ending at midnight the following Saturday or Sunday.*

*A **standard workday** is a 24 hour period beginning at an employee's regular shift start time.*

   Supervisors who require employees to work in excess of times defined by law increase their labor costs by 50 percent. An employee whose regular pay is $10 per hour must be paid $15 per hour for all excess time worked.

Standard work year is defined as 2,080 hours.

2. A **standard work year**, as defined by the law, is 2,080 hours. This is easily computed by multiplying 52 weeks per year by 40 **straight-time** hours per week. Of less importance, but still a useful figure to know, is that a **standard work month** is 173.33 hours (2,080 hours divided by 12 months). Vacation and sick leave benefits are sometimes accrued on a monthly basis.

Standard work months are 173.33 hours.

3. Another important provision of the law is the concept of minimum wage. Congress determines the national minimum wage and no employee may be paid less, with certain exceptions for trainees and specific part-time activities usually performed by minors, such as delivering newspapers, babysitting, lawn mowing, or other minor jobs.

Exempt employees are
those for whom the wage
and hour provisions of
the Fair Labor Standards
Act do not apply. These
are usually management,
professional, and
high-level administrative
members of an
organization paid for
level of responsibility
rather than time worked.

Nonexempt employees
are covered by the wage
and hour provisions of
the Fair Labor Standards
Act. They hold hourly
paid jobs and must be
paid overtime rates for
work in excess of 40
hours per week or, in
some cases, eight hours
per day.

Pay for time worked
consists of pay for actual
hours worked.

Pay for time not
worked includes
vacations, holidays, break
periods, and sick-leave
time taken.

4. Not all jobs are covered by the law. Managers, outside sales-people, and professionals (e.g., lawyers, physicians, engineers, professors, etc.) are exempt. Employees who are exempt from the law need not be paid overtime. Most supervisors work more hours than their employees and few earn any extra money for doing so. In some instances hourly employees who regularly work overtime may have gross earnings in excess of those of their first-line manager. Accountants recognize that organizations may have both **exempt** and **nonexempt employees.**

Although overtime is considered to be **premium pay** by employees, it is actually a penalty for managers. Supervisors who, through inefficiency, must work employees excess hours find their labor costs excessive. Premium pay, however, is only a small part of the total time crunch.

Know What Time Costs

In work organizations there are two major types of hourly wages: **pay for time worked** and **pay for time not worked**. Most supervisors understand pay for time worked reasonably well. An employee earns an agreed-to rate of pay for each hour worked. Although seldom realized by employees, their compensation also includes costs of benefits, such as medical benefits, that are not seen as part of a person's gross pay before mandatory deductions. Pay for time not worked directly affects the cost per hour of work, exclusive of benefits. Some pay for time not worked is based on organizational policy and cannot be directly controlled by supervisors. Even more time not worked but paid, however, is the result of poor time management.

Based on estimates for an average employee who has been with an organization for five years, policy-mandated pay for time not worked includes

1. **Vacation**—Three weeks or 120 hours each year.

2. **Holidays**—Ten days or 80 hours per year.

3. **Break periods**—Two 15-minute periods each day or 125 hours each year.

4. **Sick leave**—Approximately six days or 48 hours taken each year, even though more is earned.

5. **Miscellaneous**—Bereavement, jury duty, and other special leave not included in the estimate.

Total legitimate time paid but not worked equals approximately 373 hours per year.

Although an employee may be paid for 2,080 hours, the legitimate number of hours worked is only 1,707. An employee who is paid $10 per hour is actually being paid $12.19 for time worked. This does not include time paid but not worked that can be effectively reduced by good time management. Some examples are

Start-up time is the nonwork-related time employees often use when they first report for work.

1. **Start-up time.** Many if not most employees on reporting to work have a cup of coffee, read a paper, visit with other employees, and prepare themselves mentally for the day's work. Although it may vary, it is fair to estimate start-up time at a minimum of 15 minutes per day for many employees. Production operations probably have less start-up time delay than office, sales, or other service activities.

Shut-down time is the time taken by employees to end their workday. It shortens the work period.

2. **Shut-down time.** Near the end of a workday employees start putting papers away, joking with other employees, and preparing to leave work. Like start-up time, shut-down time is approximately 15 minutes per day.

3. **Before and after lunch.** Many employees go through somewhat shorter start-up and shut-down times before and after lunch breaks. A reasonable estimate for these mini start-up and shut-down times is an additional 15 minutes per day.

If these estimates are reasonable, we can reduce our 1,707 hours of legitimate effort by an additional 128 hours. An employee being paid $10 per hour, exclusive of the costs of benefits, is actually being paid $13.17 for time worked. This does not, unfortunately, include other types of major time wasters for both employees and supervisors. Table 9.1 lists a few major ways time is consumed inefficiently in nearly every place of work.

■ ESCAPING THE TIME CRUNCH

Knowledge of typical time wasters is not helpful unless people know techniques for minimizing them. Techniques that work are not difficult to learn and in most cases are self-evident but unused. We know what to do but fail to take needed actions. In the 1970s and 1980s Alec Mackenzie,[2] Alan Laken,[3] F. D. Barrett,[4] and Robert D. Rutherford[5] made time management a popular subject. Their books have been republished many times and can be found in most bookstores that carry management texts. More recent publications on time management add very little to the recommendations of those made over 20 years ago.

All effective time management requires effort and establishing new habits. It's just too easy to put off dull, uninteresting tasks, spend unnecessary time on the telephone, be drawn into interesting meetings that are not directly job-related, and socialize on the job unless a deliberate effort is made and old habits change.

Management by exception is an effective time management technique. More time is spent on problem areas that those that are operating without difficulty.

Many managers have found the principle of **management by exception** to be a useful time management tool. Managers who concentrate on specific areas that require special attention rather than spread their efforts equally over all activities make effective use of their time. They save time by helping to solve problems immediately rather than finding themselves in a time bind because of misplaced priorities. Management by exception means giving higher priorities to problem areas than to those being performed satisfactorily.

It must also be remembered that as time passes, change takes place. Priorities must be constantly reordered, schedules must be made and kept, and unanticipated problems and events are certain to occur. Part of effective time management is recognizing that managing time is also managing change.

Getting Started in Time Management

Here are some steps that can be taken that will lead, with self-discipline, to better usage of available time.

Analyze time expenditures. One of the simplest ways to find out how time is being spent is to keep a **time log**. This can be done

TABLE 9.1 ■ Typical Time Wasters

1. Visiting	Some employees and a few supervisors spend an unwarranted amount of time socializing with others. While some nonwork communication is normal and expected, it frequently abuses time needed for work-related activities.
2. Meetings	Conferences and staff meetings are essential forms of communication in most organizations. All too frequently they include people who have little to contribute or very little interest in the topics discussed. Some organizations are meeting-happy. Supervisors and employees are requested to attend meetings on issues that could be better handled by a smaller group of well-informed people directly concerned with the problem.
3. Paperwork	Although paperwork in some organizations has been replaced by computer-based mailboxes, databases, and message centers, it is still an important time problem for many supervisors. Memoranda, letters, reports, schedules, information bulletins, professional journals, advertisements, policy interpretations, new procedures, and a variety of other types of paper are daily time consumers for supervisors.
4. Telephone	Some supervisors spend up to 25 percent of their communication time on the telephone with other department managers, various specialists, their immediate bosses, vendors, customers, and other members of their organization. Both employees and supervisors can be guilty of using the telephone to visit or conduct personal business that has no relationship to their work.
5. Waiting	Delays can result from many causes: equipment breakdowns, late supplies, lack of information, waiting in line to use copiers, obtaining supplies, power outages, unmade decisions, and uncertain priorities.
6. Procrastination	There is little doubt that putting things off or delaying the start of an essential activity is the greatest time problem of all. Most people who rationalize by saying they did not have enough time procrastinated in getting work started or finished.
7. Vacillation	Reluctance to make a choice between alternatives is, like procrastination, a major thief of productive time. In some instances an incorrect decision is better than no decision.
8. Special interests	Supervisors often have pet projects that they enjoy. As a result they may neglect others. Sometimes interests outside of work may consume time needed for essential organizational projects.
9. Professional development	Reading, professional seminars, training, and other educational activities are necessary. They should not, however, become an all-consuming activity that prevents first-line managers from effectively doing their job.

*Maintaining a **time log** that represents actual time spent on daily activities is an effective technique to analyze personal time utilization.*

easily and is an essential starting point in time management. Most people are familiar with day planners or personal schedules. These are usually to-do lists written on a calendar, back of an envelope, or, in some instances, on prepared forms. Time logs start with a blank form or sheet of paper. At the beginning and end of any activity, a record is made of the time started and the time finished. An easy method is to prepare a simple form similar to the one shown in Table 9.2.

For the log to be useful, activities must be recorded as specifically and as accurately as possible. Above all it must be honest. Telephone calls, idle conversation, reading (including newspapers and magazines), time spent at lunch, meetings, paperwork, report preparation and analysis, and all other activities are included on the log.

While estimates and guesstimates may be useful in planning, they should not be included on the log. Both omit useful details.

TABLE 9.2 ■ Time Log

Date:	
Time	*Activity*
8:00–8:30	
8:30–9:00	
9:00–9:30	
9:30–10:00	
10:00–10:30	
10:30–11:00	
11:00–11:30	
11:30–12:00	
12:00–12:30	
12:30–1:00	
1:00–1:30	
1:30–2:00	
2:00–2:30	
2 :30–3:00	
3:00–3:30	
3:30–4:00	
4:00–4:30	
4:30–5:00	

An **estimate** is the projected length of time required to perform a task or activity based on knowledge and experience. **Guesstimates** are approximations of time required for new activities where there is little or no experience. Neither is helpful in making an analysis of actual time usage.

*An **estimate** is the projected time, based on knowledge and experience, required to do a job.*

After a daily log has been made for a minimum of three days, an evaluation is made to determine where time has been both spent and misspent. Logs that include all of the activities actually performed rather than large generalized blocks (e.g., paperwork and meetings) help identify areas where improvement is needed. An important part of the evaluation process is to determine how much time is allocated to accomplishing major work goals compared to the amount of time spent on incidental activities. After the analysis has been completed, it is helpful to make a short written summary of ways time utilization can be improved.

***Guesstimates** are approximations of time required when there is little or no experience in performing the tasks.*

Plan forward. Many supervisors believe that it is impossible to predict what is going to happen. They agree that time means change and feel most change is unpredictable. Managers who are well organized, however, take two essential planning steps. At the end of each day they develop a **priority list** of activities to be accomplished the next day. Based on the priorities, schedules are prepared for starting and completing each of the priority items. Andrew Carnegie, one of the most successful steel executives of the early 1900s, attributed much of his success to keeping a notepad on a table near his bed so ideas could be written and priorities rearranged any time of the day or night. He constantly scheduled and rescheduled work to be sure that high priority items were completed. Carnegie also believed that it was helpful to get those things he liked least done first unless there were other overriding priorities. In the years since Carnegie revealed his methods of managing his time, successful managers have used similar techniques.

Priority lists rank tasks in order of importance and define those that must be completed first.

Priority lists are not difficult to make. Supervisors know what is important and what must be done. If a plan is made using a simple form like the time log, tasks are more likely to be accomplished. Daily to-do lists scheduled by priority are extremely useful. Some activities are time-limited and often have high priorities. Reports that must be accomplished by a specific deadline, letters that must be mailed before a specific time, and preparations for meetings are just a few examples. It is mandatory that first-line managers recognize the difference between what is needed and what may be desirable. Necessary activities must be accomplished first. Those things that may be helpful or nice have a lower priority even though they are projects the supervisor would like to have completed. Since management is often plagued with interruptions, some items on the to-do list may not get completed. Any carryover should, ideally, be low-priority items. A pocket diary, planning calendar, or pad of blank paper can be used for both prioritizing and scheduling activities. Effective supervisors base priorities on work goals rather than on their personal preferences.

Get work started, and completed. Started work is a much stronger motivator than unstarted work. One of the best cures for procrastination is to get work started. When successful managers have an idea or concept that needs accomplishing, they do it. Doing it is much better than thinking of ways to get around to it. "One of these days I'll get around to it" usually means that it will never get accomplished. Once started, it is far more likely to be completed.

William Edwards Deming's first principle of total quality management is to "create a constancy of purpose for improvement of product and service."[6] By this Deming means that once a person has set the goal of improvement in all of their activities, they should not deviate from that goal. Priorities and schedules are not enough. Work must be initiated and completed.

Combine and eliminate activities. In one company a minimum of six separate documents were required before a simple purchase could be made. They included a purchase request, a budget authorization, a shipping and receiving notification document, an inspection control document to ensure that received purchases met specifications, in many instances a request for bid, a bid award notification, and finally a purchase order. Most of these documents required multiple approvals. A frustrated supervisor devised and, with effort, received approval for a simple, multiple distribution form that combined all of the steps except the request for bid and bid award. Form preparation and approval time were reduced by almost 75 percent. Further refinement in procedures eliminated the need for a separate notification of inspection and budget authorization, except for purchases in excess of those contained in annually approved budgets. Changes in procedures can eliminate many steps. Organizations with suggestion systems that work well know the value of constantly seeking ways to eliminate unneeded duplication of effort and to combine operations when possible.

Take time to save time. Planning, training, consulting with employees on procedural changes, analyzing data, and examining time usage are all time-consuming processes. They can also help eliminate many useless time wasters. Careful planning that minimizes duplication of effort, combines and eliminates activities, refines procedures, or involves retraining people or installing new equipment takes time. In the long run it can also result in accomplishing more tasks efficiently. Time management has as its goal *working smarter, not harder.*

Delegate, delegate, delegate. Supervisors have a tendency to do work they like but that could be easily delegated to others. Some first-line managers regularly perform excessive hours of basic clerical work that can be easily delegated to others. Supervisors seldom think they have more work than they can handle. For those who delegate, do continuous planning, develop realistic and effective priorities, and do not procrastinate or vacillate, time always seems available. Necessary tasks are completed on or before the required time. Less-effective supervisors find themselves working longer and longer hours, doing increasing amounts of work, and still not completing all of the activities that they have scheduled for themselves.

Recognize time management as a continuous process. It is very easy to slip into a comfortable routine with an orderly list of planned activities that rarely changes. Regular times for certain types of work are useful and often a good time management practice. Conditions in all organizations change, sometimes rapidly. Experienced managers know that set routines must be changed as conditions change. Good time management is a continuous process. Every day managers should examine work processes and develop methods for improving them both in the length of time necessary for their completion and the quality of their performance.

Paperwork sorting and paperwork reading. F. Mary Knowles[7] states that typical supervisors spend approximately a third of their time alone. Reports, memoranda, data analysis, budget and schedule preparation, as well as reading letters and memoranda occupy most of their alone time. It is nearly all paperwork-related. She also states that time spent with employees ranges from 25 to 30 percent of the total workday and is decreasing due to other demands. Effective first-line managers recognize that paperwork can be divided into three major categories:

1. Paperwork that requires action.

2. Paperwork that contains useful information but does not require response.

3. Junk mail.

It usually does not take very long to recognize the correct category in which paperwork should be placed. Action paperwork goes into one file folder, informational paperwork is put in another folder, and junk mail is very briefly reviewed and discarded. In "paperless" offices where most information is transmitted by computer networks, the same rules apply. Action and informational items are filed and junk is deleted. After sorting, action and information paperwork is prioritized and a special time is scheduled each day for both reviewing informational paperwork and completing reports, letters, memoranda, and other action-oriented items.

FIGURE 9.1 ■ Escaping the Time Crunch

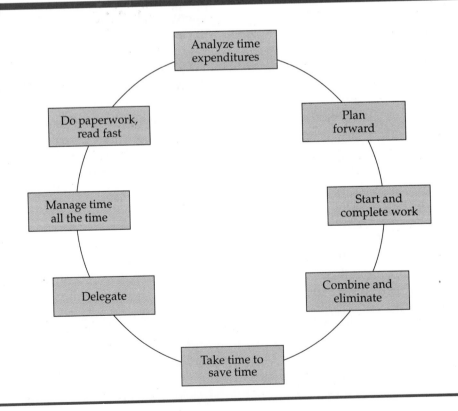

Supervisors who allocate time each day—usually about two to two and one half hours— for reviewing and completing paperwork find that they have few real paperwork problems. There are exceptions when long reports requiring extensive research are needed. If a first-line manager reads less than 600 words per minute, she or he should consider some type of reading training. Adult programs in local high schools, community colleges, and learning centers offer reading improvement at modest costs. *Fast readers forget less than slow readers.* Learning to read rapidly and accurately has many advantages. Common methods for escaping the time crunch are shown in Figure 9.1.

Ergonomics means designing equipment and facilities to fit their users' needs.

In December of 1990, San Francisco became the first city in the country to mandate ergonomic requirements for videodisplay terminals (VDTs).[8] **Ergonomics** is not a new science but it has received little public attention. It means matching equipment and methods to people. Computer terminal operators in San Francisco will have specially designed chairs, adjustable desks, and glare screens on their terminals. All are measures to make work less tiresome and to minimize health problems associated with long hours in front of a VDT screen. Comfortable, healthy employees take less time to perform tasks than those with constant complaints about working conditions.

Time has always been a philosophical and practical puzzle for most people. In work organizations it is useful to remember some of the points in Table 9.3.

■ CHANGE AND CHANGE MANAGEMENT

Time and change are inseparable. Managing time is also managing change. Managing change always involves managing time. In order to understand the impact of change in work organizations, it is important to understand both change characteristics

TABLE 9.3 ■ All about Time

- Most of what is called *cost* is the price of time. Time is an economic resource.
- Time cannot be expanded, contracted, recovered, or replaced.
- The flow of time is one-way: into the future. It cannot be reversed.
- Change takes place in time. It can be counted in seconds, minutes, hours, months, and years.
- Change is continuous, inevitable, and unstoppable.

and types of change. Both are important concepts for first-line managers.

As change occurs, it has several characteristics. Change occurs at different **rates.** Some change, such as introduction of new computers and computer software, variation in gasoline prices, and weather, occur very rapidly. Other changes occur more slowly. Geological formations, such as mountains and deserts, change at almost imperceptible rates. In work organizations most change takes place at a moderate rate. Change is generally introduced a step at a time. Personal computers, once unknown, are now a primary tool. Their introduction in most places of work occurred over a period of several years. Occasionally, when reorganization occurs or an organization restructures its basic mission, change occurs rapidly and dramatically.

Change rate refers to the speed at which change takes place. Some change is very rapid, other slow, and some is almost imperceptible.

Change also has direction. In many instances **change direction** is most apparent by increases or decreases in some part of life such as job status, salary, or relations with others. Direction of change may be up, down, or highly variable. Trend analysis is a method for predicting how changes taking place now will impact the future. Costs and wages, when plotted over a long period of time, have been moving higher. In the computer field, however, the cost for each unit of information processed has steadily declined. Moderately priced computers today can perform faster, more accurately, and have greater capacity than those costing millions of dollars in the recent past.

Change direction refers to increases or decreases in magnitude, capacity, costs, or other characteristics.

Another characteristic of change is its **magnitude** or size. Some changes are very dramatic. When a company merges with another, it affects every aspect of both organizations. Large changes are relatively rare. Most change is incremental, which means that it is done a step at a time rather than all at once. Supervisors, when faced with change, must learn to evaluate its magnitude. People can usually accept and adapt to small changes far better than to major shifts in policies, procedures, organizational realignment, or major changes in management. Planned change involves making small continuous steps toward improvement rather than radically different ways of operating. An exception is when a new organization is formed or when management must take extraordinary efforts to ensure a competitive position in the future.

Magnitude of change describes the extent, size, or impact of change.

Any change creates other changes. **Diffusion,** sometimes known as the *ripple* or *domino effect,* is an additional change characteristic. A simple act, such as reassigning an employee to different duties, can affect the perceptions and feelings of other

Change diffusion is the extent that one change spreads and creates other changes.

employees. It may also either increase or decrease productivity and quality. Changes in procedures, methods of scheduling, policies, equipment, or even a form can have effects far greater than planned. In one large aerospace company, policies allowed employees, in the event of a layoff, to bump or displace employees with less seniority, including those in lower classifications. When lack of work caused a reduction in product testing, final test technicians displaced component test mechanics who, in turn, bumped lower-grade mechanics, custodians, and finally cafeteria dishwashers. Because of a reduction of forces in the test facilities, a dishwasher found himself out of work.

■ TYPES OF CHANGE

There are many types of changes. Some of those most obvious in work environments are technological change, organizational change, social change, and economic change. Each occurs regardless of the first-line manager's preferences.

Technological Change

Technological change relates to increasing sophistication of equipment and in particular the use of electronics, lasers, genetic engineering, and other technologies that alter both work and personal life.

There is little doubt that **technological change** impacted the 1980s to a greater degree than any other decade in the history of humankind. It is very likely that these changes will continue well into the foreseeable future. What was once a curiosity is now a necessity. Knowledge workers have replaced employees with routine clerical and mechanical jobs. Personal computers moved from being a curiosity to becoming a necessity. Electronic banking developed into an accepted reality, worldwide communication networks, biotechnology, sophisticated applications of lasers, advanced diagnostic techniques in medicine, and many other technologies saw their greatest advance.

Managers have learned that technological change is often feared and resisted by employees. People do not want to be replaced by machines. They also learned that once new technology is in place, employees readily adapt and become dependent on its advantages. While technological change has eliminated many jobs, it has also created many.

As technology has become more widespread, it has also created problems. **Electronic sweatshops** are relatively common. People work with computers to handle customer complaints, place and track orders, route shipments, and even control manufacturing processes. Often their efforts are monitored by the same equipment they are using. Each second away from a terminal is recorded, lunch breaks are timed, response time to customers are reported to supervisors, and errors are highlighted. In some instances employees feel their lives are being controlled by machines. First-line managers must learn to use computer-based information not as controls or whips, but as keys to motivating employees and helping them to feel successful in their work.

Organizational Change

Organizational change is any change in an organization, such as personnel shifts, structural realignment, policies alteration, or redefinition of objectives.

Every organization experiences change. Changes in management, equipment, methods, procedures, policies, and even organization structure are common. Often such change has profound impact on both employees and first-line managers. In organizations where new changes are introduced before people can fully adapt to existing conditions, apathy, resentment, and reduction of effort are common. Lack of stability and continuity in organizations can be powerful demotivating forces. As with technological change, incremental step-by-step change on a continuous basis is a far better approach than periodic, blockbuster changes that upset the work routines of all members of the organization.

Social Change

Social change is characterized by shifts in the values and life-styles of society in general.

From time to time there are major shifts in life-styles and values in a society. One of the phenomena of the past 20 years in the United States has been the declining importance of strong nuclear family units. A consequence has been a shift in values away from the traditional close-knit, interdependent family units of the past. Another value shift has been the increase of materialistic goals of many young people with minimal regard for the welfare of others. Societal values vary greatly. In the United States, with its multiethnic, multiracial work forces and hundreds of special interest groups, there are few uniform values. Difficulty occurs when management has very traditional beliefs about what is important to people and employees think and feel differently. Not all gaps are based on age, although the so-called age gap seems to be a reality. Different life-styles, beliefs, attitudes, and values also create major social differences.

Economic and Political Change

Economic and political change are types of social change that profoundly affect the way organizations operate. Economic conditions influence marketing strategies, and politics either add or ease government regulatory requirements.

Organizations are also affected by economic and political change. Reductions and increases in the number of employees in an organization are the result of **economic change**. As market conditions improve, so do opportunities for both personal and organizational development. Some managers attempt to expand their organizations too rapidly during periods of economic prosperity and find they do not have the trained personnel necessary to make expansion successful. Like management of other types of change, step-at-a-time, continuous economic development of an organization is preferable to sudden, explosive growth.

Political change also impacts work. Changes in defense requirements, trading relations with other countries, and laws affecting specific types of work all affect people and their jobs. Figure 9.2 depicts major types of change within an organization that impact performance.

▪ CHANGE MANAGEMENT

In his 1987 *Thriving on Chaos,*[9] Tom Peters points out that in order for organizations to survive in this last decade of the 20th century, they must have **proactive** management (see Chapter 2). Rather than let unguided change occur, managers must anticipate and plan for change. Managed change requires two basic actions. Managers must first develop a sensitivity to change before it creates a crisis in their organization. They must also learn to recognize when change is needed. A useful approach to change management is to use the three basic management questions:

1. Where are we now?
2. Where do we want to be?
3. How do we get there?

Change for change's sake has little value. Managing change that will benefit the organization in accomplishing its goals or even in establishing new goals is a fundamental management activity. Since change and time are inseparable parts of each other, managing one also involves managing the other. Once objectives (i.e. Where do we want to be?) have been established, the change management process begins. First-line managers must view one of

FIGURE 9.2   Major Types of Change Impacting Organizational Performance

their roles as **change agents.** A change agent is an individual who both defines needed change and implements actions to make it a reality.

Realities of Managing Change

Successful managers use several simple principles to make change an orderly and acceptable process.

1. People both seek and resist change simultaneously. If change has apparent benefits, it is far more likely to be accepted and supported than change with unknown or potentially negative outcomes.

2. People tend to accept change if they are involved in the change process. If a procedure is to be changed, have the people who will be most directly affected review the proposed changes and make changes of their own.

3. Change in which people are not involved will not receive either support or approval unless it has highly apparent benefits.

4. Group decisions regarding change have a higher degree of acceptance than those unilaterally made by managers. If the group members are knowledgeable and well prepared, their decisions are likely to be better than individual decisions. Poorly prepared groups make poor decisions regarding change and change implementation.

5. Change should, if at all feasible, be introduced over a period of time in small steps that allow everyone affected to learn and adjust to new methods. Large, sudden change is usually difficult to understand, adjust to rapidly, or be implemented without substantial resistance by those affected.

Effective managers enthusiastically support needed change and involve their employees in making transitions as pleasant and painless as they can.

Involving People in Problems at Work

Nearly all texts, including this one, recommend involving employees in problems at work. How do supervisors involve people? Several methods usually work.

1. **Form employee focus groups** or task forces to identify, research, and solve specific work problems. Supervisors act as facilitators for the group by encouraging participation, encouraging members to select the group leader, providing a meeting place, and periodically discussing findings and recommendations. For such groups to be successful, their recommendations, if feasible, must be implemented.

2. **Individual consultation** is another technique. Rather than giving employees solutions, the supervisor encourages individual employees to identify work problems and develop solutions. In such cases the supervisor acts as a consultant, trainer, and information provider.

3. **Delegation of increased authority and responsibility** to both groups, if there is a high degree of interdependence, and individuals is also effective. Some employees are reluctant to assume additional responsibility if they have worked in systems where little thinking was encouraged or required. It is important in such cases to make very small but continuous changes rather than implement new responsibilities in large blocks.

4. Develop the belief that a supervisor's primary job is that of a **developer of people** who encourages people to take charge of their own jobs. Good supervisors do not view their jobs as rule enforcers, keep-them-in-line whip crackers, or manipulators. Their role is one of training, encouraging, and being a model for employees. They are highly visible, accessible, considerate, and listen more than they talk.

As employees learn to control their own work, they become less dependent on their first-line management for solutions. They also feel more confident, competent, and usually are more supportive of their supervisor than those who have less control or are more dependent. One way for managers to gain influence is to encourage employees to take charge of their jobs. This may require them to make decisions formerly made by their first-line manager. Effective supervisors train employees to be managers as well as workers.

▪ TIME AND CHANGE

In a work environment nothing is constant. Time flows relentlessly on and with every passing second, change of some kind occurs. Managers at all levels must learn to effectively manage both time and change. They are the inevitable conditions of the universe and are inescapable. As time passes, all things change: people, organizations, and all of the forces that make them what they are. We must learn to deal with them both for our own welfare as well as for that of others.

▪ THINGS TO REMEMBER

  I. The time crunch.

    A. Time cannot be saved, slowed, or altered.

    B. Small daily time reductions can mean large yearly reductions.

  II. Time and money.

    A. According to the Fair Labor Standards Act a standard work year is 2,080 hours; a standard workweek is 168 hours; a standard workday is 24 hours.

    B. Another provision of the Act states that work in excess of 40 hours in a week must be paid at one and one half times the base rate.

III. What time costs.

    A. Pay for time worked is based on a standard work year.

    B. Most employees receive about 375 hours per year in pay for authorized time not worked.

    C. Hourly paid employees are guaranteed overtime pay for work in excess of 40 hours per week. Salaried employees are paid for level of responsibility rather than time at work.

    D. Start-up time, shut-down time, waiting, and equipment failures are examples of time not worked but paid.

IV. Escaping the time crunch.

    A. Effective time management requires effort and establishing new habits.

    B. Priorities must be established, schedules must be made and kept.

    C. Utilizing the principle of management by exception helps manage time effectively.

V. Time management.

    A. A first step in time management is to analyze time expenditures.

    B. Time logs should not include estimates.

    C. Analysis of time spent is made based on time log data.

    D. Proactive management attempts to anticipate change and prevent crisis management.

VI. Change and change management.

    A. Managing time is also managing change.

    B. Rate of change varies greatly from one set of conditions to another.

    C. Change has direction.

    D. Change magnitude refers to the amount or size of a change.

    E. Diffusion occurs when a change in one place has effects over a wide area.

VII. Types of change.

    A. Technological change.

    B. Organizational change.

    C. Social change.

    D. Economic and political change.

VIII. Realities of managing change.

    A. People both seek and resist change simultaneously.

    B. People tend to accept change they have helped create.

    C. Group decisions regarding change have a higher degree of acceptance than decisions unilaterally made by managers.

    D. Change should be introduced over a period of time.

IX. Involving people in problems at work.

    A. Focus groups, task forces, and ad hoc committees can identify problems and recommend solutions.

    B. Individual consultations can be effective in getting people involved.

    C. Delegation can also be an effective involvement technique.

    D. A supervisor's primary job is being a developer of people.

■ KEY TERMS

time crunch	guesstimates
standard workweek	priority list
Fair Labor Standards Act	ergonomics
standard workday	change rate
standard work year	change direction
straight time	change magnitude
standard work month	diffusion
exempt employees	technological change
nonexempt employees	electronic sweatshop
premium pay	organizational change
pay for time worked	social change
pay for time not worked	economic change
start-up time	political change
shut-down time	proactive
management by exception	change agents
time log	focus groups
estimates	

■ DISCUSSION QUESTIONS

1. Record the way your time is spent on a time log for a three-day period. If you are employed, use your work hours. If you are not employed, use the regular eight-hour period in which you attend college or perform other work-type activities. At the end of the period review the way time has been spent and write a short paper on ways you currently use time and actions you can take to manage time more effectively.

2. In work environments with which you are familiar, identify some major time wasters by both managers and employees.

3. Why is effective time management vital to the success of an organization?

4. Identify some major technical, organizational, and social changes that you have observed.

5. Why do managers frequently fail to involve employees in solving work-related problems?

■ SELF-ASSESSMENT

How much do you know about and use effective time management? Remember, a 1, 2, or 3 response is disagreement with the statement; 4, 5, and 6 indicate agreement.

1. I rarely waste any time. I am willing to maintain a daily log to prove it.

   1   2   3   4   5   6

2. Usually I read 600 words a minute or faster. I have good reading skills.

   1   2   3   4   5   6

3. I fully understand the principle of management by exception.

   1   2   3   4   5   6

4. Paperwork isn't a problem on my job. I can control it.

   1   2   3   4   5   6

5. Other people's time is valuable to them. I fully respect it.

   1   2   3   4   5   6

6. Least interesting tasks should be completed after interesting ones have been completed.

   1   2   3   4   5   6

7. Started but unfinished work is more of a motivator than un-started work.

   1   2   3   4   5   6

8. I regularly plan each day's work at the end of or during the previous day.

   1   2   3   4   5   6

9. I am rarely late in reporting for work, attending meetings, or meeting with others.

   1   2   3   4   5   6

10. I willingly delegate work to others, even work I like to do and can do well.

   1   2   3   4   5   6

■ SHORT CASES

Time on Her Hands

Sheila Kilpatrick was a good listener. It was one of the character-istics that led to her promotion as office manager for Sam's Auto Glass (SAG). People would call her and talk about both business and personal matters. Sheila's employees enjoyed discussing daily occurrences with her as well. In addition to employees, customers, and vendors, Sheila was also popular with other supervisors. During an average day, two or three would visit her office for a cup of coffee and to discuss organizational changes, rumors, and their own plans. From time to time she would return the visits.

    SAG was the largest automotive-glass-installation service cen-ter in Columbia and handled a number of large commercial ac-counts as well as insurance-related claims from the general public. To keep up with the many facets of the business, weekly staff meetings were held by various segments of the organization. There were also a number of special meetings related to specific types of problems. As office manager, Sheila felt it was necessary that she attend all meetings in order to know what was going on. Although she often had little to contribute because her depart-ment was not directly affected, Sheila was one the best informed supervisors in the organization. She knew about most of the prob-lems in the organization.

    In a conversation with Laurel Pencor, head of purchasing, Sheila complained, "I seem to have less and less time to do my work. I don't procrastinate and I work hard. Why don't I have more time?"

"Perhaps you should do what I do," Laurel replied. "For the past few weeks I have been keeping a daily time log to determine where my time is spent. Believe me, it made me aware of where I was off on my priorities. I found I was doing a lot of interesting things that, unfortunately, were slowing down some of my high-priority jobs. Why don't you try it? It's easy and it might help."

1. Was Sheila a good supervisor? Explain your response.

2. What were some of her most obvious time wasters?

3. Why was Sheila not fully aware of how her time was being spent? What will her time log show if she takes Laurel's advice?

Leave It to Leavitt

Immediately after he was promoted to supervisor of Laboratory Analysis for Beckman, Anderson, and Dorfman, a large medical laboratory facility that provided services to both physicians and hospitals, Jim Leavitt called his new staff together for an introductory meeting. "I know you all liked Susan Howe, " he began. "She told me you were a great team. I'm not Sue, however, and my methods are different. To start with, there are going to be some major changes. Before joining you I developed several new analytical procedures for specimen testing that will be implemented immediately. In addition I feel that several people can benefit from new assignments. There will be a list on the laboratory bulletin board tomorrow morning. Please report to your new workstation then. Prior to taking this assignment, I discussed new equipment with the laboratory manager and have approval to purchase new computerized equipment that will completely automate many of the types of analyses you now make by hand. It, plus the new methods I've developed, will save a great deal of time now spent in analytical procedures you've used over the past few years. When the new equipment arrives, a factory representative will train those affected. Are there any questions?" Everyone rose and silently left the meeting room.

Early the next morning Jim received a telephone call from the laboratory manager. "Jim, can you come to my office? Some of your employees were here this morning seeking transfers to other sections or departments. I'll tell you about their reactions to your meeting yesterday."

1. What will the laboratory manager tell Jim?

2. Jim felt he was establishing control, asserting his power, and making changes the employees would welcome. Some were to be given an opportunity to learn new jobs and others to learn how to operate new equipment. Why were the employees' reactions largely negative?

3. What can Jim do to build confidence and trust between himself and his employees after an apparently poor start?

▪ ENDNOTES

1. Dan Costley and Ralph Todd, *Human Relations in Organizations*, 4th edition (St. Paul, Minn.: West Publishing Company, 1991).

2. Alec Mackenzie, *The Time Trap* (New York: McGraw-Hill Book Company, 1972).

3. Alan Laken, *How to Get Control of Your Time and Your Life* (New York: Signet, 1973).

4. F. D. Barrett is a professor of management at York University in Toronto. He has published many articles on time management. His 1969 article, "The Management of Time," published in the *Business Quarterly* (Spring issue), outlines his general approach to time management.

5. Robert D. Rutherford, *Just in Time* (New York: John Wiley & Sons, 1980).

6. William Edwards Deming's 14 principles of management have been published many times. His *Out of the Crisis* (Cambridge: MIT Press, 1986) is the most popular source for explanations of his principles.

7. F. Mary Knowles is an independent management consultant specializing in time management methods for work organizations. Her time management workshops have been presented to many major corporations and government agencies.

8. *San Francisco Chronicle*, December 19, 1990.

9. Tom Peters, *Thriving on Chaos* (New York: Harper & Row, 1987).

Chapter 10

First-Line Management Cost Control

Objectives

Cost control is an essential, never-ending management activity. Chapter 10 teaches first-line managers to

- Identify workable and unworkable cost-management activities.
- Utilize Pareto's law of maldistribution in developing cost controls.
- Recognize the importance of cost consciousness as a cost-control tool.
- Strive for profitability as a goal rather than constant cost reduction.
- Emphasize quality as a major cost-saving method.

Thought Starter

Profits have always been more important than costs. This does not mean that costs should not be controlled or managed. Even in economic downturns when costs are crucial and reductions may be necessary, profits must continue.[1] Part of Chapter 10 addresses the profit versus cost confusion. We want our readers to understand that the two ideas are inseparable in well-run organizations. Cost control is often misused. As a consequence profits are reduced when they should not be.

All first-time managers must recognize that they have important cost-control responsibilities. As they become more experienced, they begin to realize that in order to reduce costs, it may be necessary to make substantial expenditures. They also know that out-of-control costs usually occur in specific areas.

Effective managers learn to quickly recognize areas of excessive costs. They concentrate on finding the cause of costs overruns and then take appropriate corrective actions.

■ *There is an old story of a man who had little education but had a willingness to work hard to support his family. He set up a hot-dog cart on the street corner and tried to sell the best dogs in town. Over time his business prospered and he was able to open a small hot-dog stand on a busy highway. His large, colorful signs attracted people and soon he had a regular clientele of devoted Doggone Dogs fans. As the business prospered, so did his family. One of his proudest moments was when his son graduated from college with a degree in business. As he escorted his son around the newly refurbished business that had grown far beyond the original Doggone Dogs, the son remained silent. When he finally spoke, he said, "Dad, don't you know there is a recession? Why have you spent so much money enlarging the business? Times are bad, you need to cut all of the costs you can." "My son is a college graduate, he must be right," thought the man. Beginning the next day he reduced his advertising, laid off three of his employees, and began purchasing smaller and lower-quality frankfurters. He had really cut costs. Soon his business began to dwindle. Old customers went elsewhere and few new ones were gained. In a short period of time, he had to declare bankruptcy. "Our son was right," he told his wife. "We do have a recession and it has ruined our business."*

■ COSTS: WHO IS RESPONSIBLE?

Every second of time, everything an employee does or does not do, uses or does not use, represents costs to the organization. Each piece of equipment that is operating or standing idle, every telephone call, piece of paper, purchase order, sick day, power outage, or any of the thousands of activities and events that occur at work represents costs. Like time and change, costs never stop in organizations. Both managers and employees are rarely fully aware of all of the ways costs are incurred as well as the way they influence profits or, in some instances, losses.

Cost control consists of any activity taken to meet budget projections or reduce expenditures of organizational resources.

Cost consciousness is the awareness that some costs are appropriate and necessary while others may be inappropriate and harmful.

Every person, and especially every manager, in an organization has responsibility for cost control. Management of costs is often a matter of cost consciousness rather than cost control. **Cost control** consists of any activity taken to meet budget projections or reduce expenditures of organizational resources. **Cost consciousness** is the awareness that some costs are appropriate and necessary while others may be inappropriate and harmful. **Cost management** includes both the development of cost consciousness throughout an organization and implementation of cost controls to ensure that excessive costs are contained.

Sources of Cost Problems

Several years ago it was reported that losses of parts from automobiles, damage, and theft during transit from distribution points to dealers ran as high as 15 percent of the costs of many new automobiles manufactured in the United States. Carelessness and theft were only two of the problem areas. Other cost problems such as quality and failure to meet safety standards accounted for even greater difficulties.

Cost problems can originate in any segment of an organization. Some problems are more prevalent than others.

1. **Poor quality.** William Edwards Deming was correct when he stated that U.S. organizations can no longer afford poor quality. Doing things right the first time and every time minimizes waste, time lost for corrections, and customer dissatisfaction. Poor quality results not only in loss of customers but in costs for correcting mistakes and excessive waste. There is little doubt that emphasis on productivity with little concern for quality and customer concerns is a major reason for excessive costs and reduced profitability.

2. **Misplaced emphasis on cost reduction.** Profits should not be forfeited in order to cut or inappropriately control costs. While cost control is commendable, it should not be the cause of other organizational problems. Buying from the least expensive source, as an example, may be effective in controlling costs while hurting both schedules and quality.

3. **Crisis application of organizational policy.** Many organizations seem to pay little attention to cost control until a financial crisis is apparent. **Crisis-policy application**, the sporadic application of cost-control measures—often drastic—sends confusing messages throughout the organization. Rather than continuous, well-planned cost-related measures, organizations take a reactive rather than a proactive stance.

4. **Failure to develop cost consciousness throughout the organization.** Cost consciousness concentrates awareness of the link between personal goals and organizational health. Both first-line managers and employees frequently fail to realize that their jobs are tied to the success of the organization for which they work. When companies with declining profits are forced to reduce their labor force, the importance of continuous cost control and cost consciousness rapidly becomes a painful reality.

5. Lack of understanding of the difference between cost control and cost reduction. Cost control and cost reduction are not synonymous concepts. Effective cost control may result in reduced expenditures but its ultimate goal is improved profitability. **Cost-reduction** efforts are deliberate measures to reduce expenditures. While cost reduction can also improve profitability, in some instances it is a survival measure. If not carefully planned, cost-reduction efforts may have disastrous results. Cutbacks in services, inventories, and advertising often have just the opposite of intended results. Rather than being enhanced, profits are reduced due to lost customers or clients. There are many other reasons for cost problems in organizations. Each organization has unique problems and each must be treated in a different way.

Downsizing means reducing the size of either the whole organization or some of its units in an effort to reduce costs.

6. Substituting downsizing for rightsizing.[2] Over time organizations acquire unneeded functions and people who lack appropriate skills, too many managers and support personnel, and duplication of functions develop. Many organizations attempt to become leaner and meaner, but only become leaner. They reduce people but do not improve functions. Some of the recommendations experts make are to

- Eliminate unnecessary work.
- Put quality first.
- Empower people.
- Communicate.
- Spare the work and spoil the worker.

■ FIRST-LINE MANAGERS AND COST MANAGEMENT

In many organizations the supervisor's role in cost management is minimized. Most decisions affecting expenditures are done by higher levels of management or departments with financial-planning responsibilities. Even when such limitations exist, understanding the numbers is an essential supervisory skill. First-line managers, like all other levels of management, must have a grasp of operational costs.

While financial statements are often complex and confusing to most people, budgets are usually relatively simple and easily grasped. A **budget** is a financial plan. Budgets may apply to entire organizations, departments, sections, specific programs, or groups of activities. Most people are familiar with household and

*A **budget** is a financial plan. Budgets are made for entire organizations, departments, sections, specific programs, or groups of activities.*

personal budgets. Bills have to be paid by certain dates, groceries must be purchased, and other expenses must be planned. People who make and use budgets seem to have fewer financial problems than those who do not.

Budgets in organizations are similar to personal financial plans but are usually more formal. A budget has four primary purposes:

1. A specific amount of money is allocated to operate an organization. From the total organizational budget, money is allocated to various organizational units, projects, or activities. Budget amounts of money represent, in most instances, the maximum allowable expenditures for a particular item, which may be an activity, supply, or piece of equipment. This type of expenditure plan is called a **line-item budget**. Each budget item is a line on a budget form.

Line-item budgets are the most common budgetary format. Each budget item is a line on a budget form.

In some instances very expensive pieces of equipment and facilities are on separate budgets. Expenditure allocations for such nonexpendable items that are relatively permanent installations are often part of a **capital budget**.

Capital budgets are made for nonexpendable items, such as equipment, facilities, and land.

2. Budgets are made for a specified period of time. In most organizations budgets are made for a fiscal year. A fiscal or financial year may not be a regular calendar year. Its beginning and ending is defined by organizational policy. Budgets may be for shorter or longer periods, depending on the budget's purpose.

3. Money in budgets is allocated for specific purposes. Budgets contain lists of items for which money will be spent: labor, supplies, equipment, maintenance, and any other planned expenditures. Good managers anticipate costs and make budgets based on their analysis of the costs of operating their organizational units. Some organizations have budget-planning meetings at which requirements for the coming year are reviewed and managers submit their requirements for the coming year. Budgets are then finalized based on projected availability of money to meet requirements.

In some instances supervisors may deal with budgets that are relatively limited when compared to those of a major division of a large organization. In some instances they are given prepared budgets with very little opportunity for input of their own. Their performance is rated, in part, on how well they are able to meet budgetary limitations.

Time-phased budgets are the planned expenditures of funds over the life of the budgets.

4. Budgets are time phased. Not all money in a budget is spent the same day. Expenditures are made over the period the budget covers. Supplies are ordered when it is apparent that the current inventory is low, equipment is maintained on a scheduled basis, and labor costs are continuous throughout the budget period. As conditions change, so do budgets. Although budgets may be changed, they are always valuable tools for every level of management involved in the development of cost controls.

Common Budget Fallacies

A common practice in many organizations, especially large companies and government agencies, is to base budgets on expenditures for the previous year. Ideally increases in costs based on inflationary factors, new equipment, additions of the current work force, costs for new projects, and other increases or decreases form the basis for the new budget. Each budget represents an adjustment of the budget for the previous budget period. Managers quickly learn under such systems that if they want a budget they can meet without undue pressure, they must submit inflated budget requests. They realize that some of the items will not be approved. Their goal is that, after usual reductions, their new budget will be higher than the previous year's. Rather than encouraging positive cost management, the system almost dictates that managers fudge their requirements.

In addition to the fudge or exaggeration factor, managers also learn that to justify an adequate budget for the next period they must spend their current allocation entirely before the end of the budgetary period. It is common practice for managers to authorize orders of unneeded equipment and supplies in the few weeks before new budget requests are submitted. This allows them to show a zero balance with no expenditures or overruns in excess of the originally approved budget. Managers who have not spent all of their approved budgets may have money for the following period reduced by the amount of underexpenditures. Rather than rewarding managers for effective cost-control practices, such systems encourage overexpenditure and waste.

When Cost Controls Cost

Both small and large businesses have similar problems when faced with a financial crisis. To survive they must reduce the costs of operations. Since labor is often the largest and most obvious

FIRST-LINERS

controllable cost to most organizations, it is usually the first target of cost reduction. Other areas commonly affected are advertising, inventory, and supplies. In an effort to simplify cost-containment efforts, top management frequently orders blanket cuts. A **blanket cut** means that every component of the total organization must reduce costs by a predetermined amount, usually a percentage of their total budget. If, as an example, a 10 percent blanket cut is ordered in a department with $250,000 budgeted for employee pay, $25,000 must be cut from planned labor expenditures.

A major difficulty with blanket cuts is that both efficient and inefficient operations are equally affected. Rather than correct problems, the cuts penalize managers who have been effective in managing costs and has relatively little impact on bad managers. It is unfortunate that cuts are frequently made with little analysis of their potential effects.

Supplies such as pencils, paper clips, and paper are often reduced. Organizational units that habitually conserve supplies are hurt most, while those that have excessive supplies are not hurt. Telephone calls are usually another cost-cutting target. Neither telephone costs nor office supplies are major areas of cost difficulty in most organizations. Support employees, such as duplicating machine operators, mail distribution people, and members of the human resource management training staff, are among the first affected by blanket labor cuts. A consequence is that more highly paid employees often find themselves waiting in line for access to duplicating equipment, spending time locating and sorting mail, and going without needed training coordination.

A more productive approach to cost management in times of economic crisis is for organizations to analyze carefully where excessive costs are being generated and to correct specific cost problems rather than assume they exist equally throughout the entire organization.

Keeping Profits Up and Costs Down

First-line managers are in direct contact with most of the cost-incurring activities in an organization. Their awareness of where costs are being generated can be a key to the difference between profits and loss in their organization. Higher levels of management must also be committed to effective cost management and recognize the key role of the units actually producing the services and products of an organization. Table 10.1 lists some practical steps that can be taken to keep profits up and costs down.[3]

■ LESSONS FROM PARETO

Law of maldistribution, a concept developed by Vilfredo Pareto, states that 80 percent of problems, including costs, occur in 20 percent of the organization or population.

After completing degrees in engineering and physics at the University of Turin in Italy, Vilfredo **Pareto** worked with the Italian railway system and ultimately became its director. During his career he developed an interest in applying mathematical theory to economics. His interests lead him to accepting a professorship at the University of Lausanne in Switzerland. Pareto developed and published his now famous **law of maldistribution,** sometimes called the **law of the vital few and the trivial many.** Pareto found that most wealth was controlled by relatively few people. From his findings the now well-known 80/20 rule was derived.

1. 80 percent of errors in an organization are made by 20 percent of the employees.
2. 80 percent of cost problems occur in 20 percent of the organization's functions.
3. 80 percent of accidents are caused by 20 percent of the employees.
4. 80 percent of service and production problems occur in 20 percent of the organization.

While Pareto's law was meant to be an approximation of what actually happens, it has been proven to be remarkably accurate. Managers who are aware of the 80/20 rule realize that most of their

TABLE 10.1 ■ Practical Cost Management

1. Conduct a systems checkup.	Supervisors can conduct an analysis of their own operations. They may need help from their accounting department in setting up the right records system for tracking costs, but it will be well worth the effort. Their objective is to generate cost savings without decreasing service or product quality.
2. Buy smarter.	Review purchase orders to determine if the best price, quality, and delivery schedules are being provided by vendors. Discuss purchases with specialists in the purchasing department if the organization has one. Be careful in making bulk purchases in order to receive discounts. Breakage, careless use because of an abundant supply, and obsolescence can ultimately cost more than small discounts.
3. Manage budgets.	Budgets are often not closely monitored and appropriately adjusted as conditions change. Every aspect of the organization should be continuously reviewed to ensure that cost-consciousness efforts are being used.
4. Discuss unit prices rather than total costs with employees.	It is difficult for employees to relate their jobs to total costs. Knowledge of costs of the items, supplies, and equipment with which they work makes costs more understandable.
5. Keep a positive attitude.	Employees take their clues from managers. A "we can do it" attitude is far more likely to achieve positive results than doubts and pessimism.
6. Work with employees in developing cost-saving actions.	Honeywell, Inc. pays employees 17 percent of the first year's savings for workable cost-cutting suggestions. While not all organizations have such policies, supervisors can reward with approval, recognition, and favorable performance reviews for cost-saving suggestions.

cost problems will be specific to certain activities or areas rather than to the entire organization. Practitioners of total quality management use Pareto's law as a tool in locating specific processes that create problems. Three primary steps are required:

1. A process to be studied is identified and broken down into each of its major components.

2. Each component that is not meeting a predetermined standard, in this case a budget, is examined and alternatives for correction are developed.

3. Corrective actions are chosen, implemented, and follow-ups are made. If costs are still not meeting budgetary standards, the cycle is repeated.

Pareto charts are graphic methods for showing where problems, including cost difficulties, occur.

In defining process steps for evaluation, a **Pareto chart** is often made. Pareto charts are usually bar charts, often known as *histograms*. A simplified Pareto chart for a customer service operation is shown in Figure 10.1. Numbers on the left side of the chart represent the percentage of budget expended. Two departments, customer complaints and catalog sales, are spending in excess of their budgets. Good cost control practices will determine causes of overexpenditures in the two areas over budget, and appropriate corrections will be made. In some instances, budget increases may be justified.

An examination of the Pareto chart indicates that most processes are meeting or exceeding requirements but some are not. To correct cost difficulties, the manager must concentrate on those areas where difficulty is occurring. While Pareto charts are not the only means for cost analysis, they are useful in focusing on those specific processes where excessive costs are incurred.

Pareto's concepts are useful in other ways. Retailers, who are the bulk of business organizations in many communities, know that most of their income is derived from repeat customers. If, as

FIGURE 10.1 ■ Pareto Chart Customer Service Department Budget Expenditures

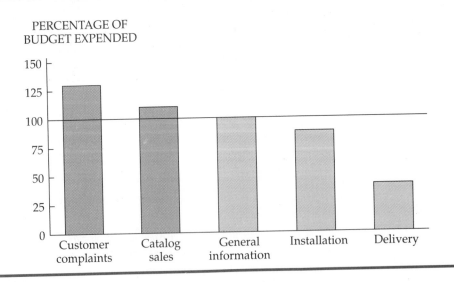

a cost-cutting measure, they reduce or eliminate items, brands, colors, or sizes that customers want, even the most dedicated customers will go elsewhere. A relatively small number of customers may be the source of most of their income. Cost reductions should, if possible, be in the form of increased efficiency and effectiveness rather than at the expense of customer services or product quality. Pareto's rule cautions against forgetting the vital few in favor of attention to the trivial many.

Perhaps the most important contribution of Pareto's law is its insistence that problems are not spread evenly. They are concentrated in specific parts of an organization.

■ SUPERVISORS AND COST MANAGEMENT

"Here we go again!" is a common reaction of employees and supervisors to annual cost-reduction drives. Rather then develop continuous cost-awareness programs that demonstrate the benefits of improved profits, job security, better working conditions, and personal commitment, many organizations react to profit declines by sudden, often poorly planned cost reduction plans. It has often been stated that the United States' massive budget deficits could be brought under control by improved management practices in government bureaucracies. In the early 1980s the famous Grace Committee made many specific recommendations that would reduce government costs by billions of dollars. Because of bureaucratic resistance and congressional apathy, few of the committee's recommendations were ever implemented. Nongovernmental organizations often act much the same way. Their cost-control programs are reactive, rarely aimed at the real causes of cost problems, and represent too little, too late approaches. It is easy to understand why some first-line managers feel there is little that they can do to control costs in their organizational units.

A Look on the Brighter Side

There is increasing evidence that managers are learning that effective cost management may mean spending money as well as saving it.[4] Improved time-saving equipment, facilities, training, and advertising are all expensive. In the long run they can result in improved profits and more soundly managed organizations.

Supervisors, especially those in organizations that recognize the value of developing cost consciousness on a continuous basis, can contribute a great deal to making cost management effective. Like all levels of management, those with first-line responsibilities must never forget that their primary responsibility is to produce services and products that not only meet but exceed customer expectations. Organizational survival in times of change make the old cut-and-slash type of cost reduction obsolete. Too many cuts may mean handing the business to a competitor willing to take risks to improve its share of the market and increase profits.

There are a number of dos and don'ts supervisors with cost-management responsibilities must learn. A number of underlying concepts are helpful in developing on-the-job cost management.

1. Forget pep talks, slogans, and posters. Cost management, if correctly implemented, is a continuous process that stems from a number of factors other than one-shot programs. While cost concerns are usually an integral part of most staff meetings, costs are best contained and even reduced when employees have a clear understanding of their organization's goals. If encouraged by sincere, interested supervisors, they will develop the same sense of concern for costs that are part of every manager's responsibility.

2. Discuss techniques, methods, and actions rather than dollars. During periods of drought in western states, members of communities are asked to voluntarily try to conserve water. In some instances as much as 30 percent reductions have been seen. Most of the conservation effort is directed toward accomplishing usual tasks while conserving water. Much the same process can be used in jobs. How can we do it better at the same or less cost is the basic question. Each job element must be examined and reexamined with the idea of improvement. Improvement usually means less cost in the long run. Simple actions like turning off equipment when it is not being used, mechanizing dull, time-consuming tasks, and combining tasks when feasible are just a few examples of cost-management techniques that can be used without reducing either quality or quantity.

3. Develop commitment. For cost management to be effective, every member of the organization must be committed to making it work. This is especially true of supervisors. As with other supervisory duties, sensitivity to both present and potential problems is essential. Cost management is part of the controlling function and involves standards, measurement, and corrective action. Cost standards are represented by budgets; measurement is made by reviewing expenditures for budgeted items; and corrective action is taken when it is apparent that budgets may be overrun. As leaders of their work units, supervisors must act as leaders in developing commitment and cost consciousness in their employees.

4. Realize that doing better isn't good enough. Although reports that show overall cost improvement are nice, they are not as valuable as knowing specific, tangible actions that have been taken to reduce costs. It is possible to have both cost reductions and increases simultaneously. Knowing the numbers is important, but it is also important to know details. Cost management involves taking the time to understand where cost problems exists, where work can be simplified, where equipment and mechanization will have long-range benefits, and where additional training will have positive payoffs. Supervisors do not have to be cost-accounting specialists. They must, however, be management minded. To do so requires knowing specifics as well as overall performance.

5. Never forget to reward others for cost efforts. Some organizations have regular cost-savings reward programs that reward individual employees or groups for their efforts in improving profitability either through cost-saving efforts or improved quality and productivity. Other organizations, unfortunately, have few real incentives for cost-reduction effort. In both types of organizations supervisors can do a great deal by positively reinforcing cost-saving efforts. Verbal and written commendations that are made part of a person's personnel file, increased merit pay, and favorable comments in a performance evaluation all tend to reinforce the concept that cost-reduction effort is worth the time and energy expended.

6. Recognize that help is needed. Effective managers know that they cannot make all decisions, all corrections, and all cost-management efforts alone. Their most valuable resource for cost-management actions are their employees. Specialists in work improvement, higher levels of management, and other supervisors who have special experience or training can all assist first-line managers in improving their cost-management skills.

7. Let employees know what is going on. Employees like to be in on what is going on in an organization. Constructive first-line managers review costs with both groups and individual employees. In very well run organizations employees are given the tools to measure their own performance in terms of productivity, quality, schedule, and costs. This has proven to be a powerful motivational tool and one that continually informs employees of their own performance. Supervisors who keep their employees informed are more likely to be informed by employees of work problems and needed corrective actions.

8. Analyze rather than criticize. It is easy to blame others for errors, budgetary overruns, and excessive waste. Rather than criticize, knowledgeable supervisors gather facts, discuss specific problems, and seek solutions. Often they find that what appeared to be mistakes were unusual circumstances that could not be controlled by the person responsible. People do make mistakes, and some have poor attitudes. Corrective action that is viewed as problem solving rather punishment or demeaning criticism is usually a better course of action. Figure 10.2 views four common cost-control fallacies and shows more positive approaches.

Ken Blanchard has pointed out that reprimands should be reserved for fully trained people who know what should be done but fail to perform.[5] Even then the focus should be on the specific problem created by the employee's failure. "Your report was two days late. It was needed for an important meeting," is a far better statement than, "You've really been making a lot of mistakes lately." He points out that it is all right for supervisors to let employees know they are disappointed, concerned, or even angry. They must also treat employees fairly and tell them that they know they can do it right. Their concern stems from knowing that a good employee failed to perform adequately rather than a desire to punish. Blanchard states that it is important for employees to feel that though they may have been chewed out, they were not mistreated. Trained, well-motivated, and committed employees know that errors cost both time and money.

9. Learn to use new technology. Some supervisors, like many employees, are resistant to change, especially technological change that is unfamiliar. While electronics and mechanization cannot cure all problems, they can, in many instances, improve efficiency, reduce errors, and make work life easier. Nearly all organizations have access to consultants or people within their own organizations who can provide useful suggestions on potentially cost-saving technology.

FIGURE 10.2 ■ Facts and Fallacies that Impact Costs

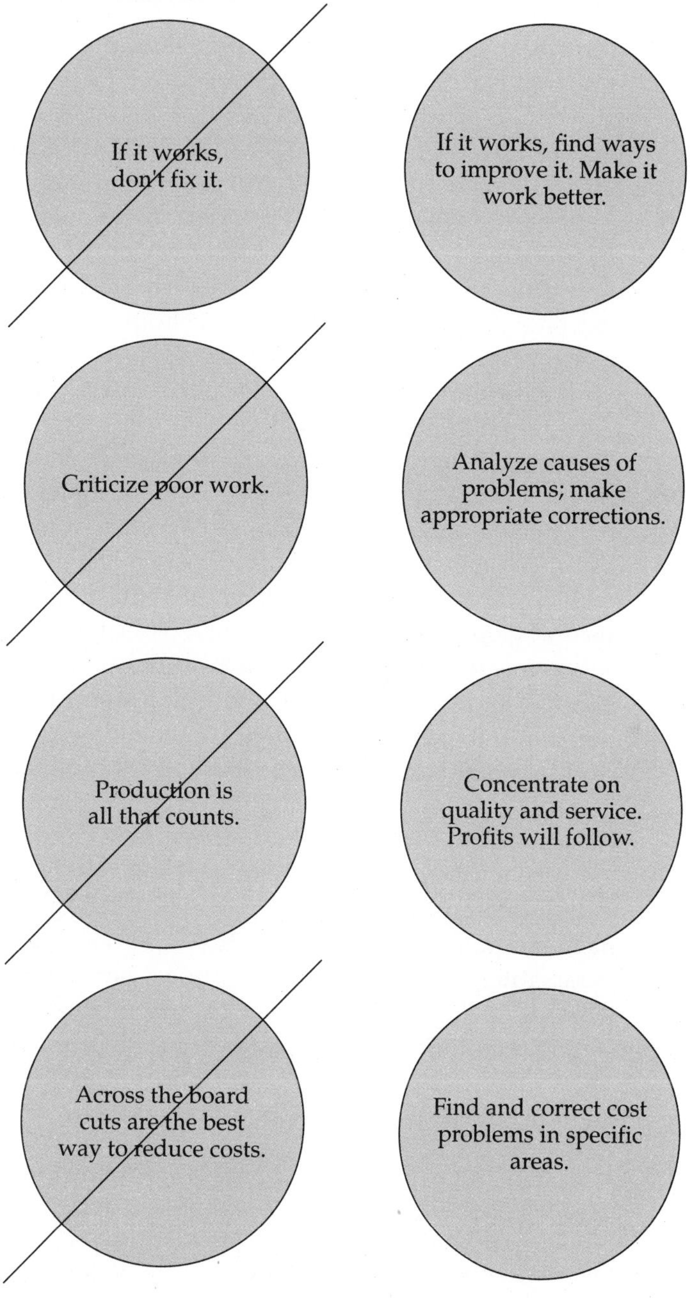

■ FACTS AND FALLACIES

One of the poorest sayings heard around many places of work is, "If it works, don't fix it." It's true that management by exception principles state that more attention should be paid to those problems that require immediate correction. Equally true is the need to know that, if it works, can it work better? Nearly every work process can be improved. Cost consciousness also breeds innovation and creativity rather than random cost cutting in an effort to reach budgetary goals. An important component of cost management is the necessity for continuous review of all functions. Those that seem to work well may offer the best opportunity for improvement. Learning to combine, eliminate, and approach tasks in new ways can improve not only costs and profitability but make work easier for those who must perform specific tasks. Like time management, cost management concentrates on doing things smarter, not harder. Improved profitability, not the amount apparently reduced from a budget, is the ultimate goal.

Crisis management rarely solves long-term problems.

Poor organizational practices can make a first-line manager's cost-management role difficult. Crisis management that sporadically engages in crash programs to reduce expenditures; lack of encouragement or incentives for cost-saving efforts; misplaced blame for problems; unclear organizational roles that lead to duplication of effort; and failure to isolate specific problem areas all contribute to cost-management difficulties.

Maintaining cost consciousness is often difficult if supervisors find other managers have little concern for budget overruns, waste, and inefficiency. Cost management cannot be effective unless every function in an organization is involved and committed to building and perpetuating positive financial plans, careful implementation of cost-saving methods, and awareness of profitability as a major long-range goal. Supervisors who find themselves working in a vacuum lacking top management support and encouragement are often trapped in an environment of mediocrity. They may either stay or seek opportunities that will both allow and encourage their development as managers.

■ FIRST-LINE COST MANAGEMENT

Decision making, communication, time management, training, motivation, leadership, and cost management are parts of the long list of management skills that first-line managers must learn. All are parts of being a fully developed manager. It is unfortunate that cost-consciousness development is frequently neglected and not understood. In many instances cost cuts are inappropriate and result in loss of profits, although cost goals on paper may be reached.

Supervisors, like other managers, should realize that profits are usually computed by subtracting costs of sales from total sales. From this amount taxes are deducted. Any remaining money represents **net profit.** Net profit to organizations is what take-home pay is to individuals. It is money available for paying stockholders, reinvesting in the organization, or spending in ways company management deems important. Since taxes are not directly controllable, increases in net profit can come only from increases in sales or reductions in costs. Although this explanation does not include many details considered in actual practice, it illustrates the importance of cost management. Supervisory attitudes and actions are major contributors to profit improvement that benefits the entire organization.

Net profit is the amount of money derived from sales after expenses and taxes have been deducted. It is the organizational equivalent of an employee's take-home pay.

In their meetings and communication with higher levels of management, knowledgeable supervisors express their cost-management philosophy. They know that influence extends both upward as well as downward in organizations. Competent managers at a policy-making level will listen to their first-line managers if suggestions and recommendations will clearly benefit the organization. Few functions are as important to top management as costs and profitability. They are, in a very real sense, primary goals of most organizations. Providing services and products to customers and employment for members of their community are important. Profits make achievement of other goals possible.

In a service-oriented economy, with the number of people employed in manufacturing declining, productivity and quality measures are more difficult to make than in the past. Both are tied directly to costs. Offices that process paperwork, such as financial institutions, insurance companies, health care providers, utility companies, and other client-oriented organizations, try to set standards based on number of loans processed, length of time to update records, customers contacted, length of time to respond to customer requests, and degree of client or customer satisfaction. All are difficult to assess.

A standard measure is to determine what percentage labor cost is of total income from sales or ongoing contracts. If the labor percentage increases and sales do not, then it may be assumed that productivity is down. More hours are required to provide the service. Supervisors, as the managers of people who actually provide services, must use experience, judgment, and careful analysis of records to determine their work unit's overall productivity and quality. Table 10.2 identifies steps that supervisors find helpful in acquiring needed cost-management expertise.

■ THOUGHTS ON THE VALUE OF MONEY

Utility of money is its use for purchasing needed goods and services.

Discretionary income is money in excess of that needed to maintain a satisfactory standard of living. In organizations it is profit beyond that expected.

Psychological value of money enhances an individual's feelings of self-esteem, security, and personal worth.

Social value of money is based on the perception, by society in general, that people who earn money are more successful and worthwhile than those who do not.

Money has several types of value for both individuals and organizations. For both the most apparent value is **utility.** Money can be used for the purchase of goods and services necessary for survival. Individuals also have **discretionary** uses for money. They can purchase items or services that improve their standard of living, increase personal pleasure, provide savings for future security, or they can help others. Organizations usually use discretionary funds for dividends to stockholders, facilities and equipment improvement, investments that provide added value to the organization, and additional funds for salaries, bonuses, and other incentives.

One of the most important values of money for individuals is **psychological.** People feel better about themselves when employed and earning enough money to maintain an adequate standard of living and also to enjoy discretionary income. Self-worth and definitions of personal success are often tied to money. Organizations, like individuals, also see money as a measure of organizational health and a measure of how well they have fared in a competitive economic market. Money also has a **social** value. Individuals are frequently judged by their income or use of money. While wealth in itself does not necessarily mean social approval (it doesn't in the case of very wealthy criminals), it often influences the way a person is perceived by others. People who are able to earn and maintain an adequate standard of living are looked on more favorably by others than those who have neither jobs nor money other than that provided by social services. In the same sense organizations that are always on the brink of financial collapse, or for which bankruptcy is a reality, are looked upon by society as failures. Their management and employees are often branded, fairly or unfairly, as being incompetent.

Both individuals and organizations that practice effective cost management are more likely to receive not only the esteem of

TABLE 10.2 ■ Making Sense out of Cost Management

1. Learn to identify where improvement is needed and define objectives.	Cost management involves developing an awareness of potential areas for improvement as well as future problems. Careful definition of what needs to be accomplished starts the process. From these objectives plans can be developed, responsibilities assigned, and actions initiated. Follow up while plans are being accomplished as well as after their completion to determine if in-process corrections are needed.
2. Involve others in cost management efforts.	Good supervisors involve others in cost management by demonstrating its benefits in improved job security, increased opportunities, and potentially better pay. If people fully understand how organizational well-being positively affects their own lives, they are more likely to show a willingness to be involved in making it even better.
3. Be a leader.	Supervisors who demonstrate their beliefs, encourage and support others, and see their primary roles as coaches and developers of people are also motivators. They are able to inspire their own enthusiasm for working to reduce errors, minimize waste, and find better ways of achieving work goals. Motivation and leadership are natural companions.
4. Establish realistic priorities.	Learn to separate the important from the trivial. Make priorities well known to everyone in the work unit. When employees know what needs to be accomplished first they respond with the required effort needed to do first things first. Part of effective cost management is assessing needs and determining priorities that support overall organizational objectives.
5. Discuss techniques, methods, procedures, and unit costs with employees.	Generalizations and slogans like "Don't waste," "Improve costs," and similar exhortations have little effect other than keeping poster designers occupied. Specific actions, such as improvement in the way things are accomplished and the cost of each operation, are far more meaningful. Leonard Sayles has pointed out that, when encouraged, employees set standards for themselves higher than those developed by their managers.[6]
6. Think *kaizen* and maintain high expectations.	*Kaizen*, as discussed frequently in this text, means improvement: continuous improvement in personal life, home life, social life, and working life. Improvement means having strong personal beliefs in the ability to improve and high expectations of others. People who expect more are far more likely to receive more than those who do not. Supervisors who believe that both they and their employees can constantly improve are the high achievers and the ones who make the vital shifts upward in their jobs and their lives.

others but enjoy a greater sense of personal achievement. Cost management can go beyond profits. It is tied directly to a sense of self-worth.

■ THINGS TO REMEMBER

I. Costs: who is responsible?

   A. Every action in a work environment affects costs.

   B. Everyone in an organization has cost-control responsibility.

   C. Cost consciousness is an awareness that certain costs are necessary while others are not.

   D. Cost control consists of activities to meet budget projections or reduce expenditures.

   E. Cost management includes both cost-consciousness efforts and cost control.

II. Sources of cost problems.

   A. Carelessness and theft.

   B. Poor quality, misplaced emphasis on cost reduction, crisis application of organizational policy, and lack of differentiation between cost control and cost reduction.

III. First-line managers and cost management.

   A. First-line managers need to understand operational costs.

   B. Budgets have four primary purposes.

IV. Common budget fallacies.

   A. Budgets encourage managers to spend rather than to save.

   B. Managers submit inflated budget requests.

V. When cost controls cost.

   A. Labor is usually the first target of cost-reduction programs.

   B. Blanket cuts involve cutting the budgets of every unit of an organization. Both efficient and inefficient organizational units are affected by blanket cuts.

   C. Expendable supply cuts and reduction of support personnel are usually ineffective cost control measures.

VI. Lessons from Pareto

   A. Pareto developed the law of maldistribution.

    B. Pareto's law estimates that 80 percent of problems occur in 20 percent of any set of activities or group.

    C. Pareto charts are used by some organizations to analyze processes.

VII. Supervisors and cost management.

    A. Employees are often apathetic to cost-saving efforts.

    B. Many organizations have reactive rather than proactive cost-management programs.

VIII. A look on the brighter side.

    A. Managers are learning that cost management means spending money as well as saving it.

    B. Supervisors can contribute to making cost management work.

    C. Too many cost reductions can result in loss of customers, quality, and productivity.

IX. Facts and fallacies

    A. Fallacy: "If it works, don't fix it."

    B. Fact: Nearly every work process can be improved.

    C. Fact: Crisis management can create many problems.

    D. Fact: Maintaining cost consciousness is difficult, especially without support from other components of the organization.

X. First-line cost management.

    A. Cost management is a fundamental management skill.

    B. Supervisors can influence upward as well as downward.

    C. Supervisors can learn to improve continuously.

XI. Thoughts on the value of money.

    A. For both organizations and individuals money has more than utilitarian value.

    B. Psychological and social values of money are very important considerations.

◼ KEY TERMS

cost control	cost reduction
cost consciousness	crisis-policy application
cost management	downsizing

budget   Pareto chart

line-item budget   net profit

capital budget   utility of money

blanket cut   discretionary money

Pareto   psychological value of money

law of maldistribution   social value of money

trivial many, vital few

■ DISCUSSION QUESTIONS

1. At your place of work or at an organization with which you are familiar, identify a minimum of three actions that can be taken to reduce costs without detracting from overall performance or customer service.

2. What are some of the primary differences between a personal budget and one developed by the supervisor of the customer services department of a large retail store?

3. As manager of a medium-size restaurant, how would you develop cost consciousness in your employees?

4. Why is the saying, "If it works, don't fix it," bad advice?

5. How can development of cost consciousness apply to personal life?

■ SELF-ASSESSMENT

Choose the response that you most agree with. Low numbers, 1, 2, and 3, indicate disagreement with the statement; 4, 5, and 6 indicate agreement.

1. Cost cutting has always been necessary to improve profitability.

   1   2   3   4   5   6

2. Effective cost management concentrates on immediate profits.

   1   2   3   4   5   6

3. Cost-reduction efforts should start before planning expenditures for the future.

   1   2   3   4   5   6

4. Supervisors in most organizations have little influence on organizational costs.

   1   2   3   4   5   6

5. Pareto's law states that the vital many are more important than the trivial few.

   1   2   3   4   5   6

6. Supervisors should actively seek employee assistance in developing cost-saving actions.

   1   2   3   4   5   6

7. Organizational analysis is the first step after cost plans are developed.

   1   2   3   4   5   6

8. Weekly pep talks and slogans are a good way to develop cost consciousness.

   1   2   3   4   5   6

9. Priorities are not necessary if several cost-control actions are obvious.

   1   2   3   4   5   6

10. Cost-control actions should apply to all situations rather than to specific areas or operations.

   1   2   3   4   5   6

■ SHORT CASES

A Case of Bills

Bill and Edwena Thompson opened their Village Offset Printing Office (VOPO) primarily to service desktop publishers. Their equipment is able to convert most computer disks with text on it directly to their presses for large-quantity production. Neither Bill nor Edwena had any concept of how popular their business would become. Many small companies with desktop publishing capability used their services for catalogs, announcements, and similar publications. Their policy of allowing 30 days for payment with discounts for early payment proved to be an added attraction for many businesses.

As demand increased, they were able to negotiate a $50,000 expansion loan to enlarge floor space, buy additional printing equipment, and upgrade their computerized color-register system. Although the 12 percent interest rate on the loan ate into their projected profits, business continued to increase. Their high-quality service and quick delivery was paying off. After two years in business they had eight employees, two delivery vans, and looked forward to the next expansion.

A few months into the second year of operations Edwena observed that they would need a loan from their bank to meet the next week's payroll. "But we have plenty of business," complained Bill, "and we're taking in lots of money."

"That's true," Edwena responded. "We also have bills to pay, and quite a few completed jobs won't be paid until the end of the month. Let's hope the interest on our loans doesn't eat up all of our profits."

1. What are some factors that could contribute to Bill and Edwena's cost problems?

2. In a business like VOPO what are some possible areas of excessive costs?

3. What obvious business problem have Bill and Edwena overlooked?

Control?

Airjet Corporation Tactical Systems' (ACT) purchasing department was large and complex. Not only was it responsible for metal-fabrication materials, plastics, supplier-made parts, and equipment, but it also ordered all office supplies and equipment and plant maintenance items. It was also responsible for material control records once supplies had been received. Although most of the department's records and reports were stored in computer data banks, it still used many standard office items. Like all similar large offices it had a centralized office supply area where employees had direct access to items they needed.

During a routine check of expendable items used by the purchasing department itself, Elaine Whitney, supervisor of records and internal supplies for the department, noticed that usage had increased dramatically. In checking with other supervisors, she could find no real reason for the apparent problem. There were no new projects, and the work load was fairly constant. No one could account for the apparent shortages. Further checks revealed that items unaccounted for included pens, pencils, gum erasers, and writing tablets. "They're the things school children could use," Elaine thought. Far more serious was the absence of a new lap top computer, ordered for use by purchasing agents when they visited vendors, and several special hand-held calculators used for estimating complex technical purchases.

"It has to be theft," Elaine reported during the weekly staff meeting with the director of procurement and other key members of the purchasing staff. "Someone is taking the material from our supply room without authorization. It could be anyone or several people. We have almost 40 employees. I doubt if members of other departments could get in and out of our supply area without being noticed. To keep our costs down, I'm issuing the following memorandum: Effective immediately, the following steps will be taken to ensure orderly distribution of office supplies in the purchasing department:

1. Ms. Janet Franklin will have primary responsibility for issuing office supplies. The supply room will be locked and only Ms. Franklin and I will have keys. Please contact her or me if supplies are needed.
2. No supplies will be issued without specific authorization from a purchasing department supervisor.
3. Quantities issued will be limited to short-term needs. Limits for single withdrawals will be posted on the supply room door. Exceptions must be approved by the authorizing department supervisor and Ms. Franklin or me.

> Elaine Whitney
> Supervisor of Records and Internal Supplies

1. How well will Elaine's control plan work?

2. How will employees and supervisors of other sections of the purchasing department react?

3. Are there other alternatives that will work equally well? Explain your response.

▪ ENDNOTES

1. "How to Profit in a World of Change," *Fortune,* January 14, 1991, pp. 12–13. Although this article is written from an investor's perspective, it stresses the importance of profits, especially in an environment of change with all of its uncertainties.

2. Ronald Henkoff, "Cost Cutting: How to Do It Right," *Fortune,* April 9, 1990, pp. 42–49. An excellent source on how to cut costs and make it stick.

3. "Keep Profits Up in a Down Economy," *Focus,* year-end issue, 1990, p. 7.

4. Brian Dumaine, "How to Manage in a Recession," *Fortune,* November 9, 1990, pp. 58–72.

5. Kenneth Blanchard is best known as co-author with Spencer Johnson of *The One Minute Manager* (New York: William Morrow and Company, 1982). He is also a prolific author, well-known management consultant, and lecturer.

6. Leonard Sayles is a well-known management author and consultant. He is best known for his text *Leadership,* 2nd edition (New York: McGraw-Hill, 1989), and the classic *How Managers Motivate,* written with William Dowling, 2nd edition (New York: McGraw-Hill, 1978).

Improving Employee Effectiveness—Training and Development

Objectives

In a world of change, constant upgrading of skills is more important now than at any time in the past. Chapter 11 will enable its readers to

- Identify three major types of learning.
- Recognize ways people learn.
- Describe different training methods.
- Avoid common training errors.
- Develop training plans.

Thought Starter

Organizations can take several different approaches in their employment philosophy. They can employ people trained and experienced in the type of work required; they can employ untrained people whom they will train; or they can employ a mixture of both trained and untrained people.

Regardless of their philosophical approach to employment, the most successful organizations have training programs available to employees. Some training is usually required, while other types are voluntary. For many years organizations in all of the developed countries of the world have realized that training is a continuous need in an ever-changing work environment. New methods, new products and services, and new technology all impact the work environment. Only through training can employees learn to cope with new working conditions.

Like many of the other skills managers must acquire, training is necessary but often neglected. Employees who are inadequately trained cannot perform satisfactorily. While some people learn by observing others as well as through trial and error, there is no guarantee that what is being learned is correct. First-line managers who understand the value of training will have workers who perform far better than workers who must learn through experience only.

■ *"In just a short five years,"* Jim Carlson observed, *"many of the skills required for our business will be obsolete."* As Human Resource Department manager for Cross Engineering, Jim was concerned with the cost and length of time required to train new personnel to become effective employees. Cross Engineering's business is developing equipment and services used in the construction of dams, bridges, and buildings in excess of six floors. Its employees included architectural designers, engineers, technical specialists, office personnel, and marketing professionals. All required a knowledge of the organization's objectives and requirements for making it one of the top international construction and engineering organizations.

In a meeting with the company's first-line managers, Jim stressed the importance of training. "No one," he began, "is as close to what is needed in work units as you. As new concepts, technology, and needs are introduced, your employees must learn new procedures, new techniques, and, in many instances, entirely new skills. Identification of training needs is an important skill. In addition you'll have to learn far more than you currently know about many new areas of skill, knowledge, and ability."

Most of the supervisors could understand Jim's concern. They knew that evaluation of training needs was important. Most also understood that, as managers, they could never learn enough and that they, like their employees, must also be trained.

■ LIVING WITH CHANGE

During their years of employment most people will change what they do several times. Although they may keep the same or similar work title, the content of their tasks will dramatically change. It is very likely that nurses will still be called nurses when the 21st century begins in a few short years. Their job content, however, is likely to be much different. Standard measurements such as blood pressure, body temperature, blood composition, and other tests are already being made by very sophisticated electronic equipment that promises to become even more versatile. In businesses, checkless monetary transactions, more fully automated offices, and increased reliance on technology will continue. These are just two of hundreds of examples of job change directly impacted by technology. Change is inevitable and unstoppable in every type of work.

Change is inevitable and unstoppable

Although secondary schools and colleges are attempting to prepare students for the future, change takes place far faster in work places than it does in the classroom. Regardless of training and educational background, lifelong learning will be a reality for those who adapt to ever-changing requirements at work. Supervisors have a prime responsibility in identification of training needs, coaching, and, in many instances, teaching others. Managers who are seen as "best" by their employees are those who see themselves as developers of people. They want their employees to be able to perform well at their current tasks and be trained in new skills, areas of knowledge, and increased ability. People must learn that as soon as a new skill or area of knowledge is acquired it may be obsolete.

Training entails learning specific job skills.

Development is preparation for increased responsibility, authority, and personal accountability.

Well-run organizations recognize the necessity for continuous training and development to upgrade competency. **Training** entails learning specific job skills while **development** is concerned with preparation for increased responsibility, authority, and personal accountability.

■ LEARNING

Three fundamental types of learning have been identified by behavioral scientists. It is important that people involved in assessing training needs, as well as trainers, themselves recognize and understand their differences.

Psychomotor Learning—Acquiring Skills

Psychomotor learning involves coordination and direction of body movements.

Psychomotor learning involves coordination and direction of body movements in specific ways. It is one of the most interesting and fundamental types of skill acquisition. When an infant learns to grope for a bottle, grasp a toy, or move its hands toward an object, psychomotor learning is involved. As the infant grows older, it learns to hold a spoon, drink from a cup, and point to what it wants. Later it learns to walk, take toys apart and put them together again, wave goodbye, and clap its hands. All of these involve complex coordination of body movements. As the infant becomes older it learns more complex psychomotor activities such as tying its shoes, riding a bicycle, and even learning a computer keyboard. All are learned psychomotor behaviors.

In a work environment psychomotor training is concerned with learning new skills. Some people learn to operate registers, adjust machinery, and perform a wide number of psychomotor activities. Most of these require accurate eye-hand coordination. Skill (i.e., psychomotor) training is unique. Once a skill is learned, the body and its muscles also seem to learn. A person trained on a standard office keyboard never thinks about which letter or key is being used to type. People who work with money do not have to stop and think when they are computing with a 10-key register or calculator. Their fingers learn where to go. Once learned, psychomotor skills are rarely lost. People who drive automobiles stop their cars at red lights without thinking. Their right foot moves from the accelerator to the break pedal as if it is self-directed. Psychomotor activities, once learned, are generally automatic.

Psychomotor training is practice dependent. Before a person can become proficient she or he usually must practice. As practice increases so does proficiency, to a point where further improvement is difficult, if not impossible.

Cognitive Learning—Acquiring Knowledge

Cognitive learning entails acquiring knowledge.

Cognitive learning is the acquisition of knowledge. Unlike psychomotor learning, cognitive learning is largely invisible. As an infant grows, it learns to identify objects, colors, sizes, and people. More complex relationships are learned as it grows older. Knowledge increases with experience. Most formal education is cognitive. Knowing, thinking, making rational choices, and understanding the physical, social, and psychological environment in which life takes place all involve cognitive learning. For practical purposes, knowledge and its use is synonymous with cognition.

In work organizations people must know rules, who is responsible for various functions, and how to assess whether work is being completed correctly or not. They must also learn to make correct decisions and understand the consequences of errors. All of our thinking activities are cognitive.

Cognitive training requires development of an understanding of often complex relationships. While using a keyboard involves psychomotor activity, writing a computer program to perform scientific calculations requires in-depth knowledge in several fields. Principles must be understood and correctly used. Both creativity and innovation are required. Both are cognitive processes. *Creativity* means developing new ideas while *innovation* is using current concepts in a different way.

Creativity means developing new ideas.

Innovation is the use of existing concepts or equipment in a new and different way.

Both knowledge and skills are acquired in many ways. Trial-and-error learning involves repetitive efforts to accomplish a task until it is mastered. A great deal of learning is based on trial and error. Another type of knowledge acquisition is based on modeling.

Modeling requires observing others and copying their behavior. Formal education is one of the most powerful tools for knowledge acquisition.

Affective Learning—Acquiring Values and Attitudes

Affective learning relates to the development of values and attitudes.

Values, attitudes, and beliefs are affective. **Affective learning** determines the way people perceive their physical and social environment. It is the most neglected area of training in both formal education and work organizations. A few large companies, such as IBM, General Electric, Hewlett-Packard, Xerox, and 3M, deliberately create a work environment that shapes both employee and management values. Excellence, customer service, innovation, and involvement in the organization are constantly emphasized. Every employee, regardless of job title, is encouraged to be an active participant. Pride in membership in the organization, rather than being a hired hand, is the norm. People feel their organization is the best and that they help maintain its status. Affective values and attitudes are acquired through association with other members of the organization. It requires an unusual commitment by top management. Commitment to excellence and belief in the worth of their organization are common employee values and attitudes in organizations that realize the value of affective training.

Some organizations, such as Johnsonville Foods, General Mills, Federal Express, 3M Corporation, Aetna Life & Casualty Insurance, and other major companies, have had outstanding affective development success with self-managed work teams.[1] Employees work in teams without direct supervision. They hire, terminate, train, set standards, determine schedules, identify and solve work problems, are their own inspectors and production-control specialists, and perform most of the other functions normally assigned to supervisors. First-line managers, what few exist, are coaches, sources of information, and trainers. They are not the traditional rule enforcers. Their primary role is that of a resource for employees. A result of improved self-determination is increased productivity, quality, and loyalty to the goals of the organization. Systems that promote teamwork, personal accountability, and increased responsibility and authority may be the most significant types of affective training.

Fundamental types of human learning are summarized in Figure 11.1.

Understanding How People Learn

No one knows precisely how people learn or even when learning begins. Psychologists have evidence that it begins very early, perhaps before birth, and continues throughout a person's life. A great deal of early learning is, as noted earlier, through trial and error and observation. Other learning is more deliberate, such as that taught by parents, peers, or in formal educational settings. There are many ways people learn. **Learning** may be defined as a change in behavior resulting from perception or experience. Much of our experience is acquired through some form of association, frequently called *conditioning*. **Conditioning** involves connecting one event, symbol, or object with another. There are two major types of conditioning.

Learning may be defined as a change in behavior resulting from perception or experience.

Conditioning involves connecting one event, symbol, or object with another.

In some organizations a bell or horn signals that work is to stop. When the sound is heard, employees automatically stop. Lights at street intersections inform automobile drivers to stop, use caution, or proceed. Interpretation is automatic. Most people stop when the light is red and go when it turns green. They do not think about their actions; they react. Automatic reaction by simple association is known as **classical conditioning.** Classical conditioning usually requires repetition of associations until a person learns to appropriately react. In work organizations employees learn to react to sounds, signals, such as flashing lights, or arrows pointing in a specific direction. Their bodies automatically react to conditioning.

Classical conditioning may be described as automatic reaction by simple association.

FIGURE 11.1 ■ Fundamental Types of Learning

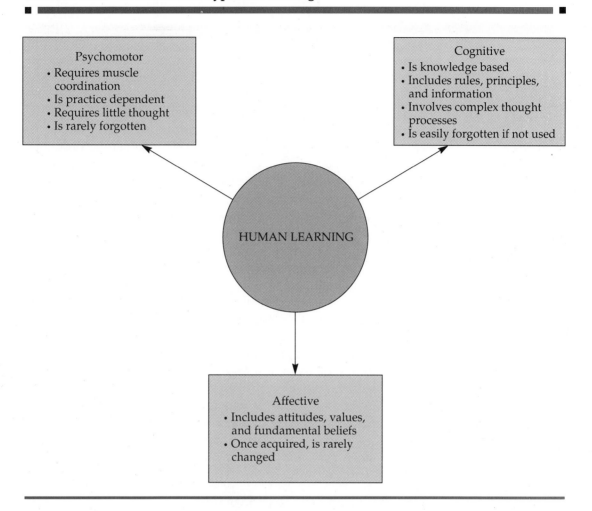

When rewards or punishments are associated with specific types of action, **operant conditioning** is developed. An employee who receives approval or praise for her or his work performance associates praise, a type of reward, with performance. If a merit increase in pay, opportunity for promotion, or additional authority and responsibility are used as a reward for accomplishment at work, a very positive type of conditioning takes place. From time to time **reinforcement** is required to strengthen and maintain the operantly conditioned response. Over a period of time, with

Operant conditioning is based on the association of specific acts with rewards or punishment.

Reinforcement is the repetition of rewards or punishment to strengthen and maintain operantly conditioned responses.

proper reinforcement, the desired employee behavior becomes habitual.

Under methods developed by the late B. F. Skinner, supervisors were trained to praise employees for correctly completing various types of work. In each type of work employees were required to keep a simple record, usually a checklist, of their activities. Supervisors would review the lists and praise employees for their efforts. In an area where goods were packaged for air shipment, error rates were reduced 90 percent in the first week of the new system. Supervisors of jobs from customer service order taking and shipment routing to truck pick-up and delivery used the Skinner system. In every instance performance improved and errors were reduced. It was found that the record keeping provided immediate feedback to employees on how well they were performing. Reinforcement was provided by the supervisors' praise. During its first two years of shaping behaviors through the use of operant conditioning, Emery Air Freight estimated savings in excess of $2 million.

Skinner based most of his behavior-shaping (operant conditioning) work on the use of positive reinforcement. He also pointed out that negative reinforcement or punishment also works, even though it may create resentment, fear, and limit creativity and innovation. Negative reinforcement teaches people to avoid certain types of behavior. A rule stating that unexcused absence or tardiness can lead to warnings, reprimands, and dismissal is a type of negative reinforcement. Employees who receive warnings or reprimands for undesirable behavior tend to avoid behavior that may not be in their best interest.

Why Some People Learn Faster Than Others

For many years Liam Hudson[2] at the University of Edinburgh and David Kolb[3] of Harvard have gathered evidence that individuals have different learning styles. These styles determine their areas of interest and predict types of occupations in which they are most likely to excel. One style of learning is convergent thinking. **Convergent thinkers** are precise, well ordered, tend to depend on rules and regulations, and pay close attention to detail. They have a low tolerance of ambiguity and want clear answers to questions. There are very few shades of gray for convergent thinkers. Things are either right or wrong.

Convergent thinkers are precise, well organized, conformist, and detail oriented.

*Divergent thinkers are
people oriented, creative,
unmindful of precise
rules, and deal with
ambiguity quite well.*

Unlike convergent thinkers, **divergent thinkers** are people oriented, creative, dislike details and precise rules, and deal with ambiguity quite well. They recognize that not all things are one way or another. Divergent thinkers do best in jobs that involve people rather than things. They are less organized than convergent thinkers and tend to have a wide variety of interests.

Trainers often notice differences in the way people learn. Some people are very good at learning tasks that require concentration on detail while others are better at those requiring imagination and creativity. Salespeople, as an example, may not be good at accounting or computer programming. Their interests lie more in dealing with people than financial or technical detail.

An additional complication in understanding factors that influence learning is evidence developed by sociobiologists that heredity influences what people can easily learn and not learn.[4] Genetic factors, sociobiologists claim, influence both interests and types of work people choose. Some seem to be able to readily learn communication skills, such as writing and making presentations, but do poorly at mathematics. Others exhibit curiosity in science but have no real interest in dealing directly with people.

All of these theories emphasize that individuals, for whatever reason, are very diverse and no two will respond to training in the same way. Learning is not necessarily a function of intelligence. It is also dependent on interests and special abilities.

*Skill transfer occurs
when job skills or
knowledge learned in a
previous place of work
are brought to a new job.*

Trainers, whether supervisors or training specialists, must also learn to recognize the effects of **skill transfer.** Job skills or knowledge learned in a previous place of employment or training are transferred when the employee changes work. Skill transfer may also occur when employees receive new assignments at their present place of employment. Qualified trainers and supervisors recognize that transfer can be either positive or negative. If an employee's new assignment is virtually identical to that previously learned, very little training may be required because of positive transfer. If there are some similarities but key differences in the sequence of work and required knowledge, then transferred work habits may be difficult to change. Employees will frequently revert to the old way of doing things. Additional post-training follow-up may be necessary to ensure that performance is not suffering due to negative transfer.

First-line managers of highly skilled or professional employees may be able to limit training to orientation of the organization and basic procedures. In such cases employees have the necessary skills and knowledge before being hired. As change in job content occurs, some training is needed to upgrade existing skills. Hospitals, as an example, maintain ongoing training programs for all levels of employees to familiarize them with new medical procedures, equipment, and administration of care. Many organizations, ranging from those in research and development of new products and services to accounting firms and educational institutions, hire people who bring their specialized knowledge with them and often are used to train and upgrade skills of the existing staff.

■ SUPERVISORS AND TRAINING

Supervisors have a number of key roles in training employees. They must be coaches, part-time instructors, and evaluators. In their role as trainers they have a number of difficult and often complex responsibilities. Some of the more important ones, briefly summarized, are:

1. **Needs assessment.** Determination of training needs and objectives is an important supervisory function in the development of programs for employees. In larger organizations with human resource management training departments, supervisors are able to obtain assistance in correctly identifying high-priority training needs. As technology changes, employee assignments shift, and new requirements are imposed, both group and individual training is necessary. Supervisors who are sensitive to change in their work units can usually identify high-priority needs and arrange necessary specialized training.

2. **Planning and facilitating.** Although supervisors do a great deal of coaching in their day-to-day contacts with employees, they usually do not have the time, knowledge or skills to be a trainer for every type of work. They must, however, know how to develop plans that identify who must be trained, when training is to take place, and how it will be accomplished. Frequently they are required to arrange training facilities and obtain people who can do the actual training.

3. **Conducting or arranging on-the-job training.** To do on-the-job training properly requires careful planning and constant evaluation of employee performance. Step-by-step procedures that allow

employees to acquire needed knowledge and skills in an orderly and correct manner are mandatory. Learning by experience is necessary but can be the very worst type of training if the experiences are not expertly guided.

4. Evaluating training results. Unless there are clear benefits in improving performance or increasing competence in the use of new skills and knowledge, training may not be worth its cost. Training for the sake of training has little real value. The primary objectives of all training programs are acquisition of new knowledge and skills and improvements in productivity, quality, and costs.

5. Encouraging self-development. Versatility as well as knowledge and skills are marks of excellent work teams. Employees who understand the benefits of self-development strive to learn and understand more about their fields of work. Best-run organizations encourage employees and managers alike to continue to learn and grow in their competency to deal with increasingly complex assignments.

■ TRAINING EMPLOYEES

There are many types of training. Each can be approached in a variety of ways. Supervisors may not use all of the possible methods of improving employee effectiveness, but it is helpful to understand some of the options.

On-the-job training is the most common type of training. Employees learn while they work.

Most training is **on-the-job (OJT).** Employees learn while they work. OJT is especially useful for new employees. It can be conducted by the supervisor or, as in most cases, by a competent employee who, under the guidance of the first-line manager, both enjoys and is competent in training others.

Characteristics of Effective Trainers

Some people find training others an uncomfortable and irritating experience. It detracts from their regular assignment, they do not like repeating job actions, and fail to understand why new trainees do not fully understand the first time they are shown how to perform a specific task. Table 11.1 briefly summarizes some of the major characteristics of good trainers.

A great deal of OJT is one-on-one. This means the person being trained interacts with only one other person. One-on-one

TABLE 11.1 ■ Characteristics of Good Trainers

1. Patience.	People in training situations are frequently nervous, eager to please, and prone to making mistakes. Competent trainers understand that learning is often a time-consuming process that requires repetition, explanation, and in many instances starting over from the beginning when the trainee obviously does not understand. Impatience shuts off communication. Trainees, fearful of being seen as stupid or inept, will not let the trainer know they lack comprehension of requirements.
2. Personal warmth and empathy.	Trainers who do not intimidate those being trained are usually more successful. They are able to perceive learning from the trainee's perspective. Like other human relationships, building trust and confidence is a valuable attribute. Effective trainers take a friendly, relaxed approach that makes learning seem easy.
3. Recognition of individual differences.	People learn at different rates. Some people learn very rapidly while others take longer. There are many reasons for such differences. From the point of view of the trainer, it is important to not compare people based on speed of learning alone. Extra time and effort with slow learners may have very positive dividends later in terms of appreciation, loyalty, and trust.
4. Careful systematic preparation.	Good trainers have a plan. They break jobs down into understandable elements and make sure that details are covered. Rather than assume all steps are covered, they use carefully prepared checklists and training procedures to help them in their efforts.
5. Willingness to use positive reinforcement.	When learners do something approximately correct, they are praised by good trainers. Ken Blanchard emphasizes that perfection isn't necessary during initial learning.[5] Positive reinforcement through praise and approval speed up the learning process and make it an enjoyable experience. Punishment for errors during learning has just the opposite effect. Fear slows down learning, increases errors, and creates dislike for the task being learned.

training may be combined with class sessions, workshops, simulations, and other group activities. In both group and one-on-one training, competent trainers must exhibit the type of behavior that encourages learning.

First-line managers must assess their own training skills and personal characteristics. Regardless of likes or dislikes, training is one of their most important and universal functions. Their personal behavior on the job trains their employees. Managers who show indifference and lack of interest in the organization or their own work are likely to have employees who act the same way. Management attitudes are copied by employees. Observation is the basis for **social learning**—learning the behavior of peers and those of higher rank—and is one of the most pervasive ways people acquire values, beliefs, and attitudes. Characteristics found in good trainers are usually the same as those found in the best supervisors.

Social learning takes place when employees learn by observing others.

■ COMMON TYPES OF TRAINING

People learn in many ways. Experience is not always the best teacher. Bad habits, incorrect and inefficient ways of performing tasks, and poor attitudes are learned just as easily as those that are correct. Well-developed training efforts improve employee performance, reduce errors, and build confidence. Employees who know how to do things correctly are more willing to accept new challenges. There are many ways to conduct training programs. There is little doubt that the most common type of training occurs on-the-job.[6]

On-the-Job Training

While on-the-job training is frequently haphazard, it can be an effective approach in many jobs. Good OJT is systematic, carefully planned, and consistent. All employees are exposed to the same steps for the tasks for which they are being trained. While supervisors can be helpful advisors and in some instances primary trainers, most OJT is a one-on-one experience between the experienced employee selected as trainer and the trainee. Trainees may be either new employees or those being trained for potential new assignments.

Shadowing involves following a person and learning by observing his or her actions.

One of the more common techniques in OJT is known as **shadowing.** Trainees are assigned to an experienced employee and instructed to observe what the employee does during a regular workday. They act as experienced employee's shadow by close over-the-shoulder watching of each move the trained employee makes. Shadowing is often accompanied by explanations of what is taking place. In well-developed OJT programs, shadowing is followed by more formal instructions.

Job instruction training (JIT), one of the most useful types of OJT, was developed almost 50 years ago during World War II. It is still a useful way to approach OJT as well as many other types of training. There are several variations of the JIT approach but, at a minimum, it consists of the following steps:

1. **Prepare to train.** Preparation consists of breaking the task to be learned into small meaningful steps so they can be mastered one at a time. It also includes developing and planning a sequence of instruction with checklists of steps, if necessary, and preparing mentally to instruct.

2. **Prepare the learner.** Put the learner at ease, find out what she or he may already know, explain the benefits of the training effort, and show enthusiasm and interest. Trainers' attitudes are often the key to the level of importance trainees attach to the training effort.

3. **Demonstrate and explain.** For short tasks it is helpful to provide an overview of the total requirements. This is followed by a more slowly presented show-and-tell of the first step in completing the task. It is important that trainers both demonstrate and explain. Learning is enhanced by both visual and verbal information.

4. **Have the learner demonstrate and explain.** Demonstration and explanation by the learner have three functions. They allow the trainer to observe the learner's performance; they provide a check of the level of the learner's understanding; they also provide practice and experience for the learner. It is essential that the trainer use positive reinforcement at this step.

5. **Provide guided practice.** Let the learner practice while being observed. This provides an opportunity for the learner to improve performance while being coached by the trainer. As in other steps, positive reinforcement of improving performance enhances the learning process. Most people respond to approval and praise. If mistakes occur, coaching rather than reprimanding is the best corrective action.

6. **Release and follow-up.** When the trainee has demonstrated proficiency, constant follow-up is no longer necessary. Employees perform the newly learned tasks as a part of their regular job assignment. Occasional follow-up helps determine if the employee retains satisfactory work habits and provides additional opportunity for both coaching and reinforcement of correct performance.

Cooperative training and apprenticeships allow people to gain job experience while attending college or other training.

In addition to OJT, there are many other types of training. Each has a special purpose. **Cooperative training** and apprenticeships provide both work experience and formal education. Many organizations, both private and public, provide internships that allow students to work part-time in an occupation that matches their college experience. Some companies find these programs a valuable method of recruiting. Apprenticeship programs combine experience in a training setting or college with work as a helper or assistant in an actual work environment. Both internships and apprenticeships are considered types of cooperative training.

Classroom training is sometimes called ***vestibule training***. *It involves demonstration, discussion, and practice.*

Simulation training involves equipment identical to that used on the job.

Vestibule training, or classroom training, takes place at a site separate from the employee's work. Vestibule training often involves actual job equipment, such as computer terminals or registers. In other instances simulators may be used. Some **simulation** equipment is very sophisticated as well as expensive. Airline pilots, astronauts, master pilots for oil tankers, and even oil-field workers are trained in a computerized environment that precisely duplicates actual experiences without endangering the real equipment or the lives of others. Problems can be introduced into the simulator that require the learner to use complex procedures and rapid reactions that may be needed in real-life situations.

Role playing, business games, conferences, and organizational laboratories are all used as training methods.

Some types of training rely largely on lectures, discussions, and familiar classroom activities. Role playing, business games, cases, conferences, and organizational laboratories are also types of simulation used to train by simulating actual experience. **Organizational laboratory** approaches use a variety of games, exercises, and problem-solving situations as team-building types of learning. People learn to work cooperatively rather than competitively in achieving specific goals.

Regardless of the type of training used, trainers must guard against common errors and assumptions. Table 11.2 summarizes some of those most frequently made.

■ EXPECTATIONS, SELF-FULFILLING PROPHESIES, AND THE PYGMALION EFFECT

Like all other management activities, expectations play an important role in training. Trainers who expect their students to learn and achieve are far more likely to have successful students than trainers who doubt their own abilities as well as those of their students. Expectations or self-fulfilling prophesies play an important role in all educational experiences. When learners make the

TABLE 11.2 ■ Common Training Errors

1. Information overload.	People can absorb a limited amount of information at any one time. Experienced trainers explain or demonstrate a single step in performing a given task. They check for understanding before moving on to the next step. Information overload creates confusion and lack of full understanding. Understanding rather than note taking is the goal of all good training.
2. "Its easy" fallacy.	Most work is easy if a person understands and is proficient. A trained pianist can easily read and play music. It is impossible for anyone lacking training to repeat their actions. Most supervisors see jobs as being simple and fail to realize that, to learners, virtually any new activity is difficult until it is understood or its movements are mastered.
3. Failure to recognize individual differences.	Some people are cautious learners. They are very slow, careful, and hesitant. Others learn rapidly and are willing to try new tasks even if they have little understanding of necessary actions. Some people learn primarily by observing, others through reading, and still others by doing. Good trainers use all of the teaching media available. Not all people learn alike nor do they react to learning experiences the same.
4. Lack of adequate preparation.	Teaching others requires more than knowing how to do a particular job. While knowledge is necessary, teaching requires careful preparation and a plan that ensures all aspects of work will be adequately covered. A common error of supervisors and employees assigned to training is the assumption that "if you know it, you can teach it." Competent trainers have to have skills in teaching as well as in performance.
5. Failure to stress benefits.	People are motivated when they clearly understand the benefits of a learning experience. Effective trainers stress advantages of acquiring skills or knowledge. Their enthusiasm and encouragement leads, rather than pushes, others into making learning both interesting, useful and enjoyable.

assumption that "I'll never learn this," they set themselves up for failure. In the same way trainers who feel, "These people will never learn," usually have students who fail.

This Pygmalion effect, the expectations people have of others, is a strong influence on learning. Many experiments have been conducted that clearly demonstrate that people tend to live up to the expectations of others as well as to expectations of themselves. When both the trainer and students have high expectations of success, those expectations are likely to be achieved.

■ EVALUATION OF TRAINING

Training is costly, time consuming, and may take people away from critical tasks. Some training needs are obvious. New employees must learn the tasks they will perform as fully competent members of the organization. All employees must understand new procedures, organizational change, and technology. While few people will deny the value and necessity of training, cost-benefit analysis is a necessary step to determine if it was worth the time and effort. Supervisors as well as training coordinators need ways of evaluating both the effectiveness and cost of training efforts.

One of the less scientific evaluation methods is simple observation of employees at work. If after training their attitudes are more positive, their performance more efficient, and their quality of work improved, then the training may have been well worth the amount of money spent. Observational methods are important but they do not adequately indicate the value of training programs.

Cost-benefit analysis is used to weigh the costs of training against its benefits to determine if the training is cost effective.

Cost-benefit analysis is required to determine the real value of training. It involves determining if the cost of training is more or less than the benefits of training results. For very practical reasons, analysis by supervisors may be somewhat more simple than that used by organizational training departments. Professional trainers measure performance before training and again after training. They can then calculate the amount of improvement after training. Another method used by professional trainers is to compare the performance of a group that has learned by itself without formal training to the performance of a trained group. An acid test is whether or not training enabled employees to attain competent levels of performance sooner than those not trained.

Supervisors, rather than make an elaborate experiment, can make some relatively simple and very practical comparisons. Table 11.3 presents a simplified model of cost-benefit comparison.

Admittedly, expenditures are far easier to precisely compute than gains. Only one gain, improvements in productivity and costs, can be given a solid dollar figure. Other factors must be judged based on the experience of the supervisor. Not all of the costs will come directly from the supervisor's training budget. In

TABLE 11.3 ■ Cost-Benefit Comparison for Training

	Expenditures	*Gains*
Salaries	Trainer, trainee(s), substitutes	Improved productivity and quality
Supplies	Texts, binders, printed material	Shared knowledge gained in training
Equipment	Special equipment or tools	Improved levels of confidence
Expenses	Food, travel, lodging, etc.	Ability to handle increased responsibility
Other	Productivity loss, substitute training	Increased loyalty

large organizations training facility, supplies, materials, equipment, and even travel and food expenses are borne by the organization's training department. Table 11.3 is a simplified model. Cost analysts in larger organizations and accounting departments in smaller ones can assist supervisors in developing methods for training evaluation in terms of direct cost.

In addition to directly measurable benefits, training also has many indirect benefits: increased loyalty, appreciation for the organization's efforts, a stronger feeling of being more than just a hired hand, and appreciation to the supervisor for providing opportunities.

Not all employees will receive equal benefits from the most carefully planned and executed training efforts. Some may find training as a way of determining whether they wish to continue in their present type of employment. Perhaps the most important consideration is that in a rapidly changing environment, training is mandatory. Supervisors must determine if the skills, knowledge, and abilities employees are acquiring are worth the time, effort, and costs to their department and the total organization.

■ SPECIAL TRAINING PROBLEMS

In an ever-changing economic, political, and technological environment, supervisors are faced with many personnel-related difficulties virtually unknown as few as 10 years ago. In their roles as trainers or training facilitators, supervisors should take special interest in four of these.

Disabled Employees

In mid-1990 the United States Congress enacted the Americans with Disabilities Act. As part of the family of civil rights legislation that began in the 1960s, it prohibits discrimination based on physical handicap. Experience indicates that handicapped employees have fewer absences, are more dedicated, and, in general, are valued employees.

Their training needs, however, may be very individual and require specialized equipment and methods. Job assignments must fit physical capabilities. Training that requires physical capability beyond that of the employee is both embarrassing and useless. Supervisors have the responsibility for training of disabled employees in activities that they can be expected to adequately perform. An additional problem, in some instances, is integrating disabled employees into the regular work force. Orientation for employees without serious disability is helpful in the integration process. Most employees will assist those who may have difficulty with some physical aspects of their work. In the future there will be increasing pressure to mainline disabled employees rather than treat them as token, isolated, and ineffective members of work teams.

Technically Obsolete Employees

During the 1980s it became increasingly apparent that **knowledge workers,** employees with special training and experience in utilizing newer technologies, were the most valuable employees. Those who had neither been trained nor had opportunities to learn new skills on the job were rapidly becoming technically obsolete. Blue-collar workers, employees with traditional mechanical skills, were rapidly being replaced by technically trained employees whose skills and knowledge enabled them to fully employ newer methodologies and equipment. Automobile mechanics became technicians, typists changed to word processor operators, and the banking industry found electronic funds transfer had revolutionized their systems. In printing, medical technology, manufacturing, office administration, and every other field of work, skilled jobs were replaced by "smart," electronic equipment. Computer programmers became the new breed of skilled workers. Employees not trained in the newer systems and methods found themselves **technically obsolete.** Without additional training they were virtually unemployable.

Thousands of employees found themselves without work and without knowledge and skills required for a changed place of work. Some states developed special retraining programs for displaced employees, but more often, workers were simply replaced. Organizations affected by changing technology had to make the critical decision to retrain employees with obsolete skills or to replace them with less costly beginners who had the required new skills or would be less resistant to training.

Supervisors in organizations are often charged with determining retraining or replacement needs. Experience has shown that when retraining that builds on old skills is possible, employees appreciate their new opportunities. In some instances employees strongly resist change. This is especially true for occupations where many years of both training and experience are required to become fully competent.

Multicultural, Multilingual Work Forces

One of the major demographic trends in the United States has been the influx of people from Asian, Hispanic, and Eastern European countries. Most bring with them a willingness to work, learn, and become productive citizens. Virtually all must be trained for the jobs they hold in the United States. Supervisors are often faced with both language and customs differences that create unusual difficulties. Some companies have developed special programs to train supervisors with **multicultural** and **multilingual employees**. Others have encouraged supervisors to learn the language of the dominant group of new employees.

Training multicultural and multilingual employees often requires a knowledge of not only language but customs different from those of more established, English-speaking employees. What may be acceptable behavior in one country is both strange and often repugnant to others. This is particularly true of the status of women. Supervisors must develop a knowledge and sensitivity to cultural differences and exercise patience with language difficulties.

Life-Style Differences

Values, attitudes, and beliefs of both individuals and groups differ. Frequently managers find employees with distinctly different values and life-styles from their own. Many so-called "new" employees have little regard for authority, are extremely materialistic, and are quick to invoke a wide range of legal protection if their defiance is challenged.

Although not explicitly protected by national law, sexual preference is an individual choice and is so protected in many states.

People with social diseases such as AIDS may also be immune, by law, from any type of discriminatory action. Civil rights protection extends to life-styles as much as it does to those specifically mentioned in various federal statutes. Supervisors must be careful that in choosing those to be trained that they do not discriminate based on not only race, color, religion, national origin, sex, age, or physical condition, but also on life-style.

While many states have hire-at-will laws that grant the right to both employers and employees to terminate their association at any time for no reason, courts have generally ruled that it is wrongful to terminate a person for his or her apparent life-style. Selection of employees for training, like all other personnel actions, must not be based on life-styles. Four categories or training problems are shown in Figure 11.2.

■ EDUCATION AS A FUNDAMENTAL VALUE

Training concentrates on development of skills and knowledge required for a specific job. Education is a much broader concept. It is directed toward increasing understanding of the world in which

FIGURE 11.2 ■ Special Training Problems

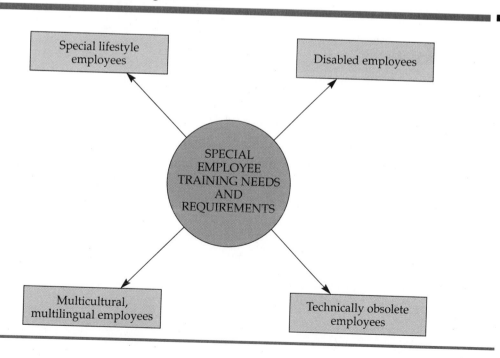

an individual lives. Unlike training, education provides principles and information that allows people to make accurate decisions, evaluate data, and critically appraise what they read or have been told. It has been frequently said that education provides choices. It is a fundamental aspect of freedom. An understanding of the physical, social, political, and economic environments in which people live is essential for those who significantly contribute to their organization and their society as a whole.

One of the great difficulties in a complex society such as that of the United States is the vast differences in levels of education of its inhabitants. Those with education tend to achieve more and enjoy the benefits of society much more than those lacking fundamental knowledge of their world. Many organizations provide training. A few encourage their members to achieve educational goals as well. Incentives such as absorbing costs associated with college or special educational programs, increased pay for successfully completing educational goals, variable work schedules that allow college attendance, and improved opportunities for promotion have proven well worth the costs and time. Supervisors who increase their own educational base and encourage others to do the same find the effort rewarding for themselves, others, and their organization.

■ THINGS TO REMEMBER

    I. Living with change.

       A. Job content is likely to change several times during a person's work life.

       B. Change occurs faster in the workplace than in classrooms.

       C. Supervisors have primary responsibility for determining training needs for their employees.

       D. Training involves learning specific job skills.

       E. Development is preparation for increased responsibility, authority, and personal accountability.

    II. Types of learning.

       A. Psychomotor learning.

       B. Cognitive learning.

       C. Affective learning.

III. Understanding how people learn.

    A. No one knows precisely how people learn or when learning begins.

    B. Learning is a change in behavior resulting from experience or perception.

    C. Conditioning involves connecting one event with another.

    D. Classical conditioning pertains to learning and reacting to events associated with each other.

    E. Operant conditioning is related to repetition of a behavior because of its association with a reward. Behavior is strengthened by repeated rewards.

IV. Supervisors and training.

    A. Most training is on-the-job. Employees learn while they work.

    B. Effective OJT is well planned and systematic.

    C. OJT may be performed by either supervisors or competent employees.

V. Characteristics of effective trainers.

    A. Effective trainers have a number of special characteristics including patience, personal warmth, recognition of individual differences, careful preparation and willingness to use positive reinforcement.

    B. People learn in many ways.

VI. Common types of training.

    A. Well-developed training programs build confidence, reduce errors, and improve efficiency.

    B. On-the-job training requires preparing to train, preparing the learner to learn, demonstrating and explaining, having the learner demonstrate and explain, guided practice, release, and follow-up.

    C. Cooperative training and apprenticeships, vestibule training, simulation, role playing, business games, cases, conferences, and organizational laboratories are all types of training.

    D. Common training errors include informational overload, the "it's easy" fallacy, failure to recognize individual differences, lack of adequate preparation, and failure to stress training benefits.

VII. Expectations, self-fulfilling prophesies, and Pygmalion effect.

   A. Learners who expect to learn and instructors who expect to succeed both have greater success than those who do not have positive expectations.

   B. Expectations of others strongly influence learning processes.

VIII. Evaluation of training.

   A. Training is costly, time consuming, and may take people away from critical work.

   B. Cost-benefit analysis is used to evaluate training.

IX. Special training problems.

   A. Disabled employees.

   B. Technically obsolete employees.

   C. Multicultural and multilingual work forces.

   D. Life-style differences.

X. Education as a fundamental value.

   A. Education enables individuals to better understand their many environments.

   B. Organizations that encourage self-development benefit from better-qualified employees.

■ KEY TERMS

training	OJT
development	social learning
psychomotor learning	shadowing
cognitive learning	JIT
affective learning	cooperative training
learning	vestibule training
conditioning	simulation
classical conditioning	organizational laboratory
operant conditioning	information overload
reinforcement	cost-benefit analysis
convergent thinkers	knowledge workers
divergent thinkers	technically obsolete
skill transfer	multicultural employees
needs assessment	multilingual employees

▪ DISCUSSION QUESTIONS

1. Give examples of psychomotor, cognitive, and affective training based on your personal experience or knowledge.

2. Lecture and discussion are the primary tools of educators. What are some of the weaknesses of this methodology?

3. In some types of work, people are hired because they have specialized knowledge that their organization is unable to provide. List five such jobs with which you are familiar.

4. What types of educational experiences do you enjoy the most? What attracts you to them?

5. Austin Kiplinger, publisher of the famous "Kiplinger Letter" and *Changing Times,* is fond of stating, "The business of the United States is education." What does Mr. Kiplinger mean by his statement?

▪ SELF-ASSESSMENT

How knowledgeable are you about training? Mark the following statements with a 1, 2, or 3 if you disagree or have a negative response or with a 4, 5, or 6 if you agree or have a positive response.

1. Once a skill has been learned and perfected, no additional training is needed.

   1   2   3   4   5   6

2. Examples set by supervisors are one type of training.

   1   2   3   4   5   6

3. Swift, but not harsh, punishment is the most effective way of improving work habits.

   1   2   3   4   5   6

4. Supervisors must be able to perform specific tasks better than their employees.

   1   2   3   4   5   6

5. Experience is, in the final analysis, the best teacher.

   1   2   3   4   5   6

6. People learn better in short sessions that in long, continuous ones.

   1   2   3   4   5   6

7. People learn specific psychomotor tasks at approximately the same rate.

   1   2   3   4   5   6

8. Talented people require little or no practice to improve their performance.

   1   2   3   4   5   6

9. Most employees prefer simple repetitive jobs to those that are difficult and challenging.

   1   2   3   4   5   6

10. Both negative and positive reinforcement works in training situations.

   1   2   3   4   5   6

■ SHORT CASES

Do It Again, Stupid

As supervisor of Southwestern Investment Company's central statistical analysis department, Burt Hall had primary responsibility for analysis of sales data, market trends, economic forecast data, and regional demographic changes. As a first-line manager with 12 highly skilled employees, his job was in some ways more enjoyable than that of other supervisors. His employees were knowledgeable, competent, and productive.

One of Burt's difficulties was new employee training. Most of his employees came from other departments and were familiar with the organization's computerized central data system. Their training was, for the most part, limited to learning specific types of reporting and methods of data retrieval required for statistical reports. These reports were used by virtually every level of management in making critical decisions. He felt obligated to do most of the training himself to make sure good work habits were established. It also allowed him to better assess new employee potential. While it was an important priority, he knew very little about effective training methods.

Esther Garza came to Burt's group from the human resource management records department with top recommendations. She had good computer skills but seemed to be having constant problems correctly gathering data and formatting the daily sales report. "It's perfectly simple!" he exploded to the almost tearful Esther.

"I've told you three times how to do it and shown you twice. Can't you get it right just once? Now watch me again." Esther nervously clutched her notepad and pencil and waited for Burt to start. As Burt started through the first steps of calling up sales data, he could not get the desired result. "Hand me that manual," he impatiently stated. After following every step and using all of his experience, the program would not work. In total frustration he called Joan Kirby, supervisor of computer operations.

"Oh," laughed Joan at Burt's questions about the procedure, "didn't someone tell you? We have a glitch in the master program and it doesn't always give the right data. It's being fixed now and should be OK by around 2:30 this afternoon."

Burt's embarrassment was apparent to Esther. Burt looked at her and said, "We'll try again at 2:30. In the meantime you can get Tom Spivey to tell you about demographics." He did not tell Esther about the defective program.

1. What must Burt do to improve his training techniques?

2. What should Burt have done before his session with Esther?

3. In the future should Burt continue to try to train or should he assign training duties to others?

Some of Our Employees

Peggy Armonde was faced with a special set of problems. In an effort to comply with the spirit of equal opportunity in employment, her company had agreed to hire a number of immigrants from Eastern European countries. All were well educated, well behaved, and could speak only fragmented English. According to the human resource department, all had worked as technicians for a major Czechoslovakian health service agency.

In her role as first-line manager for fluids and specimens at American Laboratory Services Organizations (ALSO), Peggy had major responsibility for testing and identifying human biological specimens sent to ALSO. Her employees were trained to do complex analysis with the latest biological testing equipment.

"I know these people have good potential," she stated to Dr. Sheila Kilpatrick, her immediate manager. "Their education and experience is better than most new employees. But how am I going to make them understand me? How can I teach them our procedures and the use of our equipment?" "Peggy," Dr. Kilpatrick replied. "that's why we made you supervisor. You can find a way."

1. What are some possible first steps Peggy can take in training the new employees?

2. Should companies hire employees for critical jobs who have difficulties with English? Explain your response.

3. Once they have learned to speak and understand English, should Peggy's employees be allowed to speak their native language at work?

■ ENDNOTES

1. Brian Dumaine, "Who Needs A Boss?," *Fortune*, May 7, 1990, pp. 52–60.

2. Liam Hudson, *Contrary Imaginations* (New York: Penguin Books, 1977). Dr. Hudson has published many other books and papers in more recent years. This one, however, explains his theories best.

3. David Kolb, et. al., *Organizational Psychology: An Experimental Approach,* 4th edition (Englewood Cliffs, N.J.: Prentice Hall, 1990).

4. Dan Costley and Ralph Todd, *Human Relations in Organizations*, 5th edition (St. Paul, Minn.: West Publishing Company, 1991), p. 7. Cites work of Edward O. Wilson at Harvard University.

5. Kenneth Blanchard, *Putting the One Minute to Work,* Nightingale-Conant Audio, 1988. Two audiocassettes.

6. Robert Jackson and John Madhouse, *Personnel/Human Resource Management,* 5th edition (St. Paul, Minn.: West Publishing Company, 1988), p. 262.

Part V

Stress, Conflict, and Discipline

■ Frustration, stress, conflict, and the need for discipline are, like change, inevitable consequences of life. In a work environment they become special problems for supervisors. Rather than try to eliminate frustration, stress, and conflict, and act as enforcers of discipline, excellent supervisors learn to manage and reduce tensions that ultimately create problems.

Chapters 12, 13, and 14 examine causes of frustration and stress, emphasize the importance of managing conflict, and teach that the most effective discipline is self-control. These issues affect the fundamental physical and psychological health of individuals and organizations. It is interesting that the recognition of the effects of stress, the need for conflict management, and better methods for teaching discipline are relatively new to management. Traditionally discipline and conflict management have focused on correction and punishment while the effects of prolonged stress were ignored. All are important to the functioning of organizations and their management comprises an especially difficult set of supervisory skills. Some of these skills are recognizing the symptoms of excessive frustration and stress, developing methods for stress and frustration reduction and management, distinguishing between positive and negative conflict, and assessing and correcting disciplinary problems.

Chapter 12

Frustration and Stress

Objectives

Chapter 12 examines both frustration and stress in organizations. Those who read it will be able to

- Identify major causes of frustration.
- Recognize types of inner conflict and their effects.
- Distinguish between stress and distress.
- Define major adjustive reactions.
- Apply reasonable stress-management techniques.

Thought Starter

Life changes have a way of piling up. One disastrous life event seems to lead to another. When problems at home are amplified by problems at work, minor irritations may one day become major stress points in people's lives. Thomas Holmes and Ella M. David are credited with devising the first index of the effects of life events on human health.[1] Each event they classified was a cause of stress. If, Holmes and David concluded, a person has a score on his index of stressors in excess of 200, some type of illness is likely to occur as a result of the overwhelming stress related to change. Here are the top 10 items on their social readjustment scale:

Life Event	Point Value
1. Death of a spouse	100
2. Divorce	73
3. Marital separation	65
4. Death of a close family friend	63
5. Detention in a jail or other institution	63
6. Major personal injury or illness	53
7. Marriage	50
8. Fired at work	47
9. Marital reconciliation	45
10. Retirement	45

While Holmes's life-event changes are interesting, they are not necessarily the same for every person. Divorce can be an intensely distressing event for some individuals. For others it can be a relief from stress. Change, in itself, can bring about stress but not necessarily distress. We must not forget that every person reacts to stress factors in their lives differently.

■ *Periodically the country's economy falters. Regardless of the causes, its effects are often sources of uncertainty and pressure for many people. Organizations faced with financial slowdowns tend to reduce the number of employees as a major component of their cost-cutting effort. Those directly affected must find new work in difficult circumstances. Remaining employees sense the threat of additional reductions and managers recognize that their personal survival depends on outstanding performance. Stress is real, constant, and often debilitating.*

When rough sailing for organizations is apparent, a gentle hand by management helps.[2] Team building, improved communication, and social events that show appreciation are all helpful. Major organizations such as American Steel and Wire Company, Times Mirror Magazine Company, and USX have learned that heavy-handed cutting with little concern for survivors is counterproductive. Rhodes Furniture Company, with 73 stores, put its employees in charge of finding ways to cut costs. Irwin Rhodes, CEO for Rhodes, also urged his managers to use positive reinforcement to ease the stress on employees. Both moves were effective.

In spite of moves to use a gentle hand, managers and many employees find themselves overworked and frustrated with the lack of time and employees to accomplish needed work.

■ FRUSTRATION—CONFLICT WITHIN

On a cold December morning Joe Harris, supervisor for Quick-Start Warehouse, rushed to his car. He was leaving slightly late for work where an important meeting was scheduled to start at 8:30. There was just enough time to arrive, quickly check his desk, and hurry to the meeting. As he turned the key to the ignition, the engine turned very slowly and then made no noise. After four tries, it was clear that the battery had failed. Joe's wife had already left for her job in their other car. In total frustration, he got out of the car, slamming the door. When his dog Iris ran up to him, joyous at his being at home with her, he yelled, "Get out of here!" Iris, head down, moved away.

Frustration occurs when there is any interference with goal-directed behavior or perceived inability to satisfy a need.

Frustration occurs when there is any interference with goal-directed behavior or perceived inability to satisfy a need. One of two general reactions occur to frustration. In Joe Harris's case, attack accompanied by anger resulted from interference with his goal of reaching work in time for the meeting. Another general reaction is withdrawal. Both attack and withdrawal take on many forms.

Causes of Frustration

Frustration can be caused by either external or internal conditions. An employee who works hard for a promotion and does not receive it may withdraw from any future attempts to gain promotion. Lack of confidence and resentment, both internal conditions, as well as lack of adequate opportunity in their present employment, an external condition, can increase frustration levels. Individual attitudes help shape frustration reactions. Those with positive, optimistic attitudes tend to overcome disappointment and temporary failure by showing a willingness to continue to accept challenges, while others sink into bitterness and indifference.

Conflicts Within

Unmade decisions can also lead to frustration or intensify existing tensions. When choices between alternatives must be made, frustration can continue until a decision is reached. An employee who has been given a list of tasks to perform may have difficulty with determining priorities. Without guidance from the supervisor, the employee must decide which job is most important and needed first. If the wrong choice is made, the supervisor may blame the employee.

Employees who observe cheating or wrongdoing by other employees must make the decision whether to inform their immediate manager. Lack of knowledge of the consequences of being an informer may lead to a sense of uneasiness and frustration. Decisions that involve a high degree of uncertainty or appear to have potentially negative results are especially frustrating.

Attack is a generalized reaction to frustration that takes the form of problem solving, anger, increased energy, and at times physical action against the perceived cause of frustration.

Withdrawal from frustrating conditions is a common reaction to frustration. It may take many forms, such as daydreaming, physically leaving, sleeping, or changing the topic during a discussion.

Frustration Reactions

Goal-directed behavior is any action an individual takes to satisfy a need. If the action is blocked, the person may aggressively **attack** the cause of the interference. In a job, employees having difficulty performing a task may try again, ask for help, or read procedures. Problem-solving behavior is a positive response to frustration. Problems rather than people are attacked. If problem solving fails to work, the employee may put the job aside and work on something else or temporarily leave the work area. **Withdrawal** does not solve problems but it removes the individual from the cause of frustration. Supervisors, frustrated with slower than expected performance, may first react by attack and then withdrawal.

Relatively mild frustration can result in increased energy, problem solving, creativity, and ultimately success in reaching a goal. Most people habitually attempt several times to solve the cause of their frustration. Since repeated success leads to self-confidence, mild frustration and problem solving often have beneficial results.

Prolonged Frustration

Continued frustration over long periods of time can lead to chronic irritability, anger, or disinterest. A more serious consequence of prolonged frustration is its effects on an individual's health. Nervousness, headaches, back problems, and digestive disorders have all been initiated by continued frustration. One major difficulty of extended frustration is its effect on other problems. Unable to solve pressing personal or work difficulties, individuals may develop feelings of failure, lack of confidence, and incompetency. They become hesitant, tentative, and reluctant to try new alternatives to solving their problems. Misery becomes a normal mode of life.

Supervisors who recognize employee frustration can assist in problem solving, substitute a particularly frustrating assignment for one less difficult, and positively reinforce attempts at problem solving. They must also recognize that individuals react differently to frustrating conditions. Some people have "quick triggers" and immediately react with anger or withdrawal to relatively slight barriers in achieving their goals. Less temperamental individuals will view the same problem as a challenge and patiently work toward solutions with little evidence of any real frustration. Like all other aspects of human behavior, no two people react to the same set of conditions in precisely the same way. Figure 12.1 graphically defines the frustration process.

■ STRESS

Stress is the result of any set of conditions that puts an individual off balance or increases the need for action.

There is an old saying that all pumpkins are squash but not all squash are pumpkins. Frustration produces stress but not all stress is the result of frustration. **Stress,** like the word *love*, has no precise, scientific definition. It has a variety of meanings that are best understood by the way the word is used. Anxiety, tension, strain, and pressure are common terms associated with the word *stress*. Most of the current interest in the effect of stress on people can be traced to the work of Dr. Hans Selye, an endocrinologist at

FIGURE 12.1 ■ Needs, Action, and Frustration

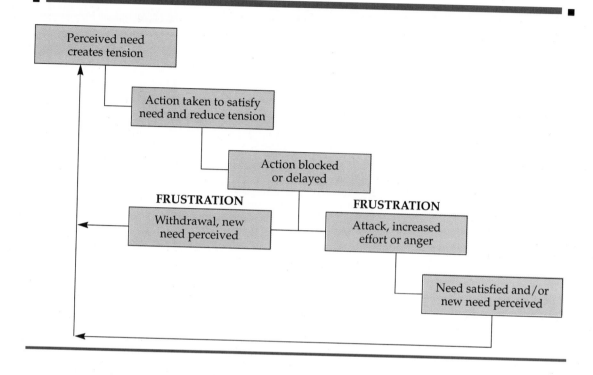

the University of Montreal. In his 40 years of research he concluded that stress is a major life factor. "Without stress," he stated, "there can be no life."[3] Stress, like perception and motivation, are normal life components. Selye's major contribution was not only bringing the attention of research to stress factors in life but recognizing excessive stress as a cause of physical as well as psychological disorder. In a work environment stress is the result of any set of conditions that puts an individual off balance or increases the need for action.[4]

Stress Reactions

Stress reactions are nonspecific. Exercise can lead to physical stress that is usually short lived and can be beneficial. Increased heart rate, perspiration, muscle tension, and changes in breathing can also be caused by threat or perceived threat to either the real or symbolic self.

When a person is physically threatened by possibility of accident, anger of another person, or forces in nature both physical

FIRST-LINERS

Attack on an individual's symbolic self, what people think an individual is, may be equally or more stressful than physical attacks.

and psychological, stress is experienced. In much the same way, threats of a person's **symbolic self** may be more common and equally stressful. When an individual is called *dumb, clumsy, incompetent,* or demeaned in other ways, their feelings about themselves are threatened. S. I. Hayakawa is credited with convincingly demonstrating that attacks on a person's self-esteem or sense of belonging can be as stressful as physical threat.[5]

Stress results from physical activity, frustration, personal illness, unsatisfied needs, or external factors, such as world conditions, economic status, political actions, and family conflict. There is no limit to the number of situations that give rise to stress. It is a normal, inevitable consequence of life.

■ STRESS AND DISTRESS

Distress is negative stress. It prevents individuals from effectively coping with the events from which stress originates.

Stress develops when an individual encounters any type of change. Its intensity depends on the degree of involvement by the individual, perceived threat, or concern for other individuals. Mild stress energizes, adds interest and challenge to life, and can lead to beneficial behavior. A need to get a job completed will lead to activity with the end effect of satisfaction when it is accomplished. Negative stress or **distress** occurs when stress reaches the point where individuals feel they cannot effectively cope with the events from which the stress originates. Most people do not recognize stress until it becomes distressful or disrupts their normal pace of living. In a job environment stress rises from not only

TABLE 12.1 ■ Typical Causes of Job Stress

Internal	External
Uncertainty of future events	Noise, temperature, vibration, air quality
Concern for self or another person	Work overload
Guilt	Unrelenting time pressures
Poor interpersonal relations	Demands by managers or others
Perceived threat or fear of failure	Difficult customers or vendors
Dislike of organization or job assignment	Poor or unfair company policy
Dislike of fellow employees or supervisor	Inadequate information or training
Insecurity	Unfair disciplinary procedures
Sense of rejection or not belonging	Incompetent management
Feelings of being in an economic trap	Poor equipment, materials, or supplies

work demands but a variety of other factors. Table 12.1 summarizes typical examples of job stress factors.

Although Table 12.1 lists a number of job stressors, it is by no means complete. Lack of responsibility and authority, unclear knowledge of organizational or work goals, lack of help in completing difficult tasks, unfair criticism, and favoritism by managers can all lead to job stress. Stress at work can come from many and often unexpected sources.

Stress management does not seek elimination of stress but attempts to keep it below the level of distress.

Stress management does not seek elimination of stress. Dull, uninteresting work in a climate with little or no change can create its own negative levels of stress. Work that is challenging with achievable goals, a sense of excitement, and an aura of high expectations results in positive stress. **Stress management** involves keeping stress at a level that places reasonable demands on members of the organization but does not push them beyond their performance limits. Supervisors should also recognize that both they and their employees have individual levels of stress tolerance. A few employees will relish difficult challenge while others will respond with fear and resentment.

■ STRESS CARRIERS AND PRESSURE WORKERS

Stress Carriers

During the early years of this century typhoid fever was one of the most dreaded diseases all over the world. In New York City a

Stress carriers are people who cause stress in others but remain relatively stress-free.

cook, who became known at *Typhoid Mary,* spread the disease to many customers for a 23-year period. Although Mary was never diagnosed as having symptoms of the disease herself, she readily transmitted it to others through food handling.

Some people are like Typhoid Mary. They never seem to suffer stress but readily create it in others. In work organizations managers who make unreasonable demands on employees, give them conflicting priorities, make special assignments that prevent regular work from being accomplished, and assign last-minute overtime work before employees have had an opportunity to change personal plans are just a few examples. **Stress carriers** rarely realize the havoc they create in the lives of others. They are usually one-way communicators and rarely listen to employee explanations or reasons for difficulties in finishing previously assigned work.

Upper levels of management, middle-managers, and supervisors may all be stress carriers. Each level carries stress to the levels below it. Supervisors with high energy levels and needs for achievement may be the worst offenders. While their enthusiasm and drive are commendable, their lack of sensitivity to the effects of their demands results in stressed-out employees. Typical employee reactions are outright anger, silent withdrawal, and developing a pattern of avoiding the supervisor when possible.

Both employees and supervisors will choose to seek other employment if the stress level reaches the point where pleasing the boss isn't worth the time and effort they are required to spend. Competent supervisors must learn to recognize that fine line between adding responsibility and authority and simply overloading employees with work.

Pressure Workers

Pressure workers work best under stressful conditions.

Frequently supervisors and employees react to lack of stress factors in their lives by seeming to deliberately procrastinate in the completion of importance projects. Even though an early start would mean time to finish well before the scheduled due date, they will delay working on difficult jobs until the approaching deadline forces them into action. These **pressure workers** are more common than those who start and complete requirements early. Pressure workers are usually self-confident, competent people who know they'll get things completed on time. They have learned that they work best under pressure.

Although pressure workers may meet most of their scheduled deadlines, they also have a tendency to not make allowances for interruptions, delays, and lack of information that can cause schedules to be missed. Pressure workers are special problems for managers. Their constant procrastination is frustrating and confusing. No one doubts their ability, but apparent inaction on needed projects creates stress not only for themselves but for others as well.

■ ADJUSTIVE REACTIONS

For many years psychologists have observed that people adjust to intolerable levels of stress in many ways. In addition to the generalized reactions of attack and withdrawal associated with frustration, other types of behavior are often exhibited. A close correlation exists between the intensity of stress and the type of behavior exhibited by an individual. Mild stress is usually dealt with by acting to solve a problem, achieve a goal, or change existing conditions. Action is taken and stress levels are reduced. As stress increases, people tend to use a wide range of behaviors to defend their symbolic self. Few people enjoy being seen or perceiving themselves as failures, incompetent, procrastinators, inattentive, or lacking credibility. They defend personal deficiencies by adopting protective measures.

Adjustive reactions are defenses people use to alleviate stress symptoms.

Although many psychology texts call them *defensive mechanisms*, we believe that the term **adjustive reactions** is more descriptive. One type of adjustive reaction is to change behavior to meet the expectations of others.

> After being laid off from Progressive Insurance due to a massive reduction in work force and elimination of her work unit, Henri (Henrietta) Santos-Coy accepted a job as office manager with Founders Health Maintenance Organization. She supervised 17 clerical employees with primary responsibility for patient medical records. Henri's management style was relatively informal and highly participative. She felt her role was that of an encourager, coach, and leader. While she submitted required weekly progress reports, most of her contact with the director of Administrative Services was verbal and informal. Her sense of humor seemed to please employees but irritate her immediate manager. On two occasions during her first month of employment she was warned for being too close to employees and not taking her job seriously.
>
> As a result of the warnings and the coolness of her manager, Henri became tense, had periods of intense anxiety, and would often

leave her office at night literally in tears. She was suffering all of the symptoms of intense job stress. As a survival technique, she began submitting a daily log of her activities to the director outlining her activities and in-progress and completed projects in her work unit. She made it a point when talking with the director to say very little other than to answer direct questions. Although her relations with employees remained good, she changed her conduct when dealing with her boss. Her former openness, candor, and sense of humor were totally suppressed. In their place she substituted seriousness, quietness, and an appearance of deference. Two weeks after the change she received a commendation for being an outstanding supervisor. She was irritated by the flattery, but realized that her survival technique worked.[6]

Not all stress adjustment is as productive as Henri's. She was fortunately able to realize that pressure would continue until she met the expectations of others. Although she does not intend to remain with her current organization due to its shortsighted view of what she believes management should be, Henri is a survivor. Survival in a work environment may mean reducing stress through changing behavior.

Common reactions to stress are attempts to relieve stress by protecting an individual's symbolic self. They do not remedy the underlying causes of stress reactions. Some of the more common types of adjustive reactions include

Rationalization takes the form of making excuses.

1. Rationalization. Making excuses for a failure that a person either caused or was responsible for is known as **rationalization.** Stress is reduced because there is a good reason, if not an honest one. "Not enough time," "Someone failed to provide information," "The equipment didn't work," "I was waiting in line," and interference by someone else are all common excuses. Like a student trying to explain a late paper, people try to relieve the stress of job failure by making excuses. There are two primary types of rationalization:

Sour grapes. There is an old fable attributed to Aesop called *The Fox and the Grapes.* According to the story a fox spies a cluster of grapes hanging from the limb of a tree. In an effort to get the grapes, the fox jumps as high as he can but misses. Again he jumps and again fails. He repeats the jumps but still does not reach the grapes. As the fox dejectedly walks away from the still-hanging grapes, he mumbles to himself, "They were probably sour anyway."

Sour-grapes rationalizations involve making excuses for a personal failure. "I didn't get the promotion because she was the boss's favorite," "There wasn't enough time," "I didn't know when it was due," and "No one told me it had to be done" are all typical sour-grapes rationalizations.

Sweet lemon. A man married a very homely woman who had a beautiful singing voice. On the morning after their wedding night he looked at his bride lying beside him. "I'm sure glad you have a beautiful voice," he whispered. Sweet-lemon rationalizations attempt to make a bad situation look good. "My job isn't that interesting but it's a good living," "It was very neat even if there were a couple of mistakes," and "He's got a sour disposition but he's a fair boss" are examples of sweet-lemon rationalizations.

Projection means blaming others who are not the cause of stress problems.

2. Projection. While rationalization may be the most common adjustive reaction, **projection** is a close second. Rene Sterns was called into her boss's office for a quick conference. "Rene," she started, "that ad you sent out for publication in *Chemical Engineering News* has two major typographical errors. One is a misspelled word. The other is an incorrect price quotation. Thank goodness Rick Moyer caught it before it went to press. You can do better than that. From now on, I want you to get Rick to proof all copy you send to publishers." Rene knew she had been chewed out. She was also angry at Rick even though he had prevented a major mistake. Her pride was hurt because she had always been trusted to complete the final proofreading. That night when she went home, her husband suggested that they go out for dinner. "What's wrong with eating here? You're in a mood to spend money," she snapped. "I was . . .," he started to explain. "Just don't say another word. I'm not in the mood for an argument," she angrily returned. Her husband quietly sat down and opened the daily newspaper. I wonder what's eating her, he thought.

Energy, in this case in the form of anger, is released by projecting it onto someone other than the cause. Rene could not attack either her immediate supervisor or her co-worker Rick. By projecting her tension toward her husband, she released some of her immediate intense feelings that generated a great deal of stress. Later when she apologized to her husband, after some of the stress was resolved by both her outburst and the passage of time, she was able to further reduce her stress by talking about her job conditions.

3. Transference. "I really need some advice," Ray Hamilton quietly spoke to Marie. "Both Sue and Howard disagree with my plan for reorganizing our schedule process. We're all on the same committee, but we can't seem to work together. What should I do?"

"Let me think it over," returned Marie. "Thanks," Ray smiled. He felt better. Marie would solve his problem. He would check with her tomorrow. Ray walked away feeling better. His problem now belonged, as least for the time being, to Marie. Marie wasn't sure why, but she felt irritable after Ray left.

Transference involves giving a problem to others to solve.

Transference is another type of adjustive reaction designed to protect self-esteem by literally *giving* a personal problem to someone else to solve. Over 60 years ago Sigmund Freud recognized transference as a means of relieving tension. Supervisors allow employees to transfer their problems to them. It is a poor practice. Employees, like all people, must learn to deal with their own problems and supervisors are not trained clinical psychologists.

4. Repression. "You can't imagine the strain I've been under." Sue Howe was near tears in her conversation with Barbara Spinx. "Yesterday I totally forgot that I was supposed to give the opening presentation at our weekly staff meeting. When the boss called on me, I was embarrassed and had to stumble through a request that my presentation be delayed until next week. Why did I forget?"

Repression means forgetting the causes of stress.

A common symptom of excessive stress is repression. **Repression** means forgetting past events that were painful, people that were particularly disliked, and tasks that interfere with other activities. It is a form of active forgetting. Stress often leads to forgetfulness of those things that can potentially add to the pressure of present conditions. Both supervisors and employees are repression prone if conditions are stressful, particularly time pressures.

5. Identification. Charles Rusk enjoyed the good life. He was dean of the School of Business and Economics at the local university, well respected, and had many friends. Early on a beautiful Saturday morning his wife, Lori, announced, "I entered a contest a few weeks ago and found out yesterday that I've won three months' free rent at the new Palace Arms apartments just off Madison Avenue." Charles looked at Lori wondering why she entered the contest. "Chuck, it just isn't working out. Tomorrow I'm moving out. You make the most money, you can have the kids. I want my own life." Charles was stunned.

Two weeks after Lori's departure members of Charles's staff observed a marked change. Chuck had his hair permed, was growing a beard, and came to work tieless with a gold chain hanging around his neck. After his divorce from Lori and his marriage to Karen, his face was again shaven, shoes shined, and gone was the gold chain and casual shirt. His friends commented, "Chuck is his old self again."

Identification occurs when people feel their present way of life if not successful. In an attempt to relieve personal stress they imitate others whom they see as successful. Young women often copy the hair styles of popular actresses, sports figures, or women they see as leaders. Men will talk, act, and dress like those who are part of the "in group." Most style fads are built on identification. If people do not like who they are, they identify with someone else and try to copy their appearance and apparent lifestyle.

Few stress reactions are more apparent than identification. Sudden changes in behavior, speech, or dress may signal serious stress reactions.

Identification occurs when a person takes on the characteristics or even the life-style of others whom they admire. It is a rejection of their personal symbolic self.

6. Regression. "It wasn't like this in the good old days," Don Hammel quietly stated. "I wish things were like they were when I was growing up."

"Stop acting childish," snapped Ellen. Bob was giggling and playing with an old yo-yo once owned by his now nearly grown children.

Both Don and Bob are showing signs of regression. **Regression** means going back in time to another style and type of life. Like identification, regression removes the person from factors currently causing stress. It is an attempt to reject a current stress-filled life. In work environments it may take the form of adult temper tantrums, pranks, horseplay, or other behavior not normally seen. Chronic regression symptoms may be relatively intense and warrant psychological counseling. It is a common intermittent behavior, however, and usually passes in a relatively short period of time. It should not be a serious concern for supervisors unless it is frequently repeated over a long period of time.

Regression means to go back in time either through remembering the "good old days" or acting childishly.

7. Reaction formation. "Management is always right," proclaimed Candice Wong. "They know best." Fellow workers felt she had gone too far. Candice, like many other employees, had just received her lay-off notice due to lack of business. She was contradicting her most basic feelings. Candice, in the deepest parts of her consciousness, knew management was incorrect in ordering random reductions in the work force as a cost-saving effort. Although she loudly proclaimed loyalty, her underlying feelings were of hate and distrust.

Reaction formation is the denial of one's own basic desires. People under extreme stress will adopt what they believe is a socially acceptable standard of behavior even though it violates their most basic needs. Highly public examples of reaction formation are television evangelists who preach against sexual sin but who patronize prostitutes, molest children, and engage in the very acts they tell others are sinful.

In a work environment people who become zealots about any topic, including theft of organizational property, alcoholism, loyalty to the organization, or the sexual behavior of others, may suffer from this odd type of stress reaction. Rather than admit their true feelings, they take a stance that they see is more socially acceptable and defend it with energy and emotion.

Texts on abnormal psychology abound with reactions to stress. Supervisors, as managers of people, must develop a sensitivity to sudden changes in behavior both in themselves and in others. Most stress symptoms will eventually abate with time. When they persist, supervisors must seek guidance from professionals in ways to help overstressed employees.

Dr. Dee Soder, a New York psychologist whose Endymion Company provides stress counseling, notes that physical symptoms may be the most visible evidence of stress that has become destructive.[7] Chronic headaches, sleep disorders, chest pains, depression, and fatigue are common signals. These symptoms are not in a person's mind but are real physical disorders brought about by the inability of employees and managers to cope with events both at work and in their lives. They are no less real than similar symptoms caused by disease or physical trauma.

■ PRACTICAL STRESS MANAGEMENT FOR SUPERVISORS

Supervisors who recognize their own symptoms are able to empathize with some of the indications of excessive stress in employees. Some of the more common responses to stress are rapid pulse rate or pounding heart, increased perspiration in hands, underarms, and forehead, tightening of jaw muscles and clamping of teeth, general irritability, excessive body movement in legs or hands, compressed lips, and tightening of facial muscles.

A number of positive stress-management steps can be taken by sensitive, observant supervisors. Simply encouraging people to talk and listening carefully to their concerns are effective starting points for stress relief. Many people find talking about their job or personal problems relieves feelings of stress even if the underlying conditions still exist.

In a work environment mutual trust between managers and employees is a primary stress-management tool. Mutual trust is developed by action. Managers who are accessible, highly visible, and willing to listen enhance trust levels in organizations. Table 12.2 briefly summarizes frequent sources of stress that can be reduced by supervisory action.

Stress Management in Practice

As a starting point in stress management, supervisors must ask themselves if they are stress carriers, tend to project their personal stress to others, or are insensitive to the feelings and reactions of their employees. They must also recognize that *stress* is a neutral term. Hans Selye used the term **eustress** to describe the type of stress that is beneficial and necessary in energizing people. Human beings are constantly adapting to both external and internal forces in their lives. These adjustments are responses that help maintain an individual's sense of being able to cope with events in their lives. Eustress and distress are contrasted in Figure 12.2.

Eustress is stress that is beneficial and necessary.

Selye emphasized that **distress**, resulting from intense, continuous stressors, creates problems for both physical and psychological well-being. Due to individual differences there is no universal optimum level of stress. There are observable symptoms of distress that first-line managers can be aware of in both themselves and their employees.

Distress creates problems for both physical and psychological well-being.

1. Difficulty in remembering important information, such as names, meeting times, appointments, and events.
2. Procrastination and vacillation in making key decisions.
3. Tendency to be overcritical of others and not admit personal mistakes.
4. Overconcern with personal errors or failure.
5. Feelings of tenseness, nervousness, and anxiety.
6. Lack of appetite, insomnia, headaches, and digestive problems.

TABLE 12.2 ■ Sources of Stress that Can Be Reduced by Supervisors

1. Unequal distribution of effort	First-line managers have the tendency to assign the most challenging work to those with proven past performance. In addition to the stress of extra work placed on the most competent employees, those not given demanding assignments feel the manager has little confidence in their ability to perform. Stress is increased for more than one member of the work team.
2. Unreasonable standards	Supervisors often make the mistake of setting standards based on the performance of their best employees. Other members of the work group may perform well but are never able to produce at the level of those who are more adept. Pressure from unreasonable performance expectations can add unneeded stress.
3. Lack of challenge	Most organizations attempt to hire the brightest, most competent, or most trainable employees available. They then make the mistake of assigning them to dull, repetitive jobs. After the initial learning period, intelligent, capable employees realize they have jobs that do not utilize their real potential. Dissatisfaction, stress, low self-esteem, and lack of interest are common stress symptoms that result.
4. Absence of priorities	One major problem that is a significant stressor is caused by lack of knowledge of priorities. Employees in many organizations must respond to requests from more than one person. In most instances they must decide which task is most important or has first priority. There is little guidance. Stress comes from the necessity to prioritize the sequence of tasks without adequate guidance.
5. Responsibility without authority	Employees who are assigned specific jobs that require requisition of transportation, materials, or information but who lack the authority to make such requests find they must rely solely on the good will of others in the organization to perform needed actions. Most people want to do a good job. They become frustrated when they realize that lack of authority prevents them from fulfilling their responsibilities.
6. Interpersonal or interdepartmental conflict	Conflicts, often called *personality conflicts,* are a source of job stress. Conflict between individual employees, employees and their supervisor, or between departments all add stress. Unmanaged conflict is a destructive force often beyond the ability of individual employees to control.
7. Unexpected change	Change of any kind induces stress. Unexpected change is especially stressful. New procedures, equipment, organizational realignment, managerial shifts, and increase or decrease in responsibility all are stressors, especially if the change has potential negative impact.
8. Rumors, misinformation, and distorted communication	Incorrect information related to changes, potential reductions in the work force, organizational change, and assignments are potential stressors. Open, candid discussion is mandatory.

FIGURE 12.2 ■ On-the-Job Eustress and Distress

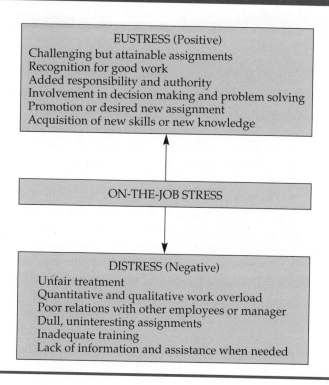

EUSTRESS (Positive)
Challenging but attainable assignments
Recognition for good work
Added responsibility and authority
Involvement in decision making and problem solving
Promotion or desired new assignment
Acquisition of new skills or new knowledge

ON-THE-JOB STRESS

DISTRESS (Negative)
Unfair treatment
Quantitative and qualitative work overload
Poor relations with other employees or manager
Dull, uninteresting assignments
Inadequate training
Lack of information and assistance when needed

7. Impatience with the performance of others both at work and in social settings, such as restaurants.

8. Constant movement, such as playing with pencils, bending paperclips, hand movements, and "bouncing" a leg while sitting.

9. Apathy, withdrawal, chronic feelings of tiredness, and reluctance to take on challenging assignments.

There are many other symptoms of stress, such as changes in consumption of alcohol, overeating, physical appearance, personal grooming, and lack of attention to details at work. When symptoms are noticed, supervisors must first examine their own actions to determine if job demands or other conditions at work can be the causes. Open discussions and willingness to listen are good tools. Large organizations frequently have skilled human resource specialists who can act as counselors and refer employees with severe stress problems to sources of professional guidance and assistance.

■ STRESS RELIEVERS

Stress relievers are any actions people take to rid themselves of stress symptoms.

People under persistent stress may attempt to resolve personal pressures with the use of alcohol, illicit drugs, or prescription tranquilizers. None of these has any long-term benefits and most have definite addictive dangers. Their appeal lies in their availability and ability to inhibit tension associated with life pressures.

Some of the more effective types of stress relievers with long-term benefits are readily available to everyone. Although those listed below are usually neither available nor practical in a work environment, they are valuable after or before work as stress-reduction techniques.

1. Physical exercise. Most texts on stress and stress management highlight the benefits of exercise as a stress-reduction technique. Organizations that encourage both employee and management exercise programs have learned that participants consistently report feelings of being able to better cope with job demands. A difficulty with exercise is that people under stress often resist the type of activities that will help them most. When a person feels "down" or is very tense from perceived pressures, exercise may have little appeal. It takes self-discipline and planning to develop a regular program of physical exercise. There is a great deal of truth in the old adage, "A healthy body make a healthy mind."

2. Meditation. Meditation is not as mysterious as it sounds. In its most basic form, meditation involves sitting quietly and mentally repeating a sound or number to make other thoughts disappear. Herbert Benson has advocated the use of meditation as a useful work-related stress-reduction technique for over 15 years.[8] Benson points out that quiet relaxation twice a day can have many beneficial results, including physical changes such as a lowered pulse rate and reduced blood pressure. Meditation can take many forms. Any pattern of relaxation coupled with a thought process that takes a person away from the pressures of work or other life situations that contribute to stress may be classified as a form of meditation. Like exercise, not many people take the time to induce the *relaxation response* that is the antithesis of stress.

3. Biofeedback. Biofeedback involves the use of special equipment that measures a variety of physical factors, such as pulse rate, blood pressure, oxygen consumption, and muscle tension. Over a period of time, with proper training and coaching, people using biofeedback learn to control physiological responses. Biofeedback and meditation are both looked on with a degree of suspicion by many people. As a consequence neither technique has gained wide popularity in most organizations.

4. Hobbies. Many people find hobbies, clubs, or social activities effective in reducing stress. Highly motivated people, who may be stress prone, often pour a great deal of energy and imagination into developing their hobbies. Hobbies as diverse as belonging to organized sports groups, woodworking, astronomy, and even tropical fish take them away from the stress associated with their jobs and provides an avenue for utilizing excess energy often associated with stressful conditions.

Stress Prevention

For most managers, attention to job design, work assignments that match employee ability, both tangible and intangible rewards for performance, and open communication that promotes trust and confidence are positive actions that reduce the probability of stress becoming excessive due to work alone. Proactive attention to potential stressors is far more productive than attempting to deal with excessive stress that may have been avoided.

Stress—Challenge Confusion

Many types of work are exciting and involve difficult challenges. Physicians, nurses, and emergency paramedical employees frequently encounter life-or-death situations. Fire fighters and police officers are routinely faced with danger. Riggers, who work on tall buildings and bridges, know that a false move could mean their own death and danger to others. Crop dusting and many other types of employment place people in exciting, challenging conditions as a regular part of their assignment. Very few people with these high-demand types of work leave their profession. When they do, it is usually for reasons of pay, excessive hours, and realization that they are in the wrong type of work rather than stress.

Exciting, challenging work that demands full utilization of an individual's training and experience may, at times, be intensely stressful. When the required task is successfully completed, the feeling of satisfaction is equally strong. Stress in such situations drives people to utilize their full capacity. Like physical exertion, the tension wears off quickly and a need for new challenges takes its place. Stress caused by challenge is very real, but for many people it is the part of their jobs they enjoy most. They know their own efforts will ultimately eliminate or reduce the primary causes of their immediate job pressures. Managers should not confuse action in response to demands on knowledge and skills with stress from seemingly insurmountable conditions of work.

■ PSYCHOLOGICAL MATURITY

Psychological maturity is the ability to successfully cope with life situations, including those that are stressful.

Psychological maturity is one of the characteristics that distinguishes superior managers from those who are mediocre. Like many other behavioral concepts, it has no precise definition. Psychologically mature people can rapidly adjust to change, cope with adversity, and recover from disaster or failure while maintaining a sense of optimism about the future. A strong sense of self-worth, knowledge of their impact on others, integrity, openness in communication, and a firm sense of what is right guide their actions.

Psychological maturity is not limited to any specific set of personality characteristics. People who are quiet, those who are people oriented, some who are known as being tough to work for, and others who are considered down to earth may all be psychologically mature. They are highly stress tolerant, tend to be analytical, and look for solutions rather than blame. Refusal to let others permanently bother them is a mark of their behavior.

Employees view psychologically mature managers as positive referents. Their attributes are both admired and respected. One of the strong assets of psychologically mature managers is predictability. Employees know they will be honest, fair, and work for the best interests of the organization and their employees. Under stressful conditions they can be depended on to be a calming influence in solving problems rather than increasing pressure to intolerable levels.

■ THINGS TO REMEMBER

I. Frustration—conflict within.

A. Frustration occurs when there is any interference with goal-directed behavior. It can be caused by either internal or external conditions.

B. Unmade decisions can also lead to frustration.

C. Employees without a clear concept of priorities are often frustrated.

II. Frustration reactions.

   A. Attack responses to frustration that are positive include trying again to complete a task, asking for help, or re-reading procedures.

   B. Withdrawal does not solve problems, but it removes a person from the causes of frustration.

   C. Mild frustration can have positive results.

   D. Prolonged frustration can lead to physical and psychological problems.

   E. No two people react to frustration the same way.

III. Stress.

   A. *Stress* has no precise definition.

   B. Stress reactions are nonspecific, positive and negative conditions can create stress.

   C. Attacks on a person's physical self and attacks on his or her *symbolic self* both create stress.

   D. Adjustment to change is a primary source of stress.

   E. Mild stress energizes, adds interest to life, and can lead to beneficial behavior.

   F. Negative stress, or distress, occurs when pressure reaches the point where individuals feel they cannot effectively cope with events in their lives.

   G. Stress management does not seek elimination of stress.

IV. Stress carriers and pressure workers.

   A. Some managers who suffer few stress symptoms themselves can transmit stress to their employees.

   B. Pressure workers are people who feel they work best under stress. They create problems not only for themselves but for others as well.

V. Adjustive reactions.

   A. Adjustive reactions are frequently called *defense mechanisms*. They are protective measures an individual may take when their symbolic self is under attack.

   B. Typical adjustive reactions include rationalization, projection, transference, repression, regression, identification, and reaction formation.

VI. Practical stress management for supervisors.

   A. Supervisors can learn to recognize many stress symptoms in themselves and their employees. Supervisors who recognize their own stress symptoms are able to empathize with the indications of problems in their employees.

   B. A number of positive stress-management steps can be taken by supervisors.

   C. Listening and responding to employees are effective stress-reduction tools.

   D. Supervisors must understand the difference between *eustress* and *distress*.

VII. Stress-relief methods.

   A. Physical exercise, meditation, biofeedback, and organized hobbies are effective stress-relief techniques.

   B. Some organizations have professional counselors or trained human resource specialists who can help in stress relief.

   C. Stress prevention through proactive analysis and planning is the most effective method for avoiding stress.

   D. Challenge that creates stress does not usually create distress.

VIII. Psychological maturity.

   A. Psychological maturity is the ability to successfully adjust to change and cope with stressful conditions.

   B. Managers who are psychologically mature are positive referents for their employees.

■ KEY TERMS

frustration	pressure workers
withdrawal	adjustive reactions
attack	rationalization
stress	sour grapes
symbolic self	sweet lemon
distress	projection
stress management	transference
stress carriers	repression

identification   **eustress**

regression   **psychological maturity**

reaction formation

▪ DISCUSSION QUESTIONS

1. How stressful is your present life? How can a person evaluate their own level of stress tolerance?

2. Why does listening and accepting another person as an individual with her or his own point of view usually reduce personal levels of stress?

3. List three types of work that you think may be particularly stressful. What job factors make them stressful?

4. Give examples of adjustive reactions to stress you may have used or have observed others using.

5. How can you recognize excessive stress in others? What positive actions can you take to help them relieve their anxieties?

▪ SELF-EVALUATION

How stress-prone are you? This questionnaire will help you focus on aspects of your life that may indicate excessive stress. Mark the number that describes your response to each of the 10 statements or questions. Remember, 1, 2, or 3 indicates disagreement or a negative response while 4, 5, and 6 is agreement or a positive reaction.

1. I rarely have time to relax and enjoy leisure activities.

   1   2   3   4   5   6

2. When eating, I usually finish well before others.

   1   2   3   4   5   6

3. Other people's lack of interest or slowness in completing work makes me angry.

   1   2   3   4   5   6

4. I often have difficulty going to sleep and may wake up during the night.

   1   2   3   4   5   6

5. People have asked me why I am impatient.

   1   2   3   4   5   6

6. I do not let occasional failure or job errors upset me.

   1   2   3   4   5   6

7. Although work is important, I find time for other activities that I also enjoy.

   1   2   3   4   5   6

8. It's more important to be liked for who a person is rather than for what they have done.

   1   2   3   4   5   6

9. Success in life doesn't depend on being rich, powerful, or recognition for accomplishments.

   1   2   3   4   5   6

10. I am rarely depressed or have feelings of anxiety.

   1   2   3   4   5   6

■ SHORT CASES

Jean's a Good Supervisor?

Jean Ramos was one of the new customer service supervisors for Price-Out Warehouses, a large catalog-ordering organization. Her employees were responsible for providing sales data, statistical reports on progress of new outlets, and a variety of customer response data including complaints and compliments. Jean was enthusiastic, filled with new ideas, and possessed a likeable, outgoing personality. She was energetic and often demanding. Her department included four senior clerks who were each leaders of four or five—depending on the work load—administrative specialists of lower classifications.

"Reed," she began in a meeting with her senior clerks, "we need that southeast marketing survey data as soon as we can get it. Don't forget the due date on the request from Sam Hurst in market research, and I need your estimate of how many of our people will be needed for the new Thompsonville site location study." She now turned to Rene Favala. "Give me a progress report on the new fresh produce distribution statistics, see if you can find out what Teri Hendrix in distribution really wants on her report, and get started on the assessment of the effects of direct mailings on our western sales." One by one she gave lists of projects to her supervisors.

"Now," she smiled, "here are some ideas for new projects we can get started." Her ideas seemed endless to the worried senior clerks. As they left Jean's office, Rene turned to Reed and sighed, "I know what will happen. Right in the middle of one report, she'll hit me with a new study. How will we ever get her under control? It's nerve-racking." Jim looked back at Rene and said, "It is really funny, but I'm not laughing."

1. What did Jean do to both frustrate and add stress to her senior clerks' lives?

2. What did Rene's reactions to Jean's instructions indicate?

3. How is it possible for employees to like a supervisor and dislike her style at the same time?

Dennis's Dilemma

When Jarvitz James opened James Enterprise Technology (JET), he was turning a hobby into a business. Since his high school days Jarvitz had been interested in sound reproduction. Over time he began to realize that no speaker was good unless it was properly mounted in an expertly designed case. After reading every book he could find on the dynamics of sound, Jarvitz developed a nearly perfect formula for correctly matching speakers to their enclosures. First friends and soon many other people knew of Jarvitz's excellent designs and superbly crafted and designed super-high-fidelity speaker systems. Going into business was a natural step.

From the outset sales of JET speaker systems outpaced Jarvitz's and his trained craftspeople's ability to meet buyers' demands. Jarvitz was approached by several large competitors to sell his basic designs to them. Companies in both Japan and Korea offered high percentages of profits for license to build JET speakers. Jarvitz was flattered, pleased, and fearful.

He found his success was not as much of a blessing as he though it would be. He was constantly faced with offers, requests, legal battles with imitators who infringed on JET patents and processes, and increasing offers to buy his business. Jarvitz also found he had difficulty sleeping, his eating habits became erratic, and his employees noticed he always seemed preoccupied.

One night he awoke bathed in perspiration with intense feelings of anxiety. "I'm making money. There are people who want to give me more. I'm at the top of my business. Why am I feeling this way?'' he thought. As he lay there he began to feel intense pain in his chest. Alone in his apartment he shakily dialed 911 and asked for help.

After an overnight stay at the local medical center and extensive examination, tests indicated no heart problem. Jarvitz was released and driven home by Fran Bowers, who was both an employee and his closest friend. "Jarvitz," Fran looked at him with deep concern, "I'm really worried. You just can't keep putting yourself under as much pressure as you do."

"Fran, I've got money, friends, and best of all you. What's wrong with me?" was his anguished reply.

1. In what ways can success create excessive stress?

2. Comment on Jarvitz's degree of psychological maturity.

3. What were some of the major causes of Jarvitz's excessive stress symptoms?

■ ENDNOTES

1. Thomas Holmes and Ella M. David, *Stress and Life Events Research* (New York: Praeger Publishers, 1984).

2. Joan E. Rigdon, "When the Sailing Gets Rough, Use a Gentle Hand," *The Wall Street Journal*, October 29, 1990, sec. B.

3. Hans Selye, *The Stress of Life* (New York: McGraw-Hill, Inc., 1976).

4. Dan Costley and Ralph Todd, *Human Relations in Organizations*, 4th edition (St. Paul, Minn.: West Publishing Company, 1991, pp. 210–11).

5. S. I. Hayakawa, *Symbol, Status, and Personality* (New York: Harcourt Brace Jovanovich, 1964).

6. Based on an interview with Henri Santos-Coy, January 4, 1991.

7. Dee Soder, "Dealing with Stress in the Workplace," *The Wall Street Journal*, January 24, 1991, sec. B.

8. Herbert Benson, *The Relaxation Response* (New York: William Morrow and Company, 1975).

13

Conflict Management and Problem Employees

Objectives

Chapter 13 addresses conflict at work and so-called problem employees. Its purposes are to enable both managers and potential managers to

- Recognize the differences between destructive and beneficial conflict.
- Develop strategies for effective conflict resolution.
- Identify typical problem employees.
- Evaluate cliques and informal groups to determine their positive and negative impact.
- Determine methods for effectively dealing with different conflict conditions and specific types of problem employees.

Thought Starter

There is very little doubt that of the developed countries of the world the United States is the most pluralistic. There is very little agreement on what is right, good, beautiful, moral, or correct. In politics, economics, and everyday life, people are divided. One of the results is conflict. Conflict is a normal, inevitable consequence of life.

Disagreement is not necessarily wrong. It often stimulates creativity, causes reexamination of beliefs and values, and can result in a creation of entirely new concepts. All too often conflict has few real benefits. People become divided, positions on issues harden, and there is little room for agreement.

In the United States there are few, if any, matters on which every person agrees. We are a people divided on political, economic, social, religious, and personal concerns. Our thinking is shaped by the influence and expectations of others, our own frames of reference, and experiences.

Regardless of our individual and group differences we live together, obey for the most part the same laws, and even develop friendships with people who have radically different outlooks from our own. Existence of conflict is not difficult to understand. More perplexing is the fact that with all of our individual and collective differences we are able to live and work together productively.

Historians in the future will ultimately decide whether the fundamental conflicts that divide us on so many issues are beneficial or the omens of future disaster. Supervisors, with employees from every segment of the earth's most heterogeneous people, have the difficult task of managing conflicts that arise at work.

■ *Until it became a victim of an unfriendly takeover by Dauntless Advertising and Marketing (DAM), Cable Action Billing (CAB) was considered one of the best organizations for which to work.[1] Employees were made to feel part of a highly successful operation that provided monthly billing services for many of the nation's largest cable television transmission companies. Shortly after DAM took over the operation, many of the original CAB managers were asked to either take early retirement or leave.*

To build what DAM felt to be a more efficient organization, over 100 employees were permanently laid off in addition to the cuts in management. Some salaried employees were reclassified to hourly jobs, benefits were reduced as cost-saving measures, and special employee programs such as incentive bonuses were eliminated.

Since the DAM restructuring of CAB there has been a steady exodus of CAB's most talented technical and administrative employees. One departing supervisor commented, "It is like a war zone. Employees need jobs but detest the new management policies; CAB managers are in constant disagreement with DAM's management team and especially those who visit from the home office. Where all this will lead is hard to tell, but it's hurting our productivity and quality already."

■ CONFLICT WITHOUT, CONFLICT WITHIN

Conflict originates from feelings of being attacked or treated unfairly or having unfulfilled expectations or disagreements.

Conflict arises from many sources. Inability to make a decision, belief that someone or something is preventing a goal from being reached, perceived competition for a limited goal that can be attained by only one person, ambiguous roles, and defensiveness are all potential sources. **Conflict** is an emotional reaction to concepts, actions, orders, policies, rules, or behavior of others, or a personal inability to make decisions that are perceived as obstacles to achieving desired goals. It can also result from expectations being blocked or feelings of powerlessness.

In the opening vignette CAB employees found themselves in conflict with the actions of their new management. DAM's policies thwarted their expectations of reward for outstanding effort, dampened pride in past promotions, and generally lowered self-esteem by reclassifying jobs. Unfair and arbitrary treatment by DAM management resulted in an almost universal emotional reaction. Employees wanted to get back at those who were perceived as causing their present difficulties. Supervisors were put in the uncomfortable position of explaining the new policies to openly hostile employees.

Conflict Reactions

In a work environment, conflict usually originates from feelings of being attacked, treated unfairly, unfulfilled expectations, and disagreement. Most conflict has a relatively low level of intensity. People argue with each other over the best way to do a particular job, the solution to a problem, who will win next week's ball game, or almost any topic. Emotional responses to minor, day-to-day conflict are usually low-level and often enjoyable and productive. New ideas are stimulated, points are clarified, and differences quickly forgotten.

Polarization means to take an extreme position in a disagreement with others.

If disagreement increases in intensity, polarization occurs. **Polarization** is the hardening of positions against a perceived opponent. Rather than drawing together in finding a common solution to their disagreement, those involved spread farther apart. On a national level polarization on major issues such as abortion, gun control, death penalties, and environmental issues have been highly publicized. As the argument becomes more heated, those involved take increasingly stronger positions to support their beliefs and disprove the stance of their opponent. There is little real communication to open up discussion or find any points of agreement.

Polarization also takes place in organizations. On an individual level employees are often in conflict with other employees, supervisors with other supervisors, and employees with supervisors. As differences continue without resolution, conflict remains unresolved and each side takes increasingly unyielding positions. Polarization is graphically portrayed in Figure 13.1.

An almost inevitable consequence of conflict is defensive behavior. When people feel they, their ideas, or things they identify with are attacked, defensive behavior is the result. When people are told the automobile they especially like is a lemon, the teams they admire are losers, or colors they wear are unflattering, they become defensive. There is a human tendency to protect beliefs, values, and preferences. Some people like cream in their coffee, others do not. Each wonders how the other can drink it that way.

Defensive behavior occurs when people feel their beliefs, values, likes, or dislikes are being attacked by someone with whom they disagree.

In a work environment a number of employees may feel that an organizational change is correct while others think it is a deliberate move to reduce their degree of influence. When their position is questioned, regardless of their feelings, they are very likely to become defensive. **Defensiveness** is a reaction to what appears to be a threat, either to an individual's physical well-being or to their

FIGURE 13.1 ■ Polarization

"I think this is a good idea"   "It's not very practical"
"You may not think so, but I do"   "It just can't be done"
"Yes it can"   No, it can't"
Yes!   No!
Yes!   No!
Yes!   No!
Yes!   No!

beliefs and values. It frequently originates from the inability to accept the beliefs and actions of others.[2] People defend their position through argument, gathering support, or withdrawal.

Defensive behavior may take several forms. Aggressive attack, the most common defensive reaction, can take the form of argument and statements of belief in an attempt to force a belief on others. Withdrawal from argument or direct confrontation is another alternative as is attempting to calm another person. In some instances adoption of the role of a problem solver is also a defensive reaction. Defensiveness is a normal human reaction. It is dangerous only when the persons involved feel that force, usually verbal, is necessary to make their beliefs or assessment of information valid. Supervisors must learn to avoid defensiveness in themselves and recognize it in others.

Group Conflict

Organizational centrism is the belief by employees or managers that their department or work unit is the most important in their organization.

Groups are frequently in conflict with other groups or, in some instances, individual people. Formal groups, such as sections or departments, often suffer from a type of **organizational centrism.** First-line managers and those who are part of their work unit begin to believe that their function is the most important in the total organization. They may also become convinced that other work units do not work as effectively or efficiently. If difficulties occur in the organization, it is always some other department's problem. In organizations that encourage competition between departments, centrism can become a source of conflict and divisiveness. Other departments are seen as competitors and voluntary cooperation is virtually absent.

Informal groups as a source of conflict is a more common problem for supervisors than conflicts between formal groups. Within any department or work unit people become associated with each other because of common interests, similar work, friendship, or feelings of insecurity. In some cases small informal groups or **cliques** within a department take positions that put themselves in conflict with other employees or management. Supervisors may, at times, believe that positions taken by these highly cohesive groups represent the view of the entire work unit. They can become a powerful and destructive force if not objectively dealt with by first-line management.

Cliques are small, informal groups within work organizations that may take positions that are in conflict with those of other employees or management.

Dampened or Dismissed Expectations

For many years Frederick Herzberg has brought to management's attention that employee dissatisfaction over unmet needs and expectations is more emotionally intense than their satisfaction with needs that are adequately fulfilled.[3] Employees who have their benefits reduced, even if they rarely use medical or sick-leave privileges, will deeply resent their being lowered. Improvement of benefits or pay will be appreciated. Their appreciation, however, will not be as emotionally intense as their resentment before changes were made.

Expectations that have been unfulfilled can ultimately lead to conflict with the person or people perceived as preventing the expectations from becoming a reality.

An employee who works hard, obeys rules, and is a strong supporter of the organization may reasonably expect to be rewarded in the form of either promotion or an increase in pay. If, after a period of time, there is little or no evidence of reward, frustration that turns into disappointment is a natural result. Unfulfilled expectations can be converted into lack of trust and confidence and ultimately be the basis of conflict between the manager and employee. When groups of employees feel expectations have not been fulfilled, the result is often a we-they relationship. Employees feel managers have taken an adversarial role against them and managers reciprocate by identifying their goals and those of employees as being essentially incompatible. For many years employee unions have been able to attract members by offering protection against unfair treatment and to help ensure that expectations will be met. Organizations that strive to meet reasonable expectations of employees rarely experience antimanagement unionizing movements.

One of the most difficult tasks of supervision is to recognize and reconcile the differences between employee needs and organization goals. Employees tend to be job centered with little responsibility and authority. Managers are concerned with achieving organizational goals. Personal and employee needs are often secondary. Some supervisors feel that if an employee is doing a job exceptionally well, the employee is meeting performance expectations. No special rewards are necessary. Those who are average are not completely fulfilling organizational objectives and do not deserve anything other than criticism. No employee deserves recognition, added responsibility, increased authority, or autonomy simply because his or her work meets or exceeds established standards.

When supervisors are perceived as being unfair or insensitive to employee expectations, conflict is certain. Table 13.1 summarizes differences between employee and first-line management expectations.

■ PSYCHOLOGICAL CONTRACTS

Psychological contracts are based on the mutual expectations managers and employees have of each other.

Very few of the items in Table 13.1, which are only a few of possible expectations, are openly discussed between employees and supervisors. Most are taken for granted as normal work expectations. These mutual expectations of supervisors and employees are known as **psychological contracts.** In work organizations trust, one of the most important concepts in human relations, is based on unspoken agreements. A person who buys a product or service, rides in an airplane, or listens to news on television trusts

TABLE 13.1 ■ Differences between Employee and Supervisory Expectations

Employee Expectations	Supervisor Expectations
Interesting work	Job effectiveness—good quality work
Fairness in treatment by supervisor	Job efficiency—productivity
Help and information	Regular on-time attendance
Adequate pay and benefits	Concern for costs
Good relationships with other employees	Support for organizational goals
Opportunity to learn and advance	Honesty
Adequate authority for responsibilities	Adherence to organization rules
Recognition for good work	Ability to work well with others
A sense of job security	Willingness to accept responsibility
Confidence and trust in supervisor	Support for supervisory decisions

Contractual trust is based on the belief that people will act responsibly, competently, and honestly.

Personal trust originates in the confidence of nonbetrayal by another person

other parties to be competent and honest. Trust is the belief that another person will honor either an implied or explicit agreement. Like psychological contracts, **contractual trust** is a fundamental human relationship.

Personal trust is somewhat more tenuous. It has its origins in the confidence of nonbetrayal by another person. Rather than arising out of normal give-and-take relationships, as does contractual trust, personal trust is founded on the assumption of total acceptance by another person.

If a supervisor or employee fails to meet the expectations of the other, trust is weakened. Employees who are tardy or fail to regularly report for work weaken the trust between themselves and their supervisors. Supervisors who are perceived as being unfair, fail to assist employees with problems, and who never recognize outstanding effort also weaken the psychological contract with their employees. Regardless of its origins, conflict is an almost inevitable result of loss or weakening of trust. Once trust has been destroyed it is very difficult to reestablish. Figure 13.2 shows the relationship between management and employee expectations in psychological contracts.

▪ CONFLICTING PRIORITIES

Supervisors depend largely on mutual cooperation to maintain effective working relationships with other supervisors. When it appears cooperation is weakened, lack of trust and conflict are certain results. In a large department store, as an example, supervisors of receiving and warehousing cooperate with various de-

FIGURE 13.2 ▪ Psychological Contracts

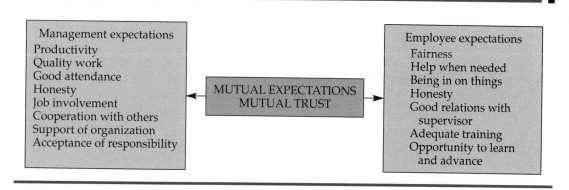

Management expectations	MUTUAL EXPECTATIONS MUTUAL TRUST	Employee expectations

Productivity
Quality work
Good attendance
Honesty
Job involvement
Cooperation with others
Support of organization
Acceptance of responsibility
		Fairness
		Help when needed
		Being in on things
		Honesty
		Good relations with
		  supervisor
		Adequate training
		Opportunity to learn
		  and advance

*Conflicting priorities
can become a major
source of conflict.*

partments to ensure adequate stocks of sizes, colors, models, or brand names of products sold. They also cooperate in ensuring prompt delivery of large items such as appliances. Conflict can arise when both supervisors have conflicting priorities. Several supervisors may want items in their departments restocked at the same time or immediate deliveries made to customers. Faced with several urgent demands, the receiving and warehousing supervisor arbitrarily prioritizes orders. Supervisors waiting for items to satisfy customer needs and those who need orders filled and shipped may feel their needs are not being given proper attention. Often conflict occurs. If the delays are repeated, conflict can become intense.

In most types of production operations conflict exists between departments because of conflicting priorities. Cooks and servers in restaurants frequently are in conflict. Servers want their orders filled; cooks, faced with many orders, operate on a strict first-come, first-served basis. Marketing people in manufacturing operations are traditionally in conflict with those in production. Like servers in restaurants, sales people in the marketing department want to provide quick delivery to customers. Manufacturing supervisors, faced with many orders, have difficulty in meeting dates committed to by salespeople. Conflict in the form of accusations is common. Supervisor-supervisor conflicts can escalate to the point where intervention by higher levels of management is required.

Priority conflicts that result in delays between interdependent work units are a primary cause of conflict between supervisors. Systems and procedures that are fully understood by everyone involved are mandatory. When the rules are clear and exceptions are made only in the most urgent conditions, serious conflict is less likely.

■ PROBLEM EMPLOYEES

In addition to disagreement, lack of trust, and diminished expectations, conflict can arise from perceived personality differences. Many psychologists effectively argue that disputes between people are not based on personality but refusal of individuals to accept beliefs, behavior, and ideas other than their own. Regardless of psychological and philosophical debate, problem employees are a reality. Some employees are extremely sensitive to criticism while others resent authority of any kind. Still more, rather than acknowledge their own responsibilities, feel their organizations exist to serve them. Employees with attitudes and behavior different from that expected are often both problems and sources of conflict.

Gorillas

For many years people's behavior has been compared to that of animals or plants. "Shy as a violet," "timid as a rabbit," "busy as a bee," "fast as a greyhound," "blind as a bat," and many other sayings are part of our vocabulary. Problem employees are often characterized by the similarity of their behavior to that of some animals.

Gorillas, because of their ability to affect an individual's life, are seen as a potential threat.

Gorillas may be, in their native habitat, peaceful. Nevertheless they intimidate other animals and people by their size, strength, and potential threat. Many employees and supervisors are gorillas. Often unknowingly, they intimidate others by their overbearing dominance. Because of their apparent power, gorillas are a threat.

Dr. William Morris[4] has observed that any person may be a gorilla to others at a given point in time. He points out that intimidation leads to both fear, dislike, and ultimate conflict. Gorillas may be managers, other employees, vendors, customers, or virtually anyone in our lives who influences our behavior by some sort of intimidation. Supervisors are often gorillas to their employees. Aggressively assertive employees can be gorillas to both their first-line managers and other employees.

Most people attempt to placate gorillas. It's the wrong technique according to Morris. Gorillas want their own ideas to prevail and are willing to ride over others to achieve their goals. Being another gorilla is the most effective method of confronting their behavior and minimizing conflict. Gorillas respect strength and confidence. They dislike appearances of weakness and will take advantage of any lack of confidence and strength in others. Psychologically mature first-line managers can successfully confront gorilla behavior by being equally assertive and refusing to retreat from positions they know are correct.

Wasps

Wasps are people who are always on the attack. They like to sting others.

Wasps are just what the name implies. They look for vulnerability and insert their stinger. In nearly every organization some employees and supervisors are excessively critical, punitive, and take every opportunity to criticize. Their stingers are always out and are used unhesitatingly. While gorilla behavior is not always vindictive or mean, wasps are dedicated to injuring others to gain advantages for themselves. In a meeting with others, a wasp is the first to observe, "Susan, you were late for the meeting. I suppose you didn't have all of your notes ready like the rest of us did."

Power is like food for wasps. They delight in stinging other employees and managers when they feel it will enhance their own position. Wasps are generally disliked and not trusted by most employees. Occasionally wasps are used by others as tools of revenge.

Wasps are masters of half-truths. They place all of their work unit's difficulties on people whom they particularly dislike. Wasps are easily identified by other employees and are frequently avoided. Lack of contact reduces chances of being stung. Supervisors must critically evaluate statements made by recognized wasps and avoid making decisions without full investigation. Half-truths, innuendos, and accusations are typical wasp weapons. First-line managers may, without recognizing wasp motives, act before thoroughly investigating a wasp's assertions. Judgment, experience, and objectivity are necessities.

Snakes

Snakes are people who use deception, camouflage, and hidden motives to manipulate others.

Snakes are manipulators. They use deception, camouflage, and secrecy to achieve their goals. Robert Morton[5] describes their behavior as manipulation of the reward structure. Snakes become involved in organizational goals only when there are clearly defined benefits.

Unlike gorillas and wasps, who are concerned with dominance and power, snakes seek advantages by remaining hidden until opportunity for personal gain appears. Their primary mode of operation depends on gathering and distorting information that can be used to punish others. They are dangerous and difficult to detect.

Supervisors who behave like snakes look through employees' desks to find incriminating evidence and spy not only on employees but on other supervisors. They constantly seek advantage by controlling information. Snakes, whether employees or supervisors, have little concern for organizational ethics. In both meetings and private conferences snakes will embarrass others by threatening to reveal confidential information or to expose alleged wrongdoing. Snakes are silent, venomous, and often unnoticed until they strike. When they strike they spread destructive rumors, accuse others of improper conduct without adequate evidence, and act as a divisive force between employees they dislike and managers in order to gain increased influence.

Baboons

Baboons depend on explosive outbursts to intimidate and control others.

Baboons are similar to gorillas but tend to depend on explosive outbursts of anger as a control method. Like gorillas, baboons depend on intimidation. Unlike gorillas, who may not be aware of their effect on fellow employees or managers, baboons have learned that people will agree with their position rather than face angry outbursts. While they have little real power and may be uninformed, their behavior allows them to achieve a degree of influence. Baboons are blind communicators. They neither want to hear the opinions of others nor have any degree of sensitivity to the way others react to their outbursts.

Supervisors who recognize baboon behavior also realize its destructive effects. People cannot effectively work in an environment where emotional outbursts disrupt the normal pace of work. It is fortunate that after a period of time most employees recognize baboon behavior as being loud but relatively harmless. Baboons when ignored tend to get louder and more threatening but will eventually suppress their outbursts if they perceive they are having little effect on others.

In some ways baboon behavior is the easiest with which to deal. Supervisors learn that the explosive anger may be, for the most part, reactions to personal frustration. If there is little or no reinforcement, either negative or positive, the undesirable behavior will eventually disappear.

Sloths

Sloths are unresponsive to both praise and punishment.

Sloths are unresponsive to both praise and punishment. Their feelings are totally hidden. Because they are impassive, they are especially difficult employees for supervisors. In the same way, impassive, nonresponsive supervisors are equally perplexing for employees.

It is unfortunate that some first-line managers feel that they should never reveal their feelings to employees. Their blank mask is frustrating and stressful. Employees never know whether they have been heard, how well their work is progressing, or how their supervisor feels about them as a person. Sloths are not born as nonresponsive individuals. They have adopted the protective coat of hiding their beliefs, values, and even their attitudes from others.

Conflict generated by sloths is the result of frustration. They simply don't react. Other people do not know whether they approve or disapprove, like or dislike, or have any type of reaction. Like good poker players, their emotions are always shielded.

Employees who are sloths have, like some supervisors, assumed a cloak of unemotional detachment as a protective shield. If emotions are not shown, the response can never be judged as being incorrect or inappropriate. It may also never be considered as an endorsement, approval, or recognition for innovative or creative ideas.

Sharks and Bleeding Sharks

Sharks attack others whom they perceive as having difficulty.

During the time he lived in Key West, Florida, Ernest Hemingway engaged in an odd sport. He and friends, with loaded rifles, would take Hemingway's large boat out into the Gulf of Mexico. Half of a cow carcass was dropped over the side and in a few minutes sharks would be attracted from many directions. As the sharks fed, the people aboard the boat would shoot a few of them. Many of the sharks would then attack those who were bleeding. Ultimately the bleeding sharks were devoured in the same way the original carcass had been.

Bleeding sharks are the victims of sharks.

When employees find themselves in difficulty because of error, inability to fit in an organization, or conflict with their supervisor or other employees, they frequently become **bleeding sharks.** Other employees take on the role of sharks. Rather than attempting to assist or defend the employee who is having difficulty, they attack by socially isolating the person, spreading rumors, and placing blame when it is unwarranted. Eventually the psychologically wounded employee quits or is fired. Supervisors, unfortunately, join the other sharks before carefully analyzing the employee's difficulties and examining possible ways of bringing them back into the mainstream work unit.

More Animals

With a little ingenuity, other problem employees can be labeled as hyenas, foxes, jackals, howling monkeys, and so on. A central

FIRST-LINERS

MY supervisor is an overbearing GORILLA!

Well MY boss is stubborn as a MULE.

At least you dont work with the monkeys I do.

Boy, this place is a ZOO!

reality of work is that people are very individualistic, and each has learned to behave in ways that satisfy his or her needs for power, recognition, anonymity, and acceptance. Notwithstanding how they are characterized, some employees will cause more problems for managers than others. Supervisors have the primary responsibility for recognizing characteristics of problem employees and their potential for causing conflict in an organization.

Robert Armsbent, as a salesperson for Conifer's Molding, a supplier of decorative wood products for architects, was liked as a person by most of his customers but seen as an oddball by fellow employees. When he was not out selling directly to customers, he, like other technical sales specialists, contacted prospective users of Conifer products by telephone. His small office was arranged so that file cabinets completely blocked one side of his desk. If someone entered his office they would be faced with a row of file cabinets with Robert safely hidden behind them.

Other employees commented that Robert was weird. He had isolated himself so much that he was not trusted by employees or the office manager who supervised the sales staff. In meetings he never sat next to other employees and became involved only when directly questioned. Clients reported he was polite but not very knowledgeable. He was liked by them for being friendly more than for being helpful. They often knew more about his products than he did.

As his refusal to become a sales team player became more apparent, Bob's isolation became more acute. Last year he was granted six months' leave for stress-related health symptoms. He also filed a law suit against his company and his supervisor claiming severe stress damage.

Although Bob's supervisor felt all employees were treated fairly and with consideration, Bob ultimately received a large settlement ($625,000) for stress-related discomfort. None of the other employees in his section had ever complained of unfair or discriminatory treatment. After the settlement Bob continued working but was even more isolated by employees, who saw him as an object of scorn. He was in conflict with every employee and level of management in the company.

Conflict, in Bob's case, was the direct result of lack of trust. Both employees and his supervisor saw Bob as unwilling to cooperate, be a team member, and join in the everyday camaraderie of the department. Self-imposed outsiders are seen as enemies by the informal group and are points of dissension and conflict.

■ PSYCHOLOGICAL DISTANCE

Psychological distance is the recognition that a manager's job and level of responsibility is different from that of other employees.

When employees make the vital shift to higher levels of responsibility and authority, conflict may arise because of the psychological distance created by their new roles. **Psychological distance** is best defined as the change in relationships resulting from altered roles, responsibilities, and levels of authority. When an employee is promoted to a leadership position, such as a first-line manager, she or he assumes an entirely different set of functions from her or his former job as a nonmanagement employee. Rather than being responsible for a specific job, the manager's concerns extend over work accomplished by all of the employees in the group. Shifts to management positions are especially difficult for employees who must supervise employees who were recently their peers.

When employees recognize that the new supervisor is no longer one of the gang, the supervisor may be perceived by some as no longer friendly, acting superior, or somehow different. This reaction is especially common when the newly promoted supervisor is younger or has less seniority on the job than the majority of employees in the work unit. In fact only the supervisor's role has changed. He or she must necessarily view the work unit as a whole in addition to assessing the performance of its individual members.

Conflict occurs when employees, formerly peers, feel the new supervisor has both responsibility and authority greater than their own. Simple recognition of differences may be a source of conflict. "Paula is one of them. She's not one of us anymore," may be a typical expression of resentment of psychological distance.

■ SUPERVISORS AND CONFLICT MANAGEMENT

One of the difficulties with conflict is that each of the parties wants to win. Supervisors who find themselves in conflict with first-line managers of other organizational units frequently develop a desire to beat the other person. They strongly feel that if there is a winner, there must also be a loser. When people believe that all conflicts can result in only winners and losers, it is called a **zero-sum game.** One side must win and the other must lose.

Zero-sum game is a situation in which one side must win and the other must lose.

Of all cultures, people in the United States are the most thoroughly indoctrinated in zero-sum philosophy. We are a country of people who, with some exceptions feel that winning, being first, and knowing we are the best are important. People are rewarded for results, not effort. Second place is never good enough. A problem with zero-sum conflict solutions is that they ignore other possibilities. Supervisors may want to look beyond zero-sum behavior and find alternatives that will not automatically create losers.

Conflict Strategy

In a conflict situation, whether between individuals or groups, there is usually a desire to win. One person or side wins, the other loses. Although this may seem to be the only possible conflict outcome, alternatives do exist. While there is some indication that people are looking for alternatives, most people in our society still believe that someone wins and someone loses in any type of conflict.

In addition to the win-lose or zero-sum stance taken by many people, alternative **conflict strategies** may be used. Some people feel that if winning is impossible, it is better to drag their opponents down rather than let them win. A lose-lose tactic is taken: "If I can't win, neither will you." For example Tom may feel that he is not likely to receive a promotion since his competition is almost sure to be promoted. One tactic may be to go to the manager who is providing new opportunities and say, "Gail will make a good supervisor. I'm sure she has licked her problem of drinking before she reports for work. Most other employees feel she has reduced her drinking at lunch also."

Rather than accept the fact that they are noncompetitors, lose-lose strategists find ways of destroying others. Regardless of what Gail says, she has been branded as an alcoholic. Her chances of receiving the promotion, like those of her accusers, have been virtually eliminated by innuendo of alcoholism. This is a *lose-lose* strategy. When win-lose tactics fail, lose-lose tactics are very likely to be the next strategy taken. A tie, even a losing one, is not as bad as an outright loss.

Rather than be combative some people take a "let them have it" stance. Rather than engage in actions that would make them winners or deliberately sabotage others, they give up. Give-up strategies are usually identified as *lose-win* positions. Lose-win strategies usually reflect a lack of confidence, unwillingness to defend a position, or simple withdrawal. "It's just not worth the effort" is the most common rationalization for adopting a lose-win strategy in reducing conflict.

One of the difficulties in understanding conflict management is the belief that someone must win and others must lose. Some years ago the well-known psychologist Carl Rogers pointed out that forcing people to feel like losers was one of the most punishing acts that can be performed.[6] It is neither necessary nor desirable to make people lose. Rogers proposed that each person in a conflict situation try to understand the basis of conflict from the other person's point of view. After more than 30 years managers are beginning to realize that a win-win strategy is far more productive than the traditional zero-sum game.

Win-win conflict reduction requires extraordinary psychological maturity. First-line managers must be willing to search for solutions acceptable, not only to themselves, but to others as well. Win-win approaches do not automatically mean some type of compromise. True win-win strategies require developing and examining common areas of agreement that may have not been part of the original points of contention. While often difficult, win-win solutions avoid making people feel like losers.

Integrative bargaining requires that each party make a good-faith attempt to fully understand the other person or group's point of view.

In collective bargaining sessions between unions and management, win-win positions are often called **integrative bargaining.** Each of the parties involved strives to fully understand the position of the other. They work for agreement rather than confrontation that can lead to polarization of positions. In normal on-the-job conflicts, problem-solving approaches are far more productive than winning. Table 13.2 summarizes conflict strategies.

TABLE 13.2 ■ Conflict Strategies

Win-lose	"If there are winners there must also be losers."
Lose-lose	"If I can't win, neither will you."
Lose-win	"You win; it's not worth the effort to me."
Win-win	"We can both gain by solving our differences."

Managing Conflict

When any group of people meet or work together, conflict is virtually certain. Since very individual perceives events differently and has beliefs and attitudes that are uniquely their own, conflict is a natural and often beneficial occurrence. Supervisors must learn to achieve a *balance* between conflict that is destructive, divisive, and counterproductive and conflict that stimulates innovation, problem resolution, and often clears the air of feelings and emotions.

Conflict management requires recognition that people approach conflict in different ways.

Conflict management requires recognition that people approach conflict in different ways.[7] Most research in conflict management indicates five fundamental tactics. While they are called by different names in various publications, their intent is the same.[8] Table 13.3 summarizes these five types of conflict behavior.

While, on the surface, problem-solving behavior seems the most productive conflict-management behavior, it may not be best for all conditions. If issues are trivial, relationships might be damaged, or if an ideal solution is not required, other styles may be appropriate.[9]

In crisis situations where there is little time for discussion and quick action is necessary, tough-battler behavior may be the most appropriate.

Problem solvers may frequently find themselves in a deadlock over decisions. Tough battlers are usually unyielding, and problem solvers insist that all ideas be examined thoroughly before decisions are made. Sometimes problem solvers will give up in frustration without resolving their differences with tough battlers.

■ SUPERVISORS AS CONFLICT CREATORS

Most people tend to be somewhat ambivalent. They have a wide range of tolerance for different types of behavior and ideas. When

TABLE 13.3 ■ Types of Conflict Behavior

Tough battlers	Tough battlers have little concern for the feelings and ideas of others. Their primary motivation is winning. Decisions are forced on others. Tough battlers tend to be dominant, confrontational, and aggressive. Power depends on beating opponents.
Friendly helpers	Consideration for the feelings of others, reduction of tension, and avoiding any indication of unfriendliness are primary friendly-helper motives. They believe it is best to not say anything if you can't say something nice. They are willing to accept both sides of a dispute in the interest of harmony. Conflict, they believe, must be avoided. Tough battlers see friendly helpers as easy to dominate. They are correct.
Avoiders	Avoiders do not want to be involved in conflict. They maintain a stance of strict neutrality when faced with differences. A typical reaction to conflict is to remove themselves either physically or mentally with little concern for people. Conflict is viewed as hopeless, useless, and punishing. They keep their opinions to themselves.
Compromisers	Getting half is better than getting nothing at all for compromisers. Compromisers try to get a solution everyone can live with but they do not avoid stating their opinion or defending their position. They tend to manipulate situations rather than force them as do tough battlers. They may express frustration when acceptable middle-ground resolution of differences is difficult.
Problem solvers	Problem solvers, like tough battlers, want to satisfy their personal goals. They also strive to satisfy goals of others. Conflict is seen as natural and potentially beneficial. Problem solvers tend to trust others, have no hidden agendas, believe everyone has a right to express their point of view, and will not sacrifice positions for the sake of pleasing others. Conflict is viewed as an opportunity to build on contributions made by everyone involved. They stick to positions they feel are correct.

they feel threatened and become defensive, the ambivalence toward and tolerance of other positions are narrowed. They seek others with views similar to their own and quickly develop "us against them" attitudes.

Supervisors who attempt to manage by dominance and fear evoke we-they feelings. Management is seen as adversarial and against employees. Conflict is often expressed subtly. Resentment is expressed by delaying work. Equipment failure, lack of materials, lack of adequate information, and misunderstanding of instructions become ways of expressing antagonism.

Managers at all levels must never forget that integrity, credibility, and trust are essential to not only their own well being but to the degree of trust employees will have in them and the organization. They must also recognize that even under the best of conditions not all problems can be solved, people problems cured, and conflict managed without some degree of difficulty.

Role Conflict

Role conflict occurs when there is uncertainty of an individual's true role. Supervisors may identify more strongly with employees than with management although they are first-line managers.

When supervisors agree with, recognize, and emotionally support the feelings of employees more than the requirements of higher-level management, **role conflict** occurs. A typical symptom of role conflict are these statements: "This is what they want us to do," "They think this is a good idea," and "I know you won't like this, but this is what we have been told." Rather than take a clear-cut management stance, supervisors will make statements that identify their support of employees and against higher-level management directives. *They,* in these instances, refers to any level of management that makes policy or issues directives. Supervisors find their role as managers in conflict with their identification with employees. In some cases supervisors may see themselves as message-passing employees rather than true first-line managers.

Another type of role conflict occurs when there is confusion over who has responsibility for certain tasks. Supervisors may, as an example, feel they have primary responsibility for determining the number of employees needed to make their own department operate effectively. Accounting supervisors, responsible for cost reporting, may disagree. They point out that their responsibility is to determine the overall budgets, including numbers of employees, for each department. Conflict is certain until the roles of each are clarified by clear definition of responsibilities or by higher-level management determination.

▪ HARD DECISIONS AND HARDER ACTION

A reality of work is that some employees will be consistently incompetent, show very little enthusiasm, and be seen not only by supervisors but by other members of the work unit as unfit. If after trying to motivate and deal with people who seem to not be able to learn or are unresponsive to training or work instructions, it may be necessary, as Ken Blanchard states, to redirect their talents.[10] What Blanchard means is that not all people fit in the same type of organization. It may be necessary, though rare, to ask a person to seek other employment.

Involuntary termination is the capital punishment of work organizations. It affects not only the person being asked to leave but other employees as well. If a person is known to have been a misfit, caused excessive problems, or been a consistent goof-off, his or her leaving may be seen as both justifiable and necessary. When termination does not seem justified, employees may view the supervisor as being arbitrary and unfair. Any negative feeling is a point of conflict. It is an emotional reaction to circumstances that are somehow threatening. "If it happened to Paula, it could happen to me" is a typical reaction. Supervisors have the responsibility for objectively evaluating all of the circumstances involved before action is taken, including their own feelings and behavior.

■ CONFLICT-MANAGEMENT SKILLS FOR SUPERVISORS

One of the primary errors that can be made in conflict situations, including those between supervisors and other supervisors, is letting the desire to win take precedence over the need to solve a problem or difference. As members of management, supervisors must never put personal goals before organizational needs.

Changing a conflict situation to one of collaboration and cooperation is usually difficult. Problem-solving behavior that seeks win-win solutions reduces emotional tension and saves face for people whose views might otherwise not be considered as part of the conflict-management process. Here are some fundamental skills that help supervisors in conflict reduction:

1. **Avoid anger, impatience, and fighting.** One of the qualities that marks management leadership is the ability to keep cool under pressure. Anger, being drawn into unproductive arguments and name-calling, and impatience block communication, make understanding difficult if not impossible, and increase tension and distrust. Skilled supervisors know that competitive people often draw others into verbal fights as a tactic and as a way of demonstrating their own power. At times anger is very difficult to suppress. Emotional control, however, is a mark of psychological maturity and ability to cope with demanding circumstances.

2. **Work for solutions that help everyone.** It is easy for a supervisor to feel that his or her work unit is the most important. Other people's problems are theirs to solve. While often difficult, the good of the entire organization rather than a single department or section must be considered. One certain way to

create conflict is to win at the expense of other work units. In dealing with individual conflicts, solutions that embarrass, belittle, or benefit only one of those concerned may be an ultimate loss for all.

David Brinkley, one of the most respected news analysts, was once asked if reporters could be objective. "Perhaps not," he responded, "but they can try to be fair." Supervisors involved in disputes, especially with other departments in their organization, may find true objectivity arduous. They can, as Brinkley advises, try to be fair.

3. **Be sensitive to emotional attitudes of others.** Supervisors who are blind to the feelings of others are doomed to failure in management of conflict. Conflict cannot be reduced if any of the parties is angry, feels threatened, or is extremely defensive. Emotions must be defused first. One of the most effective tools in reduction of emotional tension is the willingness to listen empathetically. Approval, disapproval, or judgment must be withheld until the emotions have been talked out. Active listening involves creation of understanding without arguing for or against a particular point. It is difficult to learn but a very valuable management skill.

4. **Be specific—focus on problems, not on people.** It is easy to accuse others of wrongdoing in a conflict situation. Far more productive is the willingness to define problems in terms of specific events, such as, "There have been four errors in sales data reports this week," rather than, "Your work gets sloppier all of the time. Why can't you do something right for a change?" When problems are clearly defined they can be discussed more easily and more objectively. It may have been that the errors creating the conflict were not caused by conditions the report maker could control. Depersonalize the issue.

5. **Avoid we-they distinctions.** In conflict-reduction discussions the word *you* can be made to sound like an accusation. Statements like, "You always get it wrong," "You don't know what they're doing," and "You're always complaining and not acting," make conflict reduction virtually impossible. Not only are the statements accusatory but they separate the people involved from others. We-they distinctions accuse others of causing the conflict and exempt the accuser from possibly being part of the problem.

6. **Do your homework.** Before entering any discussion related to a conflict between employees, work units, or a supervisor and

employees, check your information. Do not rely on a single source of information. Get information from everyone involved, make a careful analysis, and be prepared with workable solutions.

7. **Limit expectations to reality.** Problems involving people take time to fully resolve. In rare instances simple lack of information can be the cause of conflict. "The market research department did not understand what information was needed for the sales report" may explain why there were four errors. Investigation has resolved the conflict situation.

In most instances resolution isn't that easy. Emotions are involved, trust levels must be rebuilt, and several follow-up discussions may be necessary to complete the conflict-reduction process. Work with workable items and limit expectations to the reality of the situation and those involved. Figure 13.3 summarizes conflict management techniques.

■ CONFLICT IN GROUP DISCUSSION

In group meetings the leader has the roles of guiding, stimulating, and controlling discussion. A measure of effective groups is the willingness of members to voice their opinions, ideas, and feelings without fear of being excluded or demeaned by others. Leaders should see themselves as information gatherers, summarizers, and consensus builders rather than persuaders. Meetings aren't needed if a decision has already been made. Debate and analysis of points are encouraged. There can be a great deal of disagreement without threat or embarrassment if the leader is skilled in creating a climate of openness.

Control by the leader involves recognizing when positions on issues have been repeated several times with little change. A good tactic is to redirect a question to someone who has not voiced his position. Conflict, in the form of open discussion, can be a satisfying and productive experience. A part of control centers on keeping honest disagreement from becoming an open fight. It requires adherence to issues on the formal agenda rather than allowing hidden agendas to dominate discussion. A hidden agenda consists of the items a member of the meeting would like discussed other than those on the formal agenda.

To ensure that emotions are not allowed to escalate to the point of being uncontrollable, the leader must be able to summarize all positions, avoid attempting to sway opinions, and act as a

FIGURE 13.3 ■ Conflict Management Techniques

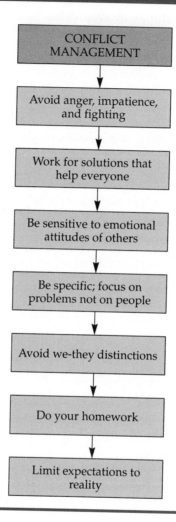

moderator and facilitator rather than a rule enforcer. Supervisors who hold regular meetings with their staff must see their roles as more than information providers and decision makers. Leaders build trust and confidence by being fair, open, and willing to listen to more than one side of a point of conflict.

■ REALITIES

Supervisors of all levels of management deal with the widest range of human behavior. Much of it is not perfect, plans do not always work, and frustration and conflict are common. A sense of humor, objectivity, and realization that individuals are complex and sometimes unpredictable is a part of being an effective first-line manager.

■ THINGS TO REMEMBER

I. Conflict without, conflict within.

  A. Blocked expectations can be a source of conflict.

  B. Most conflict has a relatively low level of intensity.

  C. As conflict increases, polarization is more likely to occur.

  D. Defensive behavior is an almost inevitable consequence of conflict.

II. Group conflict.

  A. Organizational centrism can be a point of conflict when groups try to blame other work units for most of the difficulties in an organization.

  B. Organizational centrism stifles voluntary cooperation.

  C. Cliques can be centers of conflict.

III. Dampened or dismissed expectations.

  A. Resentment about unmet needs and expectations is more emotionally intense than satisfaction with fulfilled needs.

  B. Unfulfilled expectations create distrust, dissatisfaction, and conflict.

  C. Differences in expectations arise because employees are job centered while managers focus on organizational goals.

IV. Psychological contracts.

  A. Psychological contracts are the unspoken expectations managers and employees have of each other.

  B. Contractual trust is the belief that another person will uphold an implied or specific agreement.

  C. Conflicting priorities can be a source of conflict between supervisors.

V. Problem employees.

  A. Personality differences are based on unwillingness to accept another person's behavior or beliefs.

    B. Problem-employee behavior can be compared to some of the characteristics of animals. Gorillas, wasps, snakes, baboons, sloths, sharks, and bleeding sharks abound in organizations.

VI. Psychological distance.

    A. Psychological distance is the recognition that new roles and responsibilities resulting from being promoted create a different frame of reference for both the new supervisor and employees.

    B. Because a supervisor who was once a peer is no longer one of the gang, she or he may be viewed with a certain level of distrust.

VII. Supervisors and conflict management.

    A. The belief that in every conflict someone must win while others lose is known as a **zero-sum game.** Of all cultures, people in the United States are most thoroughly indoctrinated with this philosophy.

    B. Win-lose beliefs fail to examine other alternatives.

    C. Some people adopt a lose-lose tactic if winning seems impossible.

    D. Some people take lose-win positions.

    E. Win-win conflict-reduction strategy is the most productive. Integrative bargaining is built on a win-win approach to union-management negotiations.

VIII. Managing conflict.

    A. When a group of people meet or work together, conflict is virtually certain.

    B. Conflict management requires recognition that people approach conflict in many different ways.

    C. Five types of conflict behavior include tough battlers, friendly helpers, avoiders, compromisers, and problem solvers.

    D. Conflict with management is often expressed subtly.

IX. Hard decisions and harder action.

    A. There are times when problem employees must be removed from the work force.

    B. Involuntary termination is the capital punishment of work organizations.

C. Poorly analyzed termination actions can be viewed as threatening by remaining employees.

X. Conflict management skills for supervisors.

A. Effective supervisors never let the desire to win take precedence over organizational needs.

B. Essential skills for conflict management include: avoid anger, impatience and fighting; work for solutions that help everyone; be sensitive to the emotional attitudes of others; be specific—focus on problems not people; avoid we-they distinctions; do your homework; limit expectations to reality.

C. An effective group climate encourages freedom to express feelings or opinions without feelings of fear or threat.

XI. Realities.

A. No level of management deals with a greater variety of human behavior than do supervisors.

■ KEY TERMS

conflict	bleeding sharks
polarization	psychological distance
defensiveness	zero-sum game
organizational centrism	conflict strategies
cliques	integrative bargaining
psychological contracts	conflict management
contractual trust	tough battlers
personal trust	friendly helpers
gorillas	avoiders
wasps	compromisers
snakes	problem solvers
baboons	role conflict
sloths	

■ DISCUSSION QUESTIONS

1. What types of conflicts have you encountered in work situations?

2. How do you react when your opinions or beliefs are challenged? Do you feel your reactions are always appropriate? Why?

3. Give an example of a win-win conflict resolution.

4. Why does conflict based on beliefs about abortion, gun control, support for United States peacekeeping efforts, and civil rights create strong emotional responses?

5. Under what conditions should employees be removed from the work force?

■ SELF-EVALUATION

Here are some statements related to conflict and conflict management. If you disagree with the statement, mark a 1, 2, or 3. If you agree or have a positive response, mark a 4, 5, or 6.

1. If there is a winner, there must also be a loser.

    1   2   3   4   5   6

2. Conflict has little relationship to frustration and stress.

    1   2   3   4   5   6

3. Compromise is usually the best way to manage conflicts.

    1   2   3   4   5   6

4. Problem solvers see conflict as natural and desirable.

    1   2   3   4   5   6

5. Supervisors depend primarily on friendship for effective work relationships.

    1   2   3   4   5   6

6. Tough battlers are rarely able to dominate friendly helpers.

    1   2   3   4   5   6

7. Role conflicts are relatively rare at the first-line level of management.

    1   2   3   4   5   6

8. Conflict management should focus on general conditions rather than specific occurrences.

    1   2   3   4   5   6

9. Threats to beliefs and values rarely cause defensive behavior.

    1   2   3   4   5   6

10. Employees who experience consistent difficulty are usually helped by other employees.

    1   2   3   4   5   6

▪ SHORT CASES

A Matter of Principle

Vic Flynn never wanted to be a manager. It just happened. He started with Metallic Continuous Coating Associates in the final processing area. MECCA, as the company was called, applied special coatings to a variety of metals used in the chemical, electronics, aircraft, and space-related industries. Processes were exacting and required complex controls. Vic was also a union secretary. Union members were a mixture of several large minority groups and Vic was often kidded about being one of the token whites on the union executive board. He was well liked and showed exceptional organizational skills in union activities.

Vic had been with MECCA for three years when his supervisor was required to leave the company due to severe health problems. Bob Downey, plant superintendent, asked Vic to take the job. With some reluctance, Vic accepted.

Vic immediately found that his relationship with his union friends changed. Those employees who reported directly to him acted uncomfortable when Vic made regular work assignments. He did not like telling people what to do, and he especially disliked correcting people he had worked with for three years. Bob Downey, aware of Vic's feelings, felt he was making real progress. Vic's reports were never late, his analyses of problems were accurate, and he exhibited in-depth knowledge of processes.

In spite of his success, Vic would occasionally go to Bob and ask for his old job back. Bob would always reply by stating that Vic was doing a good job and he belonged in management. Vic often felt that he understood employees better than managers. He was constantly worried and reluctant to correct employees who weren't performing well. Almost daily he felt like quitting and looking for a job with another company. From his point of view, his only reward in his new assignment was a slightly larger paycheck.

At the end of his third month as supervisor, Vic was confronted by Henry Tyson, the union president. "Vic, I want to tell you that you are in management now and the people want you to start acting like a manager. We all know you have it in you. Learn to stand up for both the company and for your people. If you have to fight the union, fight hard. We think there won't be too many conflicts."

When Vic later told Bob Downey of his conversation with Henry, Vic said, "Henry's a good man." In the following days Vic did not feel as alone as during his first few weeks. At least two people had faith in his ability, even if he was uncertain at first.

Last year when Bob Downey retired, Vic became MECCA's youngest plant superintendent.

1. What types of role conflict was Vic experiencing?

2. What could Bob have done to help Vic during this initial period as a manager?

3. Why did Henry Tyson say, "We think there won't be too many conflicts?"

Conflict Revisited

William James is called the founder of American psychology in much the same way as Frederick Taylor is known as originating scientific management. In the first volume of his famous two-volume text, *Psychology*, James wrote that people become tired, not necessarily because of hard work, but because of conflict within themselves.[11] Uncertainty about the outcomes of decisions drain energy until some definitive action is taken.

When internal conflicts are associated with conflict on the job, stress symptoms are inevitable. With Vic Flynn, conflict between his role as a manager and his desire to remain a member of the work force created unusual stress. He wanted to escape by changing jobs. Internal conflicts often distort an individual's view. Employees did not, as he imagined, resent his promotion. They were disappointed when he failed to fully take charge of his responsibilities, but they still wanted him to succeed. He was excessively fearful of conflict with employees who were once his peers.

Vic learned a great lesson. Supervisors must accept the consequences of their actions without fear of disagreement. They must realize that regardless of what action is taken, some degree of conflict is likely to exist. Conflict reduction often hinges on clear decisions about courses of action to take, decisions about ourselves, about others, and about needed actions.

1. Can you think of decisions you have been required to make that had the potential for conflict? How did you feel before making the decision?

2. In what ways can supervisors recognize potential conflict between themselves and others?

3. What are some practical approaches to conflict reduction?

■ ENDNOTES

1. Events depicted are based on interviews with employees of CAB. Company and individual names are disguised.

2. William V. Haney, *Communication and Interpersonal Relations: Text and Cases,* (Homewood, Ill.: Richard D. Irwin, 1986), p. 64.

3. Frederick Herzberg, "Workers' Needs: The Same around the World," *Industry Week,* September 21, 1987, pp. 29–32.

4. William (Bill) Morris is a management consultant and former educator. His workshops on gorilla behavior are well known.

5. Robert Morton is best known for his Organizational Laboratory. His models of management and employee behavior are well known. Dr. Morton is a fellow and diplomate of the American Psychological Association and a consultant to the American Management Association.

6. Carl Rogers, *On Becoming a Person* (Boston: Houghton Mifflin, 1961).

7. Chad T. Lewis, Joseph E. Garcia, and Sarah M. Jobs, *Managerial Skills in Organizations* (Boston: Allyn & Bacon, 1990), pp. 93–104. Several approaches to conflict management are reviewed and a clear distinction is made between conflict resolution and conflict management.

8. Kenneth Thomas, "Conflict and Conflict Management," in *The Handbook of Industrial and Organizational Psychology,* ed. Marvin Dunnett (Skokie, Ill.: Rand-McNally, 1976); Robert R. Blake and Jane S. Mouton, "The Fifth Achievement," *Journal of Applied Behavioral Science* 6 (1970), pp. 413–16. Usually credited with popularizing the five major conflict strategies used by individuals.

9. Cheryl Hamilton and Cordel Parker, *Communicating for Results,* 3rd edition (Belmont, Calif.: Wadsworth Publishing Company, 1990), pp. 305–307.

10. Kenneth Blanchard and Spencer Johnson, *The One Minute Manager* (New York: William Morrow and Company, 1982).

11. William James, *Psychology* (New York: Henry Holt & Co., 1902).

Chapter 14

Performance Evaluation, Due Process, and Discipline

Objectives

Chapter 14 focuses on the maintenance of predictable conditions at work. It requires a knowledge of the limits of supervisor action. Readers of the chapter will be able to

- Identify difficulties with most frequently used performance review methods.

- Employ techniques that enable improved performance appraisal.

- Adhere to principles of due process.

- Encourage employee self-discipline.

- Utilize combined disciplinary action and performance evaluation as management tools.

Thought Starter

In the mid-1980s a new term was added to the vocabulary of management. *Wrongful termination* became one of the many difficult problems in human resource management. It was a reflection of the many new protective laws that affect both employers and employees.

As laws become more protective of individual employee rights, supervisors are faced with the problem of how to maintain a disciplined work force without encountering either social or legal backlash. This is especially true in cases involving involuntary termination. People may be fired, but can management make it stick? An answer that was once clearly and resoundingly yes is now a tentative maybe. It is difficult for supervisors to be real first-line managers when they feel powerless in the face of aggressive and determined employees.

New questions regarding employee rights arise every day. Employees claim discrimination, lack of due process, unfair performance evaluation, lack of consideration for seniority, and a multitude of other causes as a defense against disciplinary actions or perceived unfair treatment by their supervisors.

Managers often feel powerless. Daily they are faced with employees who use company policies, union agreements, and state and federal law to resist any type of corrective action, even when it is fully justified. How far the current trends in protective legislation will go will be determined by public opinion during the next few years.

Can organizations survive in a political and social environment that, at times, ignores the necessity for adherence to rules and regulations? While isolated cases of abuse of what people know is right exist, it is our sense that a disciplined work force that rarely needs disciplinary action is the model for the future.

■ *Toni Wilson was 59 years old and had, from Carolyn Hendrix's perspective, retired on the job. Toni had, several years previously, reached the top of the pay range for her job classification. Although a review of her performance evaluations indicated satisfactory performance, she now seemed to work to minimum job requirements.*

As unit supervisor for the administrative services department of Food Additives Developers, Carolyn was responsible for providing a variety of services, ranging from report development and secretarial services to catalogs and customer-information publications. Her 14 employees were required to have multiple skills and a willingness to accept a wide variety of challenging tasks. "Frankly," Dennis Markley, employee relations supervisor, told Carolyn, "Toni is burned out. She'll retire in a year or two and just plain doesn't care much anymore."

"I don't think that's true," replied Carolyn. "It's her attitude that needs straightening out. If she wants to make it to retirement, she'll have to do more than she is doing now. Just barely meeting minimum standards is not good enough around here."

■ HOW GOOD IS GOOD ENOUGH?

How much should supervisors expect from employees? Equally important is the question, What is the best way of letting employees know how well they are performing? Answers to these questions are a difficult challenge for most supervisors. Should a senior employee with a good work record be treated the same as a relatively new employee who has no history of either good or bad performance? At times it is difficult to know the correct course of action.

Charles Moore was known for a tendency to be cocky and somewhat disdainful of authority. One of his tasks was to load and unload heavy products, such as cement, fertilizer, lumber, and building supplies. He was a skilled forklift driver and bragged to other employees he could do wheelies on one if he had an opportunity. Karen Snyder, his supervisor and manager of garden and building supplies for Home and Maintenance Stores, was fully aware of his attitude. She had twice warned him about his tendency to race equipment in the building supply yard.

One day while rapidly loading fencing from the building supply shed to a customer's truck, Charles rammed into a wooden column that supported the shed-like roof over lumber supplies. As the column snapped, roof weight was transferred to other supporting columns and the entire section collapsed. Karen witnessed the entire event.

> Charles was immediately reprimanded by Karen both in writing and in a private conference. He was given three days off without pay for unsafe use of equipment and damage to company property. Karen then called the entire department staff together. "If anyone misuses equipment, especially forklift trucks, again, it will mean immediate termination." Two days later Frank Escobar, a senior employee with an exemplary work record for seven years, backed a lift truck into a fence surrounding the outdoor decorative rock area. Karen was now faced with a problem she had created.

Discipline and Disciplinary Action

Karen, obviously, would be wrong to treat Frank Escobar the same way as Charles. With a history of good work, cooperation, and adherence to rules, Frank's accident was not the same as Charles's carelessness. In evaluating performance and applying disciplinary action, judgment and experience are necessary. While disciplinary action was justified in Charles's case, Frank neither deserved nor received the extreme penalty of termination threatened by Karen in the staff meeting. Evaluation of employee performance is rarely totally objective. Rules that may apply in one set of conditions do not apply in others.

Discipline means adherence to a set of rules.

Discipline means, in its simplest terms, adherence to a set of rules. Most employees are self-disciplined. They have learned acceptable patterns of behavior. Formal rules of an organization and commonly accepted rules of behavior are understood. Many years ago Bradford Boyd defined *discipline* as self control, and **disciplinary action** as corrective measures necessary to maintain a disciplined work group.[1] In actual practice most employees prefer to obey reasonable and understandable rules of personal conduct. Corrective action, if needed, is usually in the form of information, problem analysis, or training. Punishment, as in Charles's case, is usually an exception to most disciplinary action.

Disciplinary action focuses on correction rather than punishment.

■ PERFORMANCE EVALUATION

Performance evaluation is the judgment supervisors make concerning an employee's or group of employees' effectiveness.

Performance evaluation is the judgment supervisors make concerning an employee's or group of employees' effectiveness. Most appraisal is informal, day-to-day judgment of employee performance on specific tasks. Disciplinary action is based on an evaluation of whether an employee is meeting general performance and behavioral standards.

One of the misconceptions concerning performance evaluation is the belief that it is an annual or semiannual ritual. Employees are presented a written appraisal of their performance, there is a brief (in some instances, very brief) discussion, and the employee is asked to sign the appraisal form. It is much like a student receiving a report card. Grades are given for how well the supervisor believes employees performed various components of their jobs.

In addition to job characteristics related to productivity, quality, efficiency, and schedule adherence, employees are also rated on common rules of behavior, such as attendance, cooperation, responsibility, and observance of organizational rules and policies. Pay increases above those of normal cost-of-living adjustments are usually tied very closely to the appraisal. Although some type of formal appraisal system is virtually universal in both private and public organizations, the most significant and meaningful evaluation is that done on a day-to-day basis by supervisors. Performance appraisal and disciplinary action both have the goals of developing and encouraging predictable employee behavior. Self-disciplined employees, predictably, do what they understand as correct and necessary.

Performance Feedback

A large body of research material indicates that annual reviews, as they are often called, have little effect on employee performance. **Performance feedback** from the supervisor on specific activities is far more effective in changing work habits. Performance appraisal and disciplinary actions have the same intent. Both are directed at ensuring predictable employee work habits and behavior. They also reinforce desirable work practices.

"Dennis, that report looks great. I especially like the way it is formatted and the way data is summarized. Thanks for a good job." This is a more significant supervisory statement than "Dennis, you are doing a good job. Keep it up." Both are positive but the first lets the employee know that a specific job was well done. It ties performance to an activity and reinforces the association between approval and correct work. **Praise,** to be effective, must be associated with a specific activity. Rather than talk about the person, the supervisor praised what the employee had accomplished. It is a powerful technique in establishing predictably high standards of performance.

Praise, to be effective, must be associated with a specific activity.

"Dennis, there are some problems with the report. It is not formatted in a way that is easily understood. Let's discuss ways of improving it." This feedback is not positive, but it is also not threatening. Had the supervisor said, "Dennis, you did a lousy job on the report. Go back and get it right. You are a real disappointment," the feedback would create resentment and fear and still not correct the problem. **Corrective feedback,** like approval, must be directed to a specific problem, not the person. Regardless of whether feedback is corrective or affirmative, it is the most meaningful type of performance appraisal that an employee receives.

Debbie Tarkington works as a cashier for Bel-Wood Supermarkets. Her complaint was that she received no feedback. She assumed that she was doing a good job, but did not really know. "Every six months," she stated, "we receive a formal review. It's the only feedback we get."[2] Employees need and want to know how well they are doing. Supervisors have the responsibility for providing feedback, discussing job problems, and offering help and information. It is all part of the informal performance-appraisal process. Other benefits of on-the-job feedback include building trust, keeping lines of communication open, as well as providing the supervisor with information about employee problems, progress, and suggestions for improvement.

■ FORMAL PERFORMANCE-EVALUATION SYSTEMS

In a number of large labor unions formal evaluation systems no longer exist. United Automobile Workers and the International

Association of Machinists have taken the position that people either meet minimum standards for their jobs or they do not. They advance within union job classifications primarily by length of service or seniority. If a person is able to meet the requirements of a job description, they are qualified. Little distinction is made between minimally qualified and highly qualified. If, under union contracts that do not require formal appraisal systems, an employee clearly fails to meet minimum requirements, management may take appropriate action by lowering their classification or through discharge procedures. All such adverse actions must be reviewed for strict compliance to contractual agreements. Supervisors, under such conditions, often feel powerless. Unions, it is estimated, currently make up less than 17 percent of the total work force.

A major difficulty with the union philosophy is the assumption that meeting minimum requirements is all that is necessary. Supervisors want their employees to excel. Union leaders are quick to point out that job descriptions and formal work standards are the result of mutual agreements between management and employees. If an employee performs the tasks in the job description and meets minimum standards, they are fulfilling their job responsibilities.

Purposes of Performance Appraisal

William Edwards Deming, who has been mentioned throughout this text, advocates abolishment of formal performance evaluations.[3] He believes that formal appraisal systems tend to create fear and apprehension, which should be driven out of work environments. Not many organizations have adopted Deming's philosophy. Most have some type of performance-appraisal system. They give a number of reasons why performance-appraisal systems are necessary:

1. A historical record is needed to meet potential legal requirements in the future.
2. Performance appraisals are the primary basis for pay increases.
3. Feedback on the employee's performance during the previous report period is provided.
4. Promotions are made on the basis of past as well as present performance.

5. Performance appraisals assist in determining training needs.

6. Employees with a history of low performance or poor behavior are clearly identified.

Some management professionals feel there are two purposes of performance evaluation. One is *judgmental* and the other is *developmental.*[4] **Judgmental performance evaluation** is used as the basis for pay raises, promotions, and transfers. It can also be used as a means of whipping an employee into shape. An especially poor rating is a threatening and often humiliating experience if it is generally acknowledged that it can ultimately be used to justify demotion or termination. It is unfortunate that judgmental performance evaluations are probably the most frequently used. They are usually disliked both by first-line managers and employees. Tension, apprehension, and distrust rather than performance improvement are the results. Employees with good ratings continue to work at their regular pace; those with poor ratings become resentful and apathetic. Figure 14.1 diagrams the relationship between judgmental and developmental performance appraisal. Both provide performance feedback.

Judgmental performance evaluation is the basis for pay raises, promotions, and transfers.

Developmental performance evaluation focuses on future improvement rather than being graded in comparison to others. Employees are encouraged to work with their supervisor to develop goals. They can evaluate how well the goals they have set have been achieved independent of their supervisor's evaluation. Goals not achieved are a subject of discussion and problem solving rather than creating defensiveness. Developmental performance evaluation has many very clear disadvantages as well as advantages. For some supervisors and employees it can be time consuming and difficult. If jobs are routine and relatively repetitive,

Development performance evaluation focuses on future improvement.

FIGURE 14.1 ■ Major Types of Performance Appraisal

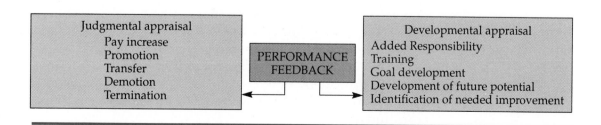

developing objectives can be especially perplexing. Employees often are unable to clearly identify activities that need improvement, and supervisors feel the time and paperwork involved are not worth the potential gain.

It is reasonably clear that most organizations use formal performance-evaluation systems as a means of justifying subsequent management action. Formal evaluations become part of the employee's permanent personnel record. They can be used as a justification for almost any management decision regarding an individual. Conversely employees may use their performance evaluation records as a defense if their job security or status is threatened.

■ METHODS OF EVALUATION

Formal performance appraisals are a means for justifying subsequent management action related to individual employees.

Virtually all of the stated purposes of annual or semiannual performance appraisals can be achieved without formal appraisal systems. Day-to-day supervisory contact with employees is more timely and accurate than an annual report card. Assessing training needs, providing feedback on performance, and determining who has earned special consideration for pay improvements or promotion can all be accomplished without formal systems. An advantage of formal systems is the provision of permanent, standardized, historical records of employee performance. Many methods have been used to grade employee performance. None is perfect.

Graphic Rating Scales

Graphic rating scales are the most common type of evaluation system. Numerical grades are given to employees for performance in predetermined job elements.

Since their origin in 1922, **graphic rating scales** have been the most popular and widely used method of evaluating employees.[5] They are simple to use and easily understood by both supervisors and employees. A graphic rating scale (see Figure 14.2) consists of a number of factors, such as quality, quantity, cooperation, job knowledge, attendance, initiative, and need for supervision. Each of these factors is rated on a scale, usually from 1 to 5, with 1 being very poor and 5 being outstanding. There are many variations of graphic rating scales. Some may have as many as 30 factors that are rated and some as few as 3. Scales can have as few as 3 evaluation points (1 — needs improvement, 2 — meets standards, and 3 — exceeds standards) or have as many as 10 or more.

Usually there is a place at the end of the form for a narrative statement that briefly describes the employee's performance in terms not included on the rating form. Regardless of how the form is constructed, ratings reflected on the form are rarely objective for a number of reasons.

FIGURE 14.2 ■ Sample Graphic Rating Scale

EMPLOYEE PERFORMANCE EVALUATION							
Instructions:	A rating of 5 indicates outstanding performance; 4 very good; 3 meets standards; 2 needs improvement; 1 poor performance.						
		1	2	3	4	5	
Productivity	Meets or exceeds productivity standards or expectations.						
Quality	Makes few errors; is concerned with quality of work as well as productivity.						
Cooperation	Voluntarily assists others; willingly accepts new assignments.						
Attendance	Is rarely absent or late for work. Attends all required meetings.						
Job Knowledge	Fully knows job requirements. Constantly improves skills.						
Use of Resources	Effectively and efficiently uses time, materials, and equipment. Is conscious of costs.						
Descriptive Comment:	In the space below write a brief description of employee's strengths and areas of needed improvement.						

_____   _____   _____
Employee signature   **Date**   **Supervisor signature**

1. External inconsistency. Supervisors in two departments may give significantly different ratings to virtually the same level of performance. In department A, the supervisor may view a person who meets all standards as average and will give a 3 on a five-point rating scale. Department B's supervisor may feel that a person who meets all standards is above average and will give a rating of 4. Each supervisor feels his or her ratings are accurate.

At times standards are difficult to determine. Members of a police force may be rated on dress. If an officer's uniform is clean, properly worn, shoes shined, and equipment properly placed, expected dress standards are being met. A persuasive argument can be made that it is impossible to earn more than an average rating for dress.

Supervisors must be well trained and fully understand rating standards to minimize external inconsistency. Most, unfortunately, have neither the training nor common understanding of standards.

2. Internal inconsistency. Supervisors often show preference in their ratings due to halo errors and stereotyping. **Halo errors** occur when a supervisor rates an employee on overall impressions, either good or bad. An employee who has good communication skills and a confident, friendly personality may receive relatively high ratings for average performance. Higher-performing employees with less confidence, poorer overall appearance, and fewer social skills may receive lower ratings than their actual performance warrants.

Beliefs about a person's behavior based on ethnicity, sex, level of education, nationality, religion, socioeconomic status, geographic origin, or any similar attribute is known as **stereotyping.** Stereotypes are common and usually have little basis in truth. "Red-haired people are hot tempered," "All lawyers are crooks," "Hungarians are moody," and "Women can't understand mechanical operations" are typical stereotypes. Supervisors who stereotype employees will rate them on the basis of what they believe about the employee's behavior. They will assign nonexistent characteristics to stereotyped employees.

Careful training and self-discipline are required to avoid letting either halos or stereotypes affect employee ratings.

3. New employee–old employee fallacies. Supervisors are often told by higher management to never give a new employee a high rating; leave room for her or him to grow. If a new employee has superior performance, she or he still gets a mediocre rating. This widespread practice is one of the most hypocritical and senseless graphic-rating-scale misuses. Performance, good or bad, should be rated correctly, regardless of length of service.

Employees who have been with an organization for several years may not be rated at all. Supervisors review the previous year's appraisals, make minor changes, and reword the narrative description at the end of the evaluation form. It is a *pro forma review.* **Pro forma** means it is done in order to meet requirements but has little real meaning. Adult behavior does not change much.

Good employees usually remain good employees and mediocre employees remain mediocre. Unfortunately, pro forma reviews do not correctly reflect improvements or declines in performance when they occasionally occur.

4. Rating tendency errors. Two other types of errors are common in employee ratings. Central tendency errors are used by cautious supervisors who want to avoid being viewed as too lenient by their immediate managers. They rate employees neither good nor bad. Nearly everyone gets a C grade simply because the rating is unchallengeable by higher levels of management and employees have a difficult time protesting being average.

Over time, employees who have been with an organization tend to be rated higher than their actual performance merits. This **seniority creep** is almost expected. Senior employees, by virtue of their experience, are expected to be better and as a consequence receive higher ratings.

5. Managerial review and forced choice. In most organizations performance appraisals made by supervisors are reviewed by higher levels of management. Supervisors are, in effect, graded on their evaluation of others. This practice frequently forces supervisors to make a forced choice. To avoid being accused of rating all employees too high, they rate most in the moderate performance level, a few are rated low, and the remaining few receive above-average ratings. Everyone is satisfied except employees who may have been rated lower than they deserve.

Other Systems, Same Problems

Ranking systems are the most simple type of employee comparisons. Employees are ranked according to their worth to the organization.

Paired comparisons, narrative ratings, and critical-incident appraisals are also used. All have disadvantages.

Many systems of employee performance appraisals have been attempted over the years since the graphic rating scale became popular. All of them, like graphic rating scales, have both advantages and disadvantages. **Ranking systems** are the most simple. Employees are compared to each other and the one with the estimated best performance is given the number one position, the next best number two, and so on. There are several forms of ranking, including **paired comparisons,** which force supervisors to compare not only overall performance but various attributes, such as job skills, to those of other employees. **Narrative ratings** require supervisors to make a written descriptive assessment of each employee's performance. **Critical-incident** appraisals involve recording both good and poor performance that deviates from the norm. If an employee does something exceptionally well, a note to that effect is added to their personnel record. Poor performance is also noted and added to the file. It is a cumbersome and difficult practice.

Objective evaluations are based on countable standards. Productivity, error rates, and schedule adherence are measured. Cooperation, innovation, and assistance to others are not considered.

Some types of jobs are appraised objectively. **Objective evaluation** compares an employee's performance against established standards. A data-entry operator may have a standard of 13,000 keystrokes per hour with less than 1 percent error. Performance is judged strictly by the employee's ability to meet or exceed standards. Objective standards in some types of work can also include cost data, schedule adherence, customer complaints, and similar measurable objectives. They do not, unfortunately, consider cooperation, innovation, creativity, leadership, and other attributes that are not directly measurable.

Management by Objectives and Behavioral Anchored Systems

MBO and BARS are difficult to prepare but are well-thought-out methods for evaluating people based against actual performance. Both measure discrete job elements.

In the late 1960s and early 1970s organizations became obsessed with **management by objectives (MBO).** Based on Peter Drucker's admonition that management can only be judged by results, organizations began to develop objectives for their total structure: divisions and departments, sections and individuals. Supervisors were required to meet with employees individually and have them state objectives they would achieve during the next 3, 6, or 12 months. Employees had a means of evaluating their own performance in conjunction with their supervisor. MBO had, and still has, many advantages. It opens lines of communication, encourages innovation and creativity, and gives employees a tool to measure their own performance. Most organizations, however, have found it cumbersome, time consuming, and too difficult to maintain. In moderately sized organizations, literally thousands of objectives would be generated. Supervisors with as few as 10 employees found that it was virtually impossible to determine whether employee goals had actually been achieved. As a consequence MBO lost much of its original popularity.

Behavioral anchored rating scales (BARS) eventually took the place of MBO in some organizations. BARS is a means of evaluating people against actual performance. A job description for various levels of performance is constructed. In a supermarket, as an example, a very good employee would be expected to answer customer questions, assist the manager in critical decisions, and be able to perform all functions, from operating checkout stations to stocking shelves, taking inventory, and knowing correct pricing as well as the location of thousands of products. BARS ratings would indicate how well employees performed each of these critical functions. Although BARS is a workable and valuable concept, it is difficult to construct, needs constant modification, and pressures supervisors to thoroughly know every action employees make. While it is used in some organizations, it has not yet been a dominant employee evaluation system.

Performance and Promotion

Potential, an individual's ability to accept and successfully perform greater levels of responsibility, is rarely evaluated.

A major difficulty with most rating scales is the lack of distinction between **performance** and **potential.** Conscientious supervisors attempt to appraise employee performance fairly. They rate their people on judgments of performance. They do not evaluate potential for promotion or increased responsibility. Present performance does not guarantee future value to an organization. A good word-processing operator, as an example, may not make a good office manager unless she or he possesses other characteristics. Leadership, communication, organizational, and planning skills may be characteristic of some excellent employees but not all. Good performance appraisal must also include assessment of potential for promotion. Guidelines for effective appraisal of employees are listed in Table 14.1.

■ DISCIPLINE AND DISCIPLINARY ACTION

Most people are self-disciplined. Their behavior is governed by expected rules of conduct. In a library people maintain silence; at ball games they cheer their favorite team. In work environments they attempt to accomplish what their jobs require. There is little need for correction other than new information, training, and assistance when unusual problems arise. Employees, in general, would rather do a good job, be independent of direct supervision, and feel like contributors to their organization. Discipline, however, must be learned. In learning environments *discipline* refers to following the rules of a field of knowledge. Mathematicians know and obey the rules of mathematics. Writers know and follow the rules of writing. *Discipline,* as stated earlier, means following the rules required to successfully accomplish any endeavor. It also means training that makes disciplinary action unnecessary. Like

TABLE 14.1 ■ Employee Appraisal for Supervisors

- Evaluate work, not people. Praise effort as well as results.
- Give credit where it is earned. Don't penalize new employees.
- Try to be fair. No one can be objective. Good supervisors are fair.
- Avoid halos. What looks good may not be good.
- Stereotypes are nonsensical. Judge performance as it actually exists, not on what others say.
- Look for potential as well as performance.
- Realize that performance evaluation is an everyday activity.
- Evaluate effort while work is in process as well as results.
- Do not tolerate errors. Correct problems, not people. Act when errors occur. Correction is not punishment. It is information, advice, and concern for performance.
- Never forget: supervisors must make organizations run correctly. To do this they must constantly assess both group and individual performance.

many words *discipline* has many meanings, depending on the way it is used. As used here, *discipline* means **self-discipline.** Supervisors who fail to encourage and maintain discipline in their work units lose the respect of their employees.

Disciplinary action, referred to earlier, involves any action that encourages and instructs people to be self-disciplined. It consists of actions that reinforce discipline. Disciplinary action is not intended to be punishment, although it may be under some circumstances. Problems in discipline must not be tolerated but corrected as soon as the supervisor is aware they exist. While corrective action is usually not punitive but helpful and informative, supervisors must be willing to face unpleasant encounters if necessary. Table 14.2 suggests ways to implement disciplinary action.

Gail Pearson was an excellent employee. As an electronic technician, Gail was an expert in diagnosis and repair of personal computers used by Systems Installation and Development (SID). She had been previously terminated from one of SID's competitors for being uncooperative and insubordinate. Gail stated flatly that her supervisor had been against women serving as high-level technicians and would not admit that she could outperform many of the male members of her work group.

Shortly after joining SID, Gail found herself embroiled in a very emotional conflict resulting from her recent divorce. She had legal

TABLE 14.2 ■ Implementing Disciplinary Action

1. Recognize potential problems	Take corrective action before more stringent measures are necessary.
2. Have clearly defined and understood standards of performance	Be certain that employees fully comprehend benefits and potential penalties for adherence to rules and standards of behavior.
3. Analyze rather than criticize	Define problems in job-related terms. Make sure that facts are orderly and thoroughly verified before taking action.
4. Correct problems rather than people	Focus all discussions on problems. Avoid accusations or criticisms of personalities. Do not demean or embarrass anyone being corrected. All corrective actions must be made in private for them to be effective.
5. Make actions reasonable	Consider all facts. Make penalties fit the degree of error or incorrect action.
6. Do not punish corrected performance	If after a period of time, usually one year, it is evident that problems have been corrected, remove potentially harmful memoranda or evidence from employee personnel files. Future promotions, transfers, or training for better jobs may be jeopardized by outdated records of corrective actions.

custody of two daughters, and her ex-husband threatened to have her arrested for kidnapping the girls if she refused to allow him full visitation rights. Both girls were afraid of their father because of abuses that led to the divorce.

At work Gail was a loner. She did not socialize with other employees, tended to resent instructions from her supervisor, and seemed withdrawn from other employees. Although SID had strict no-smoking rules in certain areas of the plant, Gail would often find a secluded spot during authorized break periods and smoke one or two cigarettes. On Monday morning she was observed by her supervisor smoking in a clearly marked no-smoking area. "Gail, I'm sorry, but you know that you are not allowed to smoke in this area. Our rules state that violation of a safety rule means an automatic three-day suspension without pay."

"You're just trying to make an example out of catching me," angrily replied Gail. "If you look around you'll see cigarette butts from other people smoking here. Even though there is a sign, people are known to use this area during their break periods. The oil drums that were once here have been removed for some time and there is clearly no danger. You know I have financial problems, and yet you're giving me three days off."

Later that afternoon Tom Blake, union steward, met with Gail's supervisor. "It looks like the company is not enforcing the no-smoking rule equally. We know Gail smoked in a no-smoking area. We also have evidence that other people have smoked there without disciplinary action. If you suspend her, we'll file a grievance based on unfair treatment."

What should Gail's supervisor do: Enforce the rule as written? Give Gail a warning and let it go this time? Enforce the rule but allow Gail to take time off one day per month? Have the no-smoking area redesignated as a smoking area? Attempt to get the rule changed? Try to find reasons for getting rid of Gail, as she is an apparent troublemaker and has had difficulties at previous jobs?

Rules and Reasonable Application

Nearly all large organizations as well as some small ones have formal rules of conduct. They specify types of behavior that are not permissible on organizational property. Use of alcohol or illicit drugs, excessive absenteeism or tardiness, sleeping at work, theft of personal or organization property, failure to perform assigned work, destruction of company property, disruption of work, and similar types of behavior are prohibited in writing. In addition common rules of behavior such as cooperation, attentiveness to instructions, and performing assigned duties are expected. Violations may result in a variety of penalties, ranging from warnings to time off without pay or, in extreme cases, involuntary termination.

Past practice is used to determine appropriate disciplinary action in the absence of a definitive policy.

In Gail's case the supervisor must weigh **past practice**. How did the company handle previous violations? Did it literally stick to the written rule or make some reasonable exceptions? In Gail's case, will lack of full enforcement set a precedent? If Gail gets off with a warning, it may be difficult to enforce the no-smoking rule in other areas. Should she receive the full penalty, it may be seen by other employees as unfair and arbitrary since her violation did not endanger anyone and others had been known to smoke in that area. If there are poor union-management relations, strict enforcement may be necessary to avoid future problems. Exceptions to the rule can be made if it is clear that the no-smoking designation was in error. When the final decision is made it will be based on analysis of a number of factors, including actions that have been taken previously in similar conditions.

Three conditions must exist for effective disciplinary action:

1. Rules must be reasonable. Employees must be able to comply with rules, and penalties must fit the severity of the infraction.

2. Employees must understand the rules and potential penalties. If a rule is violated out of ignorance, corrective action may consist of informing the violator of the rule and potential penalties.

3. Judgment must be used in rule enforcement. If, as an example, an organization prohibits gambling on company premises but employees frequently flip coins to determine who pays for coffee, are they in violation of the rule? They are engaging in a form of gambling. Reasonable enforcement would mean that as long as gambling is not for any person's monetary profit it will be tacitly ignored. Most organizations have football and baseball pools where employees, for a small amount of money, bet on the outcome of a game. Winners share in the pool of money contributed by all bettors. Past practice and reasonable judgment will decide whether such pools are a violation.

While each organization and every set of conditions is different, supervisors must consider several guidelines in rule enforcement. Some of the more important ones are briefly summarized in Table 14.3.

Implementing disciplinary actions can be emotional. Employees may get angry, challenge their supervisors' authority, and threaten action of their own through union representation, appeals to higher levels of management, or legal action. It is mandatory that first-line managers maintain their objectivity, make judgments based on fact rather than feelings, and refuse to be lured into a verbal fight. Supervisors invariably lose either respect of employees or themselves if they let anger dominate their discussions. Infractions will occur, mistakes will be made, and corrective action will be necessary. Proactive managers spend time training employees to develop a clear understanding of the type of on-the-job behavior that is expected. They firmly believe that preventive action is better than corrective action.

■ DUE PROCESS

Under English common law, on which our legal process is based, **due process** is a right of every person. It means that every person

TABLE 14.3 ■ Disciplinary-Action Enforcement

1. Disciplinary action must be corrective rather than punitive	Although it is often seen as punishment, effective disciplinary action is corrective. It is intended to build self-discipline.
2. To be effective, corrective action must be taken as soon after a rule violation as possible	Corrective action taken several days after a violation creates both questions and resentment. It is far better to take corrective action as soon as practical after a violation.
3. Get all the facts before taking action	Do not take corrective action on unsubstantiated evidence. Get all of the facts, listen to all sides of the story. Be sure to let the person who committed the violation state his or her position. Allow due process, the right of a person to have a fair hearing.
4. Make corrective action appropriate	Punishment, while frequently legitimate according to organizational rules, is not always warranted. Corrective action should be appropriate for the circumstances. Determine, from personnel records, if the infraction is a recurring pattern or an isolated incident.
5. Document, document, document	Make a written formal report of all disciplinary actions. Be specific about employee behavior, investigative evidence, dates, time, and actions taken. Give one copy of the report to the person being corrected, enter a copy in the person's personnel file, and keep a copy in personal files. These steps are necessary to identify patterns and to respond to legal actions. Without documentation, it is virtually impossible to prove charges if extreme measures are necessary.
6. Inform others	Before taking corrective disciplinary actions, discuss them with personnel specialists and immediately higher levels of management. Obtain their approval and recommendations.

Due process is the right of every person to present her or his side in a dispute, to appeal decisions to a higher level of authority, and to face accusers.

has a right to present his or her side in a dispute, to appeal decisions to a higher level of authority, and to face accusers. Due process implies that there can be no punishment for crime unless clear and convincing evidence exists that the person accused actually violated a law. In work organizations due process means that an employee has a right to appeal a supervisor's decision. Some organizations do not allow full due process and supervisors make the final decision on all disciplinary actions. Others have procedures that allow employees who feel supervisory actions are unfair or unwarranted to appeal to higher levels of management. The appeal process is usually known as a **grievance procedure.**

Grievance procedures are systematic steps used to hear employee complaints and ensure due process in the event of pending adverse actions.

In organizations where unions exist, grievance procedures are guaranteed by union-management agreements. Some nonunion organizations also have appeal processes. Typically employees who feel they have not been treated fairly by their supervisor put their complaint, called a *grievance,* in writing and submit it to either a personnel officer or to the supervisor and the next higher level of management. If decisions at the next level are not satisfactory, then the appeal is made to top management. In unionized organizations an outside person, called an **arbitrator,** may be called in to settle the differences between the employee and management. Union employees are assisted by their union representative or steward. Nonunion employees make appeals through the organization's personnel office.

*An **arbitrator** decides courses of corrective action in disputes between management and employees.*

No standard grievance process is applicable to all organizations. But organizations that allow employees to have appeal rights find that supervisors are far more careful in their implementation of corrective actions than do organizations where no due-process procedures exist.

Legal Considerations

Hire at will is the principle that either employees or managers may enter into or break employee agreements at will. No cause is necessary for termination.

A number of states have hire-at-will laws. Employers and employees have the right to enter into employment agreements of their own free will or choice and terminate employment at any time. Under **hire-at-will** conditions employers can terminate an individual's employment without notice or specific reason unless organizational policy prohibits such action. If a terminated employee applies for unemployment compensation, the organization at that time must state whether the termination has been for **cause.** *Cause,* as used in these conditions, means violation of an organizational policy, incompetence, refusal to carry out assignments, or other valid reasons. If no cause is evident, the employee is then entitled to receive unemployment compensation, provided they worked the minimum number of weeks required by law for eligibility. State laws usually define procedures although the unemployment compensation is a federally mandated program.

Cause is a legitimate reason for taking an adverse action, such as demotion, reprimand, giving time off without pay, or involuntary termination.

Wrongful termination means terminating a person without proper cause, especially if that person has a good work record or is a member of a protected class.

In some instances people terminated for clear lack of cause may claim **wrongful termination.** Wrongful termination cases are still relatively rare but they are based on the concept that employees, once hired, attain rights to their job. Their rights can be taken away only if clear and convincing evidence exists that they failed to carry out reasonable standards of work, violated established policy or rules, or otherwise acted against the interest of the organization. Court cases involving wrongful termination have established that under some conditions employees must be returned either to their former job or one of similar status and pay. They must also be compensated by the organization for time away from work and all legal fees.

It is mandatory that in disciplinary-action cases involving termination that careful and full documentation be made and that reasons for the action are well established. When supervisors give satisfactory performance ratings for unsatisfactory performance, they fail to realize the long-range implications of their actions. Employees who are terminated for cause but have a record of satisfactory performance as indicated by a history of supervisory appraisals of their work are in a strong position to challenge the termination.

■ CLINICAL AND LEGALISTIC COMPLAINTS

Need for revenge of perceived wrongs is a strong human emotion. Employees who file grievances or make formal complaints about their supervisor are often acting for clinical rather than legal reasons.

It was a wet, stormy day when Del Hamilton returned from lunch almost 10 minutes late. "Del," a tight-lipped Michelle Hanson, Del's supervisor, called to him, "you're 10 minutes late. You know we're under pressure to finish the end-of-month report. Next time you're going to get more than a verbal warning." Michelle turned away angrily before Del could respond. He had gone for lunch only to find every one of the nearby restaurants filled with people due to the rain. In an effort to keep from being late, he checked three places, only to find himself in line at a fast-food place with slow service. After waiting, he left without eating and managed to get a cold drink and a small package of crackers and peanut butter from vending machines. Although he was frustrated and concerned, he was still late getting back to work.

Two days later when Michelle asked him to work on a special project, he saw an opportunity to get back at her for the open criticism he had received two days earlier. He filed a formal grievance stating that he was required to work out of normal classification without additional pay, even though the work was usually done by higher-level program analysts. Michelle was mystified. Del had never given her any problems previously.

Del had filed a **clinical** grievance. Under most conditions he would have welcomed the opportunity to work on Michelle's special project. He enjoyed challenges. Still stinging from her open rebuke for being late from lunch, he saw an opportunity to get even. **Clinical grievances** are far more common than legal grievances. Del used a legal pretext. Technically, according to union-management agreements, any employee working in a higher classification should be paid at the higher rate. Since the assignment was temporary, Michelle did not consider reclassifying Del. As a result of her technical error Del received back pay at the higher rate for time worked on the project. Had she listened before accusing him of negligence in returning from lunch late, the grievance would have never been filed.

Clinical grievances are based on perceived wrongful treatment by a supervisor. They are a type of revenge rather than a legitimate grievance.

Legal grievances are somewhat different. They occur when the company has clearly violated one of its own policies or a union-management agreement. Failure to compensate a person for overtime work, violation of safety standards, or failure to consider seniority in promotions within union classifications are typical reasons for legal grievances. Employees are not trying to get back but are attempting to use legal, contractual, and policy protection to ensure that their rights are being upheld. Clinical grievances stem from causes often not related to the stated reason for the complaint. Legal grievances are direct responses to a violation of an employee's rights. Legal and clinical grievance relationships are summarized in Figure 14.3.

A legal grievance is an employee complaint against management based on a clear violation of due process, established policy, or union-management agreement.

▪ DIRECTING AND REDIRECTING

One of the most difficult supervisory jobs is telling employees they are not performing well, especially when it is clear they are attempting to do a good job. Not all people have the same abilities. Some are good at mathematical analysis but make terrible teachers or salespeople. Others are very good in public-contact jobs such as personnel work or acting as a company representative but incompetent in performing detailed analytical work. Supervisors are, at times, required to encourage employees to find work that they can do well. It may mean leaving their

FIGURE 14.3 ■ Major Types of Grievances

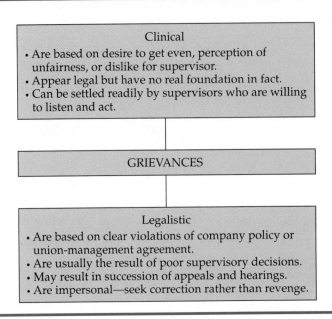

Clinical
- Are based on desire to get even, perception of unfairness, or dislike for supervisor.
- Appear legal but have no real foundation in fact.
- Can be settled readily by supervisors who are willing to listen and act.

GRIEVANCES

Legalistic
- Are based on clear violations of company policy or union-management agreement.
- Are usually the result of poor supervisory decisions.
- May result in succession of appeals and hearings.
- Are impersonal—seek correction rather than revenge.

present job. In large organizations personnel specialists can often assist supervisors with these special problem employees.

Organizations that have probationary periods for new employees allow supervisors to evaluate performance before the new person becomes permanent. Like other proactive measures that prevent problems before they develop, supervisors can assess capabilities and determine if training is effective and if new employees have the necessary job aptitudes. It is in the best interests of both the company and the failing employee to encourage **redirection** of job efforts during a probationary period rather than after they have attained permanent status.

Redirecting means encouraging employees to seek employment more closely aligned with their experience and training.

Assessment of performance and building self-discipline are daily supervisory activities. Neither should be relegated to a once-per-year ritual nor should they be reserved for application when crises in employee behavior become apparent. Supervisors who know their employees as well as work with them to build competence and confidence have few difficult people problems.

■ THINGS TO REMEMBER

I. How good is good enough?

    A. Supervisors should have reasonable expectations of employees.

    B. Rules that apply in some conditions may not apply in others.

II. Performance evaluation.

    A. Performance evaluation is not an annual or semiannual ritual.

    B. Employees are graded on other characteristics besides performance.

    C. To be effective, praise must be associated with a specific activity.

III. Formal performance appraisal systems.

    A. In a large number of labor unions, formal appraisal systems no longer exist.

    B. William Edwards Deming advocates abolishment of formal performance evaluations.

    C. Most organizations have some type of performance appraisal system.

    D. Most performance evaluation systems are judgmental rather than developmental.

    E. Organizations use formal performance evaluations to justify subsequent management action.

IV. Methods of evaluation.

    A. Graphic rating scales consider general factors such as quality, quantity, cooperation, job knowledge, attendance, initiative, and need for supervision. Measures shown on graphic rating scales are rarely objective.

    B. Ranking systems are the most simple and include paired comparisons. Employees are compared to each other and then ranked in ability.

    C. Narrative reports require written descriptive assessment in paragraph form.

    D. Critical-incident appraisals involve recording both good and bad performance as it occurs.

    E. Objective-evaluation systems compare an employee's performance against established standards.

    F. Management by objectives and behavioral anchored systems provide employees with a method of evaluating their own performance.

V. Performance and potential.

    A. High performers are not necessarily the best leaders.

    B. Good performance-appraisal systems include assessment of potential promotion.

VI. Discipline and disciplinary action.

    A. Most people are self-disciplined.

    B. Discipline must be learned.

    C. Discipline means following the rules necessary to successfully accomplish any endeavor.

    D. To be effective rules must be reasonable, employees must understand the rules and potential penalties, and judgment must be used in rule enforcement.

    E. Disciplinary action must be corrective rather than punitive.

    F. Supervisors must maintain objectivity in implementing disciplinary action.

VII. Due process.

    A. Due process means that every person has a right to present his or her side in a dispute, face accusers, and appeal to higher levels of authority.

    B. Grievance procedures provide due process in many organizations.

    C. Arbitrators may be asked to settle grievances in some conditions.

VIII. Legal considerations include:

    A. Hire-at-will laws.

    B. Termination for cause.

    C. Wrongful-termination.

IX. Clinical and legalistic complaints.

    A. Clinical grievances are based on revenge for perceived wrongs.

      B. Legal grievances are complaints based on a clear violation of a rule and are used as protective measures by employees.

X. Directing and redirecting.

      A. It is difficult to tell people who are trying to do a good job that their efforts are inadequate.

      B. Not all people can successfully learn and do their assigned tasks.

      C. Proactive measures prevent corrective actions later.

■ KEY TERMS

discipline	paired comparisons
disciplinary action	narrative ratings
performance evaluation	critical incidents
performance feedback	objective evaluation
effective praise	MBO
corrective feedback	BARS
judgmental performance evaluation	performance
developmental performance evaluation	potential
	self-discipline
graphic rating scales	past practice
external inconsistency	due process
internal inconsistency	grievance procedure
halo errors	arbitrator
stereotyping	hire at-will
pro forma review	cause
tendency errors	wrongful termination
seniority creep	clinical grievances
managerial review	legal grievances
ranking systems	redirection

■ DISCUSSION QUESTIONS

1. What is the relationship between performance appraisal and disciplinary action?
2. How should performance-appraisal interviews be conducted by supervisors?
3. After employees have received several formal evaluations, their ratings tend to change very little. Explain why this happens.
4. How can supervisors overcome personal biases such as halos and stereotypes?
5. When is a supervisor justified in using punitive disciplinary action, such as demotion, days off without pay, denial of pay increase, or involuntary termination?

■ SELF-ASSESSMENT

Here are 10 statements related to performance appraisal, discipline, and disciplinary action. If you disagree with the statement, respond by answering 1, 2, or 3. Agreement is indicated by marking a 4, 5, or 6.

1. Annual performance evaluations improve employee morale and performance.

   1   2   3   4   5   6

2. The most commonly used performance evaluations systems can be administered objectively with few difficulties.

   1   2   3   4   5   6

3. High job performers always make the best supervisors.

   1   2   3   4   5   6

4. Performance-appraisal forms provide a standardized method of recording supervisor judgments of employee effectiveness.

   1   2   3   4   5   6

5. Both MBO and BARS systems are superior to standard graphic rating scales.

   1   2   3   4   5   6

6. Discipline implies punishment.

   1   2   3   4   5   6

7. When a problem occurs, it is a good idea to let it cool off for a few days before taking action.

   1   2   3   4   5   6

8. Frequently the stated cause of grievance and the real cause are not the same.

   1   2   3   4   5   6

9. People who perform well in one type of work may fail in other job categories.

   1   2   3   4   5   6

10. Redirection means encouraging people to improve their present performance.

   1   2   3   4   5   6

■ SHORT CASES

Dirty Linen

Yung Su Pok, "Young" to her friends, enjoyed working at the receiving counter for the Hotel and Linen Supply commercial laundry. Her schedule allowed her to take morning classes at a local community college where she was an A student in computer information science. Young's job was to sort and identify linens, uniforms, tablecloths, napkins, and other items sent from restaurants and hotels for cleaning. While the job was somewhat dirty in that she handled soiled materials, she enjoyed talking with delivery people, not working in the heat and noise of the laundry, and to a large extent being her own boss. When Sue Williams, the shift supervisor, told her to cut down on the time she spent talking with delivery people, Young was upset and angry.

Two days later she asked Sue for a transfer to another assignment. "You're one of our best employees," protested Sue. "If I transferred you it would mean training another person and a loss of efficiency. There is no one else who knows sorting and identification as well as you or can do it as well. It's bad enough already when you are on vacation." Young approached Sue again, this time with the union steward at her side.

"Sue," began Paul Jacobs, the union steward, "Young has been discriminated against according to rules of the union-management agreement. She's been kept in the dirtiest job in the laundry without opportunity for transfer. We are filing a formal grievance asking for a transfer and for hazard pay for her exposure to possible contaminants and disease."

"Paul, you and I both know that there is only one job classification here, that of laundry worker. Employees can be assigned anywhere. Every task in the laundry is written into the job description. As for the dirty job, Young's assignment is no more hazardous than any other in the plant. Your grievance is being denied."

In a subsequent formal grievance hearing, Sue's position that employees could be assigned anywhere in the plant was upheld. Even so, Sue remained puzzled by Young's action.

1. What was the real cause of Young's grievance? Why didn't Sue recognize Young's feelings?

2. How should Paul attempt to change the union-management contract to prevent cases like Young's from developing in the future?

3. Give an example that distinguishes between clinical and legal grievances.

Signs of Trouble

A number of tangible warnings indicate that discipline is breaking down in an organization. These are some of the most evident ones:

■ Increased tardiness.

■ Excessive unexcused absences.

■ Increases in simple errors.

■ Failure to meet required schedules.

■ Excuses blaming equipment, materials, other departments, or faulty instructions when these have not previously been common problems.

■ Avoiding contact with supervisors.

■ Extended lunch and coffee breaks.

■ Early shutdown of work before the regular work period ends.

■ Increases in minor accidents.

■ Development of hostile work climate.

1. Select three items from the list and develop a plan for changing them.

2. List reasons discipline may break down in work organizations.

3. Why do most people respect supervisors who maintain a disciplined work force?

■ ENDNOTES

1. Bradford Boyd, *Management-Minded Supervision* (New York: McGraw-Hill, 1968), p. 164.

2. Based on an interview, February 12, 1991.

3. "A Discussion with William Edwards Deming," a national teleconference sponsored by the Department of Education, October 19, 1990.

4. John M. Ivancevich, James H. Donnelly, Jr., and James L. Gibson, *Management: Principles and Functions* (Homewood, Ill.: BPI-Irwin, 1989), p. 530.

5. Marc G. Singer, *Human Resource Management* (Boston: PWS-Kent Publishing Company, 1990), p. 209.

Part VI

Work Forces, Social Responsibility, Trends, and Careers

■ One of the most significant movements during the final third of the 20th century has been the increasingly important role of social responsibility in organizations. Supervisors face work forces vastly different from those of any other era. Multiracial, multiethnic, and multilingual problems are an everyday occurrence. Rights of people and the environments in which they live have been defined and protected to a degree not previously found in the history of humankind. Supervisors find themselves with the responsibility for ensuring compliance with complex legislation affecting employees, their organizations, and themselves.

Concern for quality and service is also increasing in U.S. organizations. Again first-line managers are directly affected by changing responsibilities. Much of what were once considered middle-management obligations now rest with supervisors. They need to make social responsibility a personal as well as organizational philosophy.

Career planning is being encouraged by forward-looking organizations. Personal development is receiving increased attention. First-line managers must continuously examine their individual strengths, weaknesses, and goals and redefine personal success. Success, they have learned, is rarely accidental.

All of these concerns are addressed in the last four chapters of the text. Supervisors are involved every step of the way.

Chapter 15

Supervision and a Changing Work Force

Objectives

Supervisors are impacted by many changes. The number and pace of these changes will probably not decrease. Chapter 15 will enable readers to

- Identify major demographic changes affecting their places of employment.
- Recognize the impact of technology and social change in their places of work.
- Confront and effectively deal with life-style issues at work.
- Effectively act as on-the-spot human resource managers.
- Act as facilitators in team building.
- Manage their technological and social environments.

Thought Starter

In 1890 Herman Hollerith, a manager with the U.S. Bureau of the Census, revolutionized the way vast amounts of statistical data could be handled by inventing the automatic tabulating machine. During the 1890 census it proved invaluable. Statistical data was sorted and tabulated faster and more accurately than at any time in the past. Hollerith eventually left the government and founded his own statistical computation organization, which became the foundation of the present-day International Business Machines Corporation. In doing so, Hollerith started the evolutionary process that has led to our present age of computers as essential tools. Work is now accomplished in ways unimaginable at the time of Hollerith's first steps in automating data processing.[1]

Knowledge workers have always been among us, but only since the mid-1980s have they been the dominant force in organizations. Few fields of endeavor have totally escaped the allure of computer systems as primary tools for information gathering, report production, analysis of data for decision making, scheduling, cost determination, projecting trends, report and proposal compilation, research, statistical analysis, and a wide spectrum of other applications.

A major problem of the U.S. work force is the degrading of our educational system to the point where we can no longer produce adequate numbers of people with necessary knowledge to be trained as knowledge workers rather than laborers or hired hands. Intelligence, training, and a solid system of personal values are necessary in effective organizations. Only those in the next century will be able to determine how well we, as a society, have met our obligations to produce excellence in every aspect of life.

■ *"Buenos dias, señorita Lopez." "Buenos, dias, señor Alonso. ¿Como esta?" "Muy bueno, señorita Lopez." So begins a morning at Fiesta Foods in the Los Angeles International Airport. Spanish is an unchallenged second language in much of southern California as well as in areas of Arizona, New Mexico, Texas, and Florida. Eric Stewart, the manager of Clifton's, a major food service company, looks at his chief cook, Jose, and Maria, his most effective and efficient hostess.*

While he understands some basic Spanish language, Eric also knows that he cannot understand their conversations completely. Lopez and Alonso are skilled and dedicated employees. Although he realizes their value, Eric is often frustrated by their use of Spanish rather than English. He realizes their familiarity with the English language is of a similar level to his of Spanish. Eric does not want to alienate his best employees but he is confused by language he doesn't fully understand.

He is faced with difficult choices. Eric can attempt to learn Spanish, require only English in the presence of customers or himself, or let Alonso and Lopez decide which language is appropriate for the situation.

■ CHANGING WORK FORCES—DEMOGRAPHICS

Demographics is the study of changes in population and how the population is distributed.

During the 1980s it became evident that organizations were being impacted by changes in the work force different from those experienced during any previous period. Employees were growing older, with the median age of 31.2 years for males and 32.3 for females. During the 1990s the dominant age group will move upward to 35 to 39 years old from 30 to 34. An older work force has many implications. People will have worked longer, be more experienced, and may have more demanding expectations of both their management and their jobs.[2] Fewer teenage entry-level employees will be available until well into the next century. Supervisors will find their leadership skills increasingly important.

De facto means "in fact." Although not formally announced, some changes become accepted realities.

In addition to an older group of employees, supervisors are already being confronted with a complex mix of ethnicities, cultures, and languages. While the United States has always been the melting pot of the world, it is more so today than at any time in the past. In parts of California, Arizona, New Mexico, Texas, and Florida, Spanish has become the **de facto second language.** Recent Hispanic immigrants, some with excellent job skills, have a willingness to learn and work hard. They have become an invaluable source of labor. Although fewer in numbers, immigrants from Asian cultures have earned a reputation for diligence and success in adapting to entirely new conditions of work. Other cultural and ethnic groups, in addition to the traditional European descendants that make up 84 percent of the population of the United States, have also enriched our society and our organizations.

African-Americans, whose history in the United States dates back to earliest colonial times, are the second largest identifiable group in the country and comprise just over 12 percent of the total population, approximately 30,330,000 individuals. Of all groups, they have had the most difficult struggle in establishing social and economic equity. While many black Americans have entered management ranks, they are still underrepresented in proportion to their total population. Work force composition in the year 2000 is projected in Figure 15.1.

Who Speaks the Right Language?

Supervisors must contend with not only job-related issues, but cultural, ethnic, and linguistic issues as well. In places as diverse as Pace Foods in San Antonio, Motorola Corporation in Los Angeles and Schaumburg, Illinois, and Del Webb Resorts in Phoenix, the question of language has been a major problem. Most memoranda, computer programs, information systems, notices, procedures, and other written material is in English. At companies like Pace Foods, where 35 percent of the work force is Hispanic, the

FIGURE 15.1 ■ Work Force 2000

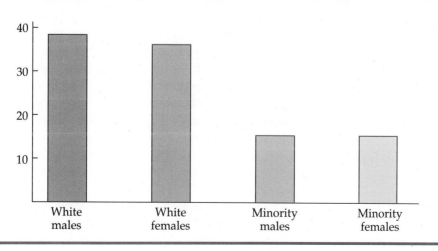

Adapted from *The Wall Street Journal*, Nov. 7, 1988.

language issue is not trivial. Supervisors are expected to learn conversational Spanish and many notices as well as other written material are printed in two languages.

A major question raised by organizations with large numbers of non-English speaking employees is whether a second language should be a requirement for promotion. An even more difficult problem is whether employees in public establishments such as hospitals, government offices, and restaurants should be required to speak English not only to clients and customers but to each other as well. Some employers have reported that customers become distrustful when they cannot understand conversations between employees.

As the century draws to an end, there is every indication that the diversity of cultures and languages in most places of work will continue to increase. Supervisors who are unwilling to learn at least some of the language of their employees and develop a sensitivity to their culturally developed beliefs and values will find themselves at a distinct disadvantage. In a world of change and ever-increasing requirements, first-line managers find adapting to changing patterns of personnel in their organizations a major challenge. Patience, willingness to learn, and adaptability are essential requirements.

Where Are the People?

During the 1980s the large population centers of the United States grew faster than at any previous period of history. By 1990 over 50 percent of the inhabitants of the United States lived in or near large metropolitan areas.[3] The fastest-growing population centers were universally in the well-known Sun Belt. Nine Florida cities, including Orlando with its giant entertainment centers as well as defense and space contractors, led the list with growth rates in excess of 40 percent.[4] Other high-growth areas included Austin, Phoenix, Sacramento, San Diego, Dallas-Fort Worth, Atlanta, and Los Angeles, with population increases in excess of 30 percent. For managers and those aspiring to be managers, the high-growth areas also represented opportunity. It also meant unusual problems for supervisors.

When people from many diverse geographic locations congregate in a single area, they bring with them their former job habits, ways of responding to authority, as well as their beliefs and values. Supervisors with a different frame of reference must learn to understand their employees' many points of view. Building effective work teams with employees from widely varying backgrounds is an often difficult task. A primary concern is preventing cliques based on regional identities from developing. It is all too easy for an us-against-them relationship to develop.

■ SUPERVISORS—THE ULTIMATE HUMAN RESOURCE MANAGERS

Human resource management is the management of all activities related to the acquisition, training, evaluation, compensation, legal mandates, welfare, maintenance, and retention of employees in an organization.

Human resource management is what many still call *personnel management*. Its activities encompass recruitment, selection, employment, training coordination, compensation determination, benefits allocation, labor-management relations, human resource planning, personnel records maintenance, and related functions assigned by higher levels of management. In large organizations human resource management departments act as a service to other functions. Responsibility for employees rests with first-line managers, who are the real human resource managers.

Although human resource management departments can be valuable resources of information, administration of virtually every personnel-related activity rests with supervisors. Supervisors must ensure compliance with civil rights, environmental protection, and safety legislation that impact their operations. Their evaluations either determine or strongly influence pay increases, transfers, training approval, promotions, disciplinary actions, needs for counseling, and development of interpersonal relations. Some of the main human resource duties supervisors perform are described in Table 15.1.

Developers of People

Effective managers are developers of people. They recognize that their personal success is tied directly to the performance of their employees. To enhance personal development they encourage employees to accept challenging assignments, make decisions that affect their jobs, take advantage of training opportunities, and participate in improving functions of their work units. They recognize that the best employees are able to work independently of constant supervision. As developers of people, first-line managers see themselves as facilitators and information providers rather than as controllers.

In addition to developing people, conscientious supervisors also identify employees capable of making the vital shift to

TABLE 15.1 ■ Human Resource Management for Supervisors

Recruitment	In most circumstances supervisors have little responsibility for attracting new applicants. Federal law requires employee selection from a pool of qualified applicants without preference or discrimination.
Selection	Most organizations encourage supervisors to make a final hiring determination from applicants screened by personnel specialists. Since employees report directly to first-line managers, good selection practices involve supervisors.
Training	Supervisors have special responsibilities for instructing new employees and upgrading the skills of those with experience. They plan and monitor on-the-job training, identify training needs, select employees for training, and arrange and schedule training for their employees (with the assistance of human resource specialists or higher levels of management).
Pay	Other than recommendation of merit increases, supervisors have minimal involvement in compensation management. Pay scales are determined by job classification, rate ranges, and established policy.
Benefits	Like pay, benefits are determined by policy. Other than sick leave and vacation administration, supervisors have little involvement.
Appraisal	Evaluation of employee performance is a primary supervisory responsibility. Supervisors must determine whether standards of performance are being met and take corrective action when necessary.
Discipline	Effective supervisors build self-discipline. They do not tolerate behavior that violates established rules or accepted standards of behavior. Disciplinary action is intended to correct rather than punish.
Contracts	Labor-management agreements are legal contracts. Supervisors are management's primary representatives in ensuring compliance with both the spirit and legal intent of contractual agreements.
Compliance	Adherence to equal opportunity provisions, environmental standards, safety regulations, and other mandates rests almost exclusively with supervisors.

increased administrative responsibility. Good supervisors want more than hired hands; they want employees to use their imagination, creativity, and intelligence to help make their organizations more effective and efficient.

■ SWANS AND CROWS

David H. Maister has studied the characteristics of excellent organizations for several years.[5] Often the difference, he has found, between a mediocre organization and one that is considered best

SWANs are Smart, Work-hard, Ambitious, and Nice employees or potential employees.

is the presence of **SWANs,** an acronym for Smart, Work-hard, Ambitious, and Nice. Quality people make quality organizations. Maister points out that in hiring practices it is relatively easy to find employees with one or two of these four characteristics but very difficult to recruit those with all four qualities. Smart, ambitious people are not always nice. Niceness, according to Maister, means they can relate effectively to other employees, managers, and clients.

By virtue of their personal qualities, SWANs are essentially self-directed. They are able to recognize what needs to be done and take appropriate action. Supervision of SWANs requires first-line managers to adopt a collegial role. There is very little psychological and social distance between themselves and their employees. Relationships with employees are largely consultive, informational, and facilitative. Supervisors are there to help when needed, but employees accept full responsibility and are totally accountable for their job efforts.

CROWs are Commonly Recruited, Ordinary Workers.

It is debatable whether **CROWs,** Commonly Recruited, Ordinary Workers, can be turned into SWANs. Many people, working with supervisors who are people developers, learn to work hard, become ambitious, and try to be nice. Training, patience, positive reinforcement of good work, and relationships built on trust and confidence help people develop their full capabilities. A reality supervisors must learn to accept is that not all people are equal. Some are more intelligent, talented, resourceful, self-reliant, and confident than others. Differences exist between people in all organizations, including companies that are recognized as having excellent work forces. It is important for supervisors who participate in employee selection to recognize and hire SWANs. CROWs are always more plentiful and many have excellent potential. SWANs can add a new dimension to a work group.

Supervisors and Superior Employees

Some supervisors both fear and resent employees whom they perceive as having qualities they may lack. They have unspoken fears that exceptionally capable employees may displace them as first-line managers or pass by them in promotions. Supervisors who feel they must be the most intelligent and knowledgeable members of the work team forget that leadership skills do not require possession of the greatest amount of knowledge or specific job skills. They must define goals, act as sources of information and

guidance, exert influence both upward and downward, and most of all have confidence in themselves as managers. Superior employees can be a supervisor's greatest resource. Their own success is judged by the success of their work unit. Managers can be successful only if their employees are successful. Good employees push managers up far more often than they push them out.

■ MANAGEMENT AND THE ELECTRONIC WORKPLACE

In early 1991 San Francisco work standards were developed for people who work with video display terminals.[6] Regular breaks from work, proper screen placement, and ergonomically designed chairs were required. It was the first official recognition in the United States of the special nature of the **electronic workplace.** During the 1980s individual computer terminals and personal computers became essential tools of business in many organizations. Today most places of work rely on their speed and versatility. Organizational changes resulting from electronic automation of offices have, in many instances, altered the role of supervisors. In addition to the creation of **electronic sweatshops,** with their motivational and employee self-esteem difficulties, supervisors find their functions have broadened.

Electronic sweatshops are places where people perform their work on computers or computer terminals and are monitored by computer network systems.

Telecommuting

AT&T, the nation's largest supplier of long-distance and business communications services, plans to eventually have 10,000 salespeople working without offices or even a desk. In an initial experiment 500 salespeople supplied with sophisticated lightweight computers do all of their work from their homes, hotels, client offices, or even on airplanes.[7] They stay in contact with their supervisors through computer and voice telephone communication. Face-to-face contact with other employees and their immediate first-line managers is rare. During the first phases of the experiment, productivity increased from 5 percent to 45 percent. AT&T estimates that eventually office costs for sales staffs will be reduced by over 50 percent.

Telecommuting involves working away from a regularly assigned place of employment by utilizing laptop or other portable computers, telephones, and fax machines.

Many companies have been involved in **telecommuting,** working away from an office or plant without direct supervision, for a number of years. While all report success, the major concern is the lack of social contact with other employees or supervisors. Jack Niles, a Los Angeles–based telecommuting consultant, recommends that employees should have some face-to-face contact with members of their organization at least twice a week.[8] Telecommuting will always be limited to clerical, creative, and sales occupations that can be performed away from a traditional place of work. As computers become more portable and increasingly versatile, telecommuting is a trend that will likely continue.

Supervisors of telecommuters have the special problem of helping them meet their need for feeling that they are still part of the organization and assisting them in developing their ability to work independently of the immediate support of an office environment.

Managing the Electronic Workplace

Supervisors in many organizations can readily access a broad range of information from computer databanks and network systems, which allow them to make decisions independent of the traditional chain of command once required. Rather than go through a series of organizational layers for information, they are able to retrieve it directly without the formal requests and approvals once required. As a consequence organizations have been dramatically flattened.[9] Large organizations have reduced their layers of middle managers significantly. A result has been a much faster reaction time to both customer and internal requirements. Supervisors find themselves routinely performing tasks once reserved for higher levels of management.

Employee productivity has also been impacted by technology-driven changes. IBM assembly workers perform tasks once done by engineers; Motorola auditors now complete reports in five days instead of 51 as in previous times; Security Pacific, Corning, USAA, and many others have also improved their productivity, especially in their clerical and administrative functions.[10] This has been done with a combination of training, improved supervision, team building, and selective use of technology. Rather than build electronic sweatshops where people resent constantly being monitored by computer reporting systems, electronic technology has been used as a tool to enhance management. A lesson that management at all levels in these highly successful organizations have learned is that technology alone does not make work perfect. It takes the effort, intelligence, and ingenuity of management and employees working together to improve methods.

Knowledge workers have specialized training and experience, usually in an information, technical, or administrative field of work.

Supervisors of knowledge workers have special problems. **Knowledge workers** have specialized training and experience in the research, design, systems development, analysis of data, financial planning, and procedures development required in most organizations. A lesson that has been learned is that productivity increases if knowledge workers have strong clerical and administrative support. Because of the availability and speed of computers, they may easily become bogged down performing their own clerical work. A primary function of supervisors of knowledge workers is to provide the support needed to free them from routine tasks better accomplished by others.

■ LIFE-STYLE PROBLEMS

Few people are without problems in their lives. For the most part individuals can deal with their personal difficulties with minimal impact on their work. In some instances their life-styles create real difficulties for their employers and especially their supervisors. A person with offensive body odor may be a source of complaints by employees who must work in close proximity. Supervisors may feel awkward and embarrassed but realize they must eventually deal with it as a matter of employee morale. Private, candid discussions, suggestions for medical examination, or referral to a company nurse, if one exists, are possible starting points. Such offenders are usually unaware of the impact on others of their poor personal hygiene or rare genetic difficulties. Good supervisors attempt to assist employees in seeking appropriate assistance.

Life-style problems include alcoholism, drug addiction, and disease.

More difficult problems exist when employees are addicted to illicit drugs and alcohol. Even more demanding are those associated with employees who have been identified as having acquired immunodeficiency syndrome (AIDS).

Alcoholism

Alcoholism is the most observable and common life-style problem.

Of all employee problems alcoholism has been the most prevalent. It has also been the subject of many studies. While it is virtually impossible to precisely estimate alcoholism's total cost, lost time, tardiness, and inefficiency cost employers in the United States between $18 billion and $27 billion annually.[11] Absenteeism, accidents, and sick leave by problem drinkers may be 16 times higher than the rates for average employees.[12]

Bill Townsend was an excellent senior electronic technician for Reming International Gateways. When his supervisor noticed that Bill left the building everyday during break times and returned somewhat more talkative and with a flushed face, he became suspicious. He asked Meridith Galloway, a competent security person, to give a report of her observations of people who passed through the plant entrance and returned during the 15-minute break periods and also during lunch breaks.

Two days later Meridith reported, "I observed Bill Townsend walking toward his automobile and followed him, unobserved. After opening the trunk, he removed a bottle of what appeared to be Early Times bourbon from a briefcase and poured approximately two ounces in a small glass. Although he looked around the area, he failed to see me approaching. After taking the first drink, he then poured another. Without warning, I asked, 'Bill is it worth another drink?' Very calmly he turned toward me and stated, 'If I can't drink on this job, I won't work here.' He then got into his car and drove off. I alerted the front gate, but the guards state that he had already left company premises." Bill never returned and his final check was sent to him, including all earned vacation and paid leave, one week later.[13]

One of the major difficulties with alcoholic employees is that they are frequently intelligent, capable employees who are willing to take the risk of being caught. They resist assistance, will not admit their difficulties, and often, because of their skills and knowledge, have relatively little difficulty in finding other jobs.

They also physically endanger themselves and other employees in many types of work, have a much higher error rate, and more accidents and illnesses than average employees. Not all alcoholics are capable and knowledgeable. Many, however, are good employees with serious problems.

Larger organizations frequently have chemical dependency rehabilitation units that assist in counseling and finding assistance for addicted employees. Their contacts with medical specialists often result in both problem reduction and, most importantly, saving talented employees. Recruitment, training, and fully integrating new employees into an organization is far more costly than rehabilitating a valuable, experienced, and usually appreciative employee.

Illicit Drugs

Illicit drugs are more difficult to detect and control than alcohol, which is usually more evident. Users of such drugs, like alcoholics, are adept at hiding their symptoms and do not have the telltale odor that often identifies drinkers. Experienced supervisors note that they can detect a druggie more by their lack of a fix than by their taking drugs. At the beginning of this final decade of the 20th century many organizations require drug tests as part of a pre-employment physical examination. Many retail establishments, such as Home Depot, one of the nation's largest do-it-yourself retail chains, openly advertise that all prospective employees will be tested for drugs prior to employment. Virtually all public transportation organizations also require testing for illegal substances.

Several difficulties exist with drug testing. Some drugs, such as cocaine and amphetamines, are very difficult to detect three days after they have been used. Marijuana can be easily detected as long as three weeks after it has entered an individual's respiratory and circulatory systems. Drug tests are often unreliable. Legal medication often is interpreted by testing laboratories as an illicit drug.

Supervisors who detect sudden and repeated changes in the behavior of individuals may have reasonable suspicions of drug addiction. In such cases human resource specialists, onsite nurses, or other medical assistants are excellent references. Supervisors should not attempt to solve addictive problems themselves. Most organizations have regular referral procedures that will assist them in controlling this difficult type of problem.

Smoking

It has been stated in the public media as well as in medical and scientific journals that more people die of tobacco use than any other cause. Tobacco is a legal drug that is highly addictive, a known cause of lung cancer, heart problems, respiratory illness, and many other diseases. Non-smokers have been able to lobby for legal constraints on smoking in work environments, airplanes, restaurants, and other public places. Some work organizations have active no-smoking campaigns and have banned smoking in buildings.

In the most extreme efforts to reduce smoking, a few organizations have banned smoking both on- and off-the-job and perform random tests of employee urine to determine if tobacco or other drugs are present. Eventually courts must decide the legality of attempts by organizations to control employees' private lives. Since tobacco use is legal and organizational policy is generated by top management, there is little supervisors can do other than encourage employees to join them in becoming nonsmokers.

Emotional Problems

Illicit drug addiction and emotional problems are more difficult to detect and assist than alcoholism.

At times the compounded effect of stress at home and stress in the workplace, separation, and financial worries will result in depression or other debilitating psychological difficulties. Both men and women tend to cut back on household chores after a stressful day at work, although women usually complain less than men.[14] Like illicit drugs, emotional problems are often difficult to detect. Sudden changes in behavior indicative of anxiety and depression are the most common symptoms. Withdrawal, hesitancy in giving opinions, reduction in communication and contacts, changes in personal grooming, observable nervousness, and excessive concern with health are all typical symptoms of emotional difficulties.

Proactive first-line managers maintain a list of references that can be used to assist employees with emotional difficulties. Most organizational health plans cover the costs of psychological problems in addition to treatment for physical problems. As in the case of alcoholism and use of illicit drugs, supervisors must realize that they are not professional clinical psychologists or medical diagnosticians. Expert assistance is far more helpful than inept and uninformed attempts to be helpful. This does not mean that supervisors should not listen, empathize, and have great patience with troubled employees.

It is fortunate that most emotional problems will cure themselves with time. When individuals recognize the sources of their difficulties and deal with them directly, anxiety and depression are often reduced. Competent medical experts are often able to control a number of emotional problems through medication and return employees to their former standards of performance.

AIDS

HIV carriers may be excellent employees with minimal or no infectious danger to other employees.

One of the more difficult issues for supervisors that has emerged during the 1980s and will continue into the foreseeable future is the status of employees who have the human immunovirus **(HIV)** that precedes the illness known as AIDS. AIDS is transmitted through exchange of body fluids. It is not contagious in the usual sense as are measles, colds, or most communicable diseases. A known precursor to AIDS is the presence of HIV in an individual's blood. Although organizations try to be fair, there is a very real fear and prejudice against people who have tested positive for HIV or who have developed AIDS symptoms.

Supervisors often have the same fears and concerns as their employees when they know people with whom they work have either tested positively for HIV or have developed AIDS. Medical experts insist that there is minimal risk for fellow employees. People who, through medical tests, have positive indications of HIV may be indistinguishable from other employees in performance, longevity, and ability to fully function. Those who have developed the disease may be able, with more recent treatment methods, to live productive and normal lives for indefinite periods. Protective measures against prejudice for HIV carriers and AIDS patients are based on the assumption that presence of the virus or the disease itself does not mean that the employee is incapable of being a productive, qualified, and even talented member of an organization. They are of little risk to others and can be valuable assets to an organization.

In order to combat fears and misinformation, supervisors have the responsibility for protecting the confidentiality of all medical records. In some states it is forbidden to report the presence of HIV in any employee with the possible exception of food service and health care employees, for whom the risk of infecting others is greater. Under rules of fairness as well as some state laws and municipal ordinances, people with minimally infectious diseases are protected from discrimination solely based on the presence of a specific condition of health. This means that HIV carriers and AIDS patients must be treated the same as any other employees. As long as their performance is satisfactory, they have a right to work. They should not be discriminated against solely because of their symptoms or indications of possible disease as revealed by authorized tests.

Supervisors have the responsibility for diffusing unfounded bias of any kind. In the case of disease that is associated with particular life-styles, their task is difficult. As in other management functions, they can become important referents for employees.

Physical Disabilities

Physical disabilities are not a cause for discriminatory treatment under the Americans with Disabilities Act of 1990.

Long before the Americans with Disabilities Act **(AWDA)**, which prohibits employment discrimination against people with physical handicaps, was enacted in 1990, organizations had learned that disabled employees were a valuable resource for many types of work. While reasonable physical standards may be required for any type of work, disqualification from employment may not be based solely on physical condition.

Supervisors of employees with disabilities may need special training. Frequently equipment, seating, and access to materials must be modified to meet disabled employees' special needs. Simple concerns such as access to toilet facilities, architectural barriers, drinking fountains, and emergency procedures are among the differences encountered. Although some problems exist, many disabled employees have excellent skills, willingly respond to training, and have minimal absenteeism due to their impairment.

It is very easy for a first-line manager to discourage employment of people they see as potentially requiring special treatment. Those who have recognized the value of human resources, however, know that hiring the disabled is a worthwhile and rewarding effort.

Sexual Preference

Some city ordinances and a few state laws protect people from discrimination based on sexual preference. At this time no federal law specifically guarantees equal employment protection based on sexual preference. Most organizations have established either policies or unwritten practices that treat life-style as an individual's personal choice. These rules apply to a variety of conditions and are of no concern to the organization as long as they do not impact the performance or well-being of others. In addition to sexual preference issues, nontraditional religious beliefs and practices that impact work schedules, poor personal hygiene, subculture speech, or unconventional dress or hair styles can all, as summarized in Figure 15.2, create employee relations difficulties for supervisors.

Supervisors are often faced with the difficult task of balancing fairness in the treatment of employees who may be homosexual against their own feelings and the bias of their employees. There is no evidence that sexual preference is related in any way to performance, talent, intelligence, or creativity. Sensible supervisors recognize that good employees, regardless of their individual differences, must be treated with the same fairness and consideration as that provided to others.

Sexual preference is an emotional issue but has no relationship to job performance, management potential, or other desirable job characteristics.

■ WORKING WITH UNIONS

Beginning in the late 1970s, all through the 1980s, and into the 1990s, unions in the United States have become less of a political

FIGURE 15.2 ■ Potential Lifestyle Problems for Supervisors

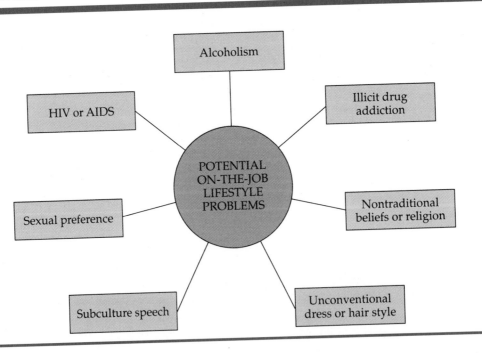

and economic force than at any time since prior to 1939. During the mid-1970s union members comprised approximately 27 percent of the total work force in the United States. At the beginning of the 1990s it was estimated that of a total work force in excess of 120,000,000, only 14,005,000[15] or approximately 12 percent were members of unions. Their power and influence must not be minimized. Small, well-organized work units often have greater influence than large numbers of employees with less dedicated goals. Although approximately 83 percent of all supervisors will never work with unionized employees, it is helpful to recognize some of the fundamental characteristics of organized work units.

When employees lack trust in their management or feel they have little influence, they may band together for **collective action,** requesting management to provide specific protections. Employees who have formally organized to bargain collectively with management on wages, effort, and other conditions of work are considered to be a **union.** Under a series of laws enacted from the early 1930s to 1959, unionized employees may legally enter into contractual agreements with management on personnel-related matters and union-management relations. Agreements between unionized employees and management are usually known as *labor contracts.* Under the Labor Management Relations Act of 1947, an amendment to an earlier law, such contracts are legally binding on both parties. Neither employees nor management may change conditions of the contract without mutual agreement. When contracts are changed, agreement is reached through a process known as *labor negotiations.* Management and employee representatives, through give-and-take discussions, reach agreements that meet the needs of each party. Table 15.2 summarizes major federal labor laws.

*A **union** is a formal organization of employees who deal collectively with management on issues related to wages, effort, work rules, and other conditions of work.*

Supervisors and Bilateral Relations

When management makes all of the rules and decisions regarding wages and conditions of work, their relationship with employees is one-sided, or **unilateral.** Contractual agreements with unionized employees are **bilateral.** Both employees and management have agreed to the rules and must conform to both their legal statements and the spirit with which they were made. Supervisors faced with union-management agreements often feel stripped of much of their power. They cannot assign employees to tasks other than those included in an employee's job description, take

***Unilateral relations** are based on management rule-making without employee participation.*

***Bilateral relations** are agreements arrived at through negotiations between management and employee groups such as unions.*

TABLE 15.2 ■ Summary of Major Federal Labor Laws

Railway Labor Act	Enacted in 1926, was the first comprehensive collective-bargaining legislation. Applies to railway and airline industries only. Guarantees employees' right to form and join unions and to collectively bargain with management.
Norris-La Guardia Act	Made yellow-dog contracts requiring employees to not join unions unenforceable. Discouraged legal injunctions against economic strikes. Enacted in 1932.
National Labor Relations Act	Famous Wagner-Connery Act that defined unfair labor practices for management and protected rights of all employees to form and join unions and bargain collectively with management. Enacted in 1935.
Labor-Management Relations Act	Written by Senators Taft and Hartley in 1947 as an amendment to the NLRA, it is the dominant labor law of today. Defines unfair practices by unions, defines bargaining practices, permits right-to-work laws, and establishes rules for suspending strikes during national emergencies. Established Federal Mediation and Conciliation Service and broadened powers of the National Labor Relations Board as administrator of federal labor law.
Reporting and Disclosure Act	As a reaction to union racketeering, protects rights of union members from victimization by union leaders, requires unions to report financial transactions and backgrounds of members of executive boards. Known as Landrum-Griffin Act, it was enacted in 1959.

disciplinary action independent of grievance procedure rules, transfer or promote employees unless contractual procedures are applied, or change any conditions of work without negotiated contractual alterations.

In most instances the presence of a union does not unreasonably restrict supervisors from carrying out their normal responsibilities. When union-management relations are adversarial, as sometimes occurs, supervisors may find that they are constantly aware of their contractual obligations under bilateral agreements.

To be effective in dealing with unionized employees, supervisors must develop a thorough understanding of their contractual obligations and make a conscientious effort to conform to required procedures. They still can make assignments, take disciplinary action, assist in selection of new employees, conduct and coordi-

nate training programs, evaluate performance, and build teamwork in their employee groups. In a very real sense supervisors in
unionized places of work may act just as they do where no unions
exist, with the exception that they must conform to contractual
agreements in their human resource management functions.

Friend or Foe?

Union-management relations publicized in the news media are
usually adversarial. Management and employees are seen as mutual enemies. In practice many modern union-management relationships are built on the premise that both employees and management must work together for the success of an organization.
Primary attractions of unions are the protections of seniority, economic gain, benefits, due process, higher wages, and union representation in relations with management. Unions usually form
when a significant number of employees distrust management or
feel they are not being treated equitably when compared to other
employees in similar types of work.

Good management practices are directed at reducing we-they
feelings. They emphasize the value of viewing employees and
management as a partnership required for the well-being of both
parties and the total organization.

Knowledgeable supervisors find that dealing with their employees honestly, fairly, without manipulation, and with adherence
to conditions of contractual agreements can build the type of relationship that avoids adversarial relationships. It often means understanding people more than the technical aspects of contracts.

Table 15.3 lists some of the common terminology of union-
management relations. It is by no means all-inclusive but is representative of some of the on-the-job terms that must be understood by supervisors of unionized employee groups.

■ INTO THE 2000s

No period has seen the social, technological, and political changes
affecting organizations as has the last half of this century. Managers no longer have total power in the sense they had in the past.
Almost every aspect of organizational life is impacted by legal
mandates, requirements for special knowledge, and fairness in
employee relations.

TABLE 15.3 ■ Contract Terminology for Supervisors

Bargaining unit	Employees who belong to a union. Some places of work may have several bargaining units. Clerical employees, maintenance workers, and technicians, as examples, may each belong to separate unions.
Management rights	Functions reserved exclusively for management. Management rights usually include hiring, firing, assignment of work, disciplinary action, and related personnel actions.
Union representatives	Employee-selected spokespersons who represent the union's position in dealing with management. Often called *stewards,* they are concerned with possible contract violations by management.
NLRB	National Labor Relations Board, the administrators of labor law in the United States. NLRB rulings determine legality of collective-bargaining practices.
Grievance procedure	Procedures that guarantee union members due process. Grievance procedures are a primary form of employee protection from unfair or unwarranted management actions. Grievances may be settled, in extreme cases, by decision a neutral third party through arbitration.
Seniority	Length of service in a company or job classification. Seniority protects employees in the event of layoffs. Those with greatest seniority in their job classification are laid off last and called back to work first. Senior employees may displace or bump employees in lower, related job-skill classifications.
Premium pay	Any pay in excess of the base hourly rate. Overtime pay and shift differential pay (pay for working other than regular day shift) are the two most common forms of premium pay.
Union security	Any measure taken to maintain and support a union organization. Includes checkoff (automatic dues deductions from check) and union or agency shop (both guarantee dues).
Economic strike	Work stoppage by employees to pressure management into concessions during contractual negotiations. Economic strikes are legal under current labor law. **Wildcat strikes,** taken even though contractual agreements exist, are illegal.
Lockout	To pressure union members into agreement during negotiations, management may prevent their entrance to the workplace. This is management's counterpart of the economic strike.

Supervisors are faced with problems and pressures unimagined in the past. Change will doubtlessly continue and supervisors in the future will find their roles altered even more than they are today. They are part of a society that has increasing numbers of undereducated employees who are difficult to train for more than routine work as well as others who are the best educated in history and have much higher expectations than those in the past.

One of the most serious societal problems facing the welfare of all organizations is the shortage of employees who can be the potential knowledge workers of the future: those with backgrounds in science, communications, and human skills that allow them to develop needed expertise in complex assignments.

New Managers

First-line managers concerned with their future will find that requirements for promotion are increasingly demanding. There is evidence that less emphasis will be placed on specialized knowledge than on generalized abilities that are highly flexible and can be used in a variety of situations.[16] Those who are able to recognize significant trends, grasp their implications, assimilate and integrate a vast array of information, and use this knowledge to make good decisions will become the real leaders.

Supervisors, for their own well-being, must be willing to educate themselves to a degree not required in the past. They can do this by learning more and improving their leadership skills to some degree every day.

■ THINGS TO REMEMBER

I. Changing work forces—demographics.

   A. Older employees are the fastest growing segment of the work force.

   B. Work groups are a complex mix of ethnicities, cultures, and languages, more so than in the past.

   C. African-Americans are a large identifiable ethnic group.

   D. In some areas Spanish is the de facto second language.

II. Supervisors, the ultimate human resource managers.

   A. Human resource management is the same as personnel management.

   B. Supervisors are responsible for most employee-related human resource problems.

   C. Effective managers are developers of people.

   D. Increased conceptual and administrative functions are assigned to supervisors.

III. SWANs and CROWs.

    A. SWANs are employees who are Smart, Work-hard, Ambitious, and Nice.

    B. CROWs are Commonly Recruited, Ordinary Workers. Fewer SWANS than CROWs are available for employment.

    C. Some supervisors fear and resent superior employees, whom they perceive as threats to their jobs.

IV. Management and the electronic workplace.

    A. Standards for VDT work are a major workplace concern.

    B. The creation of electronic sweatshops has broadened the functions of supervisors.

    C. The availability of a broad range of information via databanks and networks has resulted in the flattening of organizations.

    D. Telecommuting is a growing trend.

V. Life-style problems.

    A. Alcoholism and illicit drug use are two major life-style problems that supervisors must deal with. Absenteeisim, accidents, and sick leaves by problem drinkers is 16 times higher than the rates for average employees.

    B. Rehabilitation is often less costly than replacement of valuable employees who have alcohol or drug addiction difficulties. Large organizations often have chemical dependency rehabilitation programs.

    C. Stress at home and work can lead to emotional difficulties.

    D. Some types of depression and anxiety symptoms can be adequately treated with proper medication.

    E. Proactive first-line managers keep a list of qualified people and agencies that can assist employees with severe emotional difficulties.

VI. AIDS

    A. One of the more difficult issues for supervisors is dealing with employees who have AIDS or have been tested positive for the HIV virus.

    B. Some state laws and city ordinances protect both HIV carriers and those with the disease.

C. Supervisors have the responsibility for diffusing unfounded bias against any disease that is identified with a particular life-style.

VII. Physical disabilities.

    A. Supervisors of employees with physical disabilities may need special training.

    B. Assisting those with physical impairments can be a worthwhile and rewarding effort.

VIII. Sexual preference.

    A. Discrimination based on sexual preference is not presently prohibited by federal law.

    B. Most organizations have established either unwritten practices or policies that treat a person's life-style as an individual's personal choice.

    C. Supervisors must be able to balance fairness with their own feelings and the bias of their other employees.

IX. Working with unions.

    A. Since the mid-1970s, the power of unions in the United States has declined.

    B. Union-management relations are based on bilateral agreements or contracts

    C. Supervisors who work with union employees must understand the union-management contractual agreement.

    D. Union-management relations should be based on mutual recognition of responsibilities in developing and maintaining an organization.

X. Into the 2000s.

    A. Specialized expertise may not be as valuable for managers entering the next century as broad-based general knowledge in several fields.

    B. Supervisors are faced with problems and pressures unimagined in the past.

    C. Supervisors must be willing to continuously educate themselves.

■ KEY TERMS

demographics	**human resource management**
de facto language	**recruitment**

selection	AWDA
contracts	collective action
compliance	union
SWANs	unilateral relations
CROWs	bilateral relations
electronic workplace	bargaining unit
electronic sweatshops	management rights
telecommuting	NLRB
knowledge workers	union security
AIDS	economic strikes
illicit drugs	wildcat strikes
HIV	lockout

■ SELF-ASSESSMENT

How much do you know about the personnel management side of a supervisor's job? Mark the statements below with which you disagree with a 1, 2, or 3, depending on the strength of disagreement. For those you feel are correct, mark a 4, 5, or 6.

1. Professional human resource management departments are of little assistance to supervisors.

   1   2   3   4   5   6

2. Supervisors have primary responsibility for human resource management problems.

   1   2   3   4   5   6

3. Employees who have tested positively for presence of HIV in their bloodstreams have a highly contagious disease.

   1   2   3   4   5   6

4. Employee alcoholism is rare in most organizations.

   1   2   3   4   5   6

5. Knowledge workers need little support from other components of the organization.

   1   2   3   4   5   6

6. Unions have steadily gained political strength and influence in recent years.

   1   2   3   4   5   6

7. While other aspects of work have changed, the role of supervisors remained the same.

   1   2   3   4   5   6

8. Managers are being required to become more highly specialized in a field of knowledge.

   1   2   3   4   5   6

9. Few employees in this day and age are undereducated.

   1   2   3   4   5   6

10. A major supervisory human resource management duty is to recruit new employees.

   1   2   3   4   5   6

■ DISCUSSION QUESTIONS

1. List four specific problems that may be associated with employment of people with physical impairments. Briefly discuss each.

2. What do you feel will be some of the major human resource management trends for the next eight-year period? Justify your answer.

3. How can a supervisor detect emotional problems in employees?

4. Why do many organizations attempt to rehabilitate alcoholics and chronic illicit drug users rather than terminate them?

5. What are the primary differences between supervising in a nonunion environment and being a first-line manager with unionized employees?

■ SHORT CASES

Bad News at Bal Harbour

Bal Harbour, Florida, just north of Miami Beach, is an exclusive upscale community known as the traditional home of the annual AFL-CIO national conference. Union leaders from all over the United States converge to hear politicians courting their favor, members of government, and their own leadership discuss issues impacting the union movement in the United States.

Recently their meetings have centered on declining membership and loss of political clout. One union man states, "We don't have quite as poor a public image as we once had. It's not that we've done anything different, it's just that people don't think about us much any more. We're benefiting from our own failures."

Lane Kirkland, the well-respected president of the AFL-CIO, complains that companies are playing hardball. Companies are permanently replacing union employees on strike. He is leading an effort to attempt to get legislation passed that would make such practices illegal. In cases where unions feel strikes are justified for economic reasons, they will continue even though replacement of strikers remains a real threat. Victor Kamber, a union public relations manager, states that "Unions are willing to fight to the bitter end—even their own."

It is ironic that unions now depend on economic recession to gain members. When jobs are not threatened, no one is interested in joining or forming unions. In times of uncertainty many employees seek protections that union membership seems to offer. In spite of increased recruiting efforts and some success in organizing government employees, especially at the state level, total union membership continues to decline.

1. List a minimum of four reasons that explain the decline of union power and membership.

2. Will unions regain their former strength, remain at their present strength of about 12 percent of the total workforce, or will they continue to decline? Explain your reasoning.

3. If you were Lane Kirkland, what strategy would you use to expand union membership?

Who Speaks for Whom?

"It's pretty tough," complained Karen Matsui to Barry Stevens. "Here I am, trying to manage one of the largest assembly units of High Action Technology and I can't communicate with my employees. I'm," she stopped to laugh, "a damned minority."

Barry smiled back, "I know how you feel. Since I've been in human resource management, I find that I'm a minority too. Twenty-six percent of our employees are recent Hispanic immigrants, 14 percent are of Vietnamese origin, and another 6 percent are from Pacific island countries. Most of the islanders speak Chinese. About 8 percent more are black and the remaining 46 percent are Anglos. Frankly I think we should consider language rather than country of origin as a way of determining minority status."

"You're absolutely right," Karen interrupted. "Look at me: I'm of Japanese ancestry but I don't know any of the language. Asians around here think I am one of them, but I grew up in a predominately white-Anglo neighborhood and attended schools where English was the only language spoken. In college I studied Russian. It's not much help here. My Hispanic employees speak Spanish, my Vietnamese employees speak their own dialects and some French, and there is a smattering of other languages. On top of that they don't mix well. Each group keeps to itself. Building effective work teams is almost impossible. It's strange, but black and white employees work together better than do the other groups. They can communicate with each other. Most of my employees know some English but they speak to each other in their native language. They often don't understand what I tell them to do. They're good workers, learn fast, and want to please but have a difficult time explaining their problems. I guess we'll keep muddling through."

1. Should Karen attempt to get everyone to speak only English on the job? Why?

2. Karen can speak and understand some conversational Spanish. Should she try to learn Vietnamese and Chinese, the other dominant languages, as well? Explain your reasoning.

3. Should English be adopted as the official language of the United States? Explain.

■ ENDNOTES

1. Jerome Burstein and Edward Martin, *Computer Information Systems* (Hinsdale, Ill.: Dryden Press, 1989), p. 106.

2. U.S. Department of Commerce, Bureau of the Census, *Statistical Abstracts of the United States* (Washington, 1990).

3. "Census: 50% of Americans Live in Metropolitan Areas," *Los Angeles Times,* February 21, 1991.

4. David Shriebman, "Mobility of U.S. Society Turns Small Cities into Giants," *The Wall Street Journal,* February 8, 1991, sec. B.

5. David H. Maister, "The One-Firm Firm," *Sloane Management Review,* Fall 1985.

6. San Francisco's VDT ordinances were widely publicized in radio, television, and newspaper reports in January 1991.

7. Larry Armstrong, "Laptop Takeoff," *Business Week*, March 18, 1991, p. 124.

8. Tom Durkin, "Telecommuting," *Business Journal*, March 6, 1990, pp. 15–24.

9. Dan Costley and Ralph Todd, *Human Relations in Organizations*, 4th edition (St. Paul, Minn.: West Publishing Company, 1991), p. 399.

10. Ronald Henkoff, "Make Your Office More Productive," *Fortune*, February 25, 1991, pp. 72–84.

11. Extrapolated from Nick Correale, "Alcoholism" (unpublished research, California State University, 1990). A 4 percent inflation factor was added to Correale's estimates, which were based on research data from the U.S. Department of Labor Statistics and other sources.

12. Costley and Todd, p. 420.

13. Based on an actual incident reported to the author, November 21, 1990.

14. Alan L. Otten, "People Patterns: How Work, Home Stress Affects Working Couples," *The Wall Street Journal*, February 22, 1991, sec. B.

15. "Labor Letter," *The Wall Street Journal*, February 26, 1991, p. 1.

16. W. Brooke Tunstall, "Back to the Future," *New Management* (New York: John Wiley & Sons, 1987).

Chapter 16

Social Responsibility, Ethics, and Legal Issues

Objectives

Compliance with a myriad of federal and state laws affecting both people and the environment in which they live is a major thrust of Chapter 16. Its primary objectives are to enable supervisors to

- Define organizational responsibilities that go beyond profits and productivity.
- Deal with prejudice and intolerance in a work environment.
- Comprehend the importance of compliance administration.
- Adjust to shifting societal values.
- Discern ethical dilemmas.
- Utilize operational approaches to defining ethical issues.

Thought Starter

Tokyo Bay, the Houston Ship Canal, and the Rhine River have a common problem. They are essentially dead bodies of water. Pollution from industrial waste has killed fish, made the water poisonous, and the long-range effects on the total environment are not yet fully known. It is fortunate that in all of these cases, steps are being taken to curb pollutants and return the bodies of water to their former status as fisheries and recreational waterways. Industrial waste is not a part of nature but has been a product of humankind's misuse of the earth's resources. One of the most significant trends of the latter part of this century is the gradual realization that humans, like all other animals, need a toxic-free environment in which to live.

Humans are the only animals that have been able to alter their environment to the point that whole groups of other species have been eliminated. Tropical forests that have been weather regulators and homes for thousands of species of plants and animals are being totally destroyed at a rate that will eventually impact not only the climate, but the well-being of the lives of those who live in countries that allow their decimation.

Environmental issues are not the only problems that face organizations that depend on profits to sustain their existence. Treatment of employees is often one of the most sensitive and difficult issues with which managers must deal. Who is a minority? What does equality really mean? Are equity and fairness the same concept? Can supervisors be held personally liable for alleged injustices against employees? All of these questions and many more are the focus of Chapter 16.

Step by step, perhaps some forward and a few back, organizations are in the middle of a great social process: helping to forge a world that is both free and safe.

■ *As a part-time college student Jose Perez depended more on the advice of his professors than they really comprehended. "Here I am," he began in a discussion with Kara Robertson, his most-trusted management professor, "a professional photographer who has just been made supervisor of 12 offices, all located in different places. I was born in Brazil, grew up in Peru, moved to Costa Rica, and finally settled here. My understanding of English is good but I realize my accent identifies me as Hispanic. It's difficult when I meet with employees in relatively small cities where they may think I was promoted because I am a legal minority. They don't know how hard I've worked and how much I've been concerned about being accepted. What do you think I should do?"*

Dr. Robertson listened carefully. Jose was an excellent student who was well liked by fellow classmates. He attended an evening class where students were older and more experienced than those attending during the day. "You may be accepted more than you think." Kara replied. "People can tell phonies regardless of accent. They know you are the right person for the job."

■ FREEDOM AND EQUALITY—DIFFERENT TIMES, DIFFERENT MEANINGS

Subsistence wage is just enough money to purchase the necessities for life with no discretionary income.

In the early 1800s, during the beginnings of the Industrial Revolution, England established itself as the textile producer for the world. Cotton purchased in the new United States and other fibers obtained from its global empire made England the dominant force in the manufacture of cloth. With an acute labor shortage, children as young as eight years of age were employed as subsistence workers. **Subsistence** meant that they worked for just enough money to help their families live in the most impoverished conditions. In today's terminology it would be translated as *exploitation*. It is unfortunate that the same circumstances existed in the United States.

Robert Owen, an English textile manufacturer, was the first to try to ease the burden of children who worked 13½ hours per day with 15-minute breaks for meals.[1] Some of his employees were as young as eight years of age. When Owen proposed that no children under 10 be employed, there were howls of protest from other mill owners. He recognized that people were individuals and not machines. Owens eventually tried to establish a utopian colony in the United States that would promote his ideals of treating people as human beings rather than machines or draft animals. While he died a failure when his colony eventually disbanded, Owen will be remembered as the first industrialist who fought for both freedom and equality of those who toiled. Long before the term was coined, Owen was an advocate of civil rights.

Freedom and Equality

Equality means equal treatment, rights, and responsibilities.

Freedom provides the right of people to express themselves without fear, to agree or dissent, to select or reject any religion, to publish opinions, and to pursue happiness in ways that meet their interests and needs.

Although the Constitution of the United States declared that "all men are created equal," (until 1964 *men* meant any person regardless of sex), no person was fully equal to others except under the law. Equality and freedom have always been linked but are not precisely the same concept. **Equality** means that all people have the same rights, opportunities, and are entitled to the same treatment as other people. People may be equal under the most oppressive dictatorships: They are equally deprived of human rights.

Freedom provides the right of people to express themselves without fear, to agree or dissent, to have the right to select or reject any religion, to publish their opinions, and to pursue life, liberty, and happiness in ways that best meet their interests and needs provided such interests are for a legal purpose. It is possible for inequality of citizens to exist under political systems that allow freedom of expression and pursuit of goals. Ideally societies should promote both equality and freedom for their citizens.

■ SUPERVISORS AND PRO BONO LAW

Freedom also implies responsibility as well as rights.

Social responsibility means that organizations as well as individuals must act to support the common good of our society.

Pro bono publico law is law that is in the interest of the people.

Freedom, as it is interpreted in the United States, also implies responsibility as well as the right to agree, dissent, and choose. People are restricted only by law that prohibits them from harming themselves or others. In work organizations equal treatment under established policies, rules, and practices is a right of every employee. Freedom to accept the responsibilities of a given job or seek other employment is also guaranteed. In organizations supervisors find themselves guardians of both concepts. No employee may be denied equality of opportunity nor the right to appeal perceived injustice.

Pro bono publico is a legal term that means "in the interest of the people." It is another way of defining **social responsibility.** Organizations must, under a wide spectrum of **pro bono law,** help ensure equal treatment of employees in the application of rules and policies. They must also act to protect the physical environment through pollution controls. In essence, organizations must be the leaders in promoting the public interests of the communities in which they are located. Legally, ethically, and morally, they must be socially responsible.

Supervisors, as management's first line, have major responsibility for assuring pro bono conditions. Ultimately, in places of work, whether the ideals of freedom and equality are being achieved is judged by employees. Supervisors have the responsibility of creating conditions that encourage equal treatment and protection of employee rights. They are a key component in ensuring socially responsible actions by their organizations.

■ FIRST-LINE MANAGERS AND EQUAL OPPORTUNITY

Equal opportunity means that all members of our society have equal access and equal opportunity by legal mandate.

Access is the right to be served in public or private facilities designed to serve the general population.

Opportunity implies the right to education and work without denial because of race, color, religion, national origin, sex, age over 40 years, or physical disability.

Protected classes are groups, defined by law, specifically protected against discrimination in equality of opportunity and access.

In 1965, shortly after the death of President John F. Kennedy, his successor, Lyndon Johnson, opened his inaugural address by saying, "For over 200 years we have advocated freedom and equal opportunity. It is now time to make it a reality." Johnson may be best remembered for his power brokering and the Vietnam War. There is little doubt that, in spite of a somewhat tarnished image, he was the most significant civil rights figure of the 20th century.

Two primary concerns were addressed in the **Civil Rights Act of 1964. Access** meant that no person, because of race, color, religion, national origin, or sex, could be denied entrance and use of public or private facilities designed to serve the general population. This included restaurants, theaters, hotels and motels, retail establishments of all kinds, and all governmental service locations. The Civil Rights Act also addressed **opportunity.** No person because of race, color, religion, national origin, or sex can be denied opportunity for education, employment, and the pursuit of chosen fields of endeavor.

In 1972 Title VII of the Act, which dealt with equality of employment, was strengthened by the creation of the Equal Employment Opportunity Commission. Organizations, for the first time, were faced with penalties for violation of any individual's legal rights. A major feature of the law was the development of the concept of **protected classes.** Under the law any person who was a member of a group that had suffered past discrimination because of race, color, religion, national origin, or sex was part of a protected class. Patterns of discrimination were changed forever.

Getting to Where We Are

During the initial period of the enforcement of the act, efforts to make it a reality were focused on racial issues. African-Americans, with a history in the United States that predates the Revolutionary War, had suffered discriminatory practices more than any other identifiable group. A great deal of effort went into opening both education and job opportunities for black people, especially in geographic areas that traditionally denied full equality. It was fortunate that during this period a number of very able and politically astute black leaders emerged to push the effort forward. Hispanics progressed through alignment with strong labor unions.

The changed status of women is the most profound social movement of the 20th century.

There is little doubt that the changed status of women will be recorded as the most significant social change of the 20th century. Although great progress has been made in creating equal opportunity for black people and members of other protected classes, none have been as far reaching and meaningful as the movement of women into every aspect of work life in the United States.

■ TITLE VII FOR SUPERVISORS

Title VII of the Civil Rights Act of 1964 and its amendments guarantees equality of employment opportunity under rules of the Equal Employment Opportunity Commission.

Like other laws, the Civil Rights Act of 1964 is divided into a number of parts. Each part is called a *title*. Titles are like chapters in a book. **Title VII,** known as the *Equal Employment Opportunity Act*, is the most important. It defines what organizations must do to ensure equal treatment for all employees as well as applicants for employment. Since being enacted in 1964, Title VII has been amended several times. In 1972 the Equal Employment Opportunity Commission, known as the **EEOC,** was designated as the Act's administrator with the right to investigate complaints of discrimination and to bring offenders to court if other measures do not correct problems. Uniform guidelines for employment were added in 1978. Although nearly every year some amendments are made, the 1978 version is most important for first-line managers. Supervisors must have a working knowledge of its requirements in order to avoid costly and personally damaging errors. Some of the more important concepts are summarized below:

1. Exemptions. Not all organizations are subject to the provisions of Title VII. Some of the more important exemptions include:

- Businesses with fewer than 15 employees are exempt from Title VII unless they have government contracts. In such cases the Office of Federal Contract Compliance issues guidelines for compliance with equal opportunity laws.

- Members of Congress, some of whom have in excess of 750 employees, are also exempt from Title VII.

- Technically the federal government is also exempt from Title VII, although it adheres to equal opportunity provisions. Violations are reported to the Attorney General's office rather than to the EEOC.

- Indian tribes that own businesses are also exempt, regardless of the number of employees hired.

- Religious organizations may hire only members of their own sect if they can demonstrate a valid reason for doing so. Such exemptions may be made invalid if any people who are not members of their religion are employed.

- Private country clubs are also exempt, provided their primary purpose is not related to other public purposes, such as business.

- United States companies operating in other countries are subject to the labor laws of the host country and are also exempt.

Under a number of other conditions some businesses, while not exempt, are not usually pressured to comply. Family-owned farms that rely on transient workers and ethnic restaurants are two examples.

2. Protected class. Members of any group that has been discriminated against in the past because of race, color, religion, national origin, or sex are covered by all provisions of the Act as well as Title VII. Employers may give preference to an applicant of a protected class in order to balance the ethnicity or sex of employees if the applicant's qualifications are essentially the same as that of an applicant who represents the majority of the population. Figure 16.1 lists major federally mandated protected classes in the United States.

3. BFOQ. Employers may have a bona fide occupation qualification for limiting employment (*bona fide* may be translated as "good faith"). Usually BFOQ reasons are based on physical requirements, such as accurate color discrimination of color-coded wires

FIGURE 16.1 ■ Federally Mandated Protected Classes

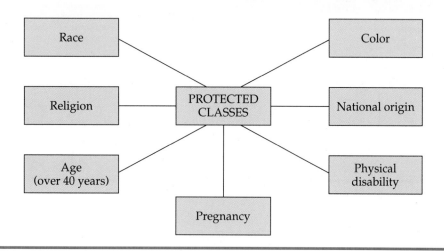

and diagrams in electronics or strength to climb poles to install and repair utility wires and equipment. There are several other types of BFOQ requirements that are relatively rare and must be handled on a case-by-case basis.

4. Disparate treatment. It is illegal to treat a group or individual different from other groups or individuals. Women, as an example, may not be selectively assigned to one type of work and men to another if both have the skill, knowledge, and ability to perform the same type of work.

5. Disparate effect. Any action that may not be intended to be discriminatory but has a discriminatory result is called **disparate effect.** Hiring "walk-ins" rather than selecting from a pool of qualified applicants, promoting an employee without considering other qualified applicants in the organization, or hiring relatives, friends, and employee-recommended applicants without considering others as well are forms of disparate effect.

6. Reasonable accommodation. Over the years since the Civil Rights Act was enacted, the courts have ruled that businesses must not set up artificial barriers to employment. They must attempt to reasonably accommodate an employee's or applicant's special conditions. One of the most famous rulings affecting **rea-**

FIRST-LINERS

sonable accommodation involved a Trans World Airlines flight attendant named Hardison.[2] Hardison's religion forbade her working on Saturday. This made it impossible to schedule Hardison on Saturday flights, one of the airline's busiest days. TWA attempted to accommodate Hardison by reassigning her to a nonflying job. Her union objected to all alternatives TWA offered and the case eventually went to the Supreme Court. In a landmark ruling the court stated that TWA had attempted to reasonably accommodate Hardison. Her refusal to accept other assignments resulted in her termination. No discrimination existed according to the Court.

7. EEO-1. All employers with 100 or more employees must file an Equal Employment Opportunity Form 1 annually. Ethnicity and sex in various types of employment, such as managers, technicians, and clerical, skilled, semiskilled, and unskilled employees, are statistically reported on Form 1.

8. Uniform guidelines. Human resource professionals often have difficulty interpreting and complying with the provisions of Title VII Uniform Guidelines. Supervisors must remember that the guidelines state that an applicant for employment, promotion, transfer, or training assignment may not be asked questions not asked others in the same job classification. An important section of the guidelines specifies standards for selection of minority applicants. Supervisors rarely, if ever, are involved in the technicalities of the process for determining hiring ratios.

9. **Affirmative action.** Affirmative action consists of plans, policies, procedures, and practices designed to make equal opportunity a reality. It is not required by Title VII but is a requirement of the Office of Federal Contract Compliance for organizations that do business with the Federal Government. A brief summary of major Title VII concepts is given in Table 16.1.

■ OTHER LAWS

In 1990 the U.S. Congress enacted the **Americans with Disabilities Act (AWDA).** It is the most recent of a series of legal mandates

TABLE 16.1 ■ Summary of Major Title VII Concepts

Exemptions	Title VII exempts businesses with less than 15 employees, certain religious organization businesses, businesses owned by Indian tribes, members of Congress, and bona fide country clubs.
Protected class	Any group that has been discriminated against in the past for reasons of race, color, religion, national origin, sex, age, or physical impairment.
BFOQ	A bona fide occupational qualification is a legal reason for excluding some people as applicants for a particular job. Usually based on physical condition.
Disparate treatment	It is illegal to deliberately treat one group or individual differently from others if they are members of a protected class.
Disparate effect	Practices that are not intentionally discriminatory but have that effect are also illegal. Hiring by employee recommendation only is an example.
Reasonable accommodation	Organizations must attempt to accommodate the religious or physical requirements of applicants or current employees.
EEO-1	Employers must report with the EEOC the number of employees and their ethnicity, sex, and type of work to ensure compliance with Title VII.
Uniform Guidelines	Uniform Guidelines define standards for selection of employees and determine compliance with laws for equal representation of minority employees.
Sexual harassment	Title VII specifically prohibits any act that requires sexual consent as a condition of employment, promotion, transfer, or other personnel action. Any act that is sexually offensive to the extent that it interferes with an individual's work performance may be construed as sexual harassment.

defining members of protected classes. Although the law does not prohibit organizations from requiring physical examinations to determine the fitness of a potential employee, it states that such standards must be reasonable for the type of work to which an employee will be assigned. As in the Hardison case, reasonable accommodation is the basic requirement of management. When applicants with physical impairments apply for work, an organization must try to reasonably accommodate their disability.

This does not mean that unqualified people must be hired regardless of physical condition. It simply states that if a potential employee has the skills, knowledge, or ability to perform a job, she or he must be considered with all other applicants without prejudice because of physical condition. If a job requires physical activity beyond the applicant's physical capability, reasonable accommodation may be impossible. Reasonable accommodation may mean removal of architectural barriers, modifying toilets, making drinking fountains more accessible, and providing special work spaces. It does not mean assigning a visually impaired person to tasks requiring clear eyesight or putting a person confined to a wheelchair in an assignment that requires climbing stairs. A major intent of the law is to encourage organizations to utilize an often neglected source of labor.

Age Discrimination

Originally passed in 1967, the **Age Discrimination Act,** preventing discrimination against employees or potential employees 40 years old or older, was amended in 1978 and again in 1986. In its original form it prohibited discrimination between ages 40 and 65. This was extended to age 70 by the second amendment. Currently the law applies to anyone over 40 years of age with no ceiling. Employees who have reached the age of 70 may be required to take physical and mental competency tests annually under certain circumstances. Older employees who are no longer competent or who cannot meet the physical demands of a job may be terminated just like anyone else.

Some occupations, such as fire fighting, police work, and piloting commercial aircraft, may have legitimate BFOQs based on age. Mandatory retirement ages may be set in such cases as well as maximum ages for consideration as an employee. Many police forces will not consider applicants past the age of 36. For job-related purposes these types of age restrictions have been found legal.

Supervisors generally find that older employees may have somewhat slower reaction times than younger people but are loyal, accurate, knowledgeable, and have acceptable attendance records.

Equal Pay

Equal pay regardless of sex is guaranteed by the Equal Pay Act.

One of the earliest efforts to reduce inequities between men and women in the workplace was the passage of the **Equal Pay Act of 1963,** an amendment to the Fair Labor Standards Act of 1938. Under the law it is illegal to pay women lower wages than men for performing essentially the same work. Pay differences based on seniority and performance are not prohibited but differences based primarily on sex are prohibited. An important part of the law states that jobs and working conditions for men and women need not be precisely identical for the law to take effect. They must involve substantially similar duties.

Comparable worth is the concept that jobs, regardless of classification, that require similar experience, training, and responsibility should be paid equally.

Two new issues have grown out of the Equal Pay Act. **Comparable worth** concerns are related to jobs that may be different but the job with greater "worth" receives less pay. Secretaries, the bulk of whom are women, with assignments that require extensive training, experience, responsibility, and variety of duties may be paid less than custodians at the same facility. It can be argued that the secretaries' job is worth more but paid less. At this time the comparable worth issue remains unsettled. Labor market forces often create imbalances in pay.

Comparable pay means that people with the same type of work and job classifications should receive substantially the same pay.

Comparable pay issues relate to doing work similar to others but being paid less. Highway patrol officers may be paid less than sheriff's deputies, or warehouse workers in private industry may be paid less than their counterparts at government facilities.

Several states and the Federal Office of Personnel Management have adopted comparable pay policies and regulations that minimize differences in pay between those in private industry and government agencies. Private industry, out of necessity, has long attempted to equalize wages between similar industries. Prevention of comparable pay differences has also been a major union aim for many years.

Pregnancy Discrimination

One of the amendments to Title VII in 1978 included the **Pregnancy Discrimination Act,** which forbids discrimination against women because of pregnancy. It also mandates that pregnancy

Pregnancy must be treated like any other reason for medical leave under the law. Some states allow up to 16 weeks of pregnancy leave with full reinstatement rights.

must be treated as any other type of medical condition for purposes of leaves of absence and sick-leave benefits. An important part of the law permits states to establish specific return rights to the employee's former job or one of like status and pay. An interesting spin-off issue of the Pregnancy Discrimination Act has been the development of paternal leave for fathers. It is based on the assumption that women need special assistance during the early weeks after pregnancy. Some city governments allow such leave, usually without pay. By the year 2000 it may be a common practice. Table 16.2 summarizes the Pregnancy Discrimination Act and other civil rights laws.

Immigration Reform and Control Act

Because of concerns about the employment of illegal aliens, especially in those states bordering Mexico, the **Immigration and**

TABLE 16.2 ■ Civil Rights Law for Supervisors

Equal Pay Act, 1963	Prohibits pay differences based on sex for doing substantially the same work. Does not prohibit pay increases based on seniority or merit.
Civil Rights Act, 1964	Title VII of the Act, amended in 1972, 1978, 1986, and 1990, prohibits discrimination against applicants and employees based on race, color, religion, national origin, and sex in any condition of employment including selection, promotion, transfer, disciplinary action, merit increases in pay, application of seniority, and training. Other titles support equality in education, public businesses, and college sports.
Age Discrimination Act, 1967	Originally designed to protect people from discriminatory practices between ages 40 and 65, the law now prohibits discrimination against anyone, based on age, over the age of 40.
Pregnancy Act, 1978	Mandates that pregnancy shall be treated as any other medical condition. Allows states to pass specific conditions for pregnancy leave. Some states guarantee up to 12 weeks for mothers to return to jobs of like status and pay after childbirth.
American with Disabilities Act, 1990	Prohibits discrimination against applicants and employees solely for physical impairment. Uses the test of reasonable accommodation to determine placement of physically impaired employees and assignment of work.

Control Act of 1986 requires employers to verify the eligibility of workers to legally work in the United States. Forms for filing verification are available from the Immigration and Naturalization Service. Usually most organizations do not require status verification unless they are in areas where employment of illegal aliens has been a long-standing practice. For many years western states have relied on immigrant labor for farm work and many types of manufacturing, especially in the garment industry. A purpose of the law is to protect aliens from being victimized by unscrupulous employers.

State and Local Laws

Civil rights protections have been extended and reenforced by both state and local law. This is especially true in cases involving housing, lending money, and sexual preference discrimination in employment. Under national law states with procedures similar to those of the federal government have the first opportunity to settle alleged civil rights violations before they are brought before the Equal Employment Opportunity Commission.

■ PREJUDICE, DISCRIMINATION, AND RACISM AT WORK

Supervisors may be faced, in some situations, with attempting to minimize discriminatory treatment. They must understand that information alone does not eliminate prejudice. In a study of drug use by U.S. postal workers[3] it was found that black employees had a higher incidence of drug use on one hand but also were absent from work 33 percent less that whites; had about the same number of accidents but 31 percent fewer injuries. They were also 143 percent more likely to be fired than were white employees and 44 percent more likely to be disciplined. A clear finding of the study is that individual employees, regardless of race, must not be judged by general trends. Higher drug use may come from living in a cultural environment quite different from that of whites. A few members of an identifiable group can distort statistical data concerning the performance of most of its members.

Prejudice may be defined as a preconceived judgment or opinion.

Prejudice may be defined as a preconceived judgment or opinion. By and large when individuals see another person as being somehow different from themselves, preconceived notions and usually unfounded stereotypes emerge. Prejudice may be based on race, religion, national origin, socioeconomic status, level of education, geographic origins, or even the schools a person has attended. Most people will state they have no real prejudices. In fact nearly all of us identify groups and individuals with different values and beliefs from our own. We all too often identify differences as somehow making us superior.

Racism is based on the belief that some races are superior to others.

Racism is based on the belief that a given racial group is somehow superior to others. Anthropologists, psychologists, and sociologists have studied racism for many years. They have found that no race is either inferior or superior to others.

Discrimination means to treat members of a group differently from others for any reason.

Inequality of treatment is the foundation of **discrimination.** A supervisor who assigns certain types of work based on a person's race, color, national origin, sex, age, or physical condition may be inadvertently engaging in discriminatory action. This is especially true when certain types of work are reserved for women and other types for men.

Segregation is the act of keeping people of different races, religions, national origins, or sex apart from each other.

People have a tendency to associate with people they perceive to be similar to themselves. It is a common and natural form of self-segregation. In a work environment, segregated work groups, even by choice of the group's members, may be illegal if the segregation is used to exclude employees of different ethnic or cultural backgrounds. Management is held responsible under the law for prevention of segregation that has adverse effects on any person or group.

■ SEXUAL HARASSMENT

Sexual harassment is any act, statement, or display that implies sexual consent as a condition of employment or any statement or material that is offensive or causes work to be impeded because of its sexual content.

One of the most sensitive issues in places of work is **sexual harassment.** Title VII of the Civil Rights Act specifically prohibits employees and supervisors from engaging in any acts that either explicitly or implicitly require sexual consent as a condition of employment.

1. It is illegal to require or imply submission to a sexual act as a condition of employment. This includes appointment to a job, promotion, transfer, performance evaluation, transfer, and consideration for increase in pay.

2. Punishment or adverse action against an employee for rejection of sexual advances is also prohibited.

3. Any sexual act, suggestions of sex, or behavior that is sexually offensive, hostile, or otherwise adversely affects job performance is also prohibited.

A danger of sexual harassment claims is their possible use as a weapon to punish a disliked supervisor or other employees. Often the accused is presumed guilty even though evidence is totally circumstantial. More often, evidence suggests, sexual harassment goes unreported.

Another problem focuses on the definition of sexual harassment. Pictures, jokes, statues, and displays of nonsexual affection have all been subjects of legal cases involving sexual harassment. Supervisors must be able to recognize the sensitivity of the issue and train employees to avoid any behavior that may be seen by others as sexually offensive.

■ COMPLIANCE–A DEMANDING TASK

Supervisors have the difficult task of dealing with their own prejudices as well as those of employees. As society gradually moves toward elimination of some of the harmful effects of racism, discrimination, and prejudice, managers of work organizations may find that they are responsible for helping lead positive social change.

■ ENVIRONMENTAL ISSUES

For many years people have been concerned with the environmental consequences of their actions. In the United States and Europe potable (drinkable) water has been a mark of an advanced country. Good sewage and garbage disposal have also been major environmental issues. It was not until 1970 that the United States established the **Environmental Protection Agency (EPA)** to establish standards for a safe and healthy physical environment. Efforts of the agency have focused on the quality of air and water, waste disposal, chemical contamination, and the impact of buildings, highways, and other structures on the lives of people. Its successes in achieving stated goals are mixed. In some areas pollution has been reduced and better planning is evident. Both air and water quality have improved in many places, but pollution still exists.

Supervisors have the responsibility for ensuring that trash and waste products are disposed of correctly and that employees, especially in manufacturing, observe critical procedures related to use and disposal of cleaning materials and chemicals. When leakage or other problems related to contaminants are evident, supervisors must follow proper reporting procedures. It is easy, in a work environment, to become careless and insensitive to potential environmental damage from relatively small amounts of toxic pollutants. Many chemicals retain their original composition for long periods of time. Some cities have reported that the earth near manufacturing or large-scale repair facilities is contaminated to the extent that it may never be usable.

OSHA is the Occupational Safety and Health Administration, which makes and enforces national safety standards.

Most states as well as the federal **Occupational Safety and Health Administration (OSHA)** have established procedures that help ensure correct use and disposal of toxic materials. Supervisors have the responsibility for ensuring that employees are adequately trained and disciplined in compliance with the law.

■ ETHICS—DOING WHAT IS RIGHT

Ethics is concerned with adhering to societal values of honesty, fairness, and concern for the welfare of others.

Morals are usually based on religious definitions of good and evil, right and wrong.

On-the-job **ethics** is a difficult and often confusing concept. In its simplest terms it means doing right and avoiding wrong. There are two types of ethics. One type is based on personal morals. Ethics may also be based on accepted societal standards. **Morals** stem from personal beliefs that usually have a religious or cultural basis. Some cultures consider exposure of the human body as immoral. A woman may not expose any part of her body other than her eyes and hands. Other cultures accept nudity as natural and unrelated to moral behavior. Primitive equatorial societies consider clothing an unneeded encumbrance. In more temperate climates public nudity may be considered immoral by some but an expression of religious feelings by others. In work environments ethics are usually based on societal standards that may or may not be founded in religious belief. Common ethical issues are listed in Figure 16.2.

FIGURE 16.2 ■ Common Ethical Issues

Honesty
  Fairness
    Lawful conduct
      Protection of human life
        Consideration for welfare of others
          Acceptance of personal responsibility

Ethics in Organizations

In most societies, regardless of dominant religions, it is considered unethical to lie, cheat, steal, or to harm another person except in personal defense. Deception, manipulation, and taking advantage of a person's lack of knowledge is also accepted as unethical. It is understood that in democracies such as the United States, freedom is dependent on ethical constraints. Without them humanity could not survive.

> Shelia Purrington worked hard as an hourly paid financial analysis specialist for the First Bank of Columbia. Her primary task involved cataloging types of loans made into such categories as personal, commercial, new business, construction, real estate, and inventory maintenance. Her data was entered into a computer databank for further analysis by the bank's top management.
>
> Ted Murphy, analyst supervisor, recognized both Shelia's interest and drive. He encouraged her to succeed. Often Shelia worked hours after other employees had left the Bank and was usually on the job a half hour before other employees arrived at work. Ted knew that under both state and federal law, Shelia should be paid a minimum of one and one-half times her base rate for all time worked in excess of 40 hours per week. Because Shelia willingly volunteered the extra time and had never requested overtime payment, Ted declined to authorize the additional time and one-half rate that she had legally earned. Was Ted unethical in his actions?

It is entirely possible that Ted did not think he was taking advantage of Shelia. He may have considered her his best employee. Under provisions of the wage and hour section of the Fair Labor Standards Act, employees who work in excess of 40 hours per week, or in some states, eight hours per day, must be paid at overtime rates, even if the work is voluntary. Ted must have been aware of the law and his actions were illegal if not, in his eyes, unethical.

Ethics and Leadership

Concern over ethical questions is a mark of leadership.[4] Employees will forgive supervisors who fail to precisely follow plans or achieve the smoothest human relations. They will not forgive those who are unethical and unprincipled. Leaders who are not honest, who are deceptive and engage in manipulation are headed for failure. In a survey conducted by the Korn-Ferry Institute,[5] executives listed personal integrity as the most important factor in achieving their status. *Integrity* means having a sense of personal worth and clear values as guides to behavior. It is best summarized in the famous quote in Shakespeare's *Hamlet:* "This above all, to thine own self be true, and it must follow as the night the day, thou canst not then be false of any man." If a person is true to her or his own beliefs and values, those values will be applied in dealing with others.

Ethical Dilemmas

Ethical dilemmas occur when two or more ethical principles are in conflict with each other.

Although supervisors are often faced with choices or dilemmas where ethics are unclear, they must be true to their own system of values. There are situations where a person is damned if they do and damned if they don't.

> Clyde Rainwater was an exceptionally bright, well-liked member of the cost accounting department at Criswell Enterprises. As a black accounting graduate he had been recruited by several companies and joined Criswell because of opportunities in his field of interest. When an opportunity to obtain special training in managing accounting functions became available, Clyde was among the first to apply.
>
> Clyde's supervisor, Joyce Becker, was faced with a problem. Dennis Richter, a white employee with equally good qualifications, had also applied for the special training. Funding limitations and space in the program meant that only one could attend. Dennis had greater seniority than Clyde as well as more experience. No black employees, Joyce knew, had ever been sent to the program. Most people who attend the additional training were eventually promoted to supervisor jobs. Criswell had no black accounting supervisors.
>
> Joyce faced a dilemma. If she chose Clyde, she would violate a tradition of making choices based on seniority if qualifications of the applicants were essentially the same. She also knew the organization's commitment to ethnic balance in its management staff. This appeared to be an opportunity to correct a long-standing wrong. Shortly after Joyce announced Clyde as the choice for the training program, Dennis filed charges of reverse discrimination with the Equal Employment Opportunity Commission.[6]

Was Joyce correct? Dennis claimed that 24-year-old white males were the group most discriminated against in the United States. Blacks, Hispanics, Asians, and women were given preference. He went on to point out that at Criswell, young white males were indeed a minority of their own. Eventually the EEOC and courts to which their findings were appealed agreed with Joyce. While apparent discrimination had occurred, the company, as represented by Joyce, was correct in attempting to correct an apparent case of discrimination against black people in management positions.

Operational Definitions of Ethics

Reference groups are groups from which ethics are derived.

Being honest and true to one's values is not always easy. Every person has a **reference group** from which their ethics are derived. Virtually all professional groups publish codes of ethics for their members. Companies publish policy statements defining ethical positions. Supervisors may have several reference groups, all with slightly different interpretations of what is acceptable and unacceptable behavior. If Rainwater, in the case just cited, and Richter had both been members of a union, Richter would have automatically been sent to training regardless of Criswell Enterprises' goal of adding black managers. Seniority would have clearly prevailed. In several rulings the Supreme Court has recognized contractual agreements as binding on both parties provided there was no intent to discriminate.

Supervisors must make decisions based on what they know is right and is best for the organization. It often means taking risks. If a supervisor who is directly in line for a promotion learns that his immediate boss, the manager of purchasing, is accepting expensive gifts and money from successful bidders for the company's business, should it be reported to higher authority? Most supervisors are reluctant to go over their manager's head to file complaints with higher levels of authority and responsibility. It makes them seem like traitors. Discussing the issue with the purchasing manager may result in denial, covering the facts, anger, and even termination for making the accusation. In such instances supervisors must dig deeply into their own values and try to find courses of action that may be high risk but are ethically correct.

▪ SEX IN THE WORKPLACE

Many employees and managers spend more waking time with each other than with any members of their families. One of the consequences is a building of friendships, trust, and often sexual attraction. Although many organizations discourage office romances, they are a reality of work. Supervisors are especially vulnerable to sexual advances because of their perceived positions of power. Unlike harassment, willing consent of partners is not considered illegal in most states even though it may be deemed immoral. **Willing consent** means that sexual relations have been voluntary, involved without coercion, threat, promise, or other harassment by either party. Married people who have sexual liaisons outside of their marriages are frequently subjects of controversy, rumor, and emotional accusations.

Willing consent means that two people enter into a relationship with each other because of mutual desire rather than threat, fear, or potential work-related rewards.

Public knowledge of sexual misconduct, especially if it results in pregnancy, can be embarrassing to an organization. Supervisors can discourage employees from office romances by explaining the possible consequences. They must also realize that their own careers may be impeded if they are personally involved. It is virtually impossible to keep strong relationships discretely hidden. Many organizations have strict rules regarding sexual conduct, especially for managers and professional employees who may represent the organization in contacts with outside agencies, vendors, associations, customers, and other groups.

▪ SOCIAL RESPONSIBILITY, ETHICS, AND LEGAL MANDATES

Social responsibility in organizations is a real concern of many managers. Organizations, after years of resisting change from traditional authoritarian rule and total self-determination, have accepted and encouraged equal treatment of employees. They are increasingly concerned with supporting environmental and ethical issues. Although urged by legal mandates, much of what corporations do today is from their own initiative. Accidents, such as major oil spills and chemical contamination of water, will continue to be realities. They are also becoming fewer and controls over their effects more productive. Out of self-interest as well as societal standards, many organizations are concerned with their own ethical images. Questions such as the ethics of selling products banned in the United States to Third World nations, bribery of foreign representatives in order to obtain contracts, and treatment of their own employees are subjects of self-examination and improvement.

Society in the future will judge the success or failure of current efforts to build socially responsible and ethically strong organizations. How well work organizations promote issues of environmental protection, education, equality of opportunity, and the general welfare of the communities affected by their services and products will help determine the well-being of future generations.

■ THINGS TO REMEMBER

I. Freedom and equality—different times, different meanings.

 A. People in the past did not understand concepts of social responsibility as they are interpreted today.

 B. Equality means all human beings have the same rights, responsibilities, and opportunities. Freedom implies equal treatment as well as equal rights. Concepts of equality and freedom have always been linked.

 C. *Pro bono publico* means in the interest of the people.

 D. *Social responsibility* also means acting in the interests of people and their environment, and adhering to legal and ethical principles.

II. First-line managers and equal opportunity.

 A. Access and opportunity are the primary guarantees of the Civil Rights Act of 1964.

 B. Title VII of the Civil Rights Act, as amended in 1972, 1978, 1986, and 1990, affects all personnel-related activities of supervisors.

 C. Title VII defines the concept of protected class. Employers may use membership in a protected class as a qualification for employment.

 D. During its initial stages civil rights action focused on race and national origin.

 E. The status of women will likely be recorded as the most significant social change of the 20th century.

III. Title VII for supervisors.

 A. Title VII of the Civil Rights Act defines personnel-related responsibilities. Provisions of Title VII are administered by the Equal Employment Opportunity Commission.

B. Organizations with less than 15 employees, those operated by certain religious groups or owned by native American tribes, and members of Congress are exempt from compliance with the Act.

C. Bona fide occupational qualifications are conditions that allow employers to select specific types of employees for jobs with special requirements.

D. *Disparate treatment* means treating employees differently because of membership in a protected class. It is legally prohibited. Disparate effect is inadvertent disparate treatment.

E. *Reasonable accommodation* means organizations must attempt to accommodate special requirements of religion or physical impairment.

F. Uniform Guidelines are an amendment to the Civil Rights Act that set standards for employee selection and determination of equity in employment.

IV. Other laws.

A. The Americans with Disabilities Act (1990).

B. The Age Discrimination Act (1967, 1978, 1986).

C. The Equal Pay Act of 1963.

D. The Pregnancy Discrimination Act (1978).

E. The Immigration and Control Act of 1986.

V. Prejudice, discrimination, and racism at work.

A. *Prejudice* is a preconceived judgment or opinion.

B. Racism is based on the belief that a given racial group is superior to others.

C. Inequality of treatment is the foundation of *discrimination*.

D. *Segregation* means intentionally keeping a group separate from other groups.

VI. Sexual harassment.

A. It is illegal to require or implicitly require submission to a sexual act as a condition of employment.

B. Adverse action against an employee for rejecting sexual advances is illegal.

C. Any sexual act, suggestions of sex, or behavior that is sexually offensive is also prohibited by Title VII.

VII. Compliance—a demanding task.

    A. Supervisors must deal with their own prejudices as well as those of employees.

    B. Managers at all levels must realize they are leaders in defining and creating positive social change.

VIII. Environmental issues.

    A. In 1970 environmental protection laws were enacted to establish a safe, healthy physical environment.

    B. Supervisors have the responsibility for enforcing environmental protection law for their work units.

    C. The Occupational Safety and Health Administration law sets standards for both safety and healthy working conditions for employees.

IX. Ethics—doing what is right.

    A. A simple definition of ethics is doing what is right and avoiding what is wrong.

    B. Morals stem from religious or cultural beliefs.

    C. Concern for ethical questions is a mark of leadership.

    D. Effective managers are true to their own beliefs. They have personal integrity.

X. Sex in the workplace.

    A. Willing consent is different from sexual harassment.

    B. Supervisors have the responsibility for informing employees of the potential dangers of sexual involvement with other employees.

XI. Social responsibility.

    A. The success of efforts to encourage socially responsible actions will be judged by future generations.

■ KEY TERMS

subsistence	**Civil Rights Act of 1964**
equality	access
freedom	opportunity
social responsibility	**protected class**
pro bono law	**Title VII**
equal opportunity	**EEOC**

disparate treatment

disparate effect

reasonable accommodation

EEO-1

Uniform Guidelines

affirmative action

sexual harassment

AWDA

Age Discrimination Act

Equal Pay Act of 1963

comparable worth

comparable pay

Pregnancy Discrimination Act

Immigration and Control Act of 1986

prejudice

racism

discrimination

segregation

compliance

EPA

OSHA

ethics

morals

ethical dilemmas

reference group

willing consent

■ DISCUSSION QUESTIONS

1. Is reverse discrimination a reality or a claim made only by white males? Explain your response.

2. Discuss your view of changes in society toward allowing equal treatment for people of all races and national origins.

3. Has civil rights legislation made minority populations more dependent on law than on ability in securing jobs once dominated by white Anglo-Americans? Discuss your response.

4. Give an example of an unethical experience you may have witnessed or encountered.

5. How do you feel future generations of people will view antidiscrimination efforts currently in progress in the United States?

■ SELF-ASSESSMENT

Social responsibility is a relatively new and difficult issue for supervisors. Respond to the following items by marking 1, 2, or 3 if you disagree or 4, 5, or 6 if you agree.

1. The Age Discrimination Act and its amendments apply to people younger than 40 years of age.

    1   2   3   4   5   6

2. Sexual harassment is not a serious violation of Title VII, although it remains an ethical problem.

     1   2   3   4   5   6

3. Women have been, and still are, subject to disparate treatment.

     1   2   3   4   5   6

4. Ethics is more a matter of law than social standards.

     1   2   3   4   5   6

5. Racism and segregation are essentially the same type of prejudice.

     1   2   3   4   5   6

6. Work organizations have little or no responsibility for employee welfare.

     1   2   3   4   5   6

7. Environmental problems are of little or no concern to supervisors.

     1   2   3   4   5   6

8. Freedom and equality mean precisely the same thing.

     1   2   3   4   5   6

9. From a practical perspective managers cannot be concerned with sex in the workplace.

     1   2   3   4   5   6

10. Reasonable accommodation applies to physically impaired employees as well as others.

     1   2   3   4   5   6

■ SHORT CASES

Who Is Who?

When Cynthia Cisneros completed the supplemental application form for a job with the city of San Francisco, she identified herself as Hispanic. Later investigation revealed that she was born Cynthia Campbell and had married Raul Cisneros, a descendant of immigrants from Chile. Her Hispanic origins were suspect. "You have falsified your national origin identity," claimed the human resource manager of Perdanales Products, where Cynthia was employed as a regional sales representative.

"You don't understand," Cynthia retorted, "I was born and reared in Chile. In Chile many Hispanic people speak Spanish but have surnames that are neither Spanish nor Portugese in origin. Does my heritage as a Spanish-speaking immigrant make me less Hispanic? It's true I married Raul Cisneros. We met in college. His father is from a seventh-generation Spanish family that predates most other families in this state. Is he Hispanic also?"

Harland Aldridge, the human resource manager, looked uncomfortable. "You are right. Definitions prescribed by law, such as surname identification of national origin, just don't make sense. Please accept my apologies for the accusations against you. Frankly, I don't know how to distinguish one ethnic or national origin group from another."

1. Discuss reasons both for and against including national origin as a qualification for membership in a protected class. With the exception of American Indians, all people in the United States are immigrants from other countries.

2. In San Francisco[7] Captain Roybal has been accused of being an imposter. He has challenged other members of the fire department to prove their national origins. Is it discriminatory to require people claiming minority status to prove their origin but exempt others from the same requirement? Discuss your response.

3. How should Harland Aldridge, human resource manager, develop criteria for determining the minority status of employees?

Hal's Harem

When the news broke, it broke big. Not only was Hal Harvey being involuntarily terminated, but 12 of his employees were charging sexual harassment against him. Hal was originally hired as a drafting technician for Sizeman Engineering and Technical Company because of his skill with computer-assisted design and computer-assisted manufacturing.

Hal's technical expertise and work quality quickly led to his promotion as supervisor of Drafting Services. Hal hired technically competent employees and formulated a training program that became a model for other departments. Upper-level managers considered Hal as a primary candidate for advancement to higher levels.

In filling vacancies in his department, Hal usually selected talented single women who were divorcees with young children.

Human resource management people supported his efforts to advance women in a male-dominated occupation. After training, Hal's women, as they were called, earned enviable records for productivity and quality. Although there were jokes about "Hal's harem," no one took them seriously until Peggy Krause blew the whistle.

"Let me tell you," Peggy began in a meeting with the managers of engineering and human resource management, "the only way to keep a job in the design department is to please Hal after work. None of us admits liking it but it's the price of keeping our jobs. When I refused to spend the night in a motel with him, he stated that he would make life less happy for me, and he has. I'm quitting and others are afraid to talk." An investigation of Peggy's claims proved them correct. Most of the women in Hal's department confessed that they had yielded to his demands. Some attempted to defend his actions but the majority felt it was a demeaning experience.

Based on overwhelming evidence, Hal was terminated.

1. How can unpleasant incidents like those in Hal's department be avoided?

2. Should Hal have been fired or given a warning? He was an excellent resource and manager for the corporation. Discuss reasons for keeping him as well as terminating his employment.

3. Why are sexual harassment cases more difficult than others to prove?

■ ENDNOTES

1. Daniel Wren, *The Evolution of Management Thought*, 3rd edition (New York: John Wiley & Sons, 1987), pp. 57–58.

2. Robert L. Mathis and John H. Jackson, *Personnel/Human Resource Management*, 5th edition (St. Paul, Minn.: West Publishing Company, 1987), p. 148.

3. Science and the Citizen, *"Postal Mortem," Scientific American*, February 1991, pp. 22–23.

4. George Manning and Kent Curtis, *Ethics at Work*, (Cincinnati: Vita Systems, 1988), p. 86.

5. Korn-Ferry is the nation's largest executive search firm. It has established an institute for the study of management at the University of California in Los Angeles. The survey quoted here was taken in 1989.

6. Based on *Kaiser Aluminum v. Weber*, a landmark case ruled on by the Supreme Court in 1979.

7. Charles McCoy, *"Taking Advantage," The Wall Street Journal*, February 12, 1991, sec. A.

Chapter 17

Supervisors, Trends, and the Ever-Present Future

■ ————————————————————————————— ■

Objectives

Chapter 17 is somewhat divided. It looks at both present and possible future trends. No one can be totally accurate in predicting the future. Supervisors and potential supervisors will learn to

- Identify process improvement techniques that lead to total quality management.
- Recognize and utilize the value of in-process recognition as well as results-oriented reinforcement.
- Employ simple process-control techniques.
- Define and utilize PADC.
- Utilize *kaizen* both in their lives and at work.
- Delineate their roles as change agents.
- Learn to learn from others.

Thought Starter

David Halbertson[1] and Mark Helprin[2] both feel the United States faces one of its most difficult eras. Halbertson points out that while we as a nation were obsessed with defense and war, Japan, and more recently South Korea, Thailand, Malaysia, and Indonesia, were obsessed with commerce. Japan set its goals as becoming a world-class exporter rather than a world-class military force. By any measure they have been successful. Their product design, quality, and marketing are constant and perplexing challenges to United States organizations.

Helprin's research focuses on the United States' heavy investment in military defense and establishing itself as the police force of the world rather than dealing with much more vital issues, such as our decaying infrastructure, declining educational standards, and impotency in dealing with floods of illegal aliens. While these issues may seem remote to most supervisors, they have an enormous impact on organizations and the way they are managed.

Executives in the United States realize that our ability to compete in global markets depends on quality and service. Supervisors have the responsibility for converting these goals into reality. With the emergence of the European Common Market, which possesses a workforce that is well educated, self-disciplined, has a driving desire to excel, and is one third larger than that of the United States, the vital role of all levels of management in the United States becomes even more significant.

American businesses are the driving force of our economy. They must achieve the quality, productivity, levels of innovation, and long-range views of global competitors. First-line managers must know more, be able to do more, and more accurately assess their effectiveness than at any time in the past.

■ *Tom Peters popularized a reality before it became fully realized in work organizations. In his best-selling* Thriving on Chaos,[3] *Peters points out that old ideas about management are not only outdated, but they force organizations into failure. He goes on to identify three driving forces that will influence the way managers conduct themselves both now and in the future.*

1. *Change will continue to accelerate in often unpredictable directions. Plans will be mandatory but in a state of constant alteration to meet new needs. Employees will require constant training to be able to meet organizational demands. Supervisors will become change agents. They will direct forces that affect employee effort.*

2. *Quality will be a driving force. Management in the United States has gradually, and often grudgingly, accepted the evidence that quality is both cost effective and mandatory for productivity. Quantitative standards are no longer supreme. How well people do things has become more important than how much they do.*

3. *Customers and clients determine whether an organization is performing adequately. "Take it or leave it," "caveat emptor" (let the buyer beware), and "more is better" approaches to managing are shortcuts to disaster.*

Supervisors are finding that they must deal with increasing higher-level management demands and work forces that are frequently undereducated and have little motivation to excel. They must be teachers, example setters, and motivators. It is a job that requires a sense of humor, insight, and willingness to work toward excellence.

■ LOOKING BACKWARD AND FORWARD

"When I was younger," Wolfe Nash began in a meeting with department heads and supervisors of manufacturing operations who reported to him, "I wanted to travel into the future. Now that I'm older, I find I have." There were smiles from younger members of the group and thoughtful looks from others.

"What was it like in *your* day, Doctor Nash?", Teri Perkins questioned, with part of her smile still remaining. "Damn it, Teri, this *is* my day! And so have been all of the others!" Wolfe's response was quick and emphatic. Teri joined others in the group in applauding Wolfe's recognition that today is not yesterday.

Wolfe Nash had worked for three major defense contractors after receiving a master's degree in organizational psychology from Yale University. His first assignment out of college was in personnel management as an employment interviewer. He quickly advanced to senior personnel specialist and then to department manager of employment. Looking back, he remembered that people were considered commodities much the same as machinery.

His job was focused on recruiting the best available people for the wage levels of their initial assignments, and then seeing that they were maintained, like machines. Benefits, fair treatment, simplified jobs that required minimal training, limited responsibility, and disciplinary action for deviations from rules were the oil and fuel that kept the work force intact. Procedures rarely changed and work was deliberately routine and repetitive. Once people learned a job, it was assumed their work would continue to meet standards barring unusual conditions such as equipment failure, supply shortages, or power outages.

In his second job as chief of personnel operations for a major aerospace company, Wolfe continued to see people as instruments of management. They were given orders, did what they were told, and received their pay. Relationships between managers and employees were impersonal and production oriented.

During this period Wolfe became aware of the emerging challenge of other countries as well as other organizations. He began to rethink the validity of bottom-line thinking that most universities were teaching as a fundamental management philosophy. Wolfe currently works as vice president of manufacturing for the same company. He continues to search for ways of improving the organization.

Bottom-Line Thinking

Bottom-line thinking concentrates on immediate profits rather than long-term organizational goals.

During the 1970s and 1980s when Japanese, European, and South Korean products began to gain dominance in some segments of consumer markets, United States managers focused on making as much money in the shortest period of time as possible. Their concern was the bottom line on an income statement. Executive performance was measured, and still is in many industries, by the profits a manager could generate in a given time. In order to enhance their positions, executives emphasized short-term goals that yielded a favorable bottom line. Long-range results of **bottom-line thinking,** taught by some of the country's most prestigious schools of business have been disastrous. Our products, compared to those of Japan and much of Europe, lacked imagination and quality.

Looking Forward

During the late 1980s it became apparent that changes were needed if we were ever to regain our competitive position in services and products. Some economists recognized that our overall standard of living was slipping when compared to other countries, and that if trends continued we would become little more than a source of cheap labor for our more powerful world competitors. Gradually, and often reluctantly, organizations in the United States have begun to realize that a new model, sometimes called a **paradigm,** was necessary.

A paradigm is a model or example.

Many useful management models have been developed during this century. All have contributed to improving operations at the time they were introduced, but no model has remained as it was originally conceived. Scientific management, human relations, management leadership style analysis, management by objectives, corporate culture development, and even cult-laden popular psychological theories and training have been used. It seems that organizations have been unable to find a persistent, workable way of building long-term effectiveness.

■ BUILDING A NEW MODEL

Concerned managers are attempting to restructure organizations to ensure their long-term competitive position. Three strongly related trends have emerged:

1. **Total quality management.** Total quality management is an evolving concept built on the quality management concepts of W. E. Deming, J. M. Juran, Phillip Crosby, M. Imai, S. Nakajima, K. Ishikawa, and their followers. Basic methodology was developed over 40 years ago but continues to be refined.

2. **Concern for customers.** Pleasing customers beyond their expectations is the key to long-term success. No advertisement is as effective as pleased customers who return with others.

3. **Team building.** Like total quality management and concern for customers, team building is not a new concept. It has, however, gained emphasis, with much of the social distance between employees and managers being minimized.

Organizations are beginning to pay more than lip service to these concepts. In 1989 John Walter Donnelly, chief executive officer of R. R. Donnelly & Sons, decentralized his organization in order to give customers more influence.[4] Like many others, Donnelly recognizes the importance of customers as a key to not only survival but growth in the future.

Speed has also become a tool for luring new customers and pleasing those who have supported organizations that meet their needs. The Limited, a major, innovative women's clothing retailer, rushes designs from the drawing board to its 3,200 stores in less than 60 days. Most clothing companies order in December what they expect to receive in May, 90 days longer than the Limited's cycle.

At Corning Glass Works, the nation's preeminent glass products organization, managers and employees have adopted quality as their central long-term value.[5] "Every employee," Corning's chief executive officer, Jamie Houghton, declares, "will spend a week or two more on additional training than we do now." Corning Glass is only one of the major corporations in the United States to recognize the value of quality.

In an environment of frequent change, increasing demands, and need for fast reaction times, teamwork is fast becoming more than an ideal. Many organizations see it as the core of their success. Supervisors are the key components of team building and team maintenance.

There is evidence that team building pays off. Top organizations such as General Electric, AT&T, Hewlett-Packard, Ford Motor Company, Brunswick, and Xerox have spent many hours training supervisors to become team builders and team leaders. In organizations of the next century differences between levels in jobs will diminish. Employees and managers will view their roles as different from each other but not necessarily inferior or superior.

Subordinate, a military term that designates someone of lesser status, is disappearing in many work organizations.

Subordinate, a military term to designate someone of a lesser status, will disappear in most organizations. People are already beginning to see teams as people with different skills, knowledge, and abilities but all necessary to make an organization effective.

■ TOTAL QUALITY MANAGEMENT

Over 40 years ago **W. Edwards Deming** realized that the key to profitability, cost effectiveness, and ultimate organization success depended on building quality into each step of every process in an organization. He strongly believed that the application of statistical-process control techniques to each step required to perform a task was more practical than inspecting the final product and

Total quality management concentrates on continuous improvement, statistical process control, and driving fear out of the workplace.

then making corrections. It proved to be a slow but highly effective way of improving quality, reducing costs, and providing customer satisfaction. Deming's concepts were initially viewed as too visionary or unneeded by management in this country. Quality control based on statistical sampling of completed operations was well established. Deming unsuccessfully argued that quality could not be inspected *into* a product after it was already made. It was necessary to control every step in manufacturing and every step in service operations.

Deming first presented his concepts at a time when Japan and Europe were still rebuilding their basic industries after World War II. U.S. industry dominated the world of international trade, and management felt secure in utilizing methods that had served them well for over 70 years.

When Deming took his message to Japan, it was embraced as a way of improving their manufacturing methods. J. M. Juran, a dedicated authority in application of statistical techniques to quality control, and Deming worked closely with Japanese industrialists and university staffs who taught their techniques. In a very short time Japan's image as a producer of second-rate goods with little ability to innovate changed. It rapidly reached a position of dominance in almost every area of manufacturing. Managers in the United States began to grudgingly admit change was needed in the mid-1980s. Years of work will be required to change systems to meet the challenge of not only Japan, but of Europe and other Asian countries as well.

Deming's Message

While statistical process control (SPC) remains a core concept, total quality management **(TQM)** has developed far beyond its early beginnings. Deming and others who envision total quality management as an always-developing process stress the need for change in traditional organizational thinking. There are many types of change-management techniques. Whether or not they are successful depends on the way they are used. Small step-by-step changes may be more significant over long periods of time than massive reorganization.

Kaizen means constant improvement on a daily basis. Small changes can make large differences over time.

TQM reexamines many traditional concepts. "If it works and works well, don't fix it," a common belief in many organizations, has been changed to, "If it works and works well, improve it." Constant improvement, the Japanese concept of *kaizen* (Ky'-zen), a recurring theme throughout this text, is the driving force of TQM. Employee-driven systems are another key. People do the work. They must be involved in every aspect of their work, including being able to measure their own effectiveness. As used in most organizations, other fundamental TQM concepts include:[6]

1. **Doing the right things and doing them right the first time and every time after with the goal of constant improvement.** This requires ongoing examination of every aspect of an organization to determine if it is in the best interest of the organization, its customers, employees, vendors, government agencies, employee groups, and others who interface with it.

2. **Close attention to each step in a work process with the intent of continual improvement that ensures correct results.** *Correct* means without variation from quality standards. This ensures that the final product or service will always be precise and accurate.

3. **Expansion of the term *customer* to include not only outside customers but managers, other departments, employees, vendors, and any group a company deals with.** Everyone to whom a company provides service, information, direction, or assistance is a customer. Customers are the people it depends on and who depend on it. This is a key to building effective working relationships under TQM.

4. **Recognition that *effort* while work is in progress should be rewarded as much as results.** Desired results are the product of correct effort and must be reinforced.

5. **Involving everyone in the organization in promoting its evolution toward constant improvement.** One of the distinguishing TQM assumptions is that managers alone cannot create total change toward improvement. Every segment of the organization must be involved.

Table 17.1 lists 14 principles of management change that Deming formulated as guidelines for development of total quality management in an organization.

Minimizing Resistance to TQM

One of the major impediments to organization improvement is the reluctance of managers to share power and relinquish some of their control. Executive management has the task of setting exam-

TABLE 17.1 ■ Deming's 14 Principles of Management Change

1. Create constancy of purpose toward management of products and services with the aim to become competitive, to stay in business, and to provide jobs.

2. Adopt a new philosophy. We are in a new economic age created by Japan. We can no longer tolerate delays, mistakes, or defective products.

3. Cease dependence on inspection to achieve quality. Eliminate inspection on a mass basis by building quality into the product in the first place.

4. End the practice of awarding business on the basis of price tag. Instead minimize total costs.

5. Improve constantly and forever the system of production and service to improve quality and productivity and thus decrease costs.

6. Institute training on the job.

7. Institute supervision. The aim of supervision is to help machines, people, and gadgets do a better job. Management at all levels must be overhauled.

8. Drive out fear so that everyone may work effectively for the company.

9. Break down barriers between departments. Institute teamwork involving all elements of the organization.

10. Eliminate slogans, exhortations, and targets for the work force that ask for zero defects and new levels of productivity. Most of the causes of low quality and low productivity lie in the system and thus are beyond the power of the work force.

11. Eliminate work standards that prescribe numerical quotas for the day. Substitute aids and helpful supervision.

12. Remove barriers that deprive hourly workers of their pride of workmanship. Remove barriers that rob people in management and engineering of their right to pride of workmanship. This means abolishing the annual or merit rating and management by objectives.

13. Ensure a program of vigorous education and retraining.

14. Put everybody in the company to work to help accomplish the transformation. The transformation is everybody's job.

ples for middle managers who in turn train supervisors. Supervisors have the ultimate task of introducing and involving employees in the change process.

Team approaches, when correctly developed, are effective in both involving employees and instituting meaningful total quality actions. Although quality circles, as originally conceived, have had a generally poor history in United States organizations, the work-team concept seems to have fared much better. Work teams are groups of employees who make key decisions about process improvement, needs for training, production control, and even selection of new employees.

A problem with the work-team concept is that many supervisors have little experience and training in team building. Since their own roles drastically change under TQM, supervisors and employees often view introduction of TQM as just another higher-level management gimmick. It is, in fact, a new type of operating and organizing. Change should be introduced in small increments, employees must participate, and education, training, and demonstration are required.

Fundamentals of Team Building

Team building is a key component of TQM. It involves development of close, effective working relationships among groups of employees.

In organizations that have successfully adopted total quality management, **team building** starts at the top. Executive officers and managers of their major organizational units form a multifunctional team that analyzes organizational problems and works together rather than independently to solve them. Development of long-term marketing strategies, as an example, may involve contributions of not only marketing managers and specialists but of specialists in finance, production, shipping, engineering, design, human resource management, procurement, and other support functions.

At the department level multifunction teams work together to develop approaches to projects that evolve from decisions by higher-level teams. Employee teams, however, are the most vital in actual improvement of quality and productivity. Many organizations have relied on outside consultants to assist in team-building activities. Relatively few companies or government agencies have the required expertise in their staff. It is a process that cannot be rushed. Even though people may know each other, working as a team in problem identification, process improvement, and implementation planning are usually unfamiliar actions. Since team members must become familiar with the basic statistical tools as well as making suggestions for improvement, time is required for teams to become fully functional. Effective team builders must have an in-depth knowledge of group processes in order to ensure that team members see their contributions as meaningful.

It is difficult to overemphasize the necessity for a change in management attitude. Management roles are those of facilitators, information providers, and coaches. Facilitation involves scheduling and arranging meeting space, providing materials for producing charts and graphs, and assisting in reproduction of materials if necessary. As information providers, they transmit project goals, technical data, and their own expertise if required. In coaching, supervisors act as advisors, evaluators, and offer suggestions for improvement.

Needed action is identified, planned, implemented, checked, and appraised by the team. Fully functional groups need very little supervision, resent interference with their planning and take ownership of their areas of responsibility. If errors occur, they make their own corrections. Groups may draw on the expertise of specialists if needed. Organizations that have effectively developed work teams have found improvements in quality, productivity, interest in organizational success, and increased motivation. Employees see themselves as having real controls over their work and are vital parts of the organization. They have a piece of the action.

Natural units of work are groups of related tasks usually performed in sequence or as part of a cooperative effort.

Group membership is based on natural units of work. A **natural unit of work** is made up of people who work in the same organizational unit performing similar or related tasks. As a team they also select their own spokespersons or leaders. Leaders may change frequently, depending on the type of problem or improvement that has been identified. In work-team operations *supervisors are not team leaders*. A common error in many organizations is to put an authority figure in charge of group activities. Responsibility for improvement in their place of work belongs to the team. A whole new level of trust in people is required by management. Table 17.2 summarizes major considerations in team building.

TABLE 17.2 ■ Team Building

1. Selection of team members is based on natural units of work.	Ideally, team members are from the same formal organizational unit and perform similar or closely related work that has a high degree of interdependence. Each person must, in some way, depend on others to successfully perform their assigned tasks.
2. Team training is essential.	Employee-centered quality improvement programs cannot succeed unless team members have a clear idea of their changed roles. Experts in team training utilize consensus building, role playing, and work simulation problems to build cohesive working teams. Supervisors rarely have the skills or time to train teams. Consultants or experienced trainers within an organization are usually used for initial training. Training steps are similar to those used for other types of on-the-job training. True team effectiveness develops over a relatively long period of time, although some teams will show immediate improvement in both quality and productivity.
3. Supervisors must change roles from rule enforcers to facilitators, information providers, and coaches.	Well-trained teams, with management encouragement, become essentially self-directed. Members identify what needs to be accomplished, plan, implement, and evaluate both in-process work and final results. They take responsibility for scheduling work, keeping records, and improving work. In some instances teams also conduct personnel-related activities such as selecting new team members, granting short-term leaves, and determining future personnel needs. Supervisors assist rather than direct; they evaluate team progress, share experience and expertise, and assist teams in obtaining needed supplies, equipment, and support services.
4. Top-management support of team approaches is vital.	Without enthusiastic support of team approaches to work improvement at every level in an organization, failure is almost certain.
5. Recognition that team-centered work does not apply to all situations and that teams are more than short-term group activities is essential.	In organizations where work is individualized and relatively independent of the actions of other permanent teams may be unworkable. Small group discussions and temporary teams such as focus groups and task forces that center on specific problems may be used effectively but usually do not have the long-term semiautonomous characteristics of true Total Quality Management teams.

■ PDCA

*PDCA are initials for
Planning, Doing,
Checking, and Action.
They are key TQM
concepts.*

Most TQM concepts are not in themselves new or unfamiliar. They differ from traditional management concepts primarily in the concept of constant improvement and in their emphasis on employee involvement in every phase of decisions that directly affect their work. Statistical tools are relatively simple: Pareto diagrams, cause-effect diagrams, histograms (bar charts), control charts, scatter diagrams, graphs (line graphs, pie charts, etc.), and check sheets are used in different applications.[7] Both supervisors and employees can be trained to construct and use them in a few training sessions. **PDCA** is an acronym for Planning, Doing, Checking, and Action, which are steps in making TQM a reality.

Planning begins with gathering information, defining processes involved in a task, developing standards, and formulating a series of actions to best complete a task. Each step in a process may have subprocesses that also require study. In order to hire a new employee, as an example, some of the processes involved are determining personnel needs; identifying required skills, knowledge, and abilities; making an employment requisition; recruitment of a pool of qualified applicants; reviewing applications; interviewing and testing those who meet required standards; and making the final selection. Each of these actions is a step in the total process of employment. In some of them, such as recruitment, several substeps may be required. Placement of advertising in newspapers, screening applications, and preliminary interviews are all subprocesses of the recruitment process.

Each process is studied and methods and standards incorporating improvements are included in the plan. Everyone involved in the employment activity is also part of a planning team that identifies the processes and the needed improvements. When the plan has been completed, the *do* segment of TQM is initiated. Doing involves more than implementing the plan. It also includes decisions by involved employees in how best to accomplish work within the framework of the plan, how to determine if it is being done correctly, and whether or not it meets standards. If potential improvements are evident, they will be incorporated in the next plan.

Checking is just what the name implies. Each process is examined to determine if standards are being met. In the case of employment, examination of effectiveness of the recruitment effort, screening techniques, testing and interviewing, and final selection will all be measured as they occur.

Action requires identification of errors and developing methods for preventing their recurrence. Based on experience in the doing and checking phases, new plans are made to incorporate changes to both improve processes and prevent repetition of errors. New standards are not set until the process has been stabilized. *Stabilization* means that work is accomplished at a predictable rate with predictable accuracy. Rather than PDCA, SDCA (Stabilization, Doing, Checking, and Action) is necessary before a new PDCA cycle is initiated. Figure 17.1 depicts the PDCA cycle.

SDCA, Stabilization, Doing, Checking, and Action, is necessary before a new PDCA process can begin.

■ KAIZEN—CONSTANT IMPROVEMENT

Cultural patterns in the United States are more complex than those of Japan. Japan has a very homogeneous society with stable values and an exceptionally long history of traditional ways people relate to each other in different environments. Reactions are much more predictable than those of a heterogeneous society where people have many cultural values and relatively unstable relationship patterns. Many American ideals, such as honesty, fairness, hard work, helping others, and individual responsibility, are not always ingrained as deeply as they are in older societies. Our independence is an unusual strength that also builds a frequently nonconformist work force.

Regardless of our complexity, the Japanese concept of *kaizen* can be a valuable asset. In its simplest terms it means ongoing improvement in our work, our social life, our personal life, and our home life. In work organizations *kaizen* applies equally to executives, supervisors, and employees.

FIGURE 17.1 ■ PDCA—Basic TQM Events

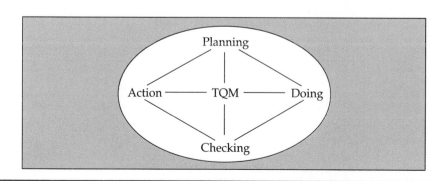

As a philosophy *kaizen* has the added advantage of showing people ways of improving all aspects of their lives. Small improvements on a daily basis mean large improvement over time. It requires a willingness to identify problems or weaknesses and then work on ways of solving or improving them, one step at a time. Table 17.3 lists some aspects of *kaizen* applied to organizations.[8]

■ TQM IN PRACTICE

Many U.S. organizations, including the Air Force Logistics Command,[9] Procter & Gamble, Hewlett-Packard, Ford Motor Company, Motorola, and Xerox, are finding total quality management concepts work and work well if properly and diligently applied. They require patience, which is often in short supply in many organizations, a willingness to look at long-term potential rather than short-term results, and reliance on people-driven systems.

Constancy of purpose is the driving force behind TQM. Once a philosophy has been adopted, it must be fully implemented for long periods of time.

Deming's first TQM principle, **constancy of purpose,** may be the most important and difficult for most managers. Time, patience, training, and believing that improvement is an unending goal are required. While near-perfection can be reached, change in technology, needs, and demands of people always offer new challenges.

TQM in the United States

Quality circles, a group involvement technique, have not had a high degree of success in the United States.

In the early 1980s **quality circles** became a popular concept in the United States. Managers, in their quest for improvement, have often been prone to adopt the latest fad in the same way that each season brings on new styles in clothing, hair, and other aspects of

TABLE 17.3 ■ *Kaizen* in Organizations

- Long-term, long-lasting, but undramatic improvement.
- Change is made in small steps.
- Improvement is continuous, a step at a time.
- Everyone in the organization is involved in change toward improvement.
- Teamwork rather than individualism is emphasized.
- Both conventional know-how and state-of-the-art techniques are used.
- Little investment but great effort is required to maintain continuous improvement.
- Improvement is people centered. Employees are the most important resource of an organization.
- Evaluation of processes and efforts has ultimately higher yields than evaluation of results.
- Visible results are slower than most U.S. managers desire.

life. Each lasts until it seems no longer applicable and is dropped. Quality circles grew out of TQM. In many Japanese companies, employees met and identified areas where improvement was needed. They set goals and charted their progress in achieving them. When quality circles were tried in the United States, unions objected because they saw them as a trick by management to increase productivity without increasing wages. When they were tried, little effort was given to building teams, an essential part of their success. Eventually they became less significant and now exist in a few isolated industries.

In organizations that have fully adopted TQM, team building has been an essential first step. As a nation that has stressed individual rather than collective effort, team effort is an often difficult ideal. It requires time for people to learn that they can achieve more working together in support of common goals than they can possibly achieve individually.

Supervisors can help build work teams, but they must let teams be their own managers. This requires a willingness to empower others to make decisions and take action. An extraordinary degree of trust in the intelligence and ability of employees is necessary. Training and viewing the role of supervisor as coach, evaluator, and goal setter rather than rule enforcer, disciplinarian, and director are essential.

■ MANAGEMENT—EVOLUTION OR REVOLUTION?

Supervisors, by the nature of their jobs, have always been concerned with the practical matters of getting work accomplished through people. They are charged with translating policy and resources into products and services. Theory, long-range views of the direction of their organization, and speculation about future changes are, for most supervisors, interesting but not significantly important. In an era of erratic change, those who intend to make the vital shift to increased responsibility and influence must develop a feel for major issues confronting management in general.

Management analysts have always been visionaries. Most of them, like Peter Drucker, Douglas McGregor, Frederick Herzberg, Rensis Likert, as well as the founders of management theory, Frederick Taylor, Henri Fayol, and Max Weber, had extensive direct experience in managing. Their writings are based on their personal encounters with organizational life as well as investigation and consultation. Each has offered his views of the way managers should manage.

Recent writers, including Drucker, have identified the adaptability and eagerness to meet new challenges head-on as essential in dealing with an environment of erratic change. As counseled by Deming, supervisors must also maintain a constancy of purpose. They should be able to define the goals of their organizations and work toward their achievement.

Management is evolutionary rather than revolutionary. Sudden changes in thinking are rare. New approaches to improvement are usually examined and tested before they become a permanent part of an organization's way of operating. While many concepts of the past are retained, new ones that modify past practices are introduced when need for change is apparent. Management is neither an art nor a science as much as it is a way of viewing organizations and understanding what is needed to make them effective.

Management in the Future

Third-wave management presumes that world changes drive change in organizations and management.

Dr. H. Alan Raymond, like other well-known management scholars, began his career with on-the-job experience. Both his organizational and academic credentials are outstanding. Raymond points to our era of management as the **third wave.** Basic changes in world civilization are reflected in the environment of managers of organizations. Prior to 1870 the world was essentially agricultural with cheap labor and cheap resources. Management consisted largely of treating people much the same way as any other work animal. Industrial-mechanical technology dominated the second wave and saw the rise of management, systems and management theory. Third-wave management which will take organizations into the next century, works in an environment of electronic-information technology with cheap information and increased knowledge. Emerging organizational forms will require new types of management thinking. Supervisors who are prepared for the changing future will be the survivors and leaders. Those who feel what works now will work in the future are already left behind.

Staying Ahead

Raymond doesn't make any distinction between middle managers and supervisors. Employees report to middle managers in his model. "If you are a middle manager [supervisor], you are the spark that keeps the organism [Raymond's definition of an organization] running and charged. Therefore you must know the corporation."[10] He goes on to state that first-line managers should write their ideas down and use them to influence the organization. "You must develop, mobilize, and stimulate people and resources." All employees, including managers and nonmanagers, should keep asking themselves, Who am I? and What do I want to be?

While Raymond's writings are somewhat poetic and philosophical, he envisions a future in which organizations are guided by four major goals:[11]

1. **Profits** allow thoughtful planning for the future and relieve undue pressure from the competitive environment. They ensure continuation of the firm.

2. **Growth** is required for an organization to remain alive and become increasingly competitive. It also provides challenge for its people on a continuous basis.

3. **Quality products and services to customers** to help build a partnership between the organizations and those who utilize its outputs. Again, this provides a stimulus for employees to excel.

4. **Creation of a great place to work** is essential to attract the best and brightest people and to keep them motivated.

In this type of environment managers must be hardworking role models who make things happen. Raymond's four goals are shown in Figure 17.2.

FIGURE 17.2 ■ Raymond's Major Organizational Goals

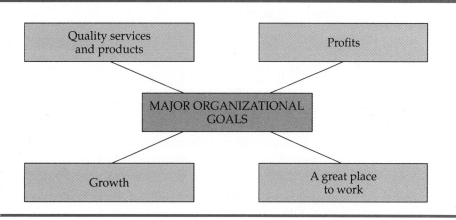

■ A NEW AGE FOR ORGANIZATIONS AND MANAGERS

As the year 2000 approaches, it is evident that a new world order is rapidly evolving. Broad alliances within the structure of the United Nations rather than unilateral actions or agreements are being relied on to solve problems. For managers the emergence of large trading blocks will have profound effects on their work and work forces. It is evident that the 1990 free trade agreement between Canada and the United States is a first step toward a western hemispheric trading block similar to that of the European Common Market Agreement of 1992. Similar agreements between trading partners of the Pacific Rim countries seem more than a possibility.

With greater access to traditionally closed markets, national economies will become less important than the total economies of major blocks. Current trends in internationalization of products and services and global operations of large organizations are certain to continue. It will matter little to managers of the next century where their organization is headquartered. Competition and cooperation will be, as it already is to a large extent, organization centered rather than focused on a specific national interest. Implications of this type of socioeconomic change are enormous. National boundaries, like those of Canada, the United States, and most European countries, already are essentially meaningless. People and trade flow from one country to another virtually unimpeded. If the present trends continue, as expected, common currencies and common languages are almost certain to emerge. Managers, including supervisors, will learn from others who may have different values, beliefs, and attitudes toward work. Learning from others as well as sharing knowledge may be the start of an emerging world culture.

■ HOW SUPERVISORS LEARN

Supervisor learning is often based on adoption of the attitudes and styles of other managers who appear successful without careful evaluation or knowledge of alternative approaches.

One of the problems in a changing environment is the way supervisors learn to be managers. Some organizations systematically prepare candidates for promotion by assigning people with additional responsibilities, making them assistants, and providing them with challenging opportunities to demonstrate their abilities. Others have formal training programs for recently promoted individuals to help them in the transition to full first-line management status.

Most people, unfortunately, who enter first-line management positions have little or no preparation. One day they were employees and the next they find themselves in charge of the efforts of others. Most of their knowledge of management has been based on what they have observed. There is a strong tendency to adopt the attitudes and styles of others who seem to be successful. New supervisors also try to gauge the expectations of their immediate manager. In their supervisory role they try to meet what they perceive as expectations and what they believe is an appropriate style. If they are in an organization that has good role models and expectations are clearly defined, their task is greatly simplified.

Those who make the shift from one level in an organization to another face the possible error of copying the wrong behavior. It is just as easy to learn incorrect attitudes and actions as it is to learn those that are positive and productive. If training programs are not offered, potential supervisors, as well as those who have made the first vital shift, can read, talk to successful managers at all levels, take advantage of training programs offered through community educational facilities, and become students of management as a career path.

Revisiting the Vital Shift

Holistic points of view picture organizations as many interacting parts that make up a whole rather than as a number of discrete parts.

Realistic self-assessment is a key requirement of all ambitious people who seek upward mobility in their lives. As organizations continue to evolve, knowledge of a specific type of work may be, in some instances, a limitation, unless it is coupled with an understanding of the total organization. Managers are increasingly required to take a **holistic point of view.** They must be able to picture their organization as many interacting parts that make a whole rather than as a series of separate functions. Their actions and decisions will affect others and to some degree the entire organization.

Political smartness, strong networking ability, high visibility, good communication skills, and willingness to accept challenge are necessary. In many organizations managers must also be willing to physically move if they make shifts upward in the organization. Those who are reluctant to accept assignments in new geographic areas will often find their opportunities for further promotion virtually eliminated. How much of my life do I want to give to an organization in order to move upward? is a question that managers must ask themselves if they find they are on any rung of the promotional ladder.

■ THINGS TO REMEMBER

I. Looking backwards and forwards.

   A. For much of this century, employees were treated like machines. Relationships between employees and managers were impersonal and production oriented.

   B. Change was forced by the emerging challenge of Japanese success in products, development, and sales.

   C. Bottom-line thinking focuses on short-range profits rather than products and services. Many organizations are guilty of bottom-line thinking.

   D. Gradually organizations have begun to realize that a new paradigm is necessary to be competitive.

II. A new model.

   A. Total quality management is an evolving concept built on the quality management concepts of W. E. Deming, J. M. Juran, Phillip Crosby, and others.

   B. Concern for customers is based on the knowledge that no advertisement is as effective as pleased customers who return with others.

   C. Team building has gained added emphasis. Social distance between employees and managers is being reduced. Use of the term *subordinate* in work organizations is fading.

III. Total quality management.

   A. W. Edwards Deming realized over 40 years ago that the key to profitability and organizational effectiveness depended on building quality into products and services.

   B. Deming's ideas are a driving force behind Japan's organizational excellence.

   C. Deming and others stress the need for change in organizational thinking.

   D. The Japanese word *kaizen* best describes the underlying total quality management philosophy. TQM requires doing the right things and doing them right the first time and every time after that. It requires constant improvement.

   E. Other steps in TQM are expressed in Deming's famous 14 points for organizational change.

IV. Minimizing resistance to TQM.

    A. A major impediment to improvement is the reluctance of managers to share power and relinquish some of their control.

    B. TQM involves employees in every step of the change process.

    C. Recognition of effort as well as results is fundamental to TQM.

    D. TQM defines customers as any individual or group to whom we provide services, information, material, or to whom we otherwise relate.

V. PDCA.

    A. *Planning* starts with organizational and process analysis.

    B. *Doing* implements the plan.

    C. *Checking* involves examining each process to determine if standards are being met.

    D. *Action* means developing methods for preventing recurrence of errors or deviations from accepted standards.

VI. *Kaizen.*

    A. *Kaizen* means continuous improvement in life and work.

    B. *Kaizen* emphasizes long-term, long-lasting, but undramatic improvement.

    C. *Kaizen* is people centered.

VII. TQM in practice.

    A. Many major companies are adopting TQM concepts.

    B. Deming's first principle, constancy of purpose, may be the most important as well as difficult for managers.

    C. Time, patience, training, and adopting an unrelenting effort to improve is required.

    D. Quality circles were generally poorly implemented in the U.S. They have become less significant and exist in few industries.

    E. An unusual degree of trust in the intelligence and ability of employees is necessary for effective team building.

VIII. Management—evolution or revolution?

    A. Management is evolutionary rather than revolutionary. Sudden change is rare.

   B. Alan Raymond views changes in society as dictating changes in management.

   C. Raymond believes that profits, growth, quality products, services to customers, and building an excellent place to work are keys to the new management era.

IX. A new age for management.

   A. European Common Market Agreement of 1992.

   B. Shrinking boundaries will change drastically the way countries trade goods and services.

X. Learning from others.

   A. Most supervisors receive very little training. They must learn from others.

   B. Realistic self-assessment is a key to self-development.

■ KEY TERMS

bottom-line thinking	**natural units of work**
paradigm	**PDCA**
subordinate	**constancy of purpose**
W. E. Deming	**quality circles**
TQM	**third-wave management**
team building	**holistic point of view**

■ DISCUSSION QUESTIONS

1. Why has the United States lost much of its competitive position in manufacturing?

2. Do you feel the United States will regain its position of leadership in the manufacture of automobiles, consumer electronics, and textiles? Justify your response.

3. Discuss your estimate of the potential success or failure of total quality management practices in the United States. Will TQM be another fad or will it be a long-lasting change?

4. Give examples of how people can apply *kaizen* concepts in their personal lives, in college, and at work.

5. Give examples you have encountered of both poor and excellent customer service. Why are some organizations able to survive even when their service is substandard?

■ SELF-ASSESSMENT

Each of the questions or statements listed below is designed to measure your beliefs, knowledge, and experience of management actions that contribute to *quality* operations. Use the scale to respond to each item by circling the number you think is correct. A 1, 2, or 3 indicates disagreement while 4, 5 and 6 show agreement.

1. Quality in organizations is best determined by the response of customers (clients, participants) to services or products.

   1   2   3   4   5   6

2. Regardless of all the theory, experience proves that **fear** is the strongest motivator: fear of failure, fear of embarrassment, fear of disapproval, and fear of being seen as incompetent.

   1   2   3   4   5   6

3. In most organizations, if not all, employees are responsible for approximately 85 percent of quality errors and management is responsible for about 15 percent.

   1   2   3   4   5   6

4. Good managers see themselves as problem solvers and crisis managers. When problems occur, they are there to solve them.

   1   2   3   4   5   6

5. Merit review systems consistently improve employee performance.

   1   2   3   4   5   6

6. Most management seminars and training are valuable ways to learn new methods and gain added knowledge.

   1   2   3   4   5   6

7. Managers with high expectations of their employees are more likely to be disappointed than those who are more realistic and expect only what they observe.

   1   2   3   4   5   6

8. One of the strongest motivators in a work environment is individual competition. Rewards for the winner, no rewards for the losers.

   1   2   3   4   5   6

9. Control means having a set of personal values and making sure others stick to them.

   1   2   3   4   5   6

10. Most people want to excel, to be challenged, and to contribute to their organization.

    1   2   3   4   5   6

■ SHORT CASES

Sony Works, and Works Well

Many standard-size Sony television sets sold in the United States are manufactured in San Diego, California. Sony's San Diego facility matches and often exceeds the quality of the company's Tokyo operations. While most of the employees who work for Sony in San Diego are U.S. citizens, their management is Japanese. All major decisions are discussed with groups of employees before they are implemented. They are frequently changed after employees have had an opportunity to make comments. There are few private offices, all managers are encouraged to eat in the company cafeteria and sit with groups of employees rather than other managers. They rotate from table to table on a daily basis. Nearly every employee knows all managers and supervisors by their first name. The only private parking place is for the company nurse.

While the pay and benefits are no higher than the average for similar work in the San Diego area, there is virtually no employee turnover. Employees tend to stay. Tardiness and absenteeism are rare. On three occasions unions have attempted to organize the employees. In each attempt the unions received overwhelming rejection. During its years in San Diego, Sony has never laid people off. During recessionary periods employees are reassigned to maintenance and clean-up work. There is an unusually strong support of the company by employees. Sony in San Diego works and works well.

1. What lessons can managers learn from Sony–San Diego's experience?
2. Why does management in the United States continue to operate in old and often ineffective ways while the world around them is changing?
3. U.S. high schools currently have a 30 percent dropout rate. What are the implications of an undereducated work force?

Working Well or on Welfare

When Janice Aldridge accepted a job with the Forest City School District as a member of the accounting department, she was eager to please, wanted to work hard and excel. After two weeks on the job learning systems and making friends with employees, Janice did her best to complete all work ahead of schedule.

"Janice," her new friend Paula Franzia told her during a break period, "stop knocking yourself out. No one around here cares if you miss a schedule. Just about everything is late. Management doesn't give a hoot one way or another." Janice was disturbed by Paula's comments.

"Here I am," was her opening statement to her husband, Harold, just after dinner, "trying to do my best and no one seems to care. I rarely see my supervisor, get my work from an in-basket with handwritten instructions, and then I read in the paper how the public is upset with our school system. It's no wonder! We operate in a vacuum. There are almost no rewards and no punishments. We have people just sitting around and doing as little as they can without getting into too much trouble. I don't even know where the cost reports I prepare every week go or if anyone even bothers to read them. There is absolutely no feedback. Why do I keep knocking myself out? It seems more like welfare than work. You get paid if you work, and you get paid if you don't."

1. If TQM was installed at the Forest City School District office, what steps would need to be taken first?

2. Give examples you may be aware of where employees have developed a "don't care" attitude.

3. Should Janice stay with Forest City School District, try to change the system, or leave for employment in a better-managed organization? Explain your response.

▪ ENDNOTES

1. David Halbertson is a well-known contributor to *The Washington Monthly.* His new book, *The Next Century,* (New York: William Morrow and Company), is fast becoming one of the most popular texts for both government officials and executive managers in organizations. It is also a valuable source of general information for first-line managers.

2. Mark Helprin is a well-known contributing editor of *The Wall Street Journal.* Helprin is considered to be an expert on foreign affairs.

3. Tom Peters, *Thriving on Chaos* (New York: Harper & Row, 1987).

4. Thomas Stewart, "CEOs See Clout Shifting," *Fortune,* November 26, 1989, p. 66.

5. Managing, "At Corning, a Vision of Quality," *Fortune,* October 24, 1988.

6. Adapted from Dan Costley and Ralph Todd, *Human Relations in Organizations,* 4th edition (St. Paul, Minn.: West Publishing Company, 1991), pp. 372–74.

7. There are several excellent sources of information on statistical tools of total quality. We recommend Masaaki Imai, *Kaizen* (New York: Random House, 1986) and The Transformation of American Industry, a set of training modules produced by Productivity-Quality Systems.

8. Adapted from Imai, *Kaizen,* p. 24.

9. Del Nelson, *"Total Quality Management and the Deming Method,"* 21st Century Leadership Conference, 1989.

10. H. Alan Raymond, *Management in the Third Wave,* (Glenview, Ill.: Scott, Foresman and Company, 1986), p. 224.

11. Raymond has examined many organizations that he feels are already in the third wave of management. Principles listed here are extracted from those utilized at the Rolm Corporation.

Chapter 10

Management as a Career

Objectives

Supervisors and employees exploring opportunities for promotion and those interested in career development will find that Chapter 18 enables them to

- Define personal success for themselves.
- Avoid common traps in career development.
- Assess their strengths and weaknesses.
- Recognize stages in career development.
- Identify personal characteristics necessary for management.
- Evaluate their life-style values.

Thought Starter

Although the figure changes as the number of employees increase and organizations adopt new patterns of operation, it is estimated that for every 10 employees there is at least 1 manager or person in a leadership capacity. With a work force of approximately 120,000,000 people in the United States, this translates into 12,000,000 management positions. If *manager* is considered to be a job title, it means that there are more managers than any other single job classification. Based on a conservative estimate, approximately 12 percent of these are replaced each year due to retirement, death, or other reasons. While our estimates are based on historical figures rather than current statistics, we believe a minimum of 1,440,000 new management positions are open each year.

Most of these, especially at the first-line level, are filled by present employees. Higher-level positions are based on promotions also if the pool of supervisors in an organization has the necessary skills, knowledge, and ability. When new departments are created or a need exists for special expertise, managers are recruited from outside sources. For employees who want to enter management jobs and supervisors who desire to make the next vital shift, the old Boy Scout motto, "Be prepared," holds true. While preparing for a management career does not mean automatic promotion, it enhances opportunities. Given a choice between two people of equal qualification, the one who has the extra education and training is more likely to be chosen.

In any career path, those who assess and upgrade their skills, prepare for the position above the one they presently hold, and build effective relationships with higher levels in their organization are candidates for promotion.

■ *When Alicia Daviu entered Congress Community College, she was like many other students. If people asked her what she would like to do after she graduated, Alicia generally responded, "Something in business, or maybe science. I think economics would be good also." It was clear that she did not have a direction she wanted to go. The Cheshire cat's advice to Alice in Wonderland was "if you don't know where you're going, any road will take you there." Alicia tried several roads. She was a good student and took courses in mathematics, computer science, business, economics, art, and literature. Her grades were excellent but she enjoyed economics and literature best. Her efforts at Congress Community College earned her a scholarship to Capital University. Since economics seemed interesting and offered an opportunity for work with a state agency after graduation, it became her major. In her junior year she obtained a job with a local television station as a traffic reporter, primarily because a friend had recommended her and she was willing to arrive at the studio every morning at 5:00 A.M. and get computer and telephone reports from the local highway patrol, police, and air surveillance. Her voice was pleasant and after a few months of being an unseen voice, she began making her reports on camera.*

At the close of her senior year at the university, Alicia was offered a graduate fellowship that would pay her fees in a master's degree program. She continued her work at the television station and acted as a teaching assistant to one of the economics professors. When one of the local news announcers suddenly left the station because of a severe illness, Alicia was asked to fill in. In a few weeks she had a regular fan club. Her appearance, her somewhat humorous approach to her fellow announcers, and intelligent questioning of guests increased her popularity. On the day Alicia received her master's degree in economics, she was also offered a full-time position as news anchor for a major television station in Chicago. Now she is seen on national television and her future looks even brighter. A major network has offered her a job as news director.

When a friend recently asked, "What does a master's degree in economics have to do with television?" Alicia smiled. "Not much, but I'm glad I have it."

■ ANY ROAD WILL TAKE YOU THERE, MAYBE

Some careers, like Alicia's, are accidental. She started out in one direction and found she fit best in an entirely different arena of work. Other careers are planned. Some children choose the same career path of one of their parents. Christie Hefner, president of Playboy Enterprises, is noted for her management ability after taking over the presidency of the company founded by her father. Three generations of the Ford family ran their automobile empire before they found professional managers could do it even better. Others find intense interests at an early age in life and make those their career.

Planned careers are built on goal-directed education and experience.

Most **knowledge workers,** with special training such as accounting, computer science, chemistry, medicine, journalism, law, architecture, art, music, and all of the hundreds of other professions, have planned their careers. They were able to define what they wanted to do, obtained the necessary education and experience, and ultimately made their plans a reality.

Getting into Management

Few people enter into management positions without work experience. Often a person's first supervision jobs develop rather quickly. Students who work in fast-food outlets and show a willingness to accept responsibility, direct the activities of others, and train new employees often get shift-leader, crew-chief, and similar assignments. In some cases they may become store managers.

Entry-level management jobs may have a variety of titles that imply leadership responsibility and authority.

Since the fast-food industry has a high employee turnover rate, opportunities are better than in most places of work for initial leadership jobs. Most organizations do not promote as readily as retail outlets that depend on short-term employees. When opportunities present themselves, employees who show initiative, intelligence, and are able to define and solve problems are primary candidates for entry-level management work.

A number of organizations hire management trainees. Typically trainees in these assignments work harder and longer hours than other employees but receive similar pay. Often the term *management trainee* is little more than an inducement to accept a relatively low-level position. Organizations also have assistant positions that are awarded to employees with management potential. Unlike the trainee, who may or may not be in a true training position, assistants frequently are acting managers and receive valuable on-the-job leadership experience.

Who Wants to Manage?

Not all people want to be managers. Rather than directing others, most people are comfortable letting others make decisions and define tasks that need to be accomplished. A number of individuals prefer to work at tasks that interest them and not be bothered with being responsible for the activities of other employees. There are probably more reasons people do not wish to enter management than there are for wanting to make it a career. Although managers do not need any definite personality characteristics, they must have good communication skills, a strong desire to get things accomplished, and a willingness to manage.

Although many people tie management positions to money, myriad jobs pay well but are not in management. Many salespeople make as much or more money than their managers. Professionals, such as lawyers, physicians, scientists, engineers, airline pilots, designers, and architects, just to name a very few, can earn as much or more than many managers. While some top management jobs pay very well, they are not the only positions that offer substantial incomes.

People who develop into managers are willing to use their influence to make things happen. Getting things accomplished is more important to them than being liked, although they are usually able to build effective working and personal relationships. They have confidence in themselves and are willing to risk failure rather than not act on things they strongly think should be accomplished. When they are a member of a work team, they tend to strongly support and defend the group's decisions. Good managers would rather report to someone who is intelligent and capable with personality characteristics they do not admire than to a manager with an outgoing, warm, and friendly personality who they view as indecisive and only marginally competent.

As a start on self-assessment, answer the questions below. They do not measure potential success or failure but do indicate some of the types of questions potential managers must ask themselves. Respond as honestly as possible.

Managers are individual human beings and vary as much from each other as does the population in general. No two have precisely the same personality characteristics, the same approach to their jobs or to people, or the same way of solving problems. Here are some thoughts about the statements in the "Do You Want to Be a Manager?" questionnaire.

1. If you answered 1, 2, or 3 it indicates others believe you have leadership or management ability. If they do, you've made the first giant step.

Do You Want to Be a Manager?

1 = Usually 2 = Often 3 = Sometimes 4 = Occasionally 5 = Rarely 6 = Never

1. People ask me to be a group leader or meeting chairperson at work and social meetings.

   1   2   3   4   5   6

2. I let other people's opinions strongly influence my actions and thoughts.

   1   2   3   4   5   6

3. It is easier for me to go along with the group than to state my own opinion.

   1   2   3   4   5   6

4. I try to have other people do things the way I think they should be done.

   1   2   3   4   5   6

5. It is easier for me to let others speak for the group than to be its spokesperson.

   1   2   3   4   5   6

6. It is easy for me to get others organized in social and work situations.

   1   2   3   4   5   6

7. It bothers me to have responsibility for the success or failure of a group.

   1   2   3   4   5   6

8. My personal values and ideas are worth more than compromise to avoid conflict.

   1   2   3   4   5   6

9. Managers tend to give their employees too much responsibility and authority.

   1   2   3   4   5   6

10. In the final analysis the way to get people to do things is to manipulate them.

    1   2   3   4   5   6

2. Managers evaluate what others say. They listen for information, analysis, and new ideas, not opinion. Good managers will answer 5 or 6.

3. Leaders are not hesitant to state their own opinion. They will answer 5 or 6.

4. A characteristic of good manager-leaders is their belief in themselves. They want things done the way they think they should be accomplished. Just as a good coach or quarterback calls the plays, good managers clearly define their expectations.

5. Managers are usually the spokesperson but will let others answer on occasions. They will answer 4, 5, or 6.

6. Part of leadership is being able to organize others. It starts at the playground and continues through life. Managers and potential managers will respond with 1 or 2.

7. A characteristic of effective manager-leaders is a willingness to accept responsibility for the actions of those who report to them. They will respond with a 5 or 6. They will take full responsibility for failure of their employees but are quick to give them credit for success.

8. When their personal values are challenged, effective managers will be true to themselves even if it means personal risk. This does not mean inflexibility in dealing with issues involving several possible alternatives. Managers will respond with a 1 or 2.

9. Many managers are reluctant to grant authority and hesitant in increasing responsibility. It is possible to give unqualified employees greater responsibility and authority than they can effectively deal with. Knowledgeable managers will respond with a 4 or 5.

10. Good managers do not have to manipulate. They explain, define, and are honest with their employees. Manipulation implies hiding facts, attempting to trick people into action, and setting people against each other. No manipulator can succeed forever. Employees are quick to sense insincerity and game playing. Effective managers mean and do what they say. They will answer with a 6.

Evaluate the results of the questionnaire carefully. Do you feel you are management material? If so, what do you need to strengthen? If your scores are not like those of managers, do you want to change or does management seem a better goal for others?

■ CAREERS AND CAREER PLANNING

A career is a sequence of jobs and work pursuits that a person does for a living.

There are many definitions of the term *career*. Douglas Hall[1] states that a **career** is "the individually perceived sequence of attitudes and behaviors associated with work-related experiences and activities over the span of a person's life." A simpler definition is *a sequence of jobs and work pursuits that a person does for a living.*[2] Careers may follow from specialized education or develop from job experiences. Over a person's work life their job content is almost certain to change, although they can remain in the same career path. A **career path** is the sequence of training, jobs, and experiences that constitute their total work history.

A career path is the sequence of training, jobs, and experience that constitutes a person's total work history.

Managers, as an example, may have been trained in accounting and began their career working in an accounting function.

Over time they may have been promoted to office manager, senior accountant, manager of financial planning, controller, and ultimately chief executive officer. Most of their career has been in the management of financial functions. Some will never leave their initial level of work and remain accountants most of their lives. This type of career path directly stems from education, interests, and available opportunity.

Necessity and Opportunity

Necessity and opportunity may be driving forces in career development rather than conscious, systematic planning.

Other career paths stem from necessity and opportunity. An individual with training in business may, out of need, accept a job as an employment interviewer, move to another human resource management assignment, such as training, labor relations, or compensation administration, and ultimately accept a management position in that field. People without specialized training usually have a series of jobs and finally settle into an activity that they have learned, can do, and enjoy doing. People tend to stay in work that offers financial security and meets other needs. People without specialized training or educational experiences may gain restricted expertise in a specific area over a period of time. **Restricted expertise,** in this sense, is knowledge and skill that is not easily transferred to other organizations.

Restricted expertise is skills and knowledge not transferable from one job to another.

When Thiokol Chemical Corporation reduced its work force at the company's Brigham City, Utah, facility due to a reduction in aerospace contracts, many workers had difficulty finding other jobs. For periods as long as 20 years they had worked in the manufacture of solid propellant rocket engines. Although the laid-off employees were experts in the manufacture of rocket engines, their knowledge and expertise could not be easily transferred to other types of work.

Skills are transferable to other organizations.

Skilled employees are those who can transfer their knowledge and experience to a variety of other organizations. People with training in computer programming, machine technology, construction, or any other knowledge-based field of work have little difficulty in transferring their skills.

Regardless of whether careers have stemmed from education or need and opportunity, careers are likely to change, even if a person remains in the same general field. It is not uncommon for people to develop several career paths over their work life. Quick learners may seek opportunities in new fields out of interest and a sense of exploration.

Career Planning

Career planning does not guarantee that an individual will follow a well-ordered career path. It does, however, provide helpful steps.

Career planning stems from what a person wants from their work and their life.[3] Although career planning does not guarantee that an individual will precisely follow a well-ordered career path, it provides a series of helpful steps. Here are a few suggestions:

1. Accept the fact that all career development is self-development. No person can decide what another should or will do. These are decisions that people must make for themselves.

2. Career planning begins with self-assessment. As a starting point, divide a sheet of paper into three columns (it may be easier to use three separate sheets). In one column list the types of things you like to do or have interest in learning. Include hobbies, recreational activities, and work. Title the next column "Things I don't like to do or have no interest in learning." Think of the types of things you dislike, procrastinate most in accomplishing, as well as those you have no interest in learning. In the third column list the things you can do whether you like them or not. People often find themselves succeeding in jobs they do not particularly like. Match the can-do list with the like-to-do list. This gives you a start on the next step.

3. Rank the items you like to do or would like to learn in order of their importance. Place 1 by the item that is most important, 2 by the next most important, and so on. Your ranking should not separate what you like to do and what you would like to learn. Some like-to-learn items may have a higher rank than like-to-do items.

4. Build goals around the highest-ranked items. Assess your strengths and weaknesses and develop plans for increasing levels of competence. What kind of additional education and experience is needed? Develop a plan for obtaining what you want and then do it. These points are reinforced by Figure 18.1.

Getting Started

Tom Peters advises people entering the field of work to find a place they would like to work, go there, and take any job.[4] Don't, he states, try to make the first job a career. That first job can offer a base for exploring other possibilities. He also advises those en-

FIGURE 18.1 ■ Career Development Facts and Actions

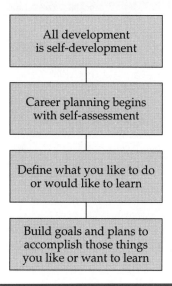

All development
is self-development

Career planning begins
with self-assessment

Define what you like to do
or would like to learn

Build goals and plans to
accomplish those things
you like or want to learn

tering the world of work to take risks. If the job a person has is one she or he does not like, she or he should find another one. His advice may not fit everyone. For those who have not focused on definite career paths, it is one way to start exploration of the world of work.

Before accepting a job offer, it is a good idea to learn something about the cost of living in the area. As an example, the same standard of living that a $32,100 salary will provide in San Diego would only require $25,000 in St. Louis. Most university libraries subscribe to the American Chamber of Commerce Researchers Association *Inner-City Cost of Living Indexes,* which are updated quarterly. A quick comparison can be made of what a salary will buy. For every $100 expenditure in food, clothing, and housing in New Orleans, which has a cost of living that represents the national average, $127 is required in Washington, D.C.

■ TRAPS

Traps are any types of behavior that prevent or slow career development.

Careers are sometimes blocked by self-imposed **traps** that people build for themselves. Most are psychological. When people reach what is often referred to as a *dead end,* they are faced with several

FIRST-LINERS

alternatives. One possibility is to stay where they are, another is to seek a job in the same or another geographic area, or they can begin a new career path. Fear may prevent any alternative other than accepting the dead end.

The thought of moving to another area is, for many, traumatic. They don't want to break away from the security blanket of parents, friends, and familiar surroundings. Fear of failure can also be a deterrent to career development. If an individual has a secure job and finds the work acceptable, they may be willing to stay where they are, even if advancement is virtually impossible. Every individual must assess their personal values. Other considerations may be more important than career development. Table 18.1 briefly summarizes some common career traps.

Working for Friday

Not everyone values a career or is genuinely interested in furthering their own self-interests. Organizations with custodial climates often create large numbers of employees who work for Fridays. **Custodial climates** are those in which management deliberately restricts employee responsibility to a specific job assignment. People know their jobs, do them, get pay and benefits and little else. They may develop friends at work, find their jobs acceptably interesting, and realize that opportunities are limited by policies that emphasize seniority over ability and conformity over innovation and involvement. Working conditions may be acceptable or good but there are few incentives other than pay and benefits or punishment if standards are not met.

Custodial climates are those in which management deliberately restricts employee responsibility to a specific job assignment. People know their jobs, do them, and go home.

TABLE 18.1 ■ Common Career Traps

Economic traps	Financial obligations are one of the primary deterrents to change. People may want to change but fear the financial consequences of leaving a job to find another. They may also fear being discovered seeking other employment and thus endangering their present position.
Inertia traps	Even though the work is no longer satisfying and they know they must eventually move in order to advance their career, some people procrastinate to the point of no return. The longer a person is in one job, the more difficult it becomes to move. This is especially true if they have not been promoted or changed assignments in several years.
Geographic traps	Unwillingness to physically move from a particular geographic area can stop or slow career development. Whether with the same organization or a new one, geographic moves often open new opportunities for career development.
Success traps	There is an old saying the "Generals can win only one battle. After that they are reluctant to try new challenges." Some people who have successfully achieved promotion or recognition are reluctant to change. The next battle, they feel, could be lost.
Outside interests	Occasionally people will confuse careers with other interests. Hobbies, avocations, friendships, or other interests are more important than career development. They must weigh their long-range values. It may be that their career is of secondary importance.

In a custodial climate people feel that they leave their brains at the door and pick them up again at night. People learn that the biggest incentive is the end of their assigned work shift on Friday. Most of their lives are spent **working for Fridays.** They find that they are in both inertia and economic traps. Their jobs provide for them and do not require too much effort. Eventually, if they stay long enough, they may receive promotions, but the climate will not drastically change. They continue to work not only for Friday but the **ultimate Friday,** when they retire.

Working for Fridays means working for the weekends and freedom from work.

Ultimate Friday is retirement.

■ CAREER DEVELOPMENT PLANS IN ORGANIZATIONS

An increasing number of organizations are encouraging employees to participate in career-development programs. In addition to providing incentives for employees, they serve as a means of identifying employees with promotion potential. Nearly all career-development plans are voluntary. Organizations will pay for additional education related to jobs and some will even sponsor graduate-level education. They also encourage on-the-job development and sponsor a number of career-development training activities.

One of the better-designed career programs has been developed by United Airlines. Every employee is given literature describing and encouraging career development. One of the pamphlets is called *Career Development Workbook*.[5] Its introduction states:

> Years ago it was not uncommon for an individual to get a job with a company at an early age and work there until retirement. Today many people change jobs and companies throughout their careers . . . .Many individuals find it difficult and intimidating to plot a course to achieve personal goals within a large company, let alone to explore a rapidly changing marketplace.
>
> United Airlines recognizes this difficulty and seeks to provide opportunities for its employees to develop their careers and achieve personal goals.

In their own self-interest as well as that of employees, organizations are recognizing the benefits of encouraging self-development. United Airlines has developed a six-step plan that guides employees through the program:

1. Values. Employees determine the importance of personal values, such as competitiveness, cooperation, economic security, job fulfillment, personal relationships, power, recognition, responsibility, self-development, and stability. Each value is compared to others and ranked. For some employees power may be ranked highly and personal relationships low. Others may have quite different rankings. Values help determine the employee's type of job interests and areas of ambition.

2. Knowledge and skills. Employees are provided forms for helping them identify and assess skills and knowledge they have obtained throughout their work history.

3. Goals. General long-term career objectives are developed and short-term goals designed to help achieve the long-term objectives.

4. Strengths and development needs. Employees determine the skills and experience required in the management job that interests them. They then compare their present skills and knowledge against the requirements to determine development needs.

5. Action plans. Plans to turn development needs into strengths are developed. Plans include specifics on what an employee

will do, when it will be accomplished, and what standards are to be achieved.

6. Meeting with first-line management. Participants in the program meet with their supervisors to discuss career development. All of their previous actions are summarized on a career transformation form to facilitate discussion and begin implementation of the action plan.

United Airlines then states that career development and advancement are not easy and do not just happen. It is an ongoing process. Benefits are a direct function of the time and resources an employee invests in making her or his plan a reality.

■ CAREER STAGES

Career stages are changes that occur in career paths during an individual's work life.

Daniel J. Levinson[6] is one of the most quoted authorities on changes in career patterns during a person's lifetime. Although Levinson and his team's studies dealt primarily with men, he found that it was impossible to separate men and women when discussing careers. Women, he states, go through the same stages. Each stage consists of approximately five to seven years of a person's life.

Ages 17–22, breaking away. This is the period when individuals must successfully break away from family ties and become their own person. Although they may still be partially dependent on parents for income (e.g., college students), they enter young adulthood as emotionally independent. Those who fail to make the break often underperform on their jobs and find breaking away later in life very difficult.

Ages 22–28, lifestyle selection. During this period people enter the adult world. Their initial formal education is completed, career and life-styles are selected. Individuals become preoccupied with getting into the adult world. Those without a career path may make extensive searches for satisfactory career goals.

Ages 28–33, transition. Personal progress is checked during this period and individuals make the decision to stay on the same track or make a break to other geographic locations and get away from their established patterns. For many it is a period of personal instability. Divorce rates are high in this age group. There is a feeling of "now or never."

Ages 33–40, settling down. Career advancement and striving to establish personal identity are a consuming interest during this period. Some may seek mentors to help steer them along the right path. Those uncomfortable with authority may find going it alone—sometimes unproductively—easier than seeking a higher-level sponsor.

Ages 40–45, mid-life crisis. For some, *transition* is a better term than *crisis*. This is the second deep assessment and often results in dramatic changes in careers and life-style. For those who are satisfied with their progress, it can be a time of reward. Feelings are often on edge. If careers have not attained the degree of satisfaction desired, sadness, resignation, anger, and other emotions may be evident. When change is made, it is usually to an entirely different career path.

Ages 45–50, middle adulthood. Old relationships are renewed, new ones are developed more consciously, and people's concern about work constraints on their personal lives and their work becomes more evident. It is in this period that people recognize that further advancement is not likely to occur. For some it can be a period of satisfaction and fulfillment as psychological maturity enables them to cope more effectively with life problems.

Ages 51–54, Transition. Awareness that retirement is approaching creates yet another transition. People review their earlier mistakes and failures and have strong feelings of self-recrimination. People who successfully weathered the mid-life crisis may undergo a degree of anxiety and feelings of dissatisfaction during this period.

Ages 55–60, End of middle adulthood. Stability and acceptance that career is ending is a common reaction. It can be a period of rejuvenation and personal enrichment. Long dormant interests may be revived and new ones developed in a noncompetitive personal environment.

Ages 60–65, retirement. Most people retire during this period. It is a period of deep reflection and change—in their view of themselves and the way they are viewed by others. Some people are happy to leave their careers and find freedom to pursue interests not allowed by pressures of the past. For others the transition is difficult and fully realizing their status is a painful experience.

Ages 65 and older, summing up. Without work pressures many find this a period of freedom. As long as their health remains good, they pursue activities that they once avoided because of work and financial pressures. Others are plagued with financial and health problems and experience a continuing period of difficulty. As one of the most rapidly growing age groups, a great deal more research is needed to fully understand the effects of this period.

■ SUCCESS

Success, the ability to define and achieve goals, is usually a matter of degree. Few people achieve what they consider total success.

Definitions of **success** are elusive. For some it is symbolized by money, status, and recognition. Success for many is embodied in being admired by others. Some people see success as rearing and providing for a family and taking pleasure in their achievements. Financial independence at retirement can also be a hallmark of success.

Success is a matter of degree. People may feel moderately successful if most but not all of their goals and ambitions have been achieved. While others evaluate the success of individuals they know or know about, the final definition rests with individuals. We may feel entirely successful in some areas of our lives but recognize failures in other areas. Ultimate success is measured by the ability to set, achieve, and evaluate challenging and enriching goals. Table 18.2 describes people by the track they are on.

People in management let success be more than another trap. It is better to have a degree of **creative discontent** than to feel that any apparent goal achievement solves all problems or entirely solves any problem. Creative discontent is the awareness that no individual or organization can stop improving and changing because of apparent attainment of difficult goals.

Allness

Allness is the belief that an individual knows all that can be known about a situation, person, or field of knowledge.

William Haney[7] has identified a special impediment to success that he calls *allness*. **Allness** is the conviction that a person knows all about a given problem, topic of discussion, group, organization, or set of conditions. This belief of total knowledge makes investigation and inquiry seem superfluous. Why examine something when everything is known? It is impossible to know all about anything. Scientists point out that every truth is only a truth until further investigation is made. We can never know or say all about anything.

TABLE 18.2 ■ Tracks and No Tracks

Fast tracks	Through a combination of resources, including preparation, selection of opportunities, effort, political sensitivity, and willingness to take personal risks, some employees advance rapidly in their career paths. These fast-track employees are usually identified by higher levels of management as having potential for management positions. Fast trackers are willing to move to other employment if they find themselves at a dead end. Fast-track employees believe in making their own luck.
Moderate and slow tracks	Some employees depend on seniority, special experience, and being in the right place at the right time for making shifts to higher levels of authority and responsibility. They represent the majority of those promoted to lower-level management jobs. Diligence, hard work, and perseverance rather than a broad knowledge of the organization powers their upward moves. Slow-track employees are often handicapped by unwillingness to move from a specific geographic area, place of employment, or to consider alternative careers.
Sidetracks	Employees who prepare for a career in a specialized field may find themselves working in an entirely different arena due to a variety of conditions. Someone trained in accounting, as an example, may find themselves working in procurement operations, human resource management, or procedures development. While they may be successful in the new career field, their original goals are sidetracked.
No track	Without preparation or planning, many employees accept jobs primarily because of availability. They learn necessary skills to adequately perform their jobs and rarely advance into management-level responsibilities. Some will resist opportunities for promotion if their jobs meet needs for a reasonable standard of living and are personally satisfying.

Managers, especially those interested in enhancing their careers, must keep an open mind that is willing to listen to conflicting points of view, investigate before making judgment, and assume that there is much that they do not know. People who quip, "Don't confuse me with the facts," may be making a joke. If their actions say the same thing, success will be an elusive goal.

■ ALL DEVELOPMENT IS SELF-DEVELOPMENT

Career development is,. in the final analysis, self-development.

Managers who are able to reach their career objectives recognize the importance of self-determination. They depend on their own resources more than those of others to make critical life decisions. Their outlook on life is from an **existential** frame of reference. Full acceptance of personal responsibility for their own success or failure typifies their behavior. They are defenders of their employees but are also their coaches. Like all coaches they know that they, not players, are given credit or fault for the performance of their team.

■ THINGS TO REMEMBER

    I. Any road will take you there, maybe.

        A. Some careers are accidental; others are planned. Most knowledge workers have planned careers.

        B. Few people enter into management positions without work experience.

        C. Trainee and assistant positions are designed to lead to management positions.

    II. Who wants to manage?

        A. No definite personal characteristics qualify a person for management, however, people entering management must have good communication skills, a strong desire to get work accomplished, and a willingness to manage.

        B. Management is not the only career that offers substantial incomes.

        C. Managers differ from each other as much as human beings do in general.

    III. Careers and career planning.

        A. A career is a sequence of jobs and work pursuits that a person does for a living.

        B. A career path is the sequence of training, jobs, and work experience that constitutes a person's total work history. Career paths often stem directly from education, interests, and available opportunities.

        C. Some career paths are influenced by necessity and opportunity more than special training and primary areas of interest.

        D. People without specialized training frequently take a series of jobs and finally settle into an activity they have learned and can adequately perform.

        E. Expertise gained in specialized organizations is frequently not easily transferable to other types of companies or job assignments.

   F. Skilled employees and those with training in knowledge-based fields of work have little difficulty transferring skills.

IV. Career planning.

   A. Career planning provides useful steps that can lead to a long-time career.

   B. All career development is self-development. It begins with self-assessment.

   C. Tom Peters advises exploring possibilities. Don't necessarily make the first job a career.

   D. Careers are sometimes blocked by self-imposed traps. Traps include economic, inertial, and success traps.

   E. Fear is the most significant obstacle to career development.

   F. Being tied to a specific geographic area can also block career development.

   G. People who work for Fridays often are in a climate where there are very few rewards or punishments if work meets minimum standards of performance.

   H. A large number of organizations provide career-development assistance in the form of educational grants, special training programs, and other incentives. One of the most clearly defined plans is offered to employees of United Airlines.

V. Career stages.

   A. Levinson has identified stages people go through in career development.

   B. Each stage is a period of approximately five to seven years when significant changes in both personal outlook and career development occur. Individuals may react differently in each of the stages that Levinson has identified.

VI. Success.

   A. *Success* can be defined in many ways: money, admiration by others, having a worthwhile job. The final definition of *success* rests with individuals.

   B. Creative discontent is the awareness that no individual or organization can stop improving and changing because of apparent attainment of difficult goals.

VII. Allness.

    A. Allness occurs when an individual believes she or he has total knowledge of a subject and is unwilling to learn more.

    B. Managers must not adopt allness points of view, which may prevent their objective examination of data.

VIII. All development is self-development.

    A. Excellent managers recognize the importance of self-determination.

    B. Good managers have developed an existential frame of reference, they recognize they are responsible for their own successes and failures.

■ KEY TERMS

knowledge workers	working for Friday
career	ultimate Friday
career path	career stages
restricted expertise	success
career planning	creative discontent
traps	allness
inertia traps	tracks
geographic traps	existential managers
custodial climates	

■ DISCUSSION QUESTIONS

1. What types of careers interest you most? Be realistic in your answers.

2. What are you currently doing to make your career interests a reality?

3. Is management a bona fide career or an outgrowth of work in a specific field? Explain.

4. How do you define *success* for yourself?

5. List some personal strengths and areas that need improvement. How are you planning to improve areas of potential weakness?

■ SELF-ASSESSMENT

Are you currently on a career path? Indicate your degree of disagreement with the following statements or questions by marking a 1, 2, or 3. A response of 4, 5, or 6 indicates degree of agreement.

1. I have clearly identified what I feel is a satisfactory career path for myself.

   1   2   3   4   5   6

2. Most of my career-choice decisions are based on advice from others.

   1   2   3   4   5   6

3. Many career paths[8] have not developed yet but will emerge in the future. Are you willing to investigate potential as well as present opportunities?

   1   2   3   4   5   6

4. Are you willing to move to another geographic area to develop your career?

   1   2   3   4   5   6

5. Your work may change several times during your career. Change does not create anxiety or fear in your life.

   1   2   3   4   5   6

6. You dislike (or would dislike) being responsible for the work of others who report to you.

   1   2   3   4   5   6

7. Periodically you assess your strengths and weaknesses.

   1   2   3   4   5   6

8. Your interests tend to focus on specific areas rather than on many subjects.

   1   2   3   4   5   6

9. It bothers you to deal with ambiguity. You want clear yes or no answers.

   1   2   3   4   5   6

10. You can clearly identify goals you would like to achieve and develop plans to achieve them.

   1   2   3   4   5   6

▪ SHORT CASES

Harry's Choice

Shortly after finishing college with a degree in chemical engineering, Harry Arden accepted a job with a large natural gas transmission company. His new organization piped natural gas from the Gulf Coast to most northeastern states. As a measurement engineer, Harry was responsible for the quality and quantity of gas that entered the company's system on the south-central coast of Texas.

As Levinson's model of change predicts, Harry's career began to develop as his family was becoming larger. His hard work and expertise paid off with promotion to regional measurement engineer and ultimately an offer from a competitor to join them as chief measurement engineer and to be in charge of two state-of-the-art laboratories designed to do very precise computer analysis of gas components.

In his new job Harry was responsible for the work of 26 other engineers scattered over the Gulf Coast from Texas to Florida. Harry's reputation as an expert in gas technology grew steadily. He was, however, surprised when an offer came for him to move to the company's headquarters in Tampa, Florida, as vice president of engineering.

After a careful assessment of what he really liked to do, his family's stability, and the necessity of uprooting their lives, he called the company president and rejected the job. Harry knew that it would be his only opportunity for further promotion. Once an opportunity is offered, it is seldom offered again.

1. Did Harry make the correct choice? Why?
2. If faced with a similar situation, what would you do?
3. What are the ultimate consequences of rejecting a job opportunity?

Building a Career Path

Early in this chapter some techniques are reviewed for identifying and implementing career plans. Develop a career plan for yourself by utilizing the methods discussed in the section of the chapter entitled "Career Planning."

It may be helpful to work with a partner after the plan has been completed to help determine if important factors have been omitted. Review the results with your instructor or a member of the counseling staff at your college.

▪ ENDNOTES

1. Douglas T. Hall, ed., *Career Development in Organizations* (San Francisco: Jossey-Bass, 1986).

2. John R. Schermerhorn, *Management for Productivity,* 2nd edition (New York: John Wiley & Sons, 1986), p. 641.

3. James R. F. Stoner and R. Edward Freeman, *Management,* 4th edition (annotated instructor's edition) (Englewood Cliffs, N.J.: Prentice Hall, 1989), p. 754.

4. Extracted from a speech given by Tom Peters to the graduating class of the University of California at Berkeley, May 19, 1990.

5. United Airlines, *Career Development Workbook.*

6. Daniel J. Levinson, et al., *The Seasons of a Man's Life* (New York: Alfred A. Knopf, 1978).

7. William V. Haney, *Communication and Interpersonal Relations* (Homewood, Ill.: Richard D. Irwin, Inc., 1986), pp. 305–307.

8. Daniel A. Burrus, "Managing Your Career," *The Wall Street Journal,* Spring 1991, p. 6.

Appendix A
Self-Assessment
Questionnaire Discussions

Chapter 1

1. (6) A primary characteristic of good managers is their willingness to accept responsibility for not only their own actions but for those of their employees.

2. (1, 2) Except in the most unusual circumstances where physical conflict may be a possibility, good supervisors perform both pleasant and unpleasant tasks without assistance. This includes both reprimands and involuntary terminations.

3. (1, 2) It is true that productive people are usually better satisfied with their jobs than those who are, for the most part, unproductive. A supervisor's job is not to create happiness but to develop conditions where people are productive, like their work, and support the efforts of the organization and its management.

4. (1) Supervisors are managers and not "just another employee." Employees expect supervisors to make decisions, properly assign work, assist them with information when needed, and most of all act like managers.

5. (1) Effective managers at all levels in an organization, including supervisors, lead rather than manipulate. Manipulation implies psychologically tricking people into some type of action. Good managers explain, coach, delegate, and assist employees. They are honest, open, and supportive of employee efforts to excel.

6. (1, 2, 3) It's true that some jobs require specific sequences of work in order for the work to be correct. Individual differences, however, make it virtually impossible for everyone to perform a given task exactly the same way. What may be best for one person is not necessarily best for another.

7. (1, 2, 3) Some types of work have been automated to the extent that complex tasks can be accomplished by literally pushing a button. For the most part newer technologies have required that employees and managers both know more and be able to do more. Innovation and flexibility are essential ingredients for most types of work affected by newer technologies.

8. (1, 2, 3) Change for the sake of change has never been a good idea. Good

managers know that no matter how well things are going, improvement can be made. They also know that, when things are going well, there is a tendency to become complacent. Many of the best supervisors have adopted the motto, "If it works, make it better," rather than the old, "If it works, don't fix it."

9. (1, 2, 3) Some U.S. products, such as aircraft, supercomputers, pharmaceutical products, and petroleum production equipment, are recognized as the best in the world. Consumer products and some manufacturing materials, unfortunately, do not have the same reputation. Our image in Japan, Korea, and most of Europe is that of a country that has sacrificed quality for productivity and price.

10. (1, 2) Good supervisors concentrate on creating conditions that lead to productivity and quality in their organizational units. Well-trained, motivated employees control themselves and correct their own errors, and little or no disciplinary action is required. Self-discipline is always better than discipline from managers.

Chapter 2

1. (1, 2, 3) Supervisors, regardless of where they work, usually perform many similar functions. Their jobs differ widely, regardless of similarities, because of differences in organizational requirements. Supervisors in a dairy have different duties and required activities than their counterparts on a construction site, in a bank, or in a large department store.

2. (1) All supervisors must know how to plan, direct, control, and organize the work of others. They must also lead, motivate, make decisions, and communicate. Ways in which these basic functions and activities are conducted depends on the type of work, the manager's personal characteristics, and the employees.

3. (1, 2) Supervisors are responsible for everything that takes place in their work unit. They are accountable for their own activities and those of their employees.

4. (1, 2) Unfortunately, supervisors are often selected before they have had any experience or training in management. Their performance, aggressiveness, and dedication to work are often the basis for selection rather than their skills in dealing with people.

5. (1) Planning is one of the most essential management skills. Effective supervisors must know what has to be done, who will do it, why it is being accomplished, when it must be completed, and how it will be done. Answers to these questions are the foundation for planning in organizations. Without planning there is no organization.

6. (1) Directing involves delegation, coaching, assigning work, training, correcting, and counseling on problems. It includes far more than simply making work assignments.

7. (5, 6) In times of crisis, dealing with employees who lack self-discipline, and solving critical problems, supervisors must frequently be direct and forceful. Management requires being *tough minded*. This means never

forgetting that the primary job of management is to accomplish, through the efforts of employees, the work of the organizational unit.

8. (1, 2, 3) A good sense of humor always helps break tensions and make work more pleasant. Even when using humor, employees should know that the supervisor is serious. A common mistake some supervisors make is using inappropriate humor about serious subjects. This can lead to employees incorrectly interpreting the urgency of a particular job.

9. (1) Control involves having standards, measuring to determine if standards are being met, and taking appropriate corrective actions if they are not being met. None of these actions are manipulative.

10. (4, 5, 6) On rare occasions employees are involuntarily terminated because of incompetence. Most people are fired because of difficulties in their relations with others, especially their management, or poor attitudes toward work. This is especially true in organizations where employees must deal directly with customers.

Chapter 3

1. (6) A primary management job is directing the activities of others. If a person feels uncomfortable doing this, she or he should stay out of management.

2. (1, 2, 3) There is usually a little guilt when a manager is not truly busy. Most experienced supervisors know that work usually comes in spurts and that there are rare moments when they find themselves caught up with their work. Such times can be used for needed reflection, assessment of future actions, and momentary relaxation. Feelings of guilt for doing a good job are unwarranted.

3. (1) Martyr complexes are very real. Supervisors who are overwhelmed with work and see others less busy often feel they are the only ones making a genuine effort to achieve.

4. (1, 2, 3) Organizing work so work will flow smoothly is a primary management function. It is a set of skills that require recognition of what needs to be done, planning, and initiating actions and coaching employees. Excellent managers see it as one of the fun parts of their jobs. For those who are inexperienced, it can be a slow and frustrating process.

5. (5, 6) With the exception of highly specialized departments such as a research and development activity, middle managers are concerned with project planning, costs, delegation of work to first-line managers, and other administrative matters that have little relationship to technical aspects of work.

6. (1, 2) Supervisors should not do work normally assigned to an employee except under the most extreme circumstances where employees are overloaded with work and emergency deadlines must be met. Employees will never learn or become competent in performing various tasks if the supervisor does the actual work. Some employees become skilled at keeping the boss busy by feigning ignorance, lack

of experience, or inability to do a specific task.

7. (4, 5, 6) It is not always necessary to assign work to the person who can do it best. Other employees will never learn a particular job if they have no opportunity to do so. It is wise to have members of a work team knowledgeable and competent in several areas in the event of absences or work overloads. Good managers spread assignments, even though they recognize employees may become somewhat specialized and very adept in certain types of work.

8. (1, 2, 3, 4, 5, 6) This is an "it all depends" statement. Highly trained, experienced employees who have worked with a given supervisor for a long period of time usually recognize what needs to be done and rarely have to be given directions. When it is necessary, they usually understand immediately. In other instances, with less knowledgeable employees or new assignments, directions must be explained, discussed, and reexplained. People do not always listen carefully and they frequently misunderstand what is wanted.

9. (6) Fear of criticism is a strong demotivator. People will avoid responsibility in order to avoid criticism. "If I don't do anything, I won't make any mistakes."

10. (4, 5, 6) Trust depends on individuals. Supervisors who have trained their employees well and have developed good interpersonal relations usually have a high degree of trust. Lack of trust in employees is usually an indication of an insecure and incompetent supervisor.

Chapter 4

1. (5, 6) Everyone has some difficulty with decision making at times. A characteristic of good managers is their willingness to make decisions for both their personal and work lives. While they evaluate available information and examine alternatives, they do not procrastinate or vacillate in making decisions.

2. (1) Alternatives are important. They cannot be developed, however, until the need for a decision or problem has been identified and objectives developed that indicate what the decision is intended to accomplish.

3. (5, 6) Good decision makers make their decisions carefully and rarely change their minds. Everyone, they recognize, is faced with decisions that must be changed under certain conditions, and good managers recognize the need for flexibility. Even so, they tend to stick to their decisions unless overwhelmingly proven incorrect.

4. (6) Some side effects of selecting a particular alternative are positive, some are negative. Working overtime, as an example, may allow a critical schedule to be met but can also add significantly to costs.

5. (1) Follow-up is always necessary. There is a degree of uncertainty in nearly all decisions.

6. (6) No decision will work in an organization unless it is accepted by both managers and employees as a positive, workable alternative.

7. (6) Frequently group decisions have a higher rate of acceptance and are of better quality than those made by individuals. If an employee or manager has special expertise or the decision must be made in a very short time period, individual decisions are best.

8. (1) Good decisions are best made when there is a precise description of the problem that includes all significant data.

9. (1) As discussed in item 1 above, good decision makers do not procrastinate.

10. (1, 2) With the possible exception of those involving mathematical equations, mechanical operations, or scientific applications, most problems have several possible solutions that are equally effective.

Chapter 5

1. (1) The positive benefits of good performance and the value of rules should be emphasized in new employee orientation. Fear and poor work attitudes in response to implied threats are powerful demotivators.

2. (1, 2) Money and security are essential for personal well-being but have little motivational value. People who get periodic increases in pay at work rarely work more effectively or efficiently. Money can be a motivator if it is tied to other goals such as status, self-esteem, or achievement.

3. (1, 2) Managers can do a great deal in helping people feel they belong and are accepted in an organization. Introducing new employees to others, expressing that they are pleased the new employee has joined the organization, and simple courtesy can all help a person fulfill social needs at work.

4. (5, 6) Good managers feel they make their own luck. It is true that they must be where opportunities exist to advance in an organization. Their dedication, degree of expertise, willingness to accept responsibility, and relations with others are the most important factors in advancement.

5. (1) Good managers must effectively work with others, communicate well, and be leaders. They do not try to manipulate or fool people into actions.

6. (1, 2, 3) Obviously exceptional people can usually be identified as well as those who lack skills, knowledge, and motivation. In most instances the performance of people depends on their attitudes, beliefs, values, and perceived relationship with their managers, other employees, and their organization. They cannot be easily classified.

7. (1) High expectations usually result in high performance. Managers who express high expectations of employees are communicating belief in their competence and ability to achieve. People usually rise to the expectations of others, especially those in positions of power and authority.

8. (1, 2) Good managers reward good performance and work to improve poor performance. They realize that many factors can cause poor performance other than an employee's unwillingness to work. Analysis and correction rather than punishment are emphasized.

9. (1, 2) It is impossible to treat all employees exactly alike in order to be fair. Conditions under which the employee is working, individual differences in behavior, and even length of service with an organization all affect management treatment of employees.

10. (1, 2) One of the most common misconceptions is that anyone can make another person think that it is his or her idea when it isn't. Sincerity beats manipulation every time.

Chapter 6

1. (1, 2) Dominant, egotistical managers deal from what they perceive is strength. Firm, factual, equally firm positions are far more effective in dealing with them than is compromise seeking and being too friendly. Dominance respects dominance.

2. (1, 2) It is usually very difficult to prove someone is wrong from their point of view regardless of evidence. A better approach is to listen without judgment and try to repeat their position back to them. People are much more willing to listen to alternative positions if they recognize that others are giving them equal consideration.

3. (1, 2) What is perfectly clear to one person may be equally unclear to another. Clarity, conciseness, and correctness in communication are invaluable tools but, in themselves, do not guarantee understanding.

4. (1, 2) For centuries managers have believed that they are the decision makers and employees are the doers. Managers are gradually realizing that one of the best ways to improve productivity, quality, and commitment to organizational goals is to involve employees in decisions that affect their jobs.

5. (1) Psychologists have known for years that eyes may be far less expressive than other facial characteristics. From the time of childhood people learn to effectively mask their true feelings. Forget about reading a person's eyes to tell her or his true feelings.

6. (1) Each level in an organization is a communication bottleneck. Too many messages must get to the next level of management. Upward communication is minimal in most large organizations.

7. (1) Information overload is an all too common reality. Supervisors frequently give employees more directions than they can absorb. As a result errors occur and mistakes are made.

8. (1) There are approximately 15,000 usages for the 500 most commonly used words in the English language. Most words are interpreted by the context in which they are used, rather than by their precise definitions.

9. (5, 6) Good managers try to reduce social distance by being highly visible, accessible, and good listeners.

10. (1, 2, 3) Compromise seekers rarely win. Tough battlers and problem solvers are far more effective. There are times when compromise is necessary. Problem definition and logical solutions are far more effective and better accepted.

Chapter 7

1. (5, 6) Good managers are the primary spokespersons for their formal group. When conditions warrant, they encour-

age employees to join with them in representing group consensus.

2. (1, 2, 3, 4) Under many conditions participative leadership works. There is, unfortunately, no one best way for managing under all conditions.

3. (1) If there is a strong degree of confidence and trust between managers and employees, control becomes a secondary issue. Employees, with rare exceptions, will control themselves. Douglas McGregor pointed out that less control means more control. It is a management paradox that is very true.

4. (1) Fear teaches people what not to do rather than what to do. In specific short-term conditions it can be a powerful motivator. At work it depresses motivation. People who are fearful of making mistakes work slower and often make more rather than fewer errors.

5. (1) There is no leadership formula. A style of leadership that works well in one set of conditions may be totally inappropriate in others.

6. (6) In a crisis a leader must be decisive, action oriented, and in total control. Followers will respond if required actions are clearly defined.

7. (1) One of the best ways to enhance power is to share it with others; especially those who are members of the same work team.

8. (1) As stated several times previously, high expectations tend to yield high results. Low expectations yield low results.

9. (4, 5, 6) Good leaders are goal oriented. They enjoy the support and friendship of followers but achievement comes first. Followers tend to rally behind success, even if they objected during the initiation of a particular task.

10. (1) As stated earlier in this questionnaire, there is no one best way to lead.

Chapter 8

1. (5, 6) Although they are not perfectly complimentary, reward power and coercive power are closely related. Both are used to induce employees to act. In many circumstances, one can be the absence of the other. Lack of coercion may be a reward, just as coercion may be lack of a reward.

2. (6) Legitimate power is often called *position* power. It is the power of the office rather than the person.

3. (5, 6) Although other types of power such as expertise and referent power are more useful, legitimate power works better at lower levels of management than at higher levels.

4. (1, 2, 3, 4, 5, 6) Expert power is useful to anyone who has expertise in a specific skill or area of knowledge. While it is especially useful for managers, it can be equally useful for employees.

5. (1) Referent power is the least tangible of all forms of power. It is based on respect, admiration, and confidence— all highly individual perceptions. Personality factors are often important in building referent power. Referent power is the most intangible of all types of power.

6. (6) Managers frequently use the expertise of nonmanagement experts in their decision making. In such cases the

nonmanagement employee has strong influence over higher level decisions and ultimate actions.

7. (1) Politics may be either positive or negative. In many instances people are helped rather than harmed by political actions.

8. (1, 2, 3, 4) Effective political action is usually based on actions that will help the organization achieve its goals. In some cases insecure and often inept managers respond to flattery, compliments, and "yes" persons.

9. (6) As stated earlier, empowering others is an effective method for gaining and enforcing total personal power.

10. (5, 6) Supervisors need the same power symbols as other supervisors in the organization. Without the symbols they are perceived as having less influence.

Chapter 9

1. (4, 5, 6) Nearly everyone wastes some time. Good first-line managers learn to use their time efficiently with minimum waste. If they are serious about time analysis and time saving they will periodically maintain a time log to determine where time is wasted and can be better utilized.

2. (5, 6) One of the most effective ways of creating extra time is learning to read fast. Fast readers remember more and are able to handle paperwork more efficiently than slow readers.

3. (6) Although it is a relatively old concept, management by exception is a good basis for prioritizing projects. Those that have the most problems are identified and corrected first; those with fewer problems are examined later. Exception means giving priority to major problems.

4. (4, 5, 6) For most first-line managers paperwork is a real problem. If they are efficient, they learn to separate junk mail from that which needs immediate attention and paperwork that can be filed. Needless to say, junk mail can be thrown away immediately.

5. (6) One of the best ways to gain time is to respect the time of others. They will extend the same courtesy to you.

6. (1, 2, 3) It is a good idea to complete least interesting tasks as soon as possible after very high-priority items. There is a tendency to procrastinate on needed actions that are not interesting. Do not wait. Get around to doing them now!

7. (1) Started work is a much stronger motivator than unstarted work. If you want to get a job completed, start it now.

8. (5, 6) Andrew Carnegie, one of the most successful managers of the early part of this century, planned each day's work at the end of the previous day. He also kept a tablet and pencil by his bed so he could replan at night. We don't need to adopt his night habits but his ideas of prioritizing work are excellent almost 100 years later.

9. (6) Tom Peters advises people to "Show up; show up on time; and show up ready to play," if they want to be successful. Good supervisors are time conscious.

10. (6) Successful managers at all levels know the power of delegation. Although they may have pet projects that they enjoy, good managers delegate as much as feasible to others.

Chapter 10

1. (1) Absolutely not! Good cost management recognizes that at times it is necessary to spend money rather than cut costs to enhance profits. Advertising, upgraded computer equipment and software, training, and a host of other activities may improve profits. Cost control, not letting costs run wild, will always be necessary.

2. (1) Effective cost management takes a long-term view. Profits in the future may be more important than the immediate bottom line.

3. (1) Planning must always precede action. Cost-reduction efforts can proceed only if there is a clear understanding of what, when, where, why, and how costs will be examined and controlled.

4. (1) Many supervisors, unfortunately, feel they have little cost-management responsibility. In actual practice cost-control effectiveness is largely dependent on supervisors and employees being conscious of the necessity for cost economy.

5. (1) Pareto's law states that the vital *few* are far more important than the trivial *many.*

6. (6) Good supervisors know that employees are one of the best sources for identification of cost problems. By seeking their involvement they not only increase commitment to effective cost control but they also involve employees in vital organizational issues.

7. (1) Organizational analysis is the first step in the development of cost-management plans. Knowledge of where duplication of effort, waste, theft, and other negative cost practices exist is vital before any reasonable planning can be accomplished.

8. (1) Weekly pep talks have little, if any, effect on cost reduction. Employees generally view them as unnecessary and unwanted.

9. (1) Priorities are necessary in cost-management activities just as in any other aspect of management.

10. (1) It has been demonstrated many times that correction of specific problems is far more effective than attempts to apply the same actions to all parts of an organization.

Chapter 11

1. (1) In a world of change, retraining has become the norm in most organizations. Obsolescence of skills due to technological change, new methods and procedures, and changes in assignments all require some degree of retraining.

2. (6) Everything a supervisor does affects employee behavior. Supervisory work habits, either good or bad, directly affect employee performance. Modeling, by copying others, is one of the most common forms of training.

3. (1, 2, 3) Punishment rarely improves performance, whether harsh or not. We advocate immediate correction of problems. Supervisors should not tolerate poor performance. Problem analysis, coaching, and encouragement are often better corrective measures. In instances of blatantly destructive or rule-breaking behavior, enforcement of prescribed penalties should be immediate.

4. (1) Employees who perform specific tasks daily can nearly always outperform their supervisors. Coaches of sports such as basketball and football know how positions should be played and how to advise their players. Like supervisors, they cannot play the game nearly as well as their trained athletes. Supervisors, like coaches, must know how to do the job but need not necessarily be expert performers.

5. (1) Experience is an unreliable teacher. Bad experience teaches the wrong things. Good experience may teach the right things but be incomplete.

6. (5, 6) Psychologists have recognized for many years that short learning sessions are more effective than long continuous ones.

7. (1) Rates of learning for individuals vary tremendously. Some people learn specific skills easily and rapidly while others labor for long periods of time trying to develop the same type of proficiency.

8. (1) Talented people frequently practice the most in order to further perfect their skills. Great pianists, golfers, artists, and others practice constantly to keep their skills at peak levels.

9. (1) Simple repetitive jobs are dull, boring, and stifling for most people. Jobs that are challenging, require utilization of training and experience, and have variety are usually preferred.

10. (5, 6) Both negative and positive reinforcement work but positive reinforcement usually works best. Negative reinforcement teaches avoidance while positive reinforcement teaches achievement.

Chapter 12

1. (1) There is a great deal of truth in the old saying, "All work and no play makes Jack or Jill a dull kid." Most successful managers find time to get away from their jobs in some form of exercise or recreational activity.

2. (1, 2, 3, 4) Fast eaters are often people who hurry other aspects of their lives as well. While fast eating can be just a bad habit, it can also be an indication of inability to relax.

3. (1, 2, 3, 4) Dedicated supervisors and employees are frequently irritated by the apparent slowness of others. Compulsively high performers expect others to meet equally high standards of performance. Few do or can. If you are one of these superascendants, try to learn to relax.

4. (1, 2, 3) One of the real indicators of excessive stress is chronic insomnia. Try to find its causes and make personal adjustments. If it continues for long periods of time, professional counseling may be warranted.

5. (1, 2) Excessive impatience is an indication of a closed-minded, compulsive personality with unreasonable expectations of both self and others.

6. (5, 6) Failure is normally upsetting for short periods of time. A psychologically well-adjusted person learns to "roll with the punches" and view occasional failure or errors as opportunities for improvement.

7. (5, 6) For many people work is their most important activity. Part of a complete life is finding other interesting and rewarding activities as well.

8. (5, 6) No matter how expert people are or how well they have done, their inner core of values, beliefs, and attitudes form the basis for solid relationships with others.

9. (5, 6) Success is the ability to define realistic goals and achieve them. Power and wealth are marks of success only if the person who has achieved them feels successful independently of other, and perhaps more important, needs.

10. (4, 5, 6) Most people have periods when they feel some degree of anxiety or slight depression. Well-adjusted personalities experience such feelings far less than those lacking psychological maturity.

Chapter 13

1. (1) Experienced managers try for win-win solutions to problems as much as possible. They know that making people feel like losers is counterproductive. Only in games and sports are losers necessary.

2. (1, 2) Conflict usually results in a degree of frustration and stress. By the same reasoning, frustration and stress can lead to conflict in an attempt to relieve their causes.

3. (1, 2, 3, 4, 5) Compromise usually means settling for something no one really likes but can accept. In some instances it is the only way to settle conflicts. Development of new ideas, problem solving, and reasoning based on accurate information is usually a more productive way of resolving conflict.

4. (5, 6) Provided the conflict is not violent or angry, problem solvers see conflict as natural and desirable in the development of good decisions and acceptable problem solutions.

5. (1, 2, 3) While friendship is always valuable, working relationships are usually based on mutual needs and co-operation to achieve mutual goals. Interdependence makes working for common objectives mandatory.

6. (1) Tough battlers stick to their decisions. They know what they want and are un-yielding even though they may be wrong. Friendly helpers do not impress them and are looked on with disdain.

7. (1, 2) Supervisors are frequently caught between requirements of upper management and needs of employees. They understand both the employee's perspective as well as that of management. This leads to the inevitable conflict of having to take the point of view of an employee or that of a manager. Role conflict is common in many types of situations.

8. (1) Conflict management should always focus on a specific problem or set of conditions.

9. (1) Threats of any kind elicit defensive behavior. This is especially true if fundamental beliefs and values are threatened.

10. (1) It is unfortunate that people who need the greatest amount of help in doing their jobs correctly often become "bleeding sharks." When other employees see a person with job difficulties, they often add to the person's misery rather than provide needed assistance.

Chapter 14

1. (1, 2) There is no evidence that annual performance reviews improve employee morale or performance. Studies made by General Electric Company researchers over a period of years indicate that annual reviews may actually depress performance. W. Edwards Deming states that they should not be given.

2. (1) Nearly all rating systems are rater dependent. This means that the rating depends on the rater. With the exception of those based solely on countable unit performance, such as the number of keystrokes a computer operator makes per hour, rating systems are to a large extent subjective.

3. (1, 2, 3) Some high performers make good supervisors. There is little relationship, however, between performance and supervisory ability. A good word processor operator may not make a good office manager or an excellent salesperson may not make an equally competent sales manager. Skills and knowledge of doing are markedly different from those of managing.

4. (5, 6) One of the advantages of performance appraisal forms is that all employees are rated the same way. Although the ratings may not reflect true performance, they are standardized for all employees.

5. (5, 6) Both MBO and BARS systems utilize actual job components rather than general terms such as productivity, quality, knowledge, attendance, and so on. Although they are difficult to both prepare and administer, MBO systems and BARS ratings have many advantages over standard rating scales.

6. (1) True discipline implies self-control. It means learning rules of behavior and following them.

7. (1) Problems should be corrected as soon as possible after they are detected. Corrective measures have much greater effect if used immediately.

8. (6) Employees who dislike their managers, other employees, or working conditions frequently file grievances out of anger and a need to act or seek revenge for perceived unfair treatment.

9. (6) People who are good accountants may make very poor salespeople. Those with expertise in computer programming may be very poor human resource specialists. Being good at a particular job does not guarantee high performance in other assignments.

10. (1) In the sense that it is used in management, redirection means a person should seek other types of work either within the organization or with other organizations.

Chapter 15

1. (1, 2, 3) Competent human resource management specialists can assist supervisors in many ways ranging from affirmative action problems to recruitment of special types of skills and knowledge. Even those human resource management departments with less competence can be valuable as sources of records, information on legal mandates, and as final arbiters of problems involving personnel policy.

2. (6) Supervisors are the primary human resource specialists in organizations. They deal with personnel problems on a daily basis and have responsibility for many policy-related functions including labor-management relations, equal opportunity, performance appraisal, training, recommendations for promotions or transfer, and disciplinary action if necessary.

3. (1) AIDS is a relatively difficult disease to transmit to others. Direct exchange of bodily fluids is its source of transmission. Presence of the HIV virus does not mean a person has AIDS. Studies indicate that periods as long as 10 years may elapse before HIV develops into AIDS. There is no indication that performance is diminished by the presence of the virus.

4. (1) Alcoholism is the most common employee life-style disorder. Few organizations have escaped the consequences of an alcohol-addicted employee. Most large organizations treat alcoholism as a disease and attempt rehabilitation before other more drastic adverse actions.

5. (1) Knowledge workers need more support than other types of employees. Clerical assistance, routine technical help, equipment maintenance, and a host of other services are needed by most knowledge workers.

6. (1) Since 1973, unions have declined from approximately 27 percent of the work force to approximately 15 percent. Both their public influence and their political strength have also declined. Whether this will continue depends on many complex factors of the market and public opinion.

7. (1) Supervisors have much more complex jobs than at any time in the past. Many perform duties that were once those of middle management. They operate in a legal, organizational, and social environment much more difficult than that of any other period of time.

8. (1, 2, 3, 4) Managers are required to be generalists rather than specialists. They must know more than just their area of specialization. Purchasing managers must understand organizational finance and strategy, accounting managers must know personnel practices, and so on. In some instances overspecialization can become a liability rather than an asset.

9. (1) One of the most unflattering truths about the United States is the woeful state of education, especially in inner cities where 40 percent of high school students typically fail to complete their basic education. A major problem for employers is finding people with levels of education that make job training possible.

10. (1, 2, 3) Supervisors are rarely involved in recruitment. While ideally they are part of the selection process, recruitment is usually accomplished by a human resource management department.

Chapter 16

1. (1) Only those people 40 years of age or older are protected by the Age Discrimination Act and its amendments.

2. (1) Sexual harassment is a serious violation of the provisions of Title VII of the Civil Rights Act of 1964. Recently it has become one of the focal points for judicial action involving civil rights.

3. (1, 2, 3) Women have been subjected to disparate treatment for many years and still are, in some cases. Most organizations, in today's work environment, no longer limit the types of work women can do or their opportunities for advancement.

4. (1) Many actions are legal but unethical. Social standards determine what is ethical and what is not.

5. (1, 2, 3, 4, 5) Racism and segregation are strongly related. Racism means perceiving another race as inferior. Segregation implies separation based on race, color, religion, national origin, or sex.

6. (1, 2) For many years employers have provided workers compensation insurance for on-the-job injuries, all or part of medical and hospitalization insurance coverage, paid sick leave, and other benefits directly related to employee welfare.

7. (1, 2, 3, 4) Supervisors often act as if environmental issues are of little concern, but in many instances waste disposal procedures, prevention of spillage of toxic chemicals, proper venting of noxious gasses, and attention to recyclable waste are supervisory responsibilities.

8. (1) People can be equally ill-treated and lacking in freedom. Freedom implies legal rights to those freedoms guaranteed by the Constitution of the United States. Equality means that all people regardless of race, color, religion, national origin, sex, age, or physical condition are treated equally and have equal access and opportunity to the benefits of society.

9. (1) Many organizations have strict rules of conduct regarding relations between sexes at work. Sexual harassment is specifically prohibited by both policy and law. Sexual conduct can be a major management concern.

10. (6) Reasonable accommodation means attempting to adjust working conditions to fit special circumstances. Religion and physical condition are the two most common reasons for attempts at reasonable accommodation.

Chapter 17

1. (5, 6) One of Deming's most important concepts is that customers determine quality. He asks organizations to not only meet but exceed customer expectation. Not only will they return but they will bring others with them.

2. (1, 2, 3, 4) Fear can be a strong motivator for individuals to protect themselves if threatened. It is a poor motivator in work environments. Fear breeds excessive caution, reluctance to try new ideas, indecision, and insecurity.

3. (1) One of the first lessons of total quality management is that management is responsible for most quality problems. Deming states that approximately 85 percent of quality difficulties are due to things employees cannot control; only 15 percent of such difficulties originate with employees.

4. (1, 2, 3, 4) Good managers are proactive. They plan to prevent crises rather than spend excessive time solving problems that could have been prevented with good planning. They are problem solvers and crisis managers

only when conditions beyond their immediate control occur.

5. (1) There is no real evidence that annual merit reviews, which are almost universally judgmental rather than developmental, improve performance. As stated earlier, many merit reviews may depress rather than improve individual productivity and quality.

6. (1, 2 3, 4, 5, 6) Some management development seminars and training programs are excellent, especially if they are specifically designed for the system in which managers work. A great deal of management training, unfortunately, is a waste of time since the principles discussed cannot be easily applied. Unless top management endorses and fully supports management development efforts, none will contribute significantly to improvement. Seminars dealing with specific topics are usually more valuable than those of a general nature.

7. (1, 2) Managers with high expectations usually are pleased with their employees' performance. People tend to rise to the expectations of those who have confidence in their judgment and ability.

8. (1, 2, 3) Individual competition may be a strong motivator for a short period of time. People who lose, however, often feel resentment and their performance decreases rather than improves. At times the desire to win can result in a lack of cooperation with others in the work group and eventual disintegration of any type of team spirit. Group incentive programs that result in rewards for all team members when goals are met or exceeded is a preferable approach to winner-take-all types of competition.

9. (1) Control involves having realistic formal or informal standards, determining if the standards are being achieved, and taking corrective action. It requires careful analysis, flexibility, and willingness to solve problems rather than blame others.

10. (5, 6) Most people want to be good employees. For most people doing a good job and contributing to the organization are more satisfying than performing at minimum levels.

Chapter 18

1. (4, 5, 6) One of the most difficult tasks faced by many people is identifying areas of work in which they would like to build a career. For some, fortunately, their likes and ambitions are very clear and well defined. We suggest seeking the help of college counseling programs designed to assist in career path development for those who have difficulty defining their long-term goals.

2. (1, 2, 3) With the exception of trained professional help, advice from others frequently has little value. People tend to advise what they like or desire rather than what a person seeking help needs.

3. (6) In a world of constant change, new potential career paths develop constantly and others will emerge in the future.

4. (5, 6) Geographic location can be a career trap. Moving to other areas may be a requirement for ambitious people who want to optimize their potential in a career field.

5. (5, 6) Well-adjusted people usually view change as opportunity rather than something to fear.

6. (1) Stay out of management if being responsible for the activities, decisions, and behavior of others bothers you.

7. (6) People who want to improve their potential and develop their career interests must periodically assess their strengths and areas of knowledge and skill that need improvement. Life-long learning is an accepted reality for those who desire to excel.

8. (4, 5, 6) Many people have broad interests and develop knowledge in several fields. In their career efforts their interests are more focused on specific objectives and areas of work than trying to do everything in which they have an interest.

9. (1) Ambiguity is a normal part of work and life. Rarely is there enough information or expertise to make all decisions certain. We live in a world of degrees of brightness rather than total darkness or total light.

10. (5, 6) Goal identification, especially concerning long-range goals, is difficult at best. Goals are necessary in planned rather than accidental career development. A key component of goal identification is a realistic approach based on known interests, strengths, and weaknesses. Intermediate goals that lead to the achievement of longer range goals form the basis of the planning process.

Appendix B
Quick-Check: Organizational Analysis for Supervisors and Employees

Quick-check is designed to provide a brief evaluation of 15 organizational characteristics. Based on the information provided by the survey, improvements can be jointly planned and implemented by employees and managers. Supervisors and other managers should complete the form before administering it to employees. After employees have contributed their responses, comparisons can be made to determine areas of difference in perception of organizational problems. Discussion of the differences between employee and management perceptions is a useful starting point for organizational improvement.

Instructions

Each of the items listed below requires three answers. On the first answer line place an **N** in the space that best represents your response evaluation of the present conditions or the way things are now. Use the second line for your evaluation of the way things should be. Place an **S** in the most appropriate spot. You may find that your **N** answers are the same as your **S** answers in some instances, or that they are significantly different. Evaluations of the importance of the factor being measured are placed on the third line. Mark an **I** to designate how important the item is to the well-being of the organization. All may be important, or some may be more important than others.

1. **Standards.** Are challenging goals related to quality, productivity, priorities, and/or services to customers and a strong commitment to their achievement fully understood and supported by both managers and employees?

	Rarely							Always
Now	1 2	3	4	5	6	7	8	9
Should be	1 2	3	4	5	6	7	8	9
Importance	1 2	3	4	5	6	7	8	9

2. **Organization.** Does work and information flow smoothly in an orderly manner with minimum confusion and chaos? Do employees and managers fully understand their roles in their organization?

	Rarely							Always
Now	1 2	3	4	5	6	7	8	9
Should be	1 2	3	4	5	6	7	8	9
Importance	1 2	3	4	5	6	7	8	9

3. **Responsibility and authority.** Are both employees and managers encouraged to accept full responsibility for their jobs, and are they granted adequate authority to perform both effectively and efficiently?

	Rarely							Always	
Now	1	2	3	4	5	6	7	8	9
Should be	1	2	3	4	5	6	7	8	9
Importance	1	2	3	4	5	6	7	8	9

4. **Communication.** Do most people in the organization feel that they are "in on things"? Do both managers and employees feel free to discuss problems, ideas, and suggestions for improvement with each other?

	Rarely							Always	
Now	1	2	3	4	5	6	7	8	9
Should be	1	2	3	4	5	6	7	8	9
Importance	1	2	3	4	5	6	7	8	9

5. **Information and assistance.** Is enough training, information, and assistance available when needed to ensure that work is accomplished with minimum difficulty?

	Rarely							Always	
Now	1	2	3	4	5	6	7	8	9
Should be	1	2	3	4	5	6	7	8	9
Importance	1	2	3	4	5	6	7	8	9

6. **Cost consciousness.** Does everyone in the organization practice good cost management? Is there minimum duplication, concern for uses of supplies and equipment, and minimal waste and theft?

	Rarely							Always	
Now	1	2	3	4	5	6	7	8	9
Should be	1	2	3	4	5	6	7	8	9
Importance	1	2	3	4	5	6	7	8	9

7. **Time utilization.** Do both managers and employees use their time wisely? Are there too many unnecessary meetings or long telephone calls, too much unnecessary waiting time for information, supplies, equipment usage, or decisions?

	Rarely							Always	
Now	1	2	3	4	5	6	7	8	9
Should be	1	2	3	4	5	6	7	8	9
Importance	1	2	3	4	5	6	7	8	9

8. **Work distribution.** Is work distributed evenly between departments and individuals within departments? Do employees feel that both quality and quantity requirements are reasonable for all members of their work units?

	Rarely							Always	
Now	1	2	3	4	5	6	7	8	9
Should be	1	2	3	4	5	6	7	8	9
Importance	1	2	3	4	5	6	7	8	9

9. **Rewards.** Do members of the organization receive recognition for exceptional work or contributions of ideas and suggestions? Are promotions and pay increases based on performance rather than personality?

	Rarely							Always	
Now	1	2	3	4	5	6	7	8	9
Should be	1	2	3	4	5	6	7	8	9
Importance	1	2	3	4	5	6	7	8	9

10. **Conflict management.** Is management willing to examine more than one point of view in resolving differences? Are conflicts usually resolved without blame or demeaning the people involved?

	Rarely							Always	
Now	1	2	3	4	5	6	7	8	9
Should be	1	2	3	4	5	6	7	8	9
Importance	1	2	3	4	5	6	7	8	9

11. **Management competence.** Do employees view their supervisors and higher level managers as knowledgeable, good decision makers, and experts in running their organizational units effectively and efficiently? Do managers respect the knowledge and expertise of other managers in the organization?

	Rarely								Always
Now	1	2	3	4	5	6	7	8	9
Should be	1	2	3	4	5	6	7	8	9
Importance	1	2	3	4	5	6	7	8	9

12. **Leadership.** Does the chief executive officer act as a true leader for the organization in development of goals, inspiring excellence, and creating a belief that the goals of the organization are important for all employees? Do lower level managers encourage, motivate, and support their employees?

	Rarely								Always
Now	1	2	3	4	5	6	7	8	9
Should be	1	2	3	4	5	6	7	8	9
Importance	1	2	3	4	5	6	7	8	9

13. **Relationship between managers and employees.** Is there a high level of trust between managers and employees? Do employees feel that management is on their side? Do managers view employees as partners in making the organization a success?

	Rarely								Always
Now	1	2	3	4	5	6	7	8	9
Should be	1	2	3	4	5	6	7	8	9
Importance	1	2	3	4	5	6	7	8	9

14. **Job involvement.** Do employees feel that the work they do significantly contributes to the overall welfare of the organization and consequently their own personal well-being? Do most employees find the work interesting, challenging, and offering opportunities for personal development?

	Rarely								Always
Now	1	2	3	4	5	6	7	8	9
Should be	1	2	3	4	5	6	7	8	9
Importance	1	2	3	4	5	6	7	8	9

15. **Quality of work life.** Do employees and lower level managers recommend the organization as a good place to work? Do they express pride in the organization and the fact that they are members? Compared to other places of employment in the larger community, do people feel that their organization is among the best?

	Rarely								Always
Now	1	2	3	4	5	6	7	8	9
Should be	1	2	3	4	5	6	7	8	9
Importance	1	2	3	4	5	6	7	8	9

■ SCORING QUICK-CHECK

On the graph below, mark the Now scores for each item with an **N**. Connect all the Ns by drawing a line from one **N** to the next. This is your graph of the way you perceive your organization now. Place your Should be answers for each item on the graph with the letter **S** and connect them with a *dotted* line to distinguish them from the solid line that connects the Ns. Repeat the same process for the **Importance** responses but connect them with lines of *plus* (+) signs. After the three-part graph has been completed, identify areas where the **N** and **S** scores are most widely separated. These indicate need for correction. Prioritize the needed corrections by examining the **I** scores. Important items will have highest priority if corrections are needed.

Item numbers are designated on the top horizontal line. Scores are listed in the vertical columns on each side of the graph.

	Quick-Check Comparison Graph															
	1	2	3	4	5	6	7	8	9	10	11	12	13	14	15	
9																9
8																8
7																7
6																6
5																5
4																4
3																3
2																2
1																1

Glossary

Access Right to be served in public or private facilities designed to serve the general population.

Accountability A component of fully accepting responsibility for reporting achievements and failures to higher levels of management.

Achievement-Oriented Leadership Leadership that sets challenging but achievable goals and has high expectations of self and others, emphasizing competence and personal responsibility.

Adjustive Reactions Defenses people use to alleviate stress symptoms.

Affective Learning Learning that relates to the development of values and attitudes.

Alcoholism The most observable and common life-style problem.

Allness Belief that an individual knows all that can be known about a situation, person, or field of knowledge.

Ambivalents People who act like ascendants if they are doing work they enjoy but take on indifferent characteristics if they are bored or faced with work they do not like.

Appearance, Speech, Manners, and Mannerisms The first nonverbal communication that is transmitted by people in face-to-face contact.

Appointed Leaders Leaders whose leadership is based on recognizing expertise, efficiency, and potential for learning management skills.

Approach-Approach Conflicts Conflicts that delay decisions because choices are similar and any choice will likely be satisfactory.

Approach-Avoidance Conflicts Conflicts that occur when the results of decisions are either uncertain or potentially harmful.

Arbitrator Person who decides courses of corrective action in disputes between management and employees.

Ascendants People who do their best at all times; they work hard and usually achieve their goals.

Attack Generalized reaction to frustration that takes the form of problem solving, anger, increased energy, and/or at times physical action against the perceived cause of frustration.

Authoritarian Leaders Leaders who see themselves as the ultimate decision makers; they take a parental role, either benevolent or judgmental, in dealing with employees.

Authority Right to act and implement necessary organizational activities, including supervision of employees.

Avoidance-Avoidance Conflicts Conflicts that result from the inability to perceive alternatives that are not painful or harmful, or have a negative outcome.

Baboons Individuals who depend on explosive outbursts to intimidate and control others.

Bilateral Relations Agreements mutually arrived at through negotiations between management and employee groups such as unions.

Blanket Cuts Reduction of the expenditures by a predetermined percentage throughout the entire organization.

Bleeding Sharks Victims of sharks.

Bottom-Line Thinking Concentration on immediate profits rather than on long-term organizational goals.

Budget A financial plan, used by entire organizations, departments, sections, specific programs, or groups of activities.

Bureaucracy Organizational structure built on authority, control, reporting, limited responsibility, and impersonality in treatment of employees, as advocated by Max Weber. Many large organizations tend to be bureaucratic in their operations.

Capital Budgets Budgets made for nonexpendable items such as equipment, facilities, and land.

Career Sequence of jobs and work pursuits that a person does for a living.

Career Development In the final analysis, self-development.

Career Path Sequence of training, jobs, and experience that constitutes a persons total work history.

Career Planning Steps that help an individual to follow a well-ordered career path; however, they do not guarantee success.

Career Stages Changes that occur in career paths during an individual work life.

Cause A legitimate reason for a manager to take an adverse action against an employee, such as demotion, reprimand, giving time off without pay, or involuntary termination.

Change Inevitable and unstoppable alteration.

Change Diffusion The extent to which one change spreads and creates other changes.

Change Direction Increases or decreases in magnitude, capacity, costs, or other characteristics of change.

Change Rate Speed at which change takes place; some change is very rapid, some slow, and some almost imperceptible.

Changed Status of Women The most profound social movement of the 20th century.

Channels Ways information is transmitted, by language, pictures, nonverbal symbols, electronics, or any other means that senses can detect.

Charismatic Leaders Leaders who are characterized by their force of personality, determination, and willingness to take extraordinary risks.

Chronemics Use of time to communicate by being late or early to meetings, by failing to meet schedules, or by being exceptionally punctual.

Classical Conditioning Automatic reaction by simple association.

Classroom Training Training that involves demonstration, discussion, and practice; Sometimes called *vestibule training*.

Clinical Grievances Grievances based on perceived wrongful treatment by a superior; a type of revenge rather than a legitimate grievance.

Cliques Small informal groups within work organizations that may take positions in conflict with those of other employees or management.

Coercive Power Power that depends on the ability to threaten, punish, or affect an individual's self-esteem.

Cognitive Dissonance Theory concerning the holding of two or more conflicting ideas at the same time.

Cognitive Learning Theory concerning the acquisition of knowledge.

Communication Understanding and being understood; involves sharing thoughts, information, and feelings.

Communication Codes Communication that may use language or some type of nonverbal communication.

Company People Individuals who are loyal, dedicated to the organizations, and responsive to higher levels of management.

Comparable Pay Concept that people with the same type of work and job classifications should receive substantially the same pay.

Comparable Worth Concept that jobs, regardless of classification, that require similar experience, training, and responsibility, should be paid equally.

Conceptual Skills Skills that require analysis, concept formulation, and visualization of the way things must be accomplished.

Concurrent Control Corrective action taken while a job is being accomplished.

Conditioning Connecting one event, symbol, or object with another.

Conflict Emotional state that originates from feelings of being attacked, treated unfairly, or having unfulfilled expectations or disagreements.

Conflict Management Management approach recognizing that people deal with conflict in different ways.

Conflict Priorities A major source of conflict.

Constancy of Purpose The belief that once a philosophy has been adopted, it must be fully implemented for long periods of time; the driving force behind TQM.

Context Definition of a term determined by the situation in which a word or words are used or by the words that either follow or precede it.

Contingency Theory Belief that an appropriate leadership style depends largely on the situation; leadership style should change as the situation changes.

Contingency-Based Management Management that recognizes there is no one best way to manage; forces in the manager, employees, and conditions of work determine appropriate management approaches.

Contractual Trust Trust based on the belief that people will act responsibly, competently, and honestly.

Control Corrective actions, derived from measurements, necessary to assure desired standards are being met.

Convergent Thinkers Individuals who are precise, well organized, conformist, and detail oriented.

Cooperative Training and Apprenticeships Job experience gained while attending college or other levels of training.

Coordination Getting things done in an organized sequence of activities; informing others what, when, where, how, and why work must be accomplished.

Cost-Benefit Analysis Weighing the costs of training against its benefits to determine if the training is cost effective.

Cost Consciousness Development of an awareness that some costs are appropriate and necessary while others may be inappropriate and harmful.

Cost Control Any activity taken to meet budget projections or reduce expenditures of organizational resources.

Creative Discontent Concept that perfection is never reached in organizations; good managers stress continuous improvement.

Creativity Developing new ideas.

Crisis Management Rarely solves long-term problems.

CROWS Commonly Recruited Ordinary Workers.

Custodial Climates Work environments in which management deliberately restricts employee responsibility to a specific job assignment; people know their jobs, do them, and go home.

De facto "In fact," although not formally announced, some changes become accepted realities.

Decision making Choosing a course of action from several possibilities or alternatives.

Defensive Behavior Behavior that occurs when people feel their beliefs and values, or likes and dislikes, are being attacked by someone with whom they disagree.

Delegation Giving to employees both authority and work that was formerly carried out by their immediate manager; granting authority is the heart of delegation.

Demographics Study of changes in population and how the population is distributed.

Demotivation Any action or set of actions that negatively impacts employee performance.

Development Preparation for increased responsibility, authority, and personal accountability.

Development Performance Performance that focuses on future improvement.

Directing Activities associated with influencing employees to perform at the level required to meet established standards.

Directive Leadership Leadership that defines goals and tasks, sets standards and priorities, and enforces rules, policies, and procedures.

Disciplinary Action Any corrective action directed toward changing behavior, attitudes, or methods of work. Actions taken to ensure that work rules are enforced.

Discipline Adherence to a set of rules.

Discretionary Income Money in excess of that needed to maintain a satisfactory standard of living; in organizations it is profit beyond that expected.

Discrimination Treating a group or groups of individuals differently from others for any reason.

Distress Negative stress that prevents individuals from effectively coping with the events from which the stress originates.

Distributive Justice Expectation that those who contribute more and take greater risks should have more.

Divergent Thinkers Individuals who are people oriented, creative, unmindful of precise rules, and deal with ambiguity quite well.

Downsizing Reducing either the total organizational size or some of its units in an effort to reduce costs.

Due Process The right of all persons to present their side in a dispute, appeal decisions to a higher level of authority, and face accusers.

Economic and Political Change Types of social change that profoundly affect the way organizations operate; economic conditions influence marketing strategies, and politics either add or ease government regulatory requirements.

Effectiveness Doing things completely and correctly.

Efficiency Performing work with minimum use of time, effort, money, and other resources.

Electronic Sweatshops Places where people perform their work on computers or computer terminals and are monitored by computer network systems.

Emergent Leaders Leaders who achieve their status through willingness to speak for their group; personality or credibility.

Entry-Level Management Jobs Position that may have any one of a variety of titles that imply leadership, responsibility, and authority.

Equal Opportunity Legal mandate stating that all members of our society should have equal access and equal opportunity.

Equal Pay Equal pay, regardless of sex, is guaranteed by the Equal Pay amendment to the Fair Labor Standards Act.

Equality Equal treatment and equal rights and responsibilities.

Equitable Pay Being paid essentially the same rates as those with similar training, experience, and job classification.

Ergonomics Designing equipment and facilities to fit users' needs.

ESOP Employee Stock Ownership Plan; uses stock ownership by employees as an incentive to increase productivity and quality.

Estimate Projected length of time required to do a job based on knowledge and experience.

Ethical Dilemmas When two or more ethical principles are in conflict with each other.

Ethics Adherence to societal values of honesty, fairness, and concern for the welfare of others.

Eustress Stress that is beneficial and necessary.

Executive (top-level) Management Chief executive officers, boards of directors, and executive committees that make key organizational decisions and formulate policies that affect the entire organization.

Exempt Employees Employees for whom the Wage and Hour provisions of the Fair Labor Standards Act do not apply; usually management, professional, and high-level administrative members of an organization paid for level of responsibility rather than time worked.

Expectancy Theory Theory that behavior is a function of the value of a reward and the expectancy of achieving the reward.

Expert Power Power dependent on the perceived degree of expertise an individual possesses; not exclusively vested in leaders or managers.

External Orientation Dependence on luck, coincidence, being liked, and higher authority for quality of life.

Fast-Track Employees Employees who work for recognition and promotion; their political smartness and ability usually identifies them as promotable material.

Fear An emotion that, when induced by a manager, teaches employees to avoid certain actions or behaviors but has little long-range motivational value.

Feedback Information gathered in response to a communication.

Filter (Communication) Any set of conditions, either within a person or a situation, that influences the way a message is interpreted.

First-Line Management Supervisors responsible for the work of individual employees and groups in performing the vital tasks of an organization.

Formal Performance Appraisals Evaluation of an employee's job performance; may be used to justify subsequent management action related to individual employees.

Formal Plans Plans in writing and formatted so they can be used by all people affected by the plan.

Formal Power Power that is granted; informal power is earned.

Formal Status Status granted by a job title or position.

Frames of Reference All of the internal and external factors that affect interpretation of events, situations, and messages.

Freedom The state wherein people can express themselves without fear, agree or dissent, select or reject any religion, publish opinions, and pursue happiness in ways that meet their interests and needs.

Frustration State occurring when there is any interference with goal-directed behavior; a perceived inability to satisfy a need.

General Status Status granted to people because of their perceived social worth or job titles.

General Supervision Supervisory style where managers inform employees of priorities and what needs to be accomplished—preferred by most; "over the shoulder" direction, however, is resented.

Gorilla Anyone who, because of her or his ability to affect another individual's life, is seen as a potential threat.

Graphic Rating Scales Numerical "grades" given to employees for performance in a predetermined set of job elements; the most common type of evaluation system.

Great Person Leadership Theory Theory stating that leaders are born, not made.

Grievance Procedures Systematic steps used to hear employee complaints and ensure due process in the event of pending adverse actions.

Group Decisions Decisions made by two or more individuals; have the advantage of greater acceptance and accuracy if group members have expertise in the problems being addressed.

Guesstimates Approximations of time required when there is little or no experience in performing a designated task.

Halos Judgments based on superficial characteristics such as appearance or speech characteristics.

Higher Level Needs Needs for social contact, self-esteem, and self-fulfillment.

Hire at Will Principle that either employees or managers may enter into or break employee agreements at will. In the case of termination, no cause is necessary.

HIV Carriers Individuals testing positive for human immune virus (HIV). They may be excellent employees with minimal or no danger of infection to other employees.

Holistic Points of view picturing organizations as many interacting parts that make up a whole rather than a number of discrete parts.

Human Relations Movement Movement that began with the work of Elton Mayo, who found that productivity increased when employees believed management was concerned with their welfare.

Human Resource Management Management of all activities related to the acquisition, training, evaluation, compensation, retention, legal mandates, welfare, maintenance, and retention of employees in an organization.

Human Skills Skills that facilitate relating effectively to employees, other managers, customers, union leadership, vendors, government agencies, and others; necessary for all managers.

Identification State when a person takes on the characteristics or even the life-style of others whom they admire; a rejection of their personal symbolic self.

Indifferents Individuals who work for money and little else; they perform to minimum standards to keep from being fired.

Informal Plans Plans made usually for the sole benefit of planner; for example, to-do lists, calendar notations, and "mental notes."

Informal Status Status granted due to an individual's ability to accomplish more for the benefit of the group.

Information Overload Giving more information to a person or group than can be fully absorbed and comprehended.

Innovation Use of existing concepts or equipment in a new and different way.

Institutional Power Power that focuses on achievement; shared power used to further the welfare of the organization and employees and organizational leaders' ability to use influence positively.

Integrative Bargaining Bargaining requiring that each party make a good faith attempt to fully understand the other person's or group's point of view.

Interactive Theories Theories of leadership stating that forces within the manager, situation, and employees determine appropriate leadership style.

Internal Orientation Dependence on a person's own resources and achievements for motivation; tendency to be existential in life approach.

Interpersonal relations Interactions that involve the way individuals deal with others.

Intrapersonal Factors Factors within an individual that may prevent the person from being effective.

Job Depth Amount of control and responsibility employees have for their own jobs.

Job Scope Number of different tasks in a job.

Judgmental Performance Evaluation Basis for improvement in pay, promotions, and transfers.

Kaizen Constant improvement on a daily basis; small changes can make large differences over a period of time.

Kinesics Use of body positions and movement to communicate; commonly known as *body language*.

Knowledge Workers Employees with specialized training and experience, usually in an information, technical, or administrative field of work.

Law of Maldistribution Concept developed by Vilfredo Pareto stating that 80 percent of problems, including costs, occur in 20 percent of the organization or population.

Leaders Individuals who are able to influence others and get people to act to achieve goals.

Leader-Member Relations The most important leadership factor identified by Fred Fiedler.

Learning Change in behavior resulting from perception or experience.

Legal Grievance Employee complaint against management based on a clear violation of due process, established policy, or union-management agreement.

Legitimate Power Power of the position; it comes with the job.

Life-Style Problems Alcoholism, drug addiction, and disease, among others.

Line-Item Budgets Budgets where each budget item is a line on a budget form; the most common budgetary format.

Lower Level Needs Needs concerning physical survival and maintenance.

Magnitude of Change Extent, size, or impact of change.

Management by Exception Effective time-management technique, wherein more time and energy are spent on problem areas than on those areas that are operating without difficulty and meeting expected levels of performance.

Management Functions A group of related activities that managers must perform.

Management in the Third Wave A management concept presuming that world changes drive change in organizations and management.

MBO and **BARS** Difficult to prepare but well-thought-out methods for evaluating people based against actual performance; both measure discrete job elements.

Middle Management Level of management that interprets top-level policies in terms of its own areas of specialization such as purchasing, finance, marketing, human resources, operations, shipping and receiving, and others, depending on the organization's structure and functions.

Morals Religious or other definitions of good and evil, right and wrong.

Motivation Forces within individuals that cause them to act to satisfy felt needs.

Motivation-Maintenance Theory Concept that some needs are necessary for personal maintenance and others for motivation to produce more and better.

Multiple Use Plans Plans that can apply to a variety of situations.

Natural Units of Work Groups of related tasks that are usually performed in sequence or as part of a cooperative effort.

Necessity and Opportunity Possible driving forces in career development rather than conscious, systematic planning.

Negative Politics Games playing, manipulation, and deception.

Net Profit Amount of money derived from sales after expenses and taxes have been deducted; the organizational equivalent of an employee's take-home pay.

No-Track Employees Employees who have few ambitions beyond their immediate assignments and are satisfied without additional responsibility.

Nonexempt Employees Employees covered by the Wage and Hour provisions of the Fair Labor Standards Act; they hold hourly paid jobs and must be paid overtime rates for work in excess of 40 hours per week or, in some cases, eight hours per day.

Objective Evaluations Appraisals based on countable standards such as productivity, error rates, and schedule adherence; cooperation, innovation, and assistance to others are not considered.

Objectives Aims and goals of individuals, groups, and total organizations, embodying the intent of those who develop the objectives.

On-the-Job Training Training employees by having them learn while they work; the most common type of training.

Operant Conditioning Concept based on the association of specific acts with rewards or punishment.

Operational Decisions Day-to-day decisions made by supervisors.

Operational Planning Day-to-day planning required to make work flow smoothly; schedules, procedures, and assignment sheets.

Opportunity Right to education and work without denial because of race, color, religion, national origin, sex, age, or physical disability.

Organizational Barriers Bottlenecks that prevent upward communication; created by both the structure and size of organizations.

Organizational Centrism Belief by employees or managers that their department or work unit is the most important in their organization.

Organizational Change Any change in an organization such as personnel shifts, structural realignment, policies alteration, or redefinition of objectives.

Organizational Chart Delineation of the organizational structure, areas of responsibility, and lines of authority.

Organizational Culture Primary values of an organization.

Organizational Hierarchy Ranking of managers from top to first line.

Organizational Processes Step-by step activities necessary to accomplish the work of an organization.

Organizational Structure Who reports to whom and major areas of responsibility.

Organizational Systems Systems that convert resources, called *inputs*, to products and services, known as *outputs*, by use of systematic steps, defined as *processes*.

Organizing Putting things in order.

OSHA Occupational Safety and Health Administration; makes and enforces national safety standards.

Paradigm Model or example.

Paralanguage Conveys meaning by the way things are spoken rather than by what is said.

Pareto Charts Graphic methods for showing where problems, including cost difficulties, occur.

Participative Leaders Leaders who encourage employee ideas, suggestions, and job involvement, and view employees as partners in the decision-making processes.

Past Practice Framework used to determine appropriate disciplinary action in the absence of a definitive policy.

Path-Goal Theory Theory that sees the leader as a person who can define goals that lead to satisfaction for those that achieve the goals; based on expectancy principles.

Pay for Time Not Worked Pay for vacations, holidays, break periods, and sick leave.

Pay for Time Worked Pay for actual hours worked.

PDCA **P**lanning, **D**oing, **C**hecking, and **A**ction; they are key Total Quality Management concepts.

Performance Evaluation Judgment supervisors make concerning the effectiveness of an employee or group of employees.

Permissive Leaders Leaders who view their role as message carriers while employees decide what needs to be done and what decisions are needed; essentially, nonleaders.

Personal Power Power used to enhance feelings of control, manipulate others, and position a person for further personal gain.

Personal Trust Confidence of nonbetrayal by another person.

Physical Disabilities Disabilities that are not a cause for discriminatory treatment under the American with Disabilities Act of 1990.

Planned Careers Careers built on goal-directed education and experience.

Planning Deciding on a course of action for the future.

Pluralistic Society A diverse society where there is very little agreement on what is right, good, bad, moral, or correct.

Polarization Taking an extreme position in a disagreement with others.

Politics Acquisition, maintenance, and use of power.

Position Power Amount of power a leader possesses as perceived by employees.

Positive Politics Attracting the attention of higher levels of management without games playing; based on common sense—show up, show up on time, and show up dressed to play.

Postcontrol Corrective action taken based on reports indicating standards defined by plans are not being met.

Potential An individual's ability to accept and successfully perform at greater levels of responsibility; it is rarely evaluated.

Power Ability to influence others.

Praise Commending an employee; to be effective, must be associated with a specific activity.

Precontrol Planning that minimizes the necessity for corrective action.

Prejudice Preconceived judgment or opinion.

Pressure Workers Those who work best under stressful conditions.

Priority Lists Ranking of tasks in order of importance and defining those tasks that must be completed first.

Pro Bono Publico Law Law that is "in the interest of the people."

Proactive Managers Managers who concentrate on problem prevention through planning to minimize the necessity for corrective action.

Procrastination To delay or postpone; a chief reason for lack of decisions.

Profit Sharing Granting employees a percentage of organization profits; the oldest and best known form of group incentives.

Programmed Decisions Decisions dictated by policies, procedures, or established practices.

Projection Blaming others, rather than oneself, for stress problems.

Protected Classes Members of groups, defined by law, that are specifically protected against discrimination in equality of opportunity and access.

Proxemics Forms of communication through the use of space; examples include personal and social space, seating arrangements, office layout and size, and office location.

Psychological Barriers to Communication Fear, lack of confidence, traumatic events, preoccupation with other events (both good and bad), and concern for the way others perceive an individual.

Psychological Contracts Mutual expectations managers and employees have of each other.

Psychological Distance Recognition that a manager's job and level of responsibility is different from that of other employees.

Psychological Maturity Ability to successfully cope with life situations including those that are stressful.

Psychological Value of Money Significance of money beyond its financial value; enhances an individual's feelings of self-esteem, security, and personal worth.

Psychomotor Learning Coordination and direction of body movements.

Quality Circles Group-involvement technique; has not had a high degree of success in the United States.

Racism Belief that some races are superior to others.

Ranking Systems Simple type of employee comparisons; employees are ranked according to their worth to the organization.

Rationalization Making excuses.

Reaction Formation Denial of one's own basic desires.

Reactive Managers Managers who see their primary role as taking corrective action when necessary.

Redirecting Encouraging employees to seek employment more closely aligned with their experience and training.

Referent Someone who has the respect and confidence of others.

Referent Power Power that originates out of respect, admiration, perceived credibility, and behavior that others admire.

Regression Going back in time either through remembering the "good old days" or acting childishly.

Reinforcement Repetition of rewards or punishment to strengthen and maintain operantly conditioned responses.

Repression Forgetting the causes of stress.

Responsibility Accepted obligation to perform necessary job requirements effectively and efficiently; *informal responsibility* means doing things right.

Restricted Expertise Skills and knowledge that are not transferable from one job to another.

Reward Power Power that stems from the ability to praise, provide pay increases, grant special favors, and provide other rewards.

Role Conflict Conflict that occurs when there is uncertainty concerning an individual's true role; supervisors may identify more strongly with employees than management, although they are first-line managers.

Role Playing, Business Games, Conferences, and Organizational Laboratories   Training methods.

Scientific Management   Concept founded by Frederick Winslow Taylor and dedicated to the use of scientific methods to find the one best way to perform every job.

SDCA   Stabilization, Doing, Checking, and Action; necessary before the PDCA process can begin.

Segregation   Act of keeping people of different races, religions, national origins, or sex apart from each other.

Self-Fulfilling Prophesies and the **Pygmalion Effect**   Forms of expectancy; in each case the individuals involved attempt to make their expectations or wishes come true.

Sensory Barriers   Any physical or physiological factor that interferes with understanding and being understood.

Sexual Harassment   Any act, statement, or display implying that sexual consent is a condition of employment, or any sexual statements or material that is offensive or causes work to be impeded because of its content.

Sexual Preference   Choice of gender of a sexual partner; an emotional issue that has no relationship to job performance, management potential, or other job characteristics.

Shadowing   Following a person and learning by observing his or her actions.

Sharks   Individuals who attack others whom they perceive as being in difficulty.

Shut-Down Time   Time taken by employees to end their workday; it materially shortens the work period.

Simulation Training   Learning on equipment identical to that used on the job.

Single Use Plans   Series of steps necessary to accomplish a specific action.

Situational Control   Combination of leader-member relations, position power, and task structure; good leaders are perceived to have all three.

Skills   Learned ability or aptitude; transferable to other organizations.

Sloths   Individuals who are unresponsive to both praise and punishment.

Slow-Track Employees   Employees who are often competent and hardworking but advance slowly because of lack of involvement in organizational politics.

Snakes   People who use deception, camouflage, and hidden motives to manipulate others.

Social Barriers   Blocks to interpersonal relations based on perceptions of differences in rank; those perceived as having higher rank are often treated with deference—communication upward is frequently intentionally limited.

Social Change   Shifts in the values and life-styles of society in general.

Social Learning   Learning that takes place when employees observe others.

Social Responsibility   Concept that both organizations and individuals must act to support the common good of our society.

Social Value of Money   Perception, by society in general, that people who earn money are more successful and worthwhile than those who do not.

Specific Status   An individual's skill or knowledge in a particular area of work.

Specific Supervision   Close observation and direction by supervisors of employee efforts.

Standard Work Months   173.33 hours.

Standard Work Times   Work times defined by the Fair Labor Standards Act of 1938.

Standard Workweek   168 hours beginning at a time defined by organizational policy—usually midnight Saturday or Sunday and ending at midnight the following week, usually Saturday or Sunday.

Standard Work Year   2,080 hours.

Standard Workday   24-hour period beginning at an employee's regular shift start time.

Standards   Expected levels of performance for specific tasks; measured by amount of productivity in a given period of time, quality, and schedule adherence.

Start-Up Time   Wasted time employees often use when they first report for work.

Status Rank given to others because of their perceived worth to a group; degree of influence or position.

Status Congruence Degree that status symbols are appropriate for a person's rank.

Status Symbol Any object, sign, adornment, or amount of space that identifies a person's rank or position.

Stereotypes Generalized biases derived from beliefs about the behavior of those of a certain ethnic background, national origin, religion, sex, or education, from a particular geographical area, performing a certain type of work, or other characteristics.

Strategic Decisions Long-range decisions that affect the operation of the total organization.

Strategic Plans Long-range plans designed to ensure the competitive position of an organization; usually expressed as policies or guidelines.

Stress Any set of conditions that puts an individual off balance or increases the need for action.

Stress Carriers People who cause stress in others but remain relatively stress-free.

Stress Management Management of stress that does not seek to eliminate it but attempts to keep it below the level of *distress.*

Stress Relievers Actions people take to rid themselves of stress symptoms.

Subordinate Military term that designates someone of lesser status; disappearing in many work organizations.

Subsistence Wage Just enough money to purchase the necessities of life with no discretionary income.

Success Ability to define and achieve goals; usually a matter of degree—few people achieve what they consider total success.

Supervision Directing, assigning, correcting, organizing, controlling, and motivating the efforts of others. Getting work accomplished through others. First-level management.

Supervisors Individuals who are responsible for planning, organizing, directing, and controlling the work of employees who perform the tasks and services of an organization.

Supervisory Learning Adoption of the attitudes and styles of other managers who appear successful without careful evaluation or knowledge of alternative approaches.

Supportive Leadership Leadership style that involves building close working relationships, demonstrating concern for employee welfare and job satisfaction, and stressing cooperative work relationships.

SWANs Smart, Work-hard, Ambitious, and Nice employees or potential employees.

Symbolic Self What people *think* they are.

Systematic Decision Making Set of step-by-step actions that lead to carefully considered decisions.

Tactical Decisions Decisions that support and make strategic decisions a reality.

Tactical Plans Plans concerned with accomplishing major projects that support strategic plans.

Task Structure Definition of what needs to be done to achieve work objectives.

Team Building Development of close, effective working relationships among groups of employees; a key component of Total Quality Management.

Technical Supervisory Skills Skills concerned with the knowledge of performing a specific task; *how* a job must be performed.

Technological Change Increasing sophistication of equipment; in particular the use of electronics, lasers, genetic engineering, and other technologies that alter both work and personal life.

Telecommuting Working away from a regularly assigned place of employment by utilizing laptop or other portable computers, telephones, and fax machines.

Theory X Douglas McGregor's designation for traditional management; assumes that people must be tightly controlled, that they dislike work, and that they are basically lazy and irresponsible.

Theory Y Managerial assumption that, given encouragement and opportunity, people will control themselves, prefer to do a good job, and will seek added responsibilities.

Theory Z William Ouchi's extension of Theory Y; states that people can be essentially self-directed, deeply involved in day-to-day job decisions, and can see themselves as partners with management in building the success of their organization.

Time Log Record of actual time spent on daily activities.

Time-Phased Budgets Planned expenditure of funds over the life of a budget.

Title VII of the **Civil Rights Act of 1964 and Its Amendments** Guarantee of equality of employment opportunity under rules of the Equal Employment Opportunity Commission.

Touch and Response Powerful forms of communication that are, with the exception of the handshake, usually socially unacceptable in our society during work.

Tough Battlers, Give-Up Communicators, Friendly Helpers, and Problem Solvers Management styles corresponding to those of blind, closed, hidden, and open communicators.

Total Listening Listening that involves hearing, interpretation of paralanguage, and observing body language, as well as use of space.

TQM—Total Quality Management Management that concentrates on continuous improvement, statistical process control, and driving fear out of the workplace.

Traditional Leaders Leaders who inherit their roles by accident of birth or kinship.

Training Learning specific job skills.

Transfer Give a problem to others to solve; or occurs when job skills or knowledge learned in a previous place of work are brought to a new job.

Traps Types of behavior that prevent or slow career development.

Ultimate Friday Retirement.

Unfulfilled Expectations Expectations that have not been met; can ultimately lead to conflict with the person or people perceived as preventing the expectations from becoming a reality.

Unilateral Relations Management rule making without employee participation.

Union Formal organization of employees who deal collectively with management on issues related to wages, effort, work rules, and other conditions of work.

Utility of Money Money's use for purchasing needed goods and services.

Vacillation Inability to decide between alternative courses of action; being wishy-washy.

Valence Value or attractiveness of a reward.

Vital Shifts Shifts that occur when people are promoted to higher levels of management.

Wasps People who are always on the attack; they like to sting others.

Willing Consent Consent whereby two people enter into a relationship with each other because of mutual desire rather than threat, fear, or potential work-related rewards.

Withdrawal Common reaction to frustration, taking forms of daydreaming, physically leaving, sleeping, or changing the topic during a discussion.

Working for Fridays Working for the weekends and freedom from work.

Wrongful Termination Terminating a person without proper cause, especially if that person has a good work record or is a member of a protected class.

Zero Sum Game Situation in which one side must win and the other side must lose.

Index